LOGIC: DEPTH GRAMMAR OF RATIONALITY

LOGIC:
DEPTH GRAMMAR
OF RATIONALITY

A textbook on the science and history of logic

PATRICK K. BASTABLE

University College, Dublin

GILL AND MACMILLAN

First published in 1975

Gill and Macmillan Limited
2 Belvedere Place
Dublin 1
and internationally through
association with the
Macmillan Publishers Group

7171 0710 8

ACKNOWLEDGMENTS

The publishers wish to thank the following for permission to include copyright material in this book: D. Reidel Publishing Company, Dordrecht-Holland, Boston-U.S.A., for J. M. Bochenski's modification of the Hilbert–Ackermann axiomatization of the logic of sentences, as presented in his *A Precis of Mathematical Logic*; the Clarendon Press, Oxford, for two passages from Jan Lukasiewicz's *Aristotle's Syllogistic from the Standpoint of Modern Formal Logic*; and Dover Publications, Inc., New York, for the axiomatization of the Boole-Schröder Algebra of Classes as presented by C. I. Lewis and C. H. Langford in their *Symbolic Logic*.

Filmset in Photon Times 11 pt by
Richard Clay (The Chaucer Press), Ltd, Bungay, Suffolk
and printed in Great Britain by
Fletcher & Son Ltd, Norwich

GENERAL CONTENTS

(Note: Detailed contents are given at the beginning of each section.)

ACKNOWLEDGMENT

Grateful acknowledgment is made to the Senate of the National University of Ireland for a generous grant-in-aid of publication.

PREFACE

The aim of this textbook is to provide a complete course on logic in the following way:

Firstly, it *prepares* the student for what is basic in the course, namely *formal logic*, which involves the use of a special symbolic language and technical procedures of proof and systematization. The preparatory section is built around the concept of X-raying meaning and brings the student into contact with Aristotle's abstractive logic; this approach has the important advantage of introducing logic by means of the work and purposes of its pioneer. The basic section of formal logic covers both standard and non-standard logics and presents the axiomatic and natural deduction approaches.

Secondly (following on formal logic itself) this textbook presents the substance and history of technical and philosophical reflection, thus making explicit the problems, underlying theories, quality and ultimate nature of formal logic. This reflection has two levels, one technical, the other philosophical; accordingly two distinct sections are called for and are named, respectively, *metalogic* and *philosophy of logic*. The writing of a metalogic is largely a matter of mapping the history of its theoretical and technical problems; however, philosophy of logic has not the benefit of either organized treatment or settled opinions—accordingly, this section, while expressing many traditional and contemporary insights, represents my own personal judgment.

Finally, the reader is provided with a substantial and systematic experience of *applied logic*. Since contemporary applied logic departs radically from tradition in being consciously interdisciplinary, the organization of content in this section must again reflect personal judgment.

As with any other science, it is in the nature of logic that the sections of a complete course, being fully and properly developed, should constitute a natural unity and should progressively clarify the nature and range of logical truth, of logical investigation and of the application of logic. A good criterion of the basic soundness of a complete course is, indeed, a reasonably apparent technical and theoretical continuity, and a thematic richness in which one's perspective on logic is always clarified and never lost.

It is unusual to present, in a single textbook, a course on all sections of logic. The value of doing so clearly, substantially and concisely (with appropriate historical settings) is very great and will, I hope, be found in sufficient measure to justify the present work.

Section A: Preparatory Section (a preliminary training for work in Formal Logic)

DETAILED CONTENTS OF SECTION A

Exercises

INTRODUCTION

I. The science of logic: its perspective and human value

We are symbol-using beings. It is this basic human fact which has created the opportunity and need for Logic. We talk and think about reality symbolically and we pore over our symbol-products in the libraries, law-courts, offices and homes of our planet. It is a common experience to scrutinize pages of printed symbols, commenting on them as a fabric of meaning—on their clarity, their richness, their truth, the weight of the evidence in them, the validity of conclusions drawn. Indeed perhaps we do not advert sufficiently to the amount of life time spent in this second-order world created by language.

This is the world in which Logic moves and such observations and discoveries as it makes are immediately concerned with the purport of symbols and symbolic expressions rather than with the physical, living human world which is first-order reality. It is not dealing with objects which *are* this or that, but with signs which *mean* or *disclose* this or that to a mind. For this reason the specific technical language of Logic is not a first-order language (an object language) referring to the world in which we live, but a second-order language which describes, and refers to, our own human symbolic talking and thinking. Of course when the logician becomes reflective about his own work (as he does in Metalogic or the Philosophy of Logic) he poses the question as to whether discoveries about the inner nature and laws of meaningful speech and thought may not be discoveries also of necessities inherent in any intelligible physical world. It is obviously possible, for instance, that in discerning what is logically contradictory we are also discerning what is physically impossible.

There are many sciences working in the world of symbols as there are many natural sciences for first-order reality. Besides Logic there are, e.g. Semiotics, Semantics, Linguistics, Grammar, Psychology. What is the specific interest and perspective of Logic? Without attempting a definition at this time (indeed this is a central question for Metalogic) we can say, broadly, that Logic is concerned with the most basic facts about the structuring of meaning and with necessities inherent in thought and speech which arise from the very nature of meaning. Above all, the logician is concerned with the phenomenon of implication: like the physicist who is interested in gravitation and radio-activity, the logician is interested in the fact that evidence has force, gravitating our intelligence to a conclusion, that a conclusion is folded up in evidence (*plex*, a fold; hence 'implied') and falls out when we scrutinize the evidence sufficiently. Historically, this phenomenon has, one way or another, occupied a central position in Logic and it would not be a bad introductory description to say that Logic is concerned, principally, with observing and analysing varieties of implication and with formulating a theory of implication that will elucidate the phenomenon in general and will provide a logical foundation for reasoned conclusions in every area of life and science. 'There are . . . other elements in the tradition of logical teaching, but the greatest logicians of modern times have taken this as the central theme, and it seems reasonable to say that everything else in the corpus has its place there because of its connection with the main enterprise of classifying and articulating the principles of formally valid inference.' (W. and M. Kneale, *The Development of Logic*, p. 739)

What is the practical value of a course on Formal Logic? Intellectually in life we find ourselves doing two different things (1) employing symbols and orientating ourselves to symbolic expressions—to words, propositions, speech, print; (2) orientating ourselves to real people and physical things. Human life requires us to combine both orientations, to respond to symbols as well as to physical nature, (using the terminology of Newman) to reach notional as well as real assents. One can say, firstly, that Logic's contribution is to the symbolic side of human life, the area of notional beliefs. Indeed it used to be common to define Logic in terms of the use that could be made of it in our own personal thinking. Sample 'definitions' were: 'Logic is the science which directs the operations of the mind in the attainment of truth', 'Logic is the science which studies the principles which should regulate human thinking', 'Logic is the science which deals with the cognitive operations of the understanding which are subservient to the estimation of evidence'. It is important to see, however, that one is not really defining or describing *the science* when one mentions secondary gains from it.

Secondly, in this age of minute analysis and of duplicating human brain work, the capacity to objectify meaning and to study in detail its structure and dynamics has become of great practical importance. Such a capacity is developed and constantly exercised, in a very generalized way, in Formal Logic. Whatever view one may have, humanly, of the type of thinking that will characterize a highly analytic computer age it is clear that the technique of analysis will draw heavily on the science of Logic.

Finally, Logic has become intimately linked with Mathematics and in this way is exercising an important influence in modern theoretical science. In the form of modern Mathematical Logic it has established its right to a position in university faculties of Science.

II. Preliminary work done in a course on formal logic

The science of logic began as an X-ray discipline. Its founder, Aristotle, discovered a way to display and study the basic forms of statements and arguments. Basically, his technique was to invent a simple language (or set of symbols) consisting of variables and constants; when properly translated or transformed into this symbolism a vernacular statement such as *All men are mortal* is drained of all its reference to the objective world of men and graves;

only basic structural meaning appears on the X-ray plate which reads *SaP*. The metaphor of X-ray photography used in medicine and empirical science is modern, but it conveys Aristotle's insight and excitement when he realized he was the founder of a new science. Working in this X-ray, abstractive way, he was able to display and study forms more basic than those presented in the grammar of Greek speech, and he achieved powerful analyses of Greek forms of argumentation and proof.

It is the primary purpose of a preparatory section on logic (1) to make us sensitive and appreciative of the wonderful varied world of meaning that is brought into existence by human speech and thought; and (2) to cover the early X-ray work done by Aristotle in this world. The X-ray apparatus may, by modern standards, be crude; the areas of meaning X-rayed may be very simple, but they constitute the origins of the science and enable us to understand its modern format and development. Indeed Aristotle's influence on the whole history of logic has been decisive.

However, one distinctive aspect of modern logic should be noted. Logical language or symbolism was used abstractively by Aristotle to X-ray *existential* speech and argument. In modern logic this X-ray function disappears (except in Applied Logic): one designs a symbolism and then uses it constructively to make (logical) statements which can be tested and organized into systems of established logical truth. Thus while the value of logical language was displayed in the original abstractive X-ray approach of Aristotle, such a language functions now not primarily as an X-ray apparatus but primarily as a medium for *making* statements. In moving from the preparatory section to the section on formal logic in this book, one will be moving from the ancient abstractive use of a simple logical language to the modern constructive use of a more complex one.

The preliminaries of the course are concerned with bringing the student to the point where he can work with ease in a purely symbol-world, where he is alive to the varying shapes and structures of meaning and to its dynamic character. Any science that is directly concerned with symbols may provide helpful observations and topics for the student during this preliminary stage. It is customary not only to anticipate some elementary facts and X-ray operations of Formal Logic itself but also to draw on Semantics, Linguistics, Grammar and Psychology. The objective is that phenomena of meaning will be *experienced* as observable and complex facts in life deserving technical, scientific study.

Formal Logic itself will then begin with a presentation of the special language (or symbolism) that is used today.

Chapter 1

THE PHENOMENON OF MEANING

I. Human thought as a fabric of meaning and a context for phenomena of meaning

In contrast with sense-awareness, e.g. visual experience, thought is meaningful awareness: it is a disclosure of meaning, plan, intelligibility in the world or affairs of life. Its logical quality is measured under the following values:

clarity: how clearly meaning is grasped and communicated in speech and writing;
precision: sensitivity to what exactly this or that judgment or statement would commit one to; a skill in finding words that communicate what one wishes to say, no more, no less;
relevance: how systematic our thinking is, maintaining a proper connection with the topic or conclusion under discussion;
consistency: sensitivity to compatibilities and incompatibilities of meanings: this ensures that in the sequence of thought incompatible judgments are not made, i.e. judgments or assertions which, in virtue of their meaning, cannot all be true;
cogency: the capacity to reason in perfect logical sequence, i.e. to so structure a sequence of thought that acceptance of the evidence compels acceptance of the conclusion.

These are key terms in the logical evaluation of thought, just as dimensions, lines, proportion, symmetry are key terms in an architectural description of a building. They represent values that characterize the judicial mind—trained, clear and accurate in its ideas and use of words, relevant and cogent in its reasoning, searching in its testing of the reasoning of others; it is characterized by discipline and accuracy, by clarity and fluency, by a sensitivity to what words mean and what the evidence given really proves.

When one looks at human thought analytically, one can notice that its building blocks, ideas or concepts, have much in common with their linguistic counterparts, words. Both the idea and the word can bring into human consciousness something other than itself: they have the power to disclose, to signify, to mean something else; each is a sign. A word like Peter brings an individual before our consciousness; the thoughts of a mechanic bring before him the plan of the motor-car he is repairing—indeed if he is obsessional in his thinking he may not be able to disengage himself, mentally, from the car until it is repaired. Physical entities may be used like words as conventional signs: due to conventional agreement, a barber's pole brings shaves, shampoos and haircuts to our mind; a green light brings to mind a conceptual traffic rule. There are also physical entities which have a natural power to signify something else, e.g. smoke is a natural sign of fire, a good complexion is a natural sign of health, a photograph is a natural sign of the person photographed.

But among all these signs, the idea or concept has a unique feature. Each of the others is an entity in its own right and can be known entitatively before that which it signifies is also brought into consciousness. In technical terms the word or physical entity, like a traffic light, is an instrumental sign (an entity *used* to convey something else to the mind). But while my ideas disclose, e.g. physical objects, to me the peculiarity about them is that they cannot be known at all in separation from what they signify. There is an immediate apprehension of what is meant, represented or signified by the idea without the idea itself being known as an entity in itself. Thus the concept or idea is *essentially* a disclosure, a disclosure of meaning. It makes known without its existence as an idea being adverted to, except by reflection. It is a *medium in quo objectum directe cognoscitur*. Such a sign is called a formal sign because formally or essentially it is simply a representation: it has no other nature or form than its signification or meaning. The only formal signs are those within consciousness—concepts, judgments and reasonings. Signs extrinsic to the knowing process have only instrumental signification.

While it is important to become sensitive to the variety of vehicles which carry meaning—thought, language and to a limited extent physical entities—logic is not at all concerned with the vehicles as such, with the psychic reality of thought or the linguistic reality of statements. The facts and phenomena it studies appear only when meaning is achieved, and the same logical phenomena—e.g. the same implication—may appear both psychically in my thought and linguistically in my script. Thus thought and language are contexts for logical work rather than a subject matter of the science.

II. Language as a fabric of meaning and a context for logical phenomena

In language the mind succeeds in putting into public and human circulation its own thinking. Language is a system of conventional signs designed and learnt for the purpose of externating and transporting thought. Some speak in an associationist way of the link between words and the ideas or judgments they signify, saying that the mind attaches to sounds and marks the meanings it conceives within itself and structures these sounds and marks into propositions and arguments. For others it is incorrect to be separating word and thought in this way and thus better to speak of verbal thought, with the word as a unit of verbal thought. All are agreed that language succeeds in embodying thought without being a facsimile of it, and that it is a fabric of meaning and a context therefore for logical phenomena. Indeed it is the context where early logical observations and discoveries were made.

Medieval logicians spoke of Logic as being concerned with discourse, i.e. with our talking and thinking rather than with the natural world. This expresses the fact that the two contexts in which logical entities and phenomena may be discovered or produced are thought and language. This is an important consideration for Metalogic but the work of the Formal Logician is done in and through the medium of language.

Most of the following observations will deal with words, statements and arguments rather than with their mental counterparts—ideas, judgments and reasonings. However, they will be in some way valid for the latter, although language must not be looked on as a facsimile of the mental. The observations will proceed systematically from atomic units of meaning to the more complex.

III. The structuring of meaning

The incessant flow of ink and of sound-waves into our lives is sufficient evidence of a human drive to communicate meaning and of skill in doing so. A basic exercise in observing this skill consists in noting the variety of words we use and how various are the shapes of symbolized meaning.

Some words name a single individual or a single group, e.g. 'Socrates', 'this man', 'this football team'; they are called *singular names*. A *common name* is one that can be used distributively of many things—it is a class name which can be applied to each member of the class taken separately, e.g. man, soldier, team. A singular name may be a uniquely descriptive one, serving both to identify the individual and to describe it in some aspect, e.g. 'the President of Ireland', 'the discoverer of penicillin', 'the capital of Ireland'. Or it may be a proper name with which we identify but do not describe. Of course proper names acquire a private meaning for acquaintances of, e.g. John Smith, but this is not a conventional general meaning (technically called connotation). In the course of time a proper name may acquire a fixed invariable meaning and so be transformed into a common or general name. We speak of an individual as being a Don Quixote, a Nero, a Solomon, a Quisling. Captain Boycott, General Shrapnel, the Earl of Sandwich and Mr Joseph Aloysius Hansom have also enriched conventional language with their names.

'The angles of a triangle are equal to two right angles,' is an imperfect statement: it is not clear from the wording whether 'angles' is meant to be understood distributively or collectively. Some words are invented especially to signify a group or collectivity, e.g. 'jury', 'team', 'army'. A *collective term* is singular if it names a single group, e.g. 'this jury', 'the Irish army'; it is general if it can be used distributively of many groups, e.g. 'fleet', 'audience'. A singular collective name may be a proper name, e.g. 'the National Library', 'the Rockies', or a uniquely descriptive name, e.g. 'the congregation here present'. Collective statements are not as vulnerable to criticism as statements about a class of things distributively; the former are not refuted by a small number of adverse particular instances.

Abstraction—focusing aspects of reality and mentally isolating them—is both a human need and a human capacity. It gives rise in language to words which name natures, qualities or actions considered in isolation, e.g. 'humanity', 'height', 'navigation'. Such words contrast with *concrete names* which signify either the full individual or a nature, quality, action in its real context, e.g. 'Socrates', 'man', 'white'; and 'running' in 'he was running'. Abstract names are plentiful in Western languages: they are easily formed from adjectives (e.g. 'height', 'devotion', 'whiteness') and verbs (e.g. 'attention', 'walking' in 'walking is a fine exercise').

The words 'as such', 'ut sic', 'qua tale' qualifying a noun make its meaning abstract, e.g. in the sentence, 'A judge as such has not the power to make law' the force of the words, as such, is to make one consider the person precisely and exclusively in his role as judge. It is only in the mind however that a person can be precisely and exclusively an official. Since abstract names refer to attributes considered in isolation from their subjects, there is not a range of subjects to which they are applicable—as there is for instance in the case of the concrete term 'man', which can be applied to Europeans, Americans, Japanese, etc. Thus the meaning of an abstract name has a reference value ('whiteness' refers to the quality of being white) but not extension.

Being *positive or negative* is a prominent feature of meaning, and indeed the phenomenon of negation is of great importance in logic. Many words signify the absence of a quality, e.g. 'colourless', 'unfit'; where the quality should normally be present the negative word signifying its absence is called a *privative* term, e.g. 'deafness'. A positive name of course signifies the presence of a quality; it may also be abstract (e.g. 'greed') or concrete (e.g. 'hot').

Logic is interested in the opposition between paired names, one positive, the other negative. Thus 'hot' and 'non-hot' are contradictories; 'hot' and 'cold' are contraries. The former are exact opposites—they are mutually exclusive and collectively exhaustive, i.e. their opposition is such that in failing to come under one, any object with a temperature must come under the other. Contraries are not opposed in this exact way and so do not collectively exhaust all possibilities.

One can make the contradictory of any term by simply prefixing 'non' to it. Such terms are thoroughly negative, indefinite or indeterminate in range since they are applicable to anything that has not a certain quality. Some of them can create obscurity: 'Institutions for the care of the non-sick' presumably does not mean 'institutions for the care of the healthy'—but the difference is not apparent.

A distinction between *relative and absolute names* develops out of the systematic quality that meaning can have. A relative name signifies a thing or quality in relation to something else, e.g. 'father'; an absolute name signifies a thing or quality simply in itself, e.g. 'man'. A relative term is paired with a correlative, e.g. 'equal', 'greater', 'father' have as correlatives 'equal', 'less', 'child'. Is 'mountain' a relative term or an absolute one?—'A mountain is so only by its elevation above the plain, and yet in calling it a mountain we have in mind many features besides this relation.'

The words of vernacular languages are subject, through constant social use, to development and change. Few are *univocal*, i.e. used always in the same sense (*una voce*). *Equivocal* terms are used in two or more equal and independent meanings (*aequa voce*), e.g. 'vice', 'bit'; equivocation is based on the clever use of such terms. Most vernacular words are *analogical*, i.e. in the course of time they develop a variety of senses which are partly but not wholly the same. Scientists try to have a system of technical terms that are fixed in meaning; in philosophy the question is discussed as to whether a language applicable univocally to both God and creatures is in principle impossible.

Of cardinal importance to logic is the distinction between *first-order* and *second-order language*, or between *object-language* and *metalanguage*. Thus when I say: ' "Cat" is the subject of that sentence,' I am talking about the language used and have to employ a new level of words invented after (*meta*) the primitive object-words. Medieval logicians made the same point in distinguishing *terms of the first intention* and *terms of the second* intention. Mental activity was imaged as a stretching towards (*intendere, intentio*) the object and grasping (*apprehendere, apprehensio*) of it. Awareness of the world in which we live was called the primary or first intention of the mind; our reflective awareness of our own thinking—psychic or verbal—was called the second intention of the mind. By extension of usage, everything discovered in the first intention was itself called a first intention. Similarly terms of the second intention referred to such features, distinctions and properties as are discovered in the second intention of the mind. These terms (e.g. 'abstract', 'specific', 'contradiction', 'predication', 'implication') obviously constitute a metalanguage.

Logic has been described as a science of second intentions: it is not concerned with the natural world; it is developed in and through reflective awareness and it operates with a second-order language.

This fact is emphasized by the concern logic has for *syncategorematic words*. These words are so-called because they can never function as subjects or predicates (*categorein*, to predicate); they go with (*syn*) the categorematic words and link them together as subject and predicate, or modify them as subject and predicate or express an operation of thought. Examples are: 'all, some, and, is, not, or, if, if and only if, if . . . then, not . . . both, both . . . and, either . . . or'. Nowadays they are often called functors, logical constants, logical operators. They are the formative elements in discourse: one can change the other (categorematic) words of a statement without changing its form: e.g. 'All *men* are *spiritual*' has the same form as 'All *animals* are *mortal*'. The categorematic words give content or matter to the two statements, but it is the words 'all' and 'are' which structure and form them.

Logic is very concerned with the formative elements in symbolized meaning. Thus in the argument: 'If all men are mortal and if Socrates is a man, then Socrates is mortal,' the logician is not concerned with men or mortality but simply with the truth of the words, 'if . . . and if . . . then'. What is the force of these words? Am I entitled to use them, i.e. is the argument in fact valid? These are formal questions and can be answered without investigating the particular content of the statements and their material truth.

IV. A dualism within meaning: sense and reference

(It is the function of definitions and classifications to give a systematic presentation of sense and reference.)

Taking a simple word like 'man', one notes that it signifies the possession of certain attributes. This constitutes the sense or connotation of the word. The process of formulating this is called definition, and the formula is the familiar dictionary meaning of 'man'. However, the word has also a reference value: it is applicable to anything that realizes the definition. The range of sub-classes and individuals to which it is applicable constitute its reference value, extension or denotation. Thus the total signification of the word 'man' is complex—a blend of sense and reference.

Some words have reference merely, e.g. a proper name: it identifies an individual without connoting any attribute present. There are words also which have sense but no individual reference, e.g. abstract words. Most categorematic words have the two dimensions of meaning—sense and reference.

An expert in any subject will not only be able to define its technical terms accurately; he will also have a wide, personal experience of their range of reference. The technical operations which formulate sense (connotation) and reference (extension, denotation) are respectively definition and classification or division. They are basic to systematic thinking; thus definitions and classifications appear in the elementary section of pedagogical presentations—inverting the order of real enquiry where they are reached laboriously.

Indeed frequently definitions are only approximate and are called 'definition' only by a polite fiction. For the purpose of a definition is not merely to ascribe a fixed meaning for a term but to do so by revealing the nature of the thing signified, i.e. to verbalize an adequate insight into reality. To quote Aristotle (in *Posterior Analytics*, p. 101[b]) 'a definition is a phrase signifying a thing's essence'. Of course there are definitions which are concerned wholly with artificial symbols—with correct usage and not at all with any *object* apart from the symbols; these simply express volition and are not true or false in an objective sense. They are called merely *nominal definitions*, as opposed to the other *real definitions*.

It is important to evaluate the kind of information which a formula proposed as a definition gives. Is it merely nominal? If real, but approximate only, it may give a concrete picture with or without metaphor. If the description is literal and enables us to identify, e.g. a disease, the definition is called distinctive—this type is valuable in medicine: it enables the physician to diagnose and prescribe with confidence even though the nature of the disease is not properly known. The description of charity in I Corinthians 13 : 4 is a distinctive 'definition' of it. Some approximate definitions give the origin of the *definiendum*, or the way in which it can be produced really or ideally, e.g. 'An eclipse of the moon is a deprivation of light from the moon caused by the interposition of the earth between the moon and the sun'; 'A sphere is a solid figure formed by the revolution of a semicircle about its diameter, which remains fixed.' Others present samples and vary greatly in value according to the sampling that is done, e.g. 'The *Iliad*, the *Odyssey*, the *Aeniad, Paradise Lost* are Epic poems.' Others again signify purpose, e.g. 'A clock is a mechanical device for showing time.'

The classic technique of defining is *per genus et differentiam*, i.e. to detect the class of things to which the *definiendum* belongs and what differentiates it from the co-ordinate sub-classes. 'Man is a rational animal' is a familiar classic definition. It would be impossible to justify the claim that this type of definition is the only genuine type. The technique, however, is extremely useful and helps to implement the following basic rules:

1. *The definition should be convertible with the word to be defined*—neither wider nor narrower in reference value. It is too narrow, e.g. to conceive a politician as a member of parliament; too wide to conceive him as a person interested in public affairs.
2. *The definition should not use or include the term to be defined.* If it does so explicitly the definition is said to be *idem per idem*; if it does so implicitly (by using an expression which can be defined only in terms of the *definiendum*) it is said to be circular. However, the writer who defines an archdeacon as one who exercises the archdeaconal functions may not be defining badly so much as conveying, humorously, that no one knows what an archdeacon does.
3. *The definition should not be expressed in obscure or figurative language*, e.g. architecture is frozen music; memory is the tablet of the mind. A definition is not obscure simply because it presupposes an educated audience.
4. *A definition should not be negative unless the definiendum is purely negative.* 'Alien' is negative and can be defined reasonably as 'a person who is not a citizen'. The schoolboy was less successful when he defined vitamins as 'things which make you sick, if you haven't got them'.

As one organizes the words of ordinary life or of any special discipline, it becomes clear that there is not an infinite regress towards simpler terms, and that there are primitive terms which are undefined and indefinable. Very general terms like 'existing', 'thing', 'good', 'unity', are so wide in reference value that it is technically impossible to formulate their sense. Terms which express elementary sense-experience or the primary sensible qualities we experience are also indefinable, e.g. sensation, pain, hardness, odour, sound, colour, shape. At the other extreme—complexity—the full reality of an individual object is not definable humanly; indeed in the Aristotelian and Thomistic philosophies it is regarded as, in principle, not completely conceptualizable.

Today every discipline seeks to so organize its body of knowledge that primitive indefinable terms are evident and that all processes of definition are brought back to them.

Reference value is organized in the processes of division and classification, and it appears as a hierarchical series of genera and species. In logical division one begins with a term which names a very wide class (the *summum genus* of the series) and by processes of division and sub-division analyses it into sub-classes and these again into more subordinate classes until the lowest level of classes is reached (the *infimae species*) whose members are simply individuals. Classification, on the other hand, begins with the individuals, sorting them into classes, these classes being then grouped under a smaller number of wider classes—in other words it constructs the hierarchical series upwards, rather than downwards from the *summum genus*.

The rules for a correct or good logical division are as follows:

1. *Each separate division or sub-division should have a single basis* (the basis being some attribute of the genus which is realized in different ways by the species). Thus in dividing the term 'building' one may use, at choice, as basis: (a) the function of buildings (there are, e.g. homes, schools, churches, businesses); or (b) architectural style (e.g. Colonial, Georgian, Byzantine, contemporary); or (c) structural material (brick, stone, frame, metal). But it is faulty to oscillate from one basis to another; thus the division of buildings into homes, schools, Georgian, contemporary, metal, stone is faulty: it is a cross-division, failing to maintain a single basis (*fundamentum divisionis*), and, consequently, to separate the constituent species (the *membra dividentia*, so called because the species are pictured as sharing the genus between them).

2. *The division should be carried out exhaustively according to the basis chosen.* Every sub-class must be listed so that the extension of the sub-classes taken together is equal to the extension of the wide class. This rule is of practical importance. If an income-tax law is being introduced, the legislators will have to divide wealth into various forms and legislate on what is to be regarded as income. If their division is not complete, people whom they intend to tax may not come under the law.

3. *Successive sub-divisions should be gradual*, i.e. each basis should be continuous with the basis of the preceding sub-division, and immediately so. *Ne fiat saltus in divisione.* If one divides quantity into continuous and discrete and then sub-divides continuous quantity into triangles, quadrilaterals, etc., there is a jump in the division. A graduated process would sub-divide continuous quantity into plane and solid, and then sub-divide plane figures into rectilinear and curvilinear before proceeding to the further sub-division of rectilinear figures into triangles, quadrilaterals, etc. In practice the work of defining and that of classifying interact. Both contribute to a total grasp of meaning and to expert knowledge in any subject-matter.

There is an interesting relationship between the sense and reference values of a word. Class names with richer sense have less reference value. Take the class-names: square, rectangle, parallelogram, quadrilateral. Each name connotes a greater number of characteristics than the names which succeed it, and it has less extension than they. It is quite clear that a term with greater connotation has less extension for the connotation of a term determines its range of application. This point is sometimes expressed as follows: connotation and denotation vary inversely. However it is not accurate to speak so mathematically in this context. Connotation is not a calculable quantity and thus there cannot be a mathematical proportion between the variations in question.

Further, the actual number of individuals existing is not of logical interest. We must distinguish the range of species over which a term extends from the range of individuals to which it is applicable. We could speak of the former (with Joseph) as the extension of the term, the latter as its denotation. Joseph says (*Introduction to Logic*, ch. 6), 'It is plain that by the extension of a term we should not mean indifferently species and individuals; to be specified in divers ways is not the same as to be found in many instances.' Logic is more concerned with extension than with denotation, even when the term, denotation, is used to cover the indefinite number of possible instances, rather than an actual number.

V. More complex meaning: propositional meaning

A word is an atom of meaning; a sentence is a molecular structure—it is a set of words which we can use to say something. *Proposition* is the technical word used for that which is said, the content of meaning or *lekton* (a term of the early Stoic logicians). The same proposition can be expressed in different sentences (e.g. in German, French, etc.) and the same sentence can express different propositions (e.g. 'I was born in Dublin' as uttered by various people). The science of logic is concerned with the proposition not the sentence. Observations about sentences fall outside it, e.g. as to whether they are grammatical, ungrammatical, spoken, written, etc.

Since propositions are not sentences but the *lekton* or meaning conveyed in sentences, it follows that the elements of propositions are not words and the form of the proposition is not simply the verbal structure. Humanly however one comes to understand *propositions* better the more one understands the varying structures of *sentences* which express them. Indeed in modern logic a great deal of time has been spent in creating a special artificial language and in studying the sentences which are constructed in this logical language.

For our purpose it is sufficient to note that even in a vernacular language such as English there is a great variety of structure in ordinary familiar sentences. For example:

S is P, S is not P: simple subject–predicate forms in which the link word is a part of the verb *to be*, present tense, indicative mood; the statement is categorical or unqualified in tone.

S must be P, S cannot be P, S may be P, S need not be P: here one has not a categorical statement but a modal one expressing the mode or manner in which *P* is asserted or denied of *S*.

a is b and c is d; *a is b because c is d* . . .: these types of statements are compound conjoining simple statements with the word *and* or with words like *because, although*, etc., which contain the meaning of *and* but add some further nuance of meaning to it.

If a is b, then c is d: this is a conditional statement; the important, structural words are 'if . . . then'.

Either a is b or c is d: this is the type of statement in which we express alternatives.

VI. The complexity of signification in predicative sentences: some elementary features

The verbal structure of 'Some men are self-sufficient' consists of a subject-term, a predicate-term, a copula ('are') and a sign of quantity ('some', which indicates that the statement is not universal but limited in range).

The subject-term. The subject-term designates the object about which we are making the predication. This object is called the supposit of predication. Thus in the sentence: 'men are mortal', 'men' is the subject-term, but the statement is not about the term but about the real men signified by the term. The supposit of predication then is the real men.

It is the function of a subject-term to designate the supposit of predication. This may be done by means of a term like 'this' or 'that' accompanied by a gesture (e.g. '*this* is a hospital') or by means of a term which classifies the supposit (e.g. '*hospitals* are necessary') or which connotes some of its attributes (e.g. '*the older patients* are difficult'). In the first case the supposit is presented at the level of perception without any formal conceptualization of it; in the other cases terms that could be used as predicates are used in the subject position as explanatory and descriptive features of the supposit.

In some cases it may be quite difficult to determine the supposit, e.g. in impersonal statements such as: 'it is raining'.

A subject-term may be related to the supposit of predication in either of two ways: (1) It may be the supposit, as in the sentence: 'man is a three-lettered word'. Here the term is employed non-significatively, materially; the statement is about the term itself and the supposition is said to be material. (2) The term may be employed as subject because of its signification; it may be used significatively. In this case it signifies the supposit. If the supposit is a mental entity signified by the term, the supposition is said to be mental (e.g. in 'Man is abstract not pictorial' we are talking about the idea, man); if it is extra-mental the supposition is said to be real (e.g. 'Man is mortal').

The supposition of terms arises from the fact that reference has direction, i.e.

a vector quality. As used in the vernacular the same term may refer to a real entity or to the idea of that entity or it may refer to itself as a word. In Logic terms which are not identical in supposition are really distinct terms: accordingly, instead of speaking of the word, man, as being self-referring and being used in material supposition, it speaks of a new, second-order word, 'man' (spelling it with inverted commas). It is not relevant to logic to go further and differentiate in its language between terms used in real supposition and those used in mental supposition. However, it is an important rule that terms which are not identical in supposition cannot be used in reasoning as identical terms.

The predicate-term. The predicate-term signifies that which is attributed to the subject (or denied of it in a negative sentence). Predicates give various kinds of information about their subjects and these are called *predicables*. Porphyry's list of predicables is the traditional one; it is based on Aristotle's and is only slightly different from the original. Worked out systematically it is as follows: If one takes a singular term, e.g. Socrates as subject, a predicate may express the essence of Socrates fully and thus give his *species* ('rational animal') or it may express the essence partially, giving either the *genus* of Socrates ('animal') or the attribute which differentiates his species from others in the same genus ('rational' is the *differentia* of the species, man); if it does not express anything essential, it may give a *property* of Socrates deducible from the type of being he is (e.g. 'free', 'risible') or an attribute that is purely individual, an *accident* (e.g. 'snub-nosed').

Thus *species*, *genus*, *differentia*, *property*, *accident* are Porphyry's list of Predicables. The original classification by Aristotle was made having in view a subject term that was general (e.g. 'man') not singular (e.g. 'Socrates'). Accordingly the first predicable was not species but definition—the predicate 'rational animal' gives the species of Socrates, but the definition of 'man'.

The copula. The fact of predication is signified by the copula. Of course the linguistic symbol of predication is fixed by convention. Vernacular languages, however, display a remarkable bias for the verb of existence (e.g. S is P, S is not P). The question arises: has every predicative sentence an existential import or is there any appropriateness in using the verb *to be* as copula? It is clear that when I assert 'Mount Olympus is the abode of the gods' or 'Jove is the king of the gods' or 'Cerberus is a fierce three-headed dog guarding the gates of Hades', I do not mean to assert that Mount Olympus or Jove or Cerberus are real, physically. But they figure in Greek mythology and my sentences make a truth-claim, claim to conform to fact in some way. Accordingly some would speak of a predicative proposition as having existential validity for some universe of discourse—whether that be the physical world, or the world of Greek mythology, etc.

However, these considerations are extra-logical. They are bound up with vernacular language, and they concern the supposition of terms (mental or real) rather than the force of predication. A study of predication should not be confused with a study of the verb of existence. Indeed Aristotle signified predication by the words 'belongs to' ('*B* belongs to all *A*' instead of 'All *A* is *B*'). In modern logical notation the verb of existence does not appear: e.g. *F* is a symbol used for any predicate, *a* is a symbol used for any subject and the expression *Fa* (read as *F* of *a*) signifies that the property *F* belongs to the individual *a*.

Quantity and quality in predicative sentences. The final elementary features of signification in predicative sentences are *quantity* and *quality*. The latter refers simply to their affirmative or negative character. The former concerns range of reference. In 'All *S* is *P*' and 'Some *S* is *P*', the words 'all' and 'some' are signs of quantity; 'all' indicates that the subject-term is to be taken in the whole range of its extension, that the statement is universal; 'some' indicates that it is to be taken in part only of its extension, that the statement is particular. The former is called an *A* proposition, the latter an *I* proposition, and traditionally they are symbolized *SaP* and *SiP* (*a* and *i* being vowels from the Latin word *affirmo*). In the negative propositions 'No *S* is *P*' and 'Some *S* is not *P*', 'no' is now the sign of universal quantity and 'some' again signifies that the statement is particular. These negative statements are respectively *E* and *O* and are symbolized *SeP* and *SoP* (using the vowels of the Latin word, *nego*).

Thus on the combined basis of quantity and quality simple predications are classified as *A*, *E*, *I* and *O* propositions.

A proposition without any sign of quantity is called an indesignate (or indefinite) proposition and, logically, its signification is defective. However, in the vernacular, certain words or phrases which grammatically are part of the predicate, function as signs of quantity, e.g. 'Never', 'nowhere', 'under no circumstances', 'in no case', 'always', 'everywhere', 'not always', 'not every-where', 'occasionally', 'once', 'somewhere'. A proposition with 'the' prefixed to the subject-term often functions as a universal, e.g. 'The horse is a quadruped'. The indesignate form may be used deliberately to express a group tendency (rather than a universal truth), e.g. 'country children are more impressionable than city children'.

It is often difficult to say how far a writer or speaker wishes to commit himself by a statement of the form 'All *S* is not *P*'. Is he conceding that 'Some *S* is *P*' but stressing the fact that 'Some *S* is not *P*'? Or is he simply going as far as stating 'Some *S* is not *P*' without excluding either the possibility that 'No *S* is *P*' or the possibility that 'Some *S* is *P*'? Where the latter two possibilities are left entirely open, commitment is minimized. It is this minimum commitment that is imposed by the words of the statement, not anything stronger— whatever be the intention of the speaker.

Where the subject-term of a modal proposition has a sign of quantity, the proposition is said to have *dictum* as well as mode—*dictum* here connotes the presence of a quantity or range in the statement. There are eight kinds of modal propositions which have dictum: necessity and impossibility may be asserted in universal or particular statements ('All *S* must be *P*', 'Some *S* must be *P*'; 'No

S can be *P*', 'Some *S* cannot be *P*'); so also may possibility both in its positive and negative senses ('All *S* can be *P*', 'Some *S* can be *P*'; 'No *S* need be *P*', 'Some *S* need not be *P*').

VII. Value as a phenomenon within meaning

A meaningful statement either possesses or lacks the value of truth. A simple inspection of meaning is sometimes sufficient to show that a statement is true, e.g. '*A* is either *b* or non-*b*'. Such a statement is called a tautology or an analytic proposition: the act of seeing its truth and the act of grasping its meaning coincide. It is also called an *a priori* proposition, one that can be known to be true prior to, and independently of, experiencing actual instances of it. At the other extreme, there are statements which are self-contradictory, i.e. their meaning is such that it could never be verified. If the incompatibilities within meaning are present at the level of the basic form of a statement, then it is called a logical or formal contradictory, e.g. '*A* is both *b* and non-*b*'.

Most meaningful statements are contingent, i.e. their truth value cannot be read off from their meaning; they are known to be true in and through experiencing the facts signified or, indirectly, through the evidence of other facts. Experience, not simply meaning, is the criterion of their truth—they are empirically true or empirically false.

VIII. Simple relationships between predicative propositions

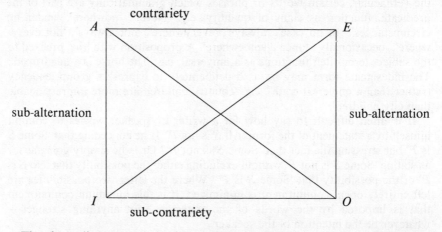

The above diagram sets out the relationships between *A*, *E*, *I* and *O* propositions which have the same subject- and predicate-terms. It is traditionally called the Square of Opposition although the relationships it displays are not all ones of opposition or conflict.

Contradictory opposition exists between propositions which differ both in quantity and quality—between a universal affirmative (*A*) and a particular negative (*O*), and between a universal negative (*E*) and a particular affirmative (*I*). Contradictories are an exact negation of each other, mutually exclusive and collectively exhausting all possibilities; thus one must be true, the other false.

A and *E* are contraries; indeed they are extreme contraries, for contrary opposition exists wherever the conflict is greater than contradiction (thus some propositions have many contraries). Contraries cannot both be true but they may both be false. Note that *I* and *O* propositions have not contraries: to contradict the *I* one must make a universal statement in the opposite direction (*E*) and there is no stronger statement remaining in that direction.

The relationship between *I* and *O* is not one of opposition although the technical name, sub-contrariety, suggests conflict. Both can be true at the same time, but both cannot be false.

Finally, the relationship between *A* and *I* and between *E* and *O* is one of sub-alternation. This is subordination not conflict: the particular affirmative is a sub-alternate of the universal affirmative, and the particular negative is a sub-alternate of the universal negative.

In some vernacular propositions quantity is signified by an adverb rather than by 'all', 'no', 'some', e.g. 'Men are always unhappy'. One can work out the full set of relationships between such propositions: e.g.

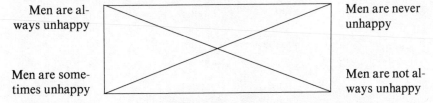

Men are al-ways unhappy

Men are never unhappy

Men are some-times unhappy

Men are not al-ways unhappy

Since, as we have seen, there are eight types of quantified modal propositions, the whole set of relationships between them is diagrammed in an octagon. The contradictory relationships may be worked out as follows:

MODAL PROPOSITIONS WITH DICTUM AND MODE

				Contradictory	
All *S* must be *P* Some *S* must be *P*	Asserts the mode, necessity,	of $\langle$ *all* *some*	Denies that mode	of $\langle$ *all* (*even of*) *some*	(Some *S* need not be *P*) (No *S* need be *P*)
All *S* can be *P* Some *S* can be *P*	Asserts the mode, possibility,	of $\langle$ *all* *some*	Denies that mode	of $\langle$ *all* *some*	(Some *S* cannot be *P*) (No *S* can be *P*)
No *S* need be *P* Some *S* need not be *P*	Negative possibility, possibility of not being *P*, is stated	for $\langle$ *all* *some*	Negative possibility is denied	of $\langle$ *all* *even of* *some*	(Some *S* must be *P*) (All *S* must be *P*)
No *S* can be *P* Some *S* cannot be *P*	Impossibility stated	for $\langle$ *all* *some*	Impossibility denied	of $\langle$ *all* *some*	(Some *S* can be *P*) (All *S* can be *P*)

Relationships of incompatibility can, of course, exist between all types of proposition, not merely between the predicative type. Every proposition has a contradictory—an exact minimal negation of its meaning—and any proposition which is stronger than this is a contrary. Formulating the contradictory of a statement is a good way of testing our grasp of its meaning.

The minimal negation of '*A* is *b* and *c* and *d*' is that '*A* is either not *b* or not *c* or not *d*'. This kind of negation is implicit in a plea of not guilty and it puts the onus on the prosecution of proving every part of the indictment. The contradiction of 'If *a* is *b*, *c* is *d*' is 'Even if *a* is *b*, *c* need not be *d*'; 'If *a* is *b*, *c* is not *d*' is a contrary. To contradict '*A* is either *b* or *c*' it is sufficient to assert that '*A* may be neither *b* nor *c*'. Finally, the contradictory of '*A* cannot be *b* and *c*' is '*A* can be *b* and *c*'; '*A* is both *b* and *c*' is a contrary.

Some predicative propositions seem to have double quantification, e.g. 'Some men are never satisfied', 'No man is always polite', 'Every man is sometimes selfish'. Here the adverbs do not function as quantifiers; they are part of the predicate and do not determine the range of the statement. The contradictories are accordingly: 'There is not any man-who-is-never-satisfied', 'Some men are always polite (the-sort-who-are-always-polite)', 'Some men are not the-sort-who-are-sometimes-selfish'.

Chapter 2

THE PHENOMENON OF IMPLICATION

I. Inference and implication

The words 'infer', 'inferring', 'inference' refer to the mental act of drawing and asserting a conclusion and since this is a personal act the mind may be gravitated towards the concluding assertion by a variety of forces. Certainly in real life reasoning is not simply structured in full and conscious conformity with logical rules of evidence. The word, implication, does not refer at all to the context of personal reasoning. It denotes a relationship between propositions such that the meaning of one proposition (the conclusion) is folded up (implied; 'plex', a fold) in the meaning of another proposition or in the combined meaning of other propositions (the evidence). The implication is objective: it is *there* whether or not any person is subjectively conscious of the fact. Thus 'All *S* is *P*' implies that 'Some *S* is *P*'; ideally, of course, my inference that 'Some *S* is *P*' should be governed by a perception of the implication. On the other hand, 'Some *S* is *P*' does not imply that 'All *S* is *P*'; notwithstanding the lack of implication, I may in real life make that kind of inference. We apply logical principles when in this or that context of personal inference we seek to discover whether the mental inference was governed by objective implications.

Synonyms for implication are 'consequence' (this gives a dynamic image of meaning: the conclusion follows on, and from, the evidence) and 'logical necessitation' (there is a compulsion, based on meaning, to accept the conclusion once the evidence is accepted).

II. Implications within the square of opposition

In virtue of their meanings, contradictories cannot both be true and cannot both be false; contraries cannot both be true but may both be false; sub-contraries cannot both be false and may both be true; if a universal is true the corresponding particular is true, if a particular is false the corresponding universal must also be false. Accordingly, the following is a table of inferences we can make on the basis of the square of opposition:

If *A* is true, *E* is false, *O* is false, *I* is true.
If *E* is true, *A* is false, *I* is false, *O* is true.

(Since the *A* and *E* propositions are of universal range, a complete set of inferences can be made when they are given as true.)

If *E* is true, *A* is false, *I* is false, *O* is true.

(Since the *A* and *E* propositions are of universal range, a complete set of inferences can be made when they are given as true.)

If *I* is true, *E* is false, *A* and *O* may or may not be true.

If *O* is true, *A* is false, *E* and *I* may or may not be true.

(Since *I* and *O* are of minimal range, the truth or falsity of any proposition other than the contradictory is simply not implied.)

If *A* is false, *O* is true, *I* and *E* may or may not be true.

If *E* is false, *I* is true, *O* and *A* may or may not be true.

(Since *A* and *E* are of universal range to know simply that they are false gives us minimal information.)

If *I* is false, *A* is false, *E* and *O* are true.

If *O* is false, *E* is false, *A* and *I* are true.

(Since *I* and *O* are of minimal range, to know they are false gives complete information about the whole set of propositions.)

The universal (e.g. *A*) implies the particular (*I*), the particular (e.g. *I*) is implied by the universal (*A*). The former implication is sometimes called superimplication, the latter subimplication.

III. Simple operations on predicative propositions which disclose implications: conversion, obversion, contraposition and inversion

Conversion is an operation in which we transpose the subject and predicate terms symbolized as *S* and *P*. Thus *S* becomes the predicate of the new derived proposition and *P* its subject. What is the converse of *SaP*? It will have the form *P S*, and it must be an implication of the original, i.e. be logically necessitated by the meaning of *SaP*. Is the converse *PaS* or *PiS*? An example would seem to counterindicate the former: 'All Frenchmen are Europeans' does not seem to imply that 'All Europeans are Frenchmen'.

At this point one must examine the relationship of evidence and conclusion: if we have not information about all *S* in the evidence we cannot say that a conclusion about all *S* is logically necessitated; similarly for the term *P*. This leads to the question: what information have we, quantitatively, about *P* in the propositions *SaP*, *SeP*, *SiP*, *SoP*? A sign of quantity tells us whether *S* is used in the whole range of its extension or not, i.e. to use a technical phrase, whether *S* is or is not distributed; thus the symbols *a* and *e* tell us that a universal affirmation or denial is being made about *S*, the symbols *i* and *o* that the affirmation or denial is particular. But there is no sign of quantity for *P*. Do the forms of these propositions disclose anything about the extension of *P*? The answer is important for the validation of operations such as conversion.

For the purpose of drawing implications from the meaning of a proposition, it is clear that a term must be treated as undistributed if it is not known to be distributed. Taking the two affirmative propositions, *A* and *I*, the *A* does not signify whether 'All *S*'s are all the *P*'s' or whether 'All *S*'s are only some of the

P's', and the *I* does not signify whether 'Some *S*'s are all the *P*'s' or 'Some *S*'s are some of the *P*'s'. Thus for the purpose of inference *P* must be treated as undistributed in affirmative propositions.

In negative propositions, on the other hand, whether we are talking about the whole range of *S* or about some *S* only, we are excluding them from the class *P*. Thus we are talking about *P* in its class extension and *P* is accordingly distributed.

The rule for inference therefore is that a negative proposition distributes its predicate, an affirmative proposition does not. On this basis the valid converse of *SaP* (where *P* is undistributed) is not *PaS* (where *P* is distributed) but *PiS* (where *P* remains undistributed). The converse of *SeP* is *PeS*; of *SiP* is *PiS*. There is no valid converse of *SoP*: the only feasible claimant, *PoS*, distributes *S* which in the original evidence is undistributed.

Obversion is an operation in which we introduce a double negation into a proposition, substituting for the predicate (*P*), its logical contradictory ($\overline{P}$) and balancing this by changing the quality of a proposition (an *A* to an *E*, an *I* to an *O* or vice versa). The original proposition is called the obvertend, the implied one is called the obverse. Thus the obverse of *SaP* is *Se$\overline{P}$*; of *SeP* is *Sa$\overline{P}$*; of *SiP* is *So$\overline{P}$*; and of *SoP* is *Si$\overline{P}$*.

When a single predicative proposition is the evidence, conversion and obversion are the basic operations on it which disclose implications. The other operations, contraposition and inversion, are a combination of conversion and obversion.

Contraposition alternately obverts and converts so as to derive a new proposition which has for its subject the contradictory of the original predicate ($\overline{P}$):

	(1) *Obverse*	(2) *Converse of Obverse*	(3) *Obverting* (2)
SaP	*Se$\overline{P}$*	*Pe$\overline{S}$*	*Pa$\overline{S}$*
SeP	*Sa$\overline{P}$*	*Pi$\overline{S}$*	*Po$\overline{S}$*
SiP	*So$\overline{P}$*	None, and thus the *I* proposition has not a contraposititve	
SoP	*Si$\overline{P}$*	*Pi$\overline{S}$*	*Po$\overline{S}$*

Thus there are two contrapositives of *A*, *E* and *O* propositives. Some writers call (2) a partial contrapositive and (3) a full contrapositive.

In inversion the derived proposition has as its subject the contradictory of the original subject, i.e. the inverse has the form $\overline{S}$ *P* or $\overline{S}$ $\overline{P}$. Actually only *A* and *E* propositions have inverses. To get the inverse of *A* you obvert first; with *E* you convert first:

SaP,	*Se$\overline{P}$*,	*Pe$\overline{S}$*,	*Pa$\overline{S}$*,	*Si$\overline{P}$*,	*SoP*
SeP,	*PeS*,	*Pa$\overline{S}$*,	*SiP*,	*So$\overline{P}$*	

If you begin converting with the *A* proposition or obverting with the *E*, the sequence of conversions and obversions leads to an *O* proposition which cannot be converted, as is the case with the *I* and *O* propositions no matter how the sequence is structured.

If one is converting, obverting, contraposing or inverting vernacular propositions it is often necessary to put them into a more appropriate shape where (1) subject and predicate are clearly indicated, (2) the copula is part of the verb *to be* in present tense, indicative mood, and where (3) there is a sign of quantity before the subject term. If the meaning of the original proposition is not clear enough to formulate in this way, then it will not be possible to convert it, etc. It is not a matter of the new form being better than the original but of its being convenient for the operations of conversion, etc. Thus one would not want to improve on 'No news is good news' or 'Men think' but to convert these propositions one must translate them into something like 'In every instance the absence of news is good news', and 'All men are such-that-they-think'. It is not a happy phrase to describe this as putting propositions into logical form, the suggestion here being that the new propositions are an improvement on the originals.

IV. The crux of inversion

The inverse of *SaP* is $\overline{S}oP$ in which the predicate is distributed while it is not distributed in the original proposition. A rule of inference seems to be violated, and yet each separate step of conversion and obversion is valid.

The inverse of *SeP* does not involve this particular formal difficulty but in it a difficulty arises which has essentially the same solution.

By analysing an example of each kind of inversion we shall see that an assumption is made in inversion, and that the process is valid or not according as that assumption is or is not verified.

Inverting an A proposition

Given: All future acts are known to God (*SaP*), the successive stages are:
No future act is unknown to God (*Se$\overline{P}$*)
Nothing unknown to God is a future act (*$\overline{P}$eS*)
Everything unknown to God is a non-future act (*$\overline{P}$a$\overline{S}$*)
Some non-future acts are unknown to God (*$\overline{S}i\overline{P}$*)
Some non-future acts are not known to God (*$\overline{S}oP$*)
(Notice by contrast that given: All Frenchmen are Europeans, the inverse: Some non-Frenchmen are not Europeans, is also a *true* proposition.)
Solution: There is an assumption that the new term $\overline{P}$, developed in this process, can be used in real supposition, i.e. that there are or can be non-*P*'s. Thus there is an auxiliary statement understood along with the original *S a P*, namely that there are non-*P*'s, i.e. there are some things which are not *P*'s—an *O* proposition with *P* distributed. It follows then of course that these things which are not *P*'s are things which are not *S*'s.

Thus the reasoning in the example can be presented fully as follows:

Granted that all future acts are known to God, *then if* there are things unknown to him, these things must be non-future acts.

Inverting an E proposition
SeP, PeS, PaS̄, S̄iP
Granted: No great poet (is one who) has actually written a flawless epic poem.
Inverse: Some non-great poets (are ones who) have actually written flawless epic poems..
Solution: It is assumed that the term *P* (poets who have produced flawless epic poems) admits of being used in real supposition, i.e. that there are such poets. The inverse that it is non-great poets who are such, follows on this assumption. Without this assumption you could not pass validly from the original negative statement *(SeP)* which does not involve the existence of *P*, to the positive assertion *S̄iP* which does involve the existence of *P*.

As a general conclusion one can say: Only those *A* propositions have a valid inverse in which the term *P̄* has designation (i.e. in which there are non-*P*'s); and only those *E* propositions have a valid inverse in which the term *P* has designation (i.e. in which there are *P*'s). Thus the operation, inversion, is not absolutely self-guaranteeing—it will not develop a true conclusion from an original truth under all conditions. The solution to the crux of inversion lies in formulating the conditions under which it is valid. The governing rule is that we are not entitled to use a term in real supposition in a conclusion, if the evidence does not use it in real supposition. And the requisite conditions are that in the case of the *A* and *E* propositions respectively, *P̄* and *P* be *given* in real supposition.

V. Other simple implications

Immediate inference by added determinants consists in adding the same qualification to the subject and the predicate of the original proposition, e.g. 'A statue is a work of art' implies that 'A beautiful statue is a beautiful work of art'. This kind of inference is valid provided the qualification has an identical meaning when applied to both subject and predicate. 'A cottage is a building' does not imply 'a huge cottage is a huge building'—'huge' is a relative qualification.

Immediate inference by omitted determinants is an inference in which from a proposition affirming of a given subject an attribute qualified by a determinant, we infer a proposition affirming of the same subject the attribute without qualification. Thus 'God is an infinite spirit' implies 'God is a spirit'. An inference of this kind is not valid if the determinant negatives the attribute: 'this is a bad shilling' does not imply 'this is a shilling'.

Immediate inference by complex conception consists in employing both the subject and the predicate of the original as parts of a more complex conception: 'A horse is a quadruped' implies 'The head of a horse is the head of a quadruped'. Similar errors may occur here as in the other types mentioned.

Immediate inference by converse relation consists in inferring correlations. Thus the proposition 'A is older than B' implies that 'B is younger than A'.

Finally *immediate inference by modal consequence* consists in inferring that a thing *can* be so from the fact that it *is* so; or in inferring from the *necessity* of it being so that it *can* be so, and also that it *is* so; or in inferring that it *is not* so from the fact that it *cannot* be so.

VI. Complex implications: the simple categorical syllogism

In syllogistic reasoning two propositions (called premisses) are so combined as to imply a third proposition (the conclusion). The syllogism is named after the type of propositions which constitute it; accordingly where premisses and conclusion are simple categorical propositions the syllogism is called a simple categorical one. Aristotle analysed it fully and in studying his presentation of its mechanism one is experiencing a Formal Logician at work.

> All things which reproduce their kind are living
> All viruses are things which reproduce their kind
> _____
> Therefore all viruses are living
> _____

This is an argument in biology, but one can abstract from the biological content and focus the general structure. Two terms ('virus' and 'living') are linked up in the conclusion through being alternately linked in the premisses with a third term ('things which reproduce their kind'). Aristotle saw that by using variables for these terms (S for the subject of the conclusion, P for the predicate of the conclusion, and M for the common middle term) he could isolate and completely analyse the basic structure of this kind of argument. Just as the chemist in his laboratory physically isolates chemical entities, so too the logician by his use of variables succeeds in isolating structures of meaning. The chemist and logician work in two different worlds but there is a basic identity about their needs and about the movements of their intelligence.

Substituting variables the biological argument becomes

> All M is P (MaP)
> All S is M (SaM)
> _____   _____
> Therefore all S is P (Therefore SaP)
> _____   _____

To present the argument in a completely formal way, eliminating any suggestion of personal belief in the constituent propositions and focusing simply the fact of implication, one can use the format

If all M is P	(If MaP)
and if all S is M	(and if SaM)
then all S is P	(then SaP)

What is asserted here is simply and solely a logical fact, the truth of the words 'If ... and if ... then.' The syllogism then is simply a single continuous implicative statement.

From this point a complete treatment of the categorical syllogism almost writes itself. There are four possible Figures according to the position of M in the premisses:

First Figure	*Second Figure*	*Third Figure*	*Fourth Figure*
$M - P$	$P\ M$	$M\ P$	$P - M$
$S - M$	$S\ M$	$M\ S$	$M - S$
$S - P$	$S\ P$	$S\ P$	$S - P$

The premiss in which P appears is called the major premiss and by convention is written first. P is called the major term and S the minor term. The premiss in which S appears is called the minor premiss. In the First Figure S and P occupy their natural positions: S is subject in the conclusion and in its premiss, P is predicate in both the conclusion and its premiss. Reasoning which embodies this First Figure format is very natural and fluent. In the Fourth Figure on the other hand S occupies the predicate position in the minor premiss and P the subject position in the major. It is not easy to experience the cogency of valid reasoning when it is in this form. Aristotle regarded the First Figure as the perfect form. Actually, the Fourth Figure is not frequently used.

Since simple categorical propositions are of four kinds, A, E, I and O, categorical syllogisms may consist of various combinations of these. The same combinations are not valid in every figure. In the First Figure the following sequences (for major premiss, minor premiss, conclusion) are valid: AAA, EAE, AII, EIO are valid; all other possible sequences would violate some rule governing the syllogism. There is a medieval latin mnemonic for memorizing the valid combinations (or *moods*) of each Figure through the sequence of vowels in each word:

> Barbara, Celarent, Darii, Ferioque prioris. Cesare, Camestres, Festino, Baroco secundae. Tertia Darapti, Disamis, Datisi, Felapton, Bocardo, Ferison, habet. Quarta insuper addit Bramantip, Camenes, Dimaris, Fesapo, Fresison.

This mnemonic is quite dispensable as the general rules of the syllogism are simple and their application to each figure is not difficult. However, it contains a code also for reducing all syllogistic reasoning to a first figure format.

The general rules of the simple categorical syllogism refer to structure, quantity and quality:

Rules of structure
(1) A syllogism must contain three and only three propositions.
(2) It must contain three and only three terms.

Since the implied relationship between S and P is rooted in their separate relationships to a common term, it follows that a syllogism is defective if it fails to have a term common to both premisses. This is the logical flaw or fallacy of *Quaternio Terminorum*—having a set of four terms instead of three. Sophistical arguments sometimes commit this fallacy, e.g.:

> Every rare thing is a dear thing
> But a-horse-for-a-penny is rare
> _____
> Therefore a-horse-for-a-penny is dear

Rules of quality
(1) From two negative premisses there can be no conclusion.
(2) If one premiss is negative, the conclusion must be negative; and if the conclusion is negative one premiss must be negative.

Information that neither S nor P is linked with M does not imply any particular interrelationship between them; again information that one is positively linked with the common term and the other is not can at most imply a negative interrelationship.

Rules of quantity
(1) The Middle Term must be distributed in one at least of the premisses.
(2) No term may be distributed in the conclusion unless it has been distributed in its premiss.

If the reference in both premisses is to some M merely, then the M's to which S is related need not necessarily be any of the M's to which P is related, so that there is not effectively any common term. Distribution of M in one premiss ensures a common area of reference. Violation of this rule is called the fallacy of *Undistributed Middle*. With regard to the quantity of S and P, quite clearly one cannot draw a valid conclusion about 'all S' or 'all P' if one has information about only some S or some P in the relevant premiss. Violations of this rule are called an *Illicit Process of the Minor Term* (S) or an *Illicit Process of the Major Term* (P).

> *Every detective is armed*
> *But No criminal is a detective*
> _____
> *Therefore No criminal is armed*

Here an Illicit Process of the Major Term is committed—P is distributed in the negative conclusion but is undistributed in the major premiss where it is the predicate of an affirmative proposition.

Corollaries

(1) From two particular premisses there can be no conclusion.

Proof: Both premisses cannot be negative. The remaining possibilities are that only one premiss is negative or that neither premiss is negative.

If one of the premisses is negative, the conclusion must be negative and *P*, consequently, be distributed in it. Since the premisses are particular none of the subject terms are distributed, and of the predicates only the predicate of the negative premiss is distributed. Thus there is not provision for the distribution of *P* along with *M*; there must be then either an Illicit Process of the Major Term or an Undistributed Middle.

If both premisses are affirmative (as well as particular) there is not any term distributed in them. Consequently there is the fallacy of Undistributed Middle.

(2) If one premiss is particular, the conclusion must be particular.

Proof: If both premisses are affirmative only one term can be distributed, the subject of the universal premiss. For validity it must be *M*. Accordingly *S* is undistributed in its premiss and may not be distributed in the conclusion.

If one premiss is negative, an additional term is distributed, the predicate of the negative premiss. But since the conclusion must now be negative and distribute *P*, the extra term distributed in the premisses must be *P*. Thus *S* is still undistributed in its premiss and may not be distributed in the conclusion.

These general rules and corollaries enable us to eliminate some of the 16 possible combinations of *A E I O* in the premisses:

AA	AE	AI	AO
EA	~~EE~~	EI	~~EO~~
IA	IE	~~II~~	~~IO~~
OA	~~OE~~	~~OI~~	~~OO~~

Special rules may be worked out for each figure determining the moods that are valid in each. In the First Figure (1) the minor premiss must be affirmative and (2) the major premiss must be universal. If the minor premiss were negative, the major premiss would have to be affirmative (with *P* undistributed in it) and the conclusion would be negative (distributing *P*) involving an illicit process of the major term. The major premiss must be universal to distribute its subject, *M*. (Thus *AAA, EAE, AII, EIO* are the only valid First Figure moods.)

In the Second Figure, (1) one premiss must be negative (to distribute *M*) and (2) the major premiss must be universal (to distribute *P* and so avoid an illicit process of the major term.) Thus *EAE, AEE, EIO, AOO* are the valid moods of the Second Figure which is sometimes called the figure of exclusions because its conclusions are negative.

In the Third Figure (1) the minor premiss must be affirmative for the same reason as in the First Figure. Consequently, (2) the conclusion must be particular as *S* is predicate of the affirmative minor premiss and so undistributed in it. *AAI, IAI, AII, EAO, OAO, EIO* are the valid moods of this Figure, called the figure of examples because its conclusions are particular, being used either to contradict or prepare the way for a universal.

The rules of the artificial Fourth Figure are only listed for the sake of completeness: (1) If the major premiss is affirmative, the minor must be universal; (2) If the minor premiss is affirmative, the conclusion must be particular; and (3) If either premiss is negative, the major premiss must be universal. Thus *AAI, AEE, IAI, EAO, EIO* are the valid Fourth Figure moods.

Nineteen valid moods are listed in all. Of these, fifteen are called fundamental moods. The other four are called strengthened moods; two of them are from the Third Figure *AAI* (Darapti) and *EAO* (Felapton) and two from the Fourth Figure *AAI* (Bramantip) and *EAO* (Fesapo)—in each case the two premisses need not be universal in order to imply the conclusion. Finally, the number of valid moods can be brought from nineteen to twenty-four, as in five of the moods the conclusion is universal so that there is room for five more weakened moods in which the conclusions are particular.

(*Note:* In translating vernacular arguments into the *S, P, M* symbolism, it is important to remember that although singular propositions are not universal they are symbolized as *A* (affirmative) or *E* (negative). This convention is based on the fact that there is a sufficient identity of behaviour within the syllogistic context to warrant this extended use of the symbols. Thus the classic syllogism, 'All men are mortal, but Socrates is a man; therefore Socrates is mortal' is symbolized '*MaP*, but *SaM*; therefore *SaP*.')

VII. Some exercises on the rules of the simple categorical syllogism

Procedure in doing the exercises:
(1) Work out your answer roughly, if necessary by testing the problem in the separate figures; but have as your aim to find a reason from the *general rules* of the syllogism.
(2) Formulate your final answer fully but concisely.

Samples of formulated answers:
First Exercise: Why do not the premisses *IE* yield a valid conclusion in any figure while the premisses *EI* yield a valid conclusion in every figure?

The premisses *IE* yielding a negative conclusion (with *P* distributed in it) involve an illicit process of the major term (*P* being undistributed in the major premiss whether in subject or predicate position).

The premisses *EI* provide for the distribution of two terms (*M* and *P*) in the major premiss. If the conclusion is particular no other term need be distributed in the premisses for validity.

Second Exercise: Prove that when the minor term is predicate in its premiss the conclusion cannot be *A*.

The symbol *A* connotes a proposition that is affirmative and universal. If the conclusion were *A*, both premisses would have to be affirmative. *S* being the predicate of an affirmative premiss would be undistributed and so it would have to be undistributed in the conclusion—that is to say, the conclusion would have to be particular.

Third Exercise: If the major term be predicate in the major premiss, what do we know about the minor premiss?

The minor premiss must be affirmative. If it were negative the conclusion being negative would distribute *P*. Further the major premiss would have to be affirmative leaving *P* undistributed in it (as predicate). Thus there would be an illicit process of the major term.

Fourth Exercise: Why can an *O* proposition occur as a major premiss only in Fig. 3 and as a minor premiss only in Fig. 2?

An *O* premiss gives rise to a negative conclusion in which *P* is distributed. Consequently *P* must be distributed in its premiss, i.e. be predicate of the *O* major premiss. This rules out Figs 2 and 4 where *P* is subject in its premiss. In Fig. 1, *M* is not distributed in the major (being subject of *O*) and cannot be distributed in the minor premiss (which is affirmative and has *M* for predicate).

An *O* minor premiss also gives rise to a negative conclusion in which *P* is distributed. It involves the major premiss being affirmative. In Figs 1 and 3 where *P* is predicate in its premiss this means that an illicit process of the major term cannot be avoided. In the 4th Figure, *M* is undistributed in both minor premiss (which is *O* and has *M* for subject) and in the major premiss (which has to be affirmative and has *M* for predicate).

Fifth Exercise: Prove that an *A* proposition can be proved only in Fig. 1.

None of the other figures can prove a conclusion that is both affirmative and universal. Fig. 2 proves only negative conclusions (one of the premisses must be negative to distribute *M* once). In Figs 3 and 4, *S* is predicate in its premiss. If the conclusion is universal it will have to be distributed in its premiss which must then be negative. But a negative premiss cannot give rise to an affirmative conclusion.

Sixth Exercise: Prove that if the middle term is distributed in both premisses the conclusion must be particular.

If both premisses are affirmative only two terms can be distributed in them (the terms occupying the subject positions). Actually *M* is distributed in each. Thus *S* is not distributed in its premiss. Consequently the conclusion must be particular.

If one premiss is negative an extra term is distributed but this must be *P* which is now distributed in the negative conclusion. Once again *S* is not distributed in its premiss and consequently the conclusion must be particular. No conclusion follows from two negative premisses.

VIII. Is there any real inference in the simple categorical syllogism?

Even in Aristotle's time it was urged that a simple categorical syllogism begs the question, i.e. assumes the conclusion in the very course of the proof. The English logician, John Stuart Mill, formulated the objection very clearly: 'It must be granted that in every syllogism, considered as an argument to prove the conclusion, there is a *petitio principii*. When we say, *All men are mortal, Socrates is a man, therefore Socrates is mortal*, it is unanswerably urged by the adversaries of the syllogistic theory, that the proposition, *Socrates is mortal*, is presupposed in the more general assumption, *All men are mortal*, that we cannot be assured of the mortality of all men, unless we are already certain of the mortality of every individual man.' (*A System of Logic*, Bk II, ch. 3, § 2)

Throughout history, logicians who are radical or extreme empiricists in their philosophy (believing that human knowledge is exclusively an organic sense knowledge) classify universal propositions as numerative. *SaP* means simply that every instance of *S* is *P*: it is either a valid shorthand expression if our experience is comprehensive or it is an excessive generalization if our experience is incomplete. In our reasoning therefore a universal proposition functions either as shorthand for complete numeration of instances or as an acceptable practical guide when our experience is extensive. In the latter case the real evidence present is not the universal proposition but such experience as we have and which has induced us to formulate the universal as a practical guide. Mill puts the point very forcibly: 'All inference is from particulars to particulars. General propositions are merely registers of such inferences already made, and short formulae for making more: The major premiss of the syllogism, consequently, is a formula of this description; and the conclusion is not an inference drawn *from* the formula, but an inference drawn *according to* the formula: the real logical antecedent or premiss being the particular facts from which the general proposition was collected by induction.' (*A System of Logic*, Bk II, ch. 3, § 4)

Concerning, e.g. the syllogism 'All men are mortal, Socrates is a man, therefore Socrates is mortal' it is also objected that to know the minor premiss is true, one must know that Socrates has all the attributes of man including mortality. Inevitably again (it is contended) the conclusion must be known or assumed in the course of an alleged proof.

Sir W. D. Ross summarizes Aristotle's contribution to an answering of these objections:

> Aristotle is not unaware of the objection that has been brought against the syllogism, that it involves a *petitio principii*. If I argue 'All *B* is *A*, All *C* is *B*, Therefore all *C* is *A*', it may be objected that I have no right to say All *B* is *A* unless I already know *C* (which is a *B*) to be *A*, and that I have no right to say All *C* is *B* unless I already know *C* to be *A* (which is implied in its being *B*). These objections rest on erroneous assumptions. (1) The first rests on the assumption that the only way of knowing that All *B* is *A* is to examine all the instances of *B*. As against this Aristotle is aware that in dealing with certain types of subject-matter (e.g. in mathematics) a universal truth may be ascertained by the consideration of even a single instance—that the generic universal is different from the enumerative. (2) The second objection rests on the assumption that, to know that All *C* is *B*, you must know it to have all

the attributes involved in being *B*. This objection he implicitly meets by his distinction of property from essence. Among the attributes necessarily involved in being *B* he distinguishes a certain set of fundamental attributes which is necessary and sufficient to mark *B* off from everything else; and he regards its other necessary attributes as flowing from these and demonstrable from them. To know that *C* is *B* it is enough to know that it has the essential attributes of *B*—the genus and the differentiae; it is not necessary to know that it has the properties of *B*. Thus each premise may be known independently of the conclusion. And even both may be known without the conclusion being known. The drawing of the conclusion involves the 'conjoint contemplation' of the premises, and if they are not thus viewed in relation to one another, we may be ignorant of the conclusion, and may even believe its opposite without thereby explicitly breaking the law of contradiction. The advance from premises to conclusion is a genuine movement of thought, the explication of what was implicit, the actualising of knowledge which was only potential. (*Aristotle*, ch. II: Logic, Published by Methuen, pp. 37–8)

Thus the fundamental position of Aristotle and of all moderate empiricists is that human thinking is not simply a sense knowledge: we possess and often display a capacity for insight into what is so universally and what is so by necessity, and the most valuable universal propositions that we have mean, primarily, that *S* *is essentially P*—the quantitative meaning, *every instance of S is P*, being subordinate. Of course where a universal proposition is purely numerative (e.g. 'All the days of last week were wet') we cannot reasonably adduce it as proof of any instance (e.g. 'Wednesday of last week was wet').

IX. Syllogisms other than the simple categorical type

Abbreviated forms. Concrete reasoning is rarely formulated fully; perhaps indeed in argument we differ most in what we do not say. Often a syllogism is abbreviated by the omission of a premiss or of the conclusion; such an abbreviated syllogism is called an *enthymeme*—a part of it is *en* (in) *thumos* (the mind)—and according as the major premiss, minor premiss or conclusion is tacit, it is said to be of the first, second or third order. An example is the statement: 'That war was long and bitter, for it was a civil war.' Fully formulated the argument is 'All civil wars are long and bitter, that war was a civil war, therefore that war was long and bitter.' This example illustrates an interesting fact: we often know a proposition is true (e.g. an historical fact) before we are able to discover the premises which will prove and therefore explain it. For Aristotle one is able to explain a proposition when one can show the general principle from which it can be deduced. Thus we often construct a syllogism not to prove the conclusion is a true proposition but to show why it is true, to demonstrate or explain it.

Sometimes a reason is annexed to one or both premisses in support of it. Such a premiss can be expanded into a syllogism; thus there are really two or more syllogisms telescoped into one. The abbreviated syllogism is called an *epicheirema* (so called, perhaps, in Aristotle's logic because it was a weapon in Greek debate). An example is 'Every *M* is *P* because it is *N*, every *S* is *M*, therefore every *S* is *P*.' The major premiss can be expanded into the distinct syllogism 'Every *N* is *P*, every *M* is *N*, therefore every *M* is *P*.' This is a single Epicheirema; in a Double Epicheirema a reason is annexed to both premisses.

A polysyllogism is any chain of syllogisms. It is called a Sorites (from the Greek *soros*, a heap) if the intermediate conclusions are suppressed. There are two kinds of Sorites, the Aristotelian and Goclenian (named after Rodolfus Goclenius, Professor at Marburg at the end of the sixteenth century). In the former one advances to terms of greater extension and each conclusion becomes the minor premiss of the following syllogism. An example is '*A* is *B*, *B* is *C*, *C* is *D*, *D* is *E*'; this expands into three syllogisms; '*B* is *C*, *A* is *B*, therefore *A* is *C*; *C* is *D*, *A* is *C*, therefore *A* is *D*; *D* is *E*, *A* is *D*, therefore *A* is *E*.' The special rules for an Aristotelian Sorites are (1) only the last premiss may be negative; and (2) only the first premiss may be particular.

In a Goclenian Sorites the terms are of decreasing extension, i.e. are regressive in extension, and each conclusion becomes the major premiss of the following syllogism. An example is '*D* is *E*, *C* is *D*, *B* is *C*, *A* is *B*, therefore *A* is *E*'; this expands into '*D* is *E*, *C* is *D*, therefore *C* is *E*; *C* is *E*, *B* is *C*, therefore *B* is *E*; *B* is *E*, *A* is *B*, therefore *A* is *E*'. The special rules for a Goclenian Sorites are (1) only the first premiss may be negative; and (2) only the last premiss may be particular.

The modal syllogism. It includes one or more modal propositions, e.g. 'All *M* must be *P*, all *S* may be *M*, therefore all *S* may be *P*.' Here, although the major premiss affirms necessity, the conclusion follows the weaker mode of the minor premiss.

Compound syllogisms. There are as many varieties of compound syllogisms as there are varieties and combinations of compound propositions, e.g. compound categorical, conditional, alternative, disjunctive syllogisms.

Examples of *compound categorical syllogisms* are '*A* is both *b* and *c*, *D* is *A*, therefore *D* is both *b* and *c*'; 'An eternal being is immortal, only God is eternal, therefore only God is immortal.' This latter syllogism is invalid: its conclusion consists of two statements, 'God is immortal' and 'No one else is immortal'; in the latter statement *P* is distributed although it is not distributed in the major premiss.

The purely *conditional (or hypothetical) syllogism* consists exclusively of conditional propositions, e.g. 'If *A* is *B*, *C* is *D*, and if *E* is *F*, *A* is *B*, therefore if *E* is *F*, *C* is *D*.' If one of the premisses is categorical, the syllogism is called a *mixed conditional (or hypothetical) syllogism*. It has two very important valid forms:

If *A* is *B*, *C* is *D*

A is *B*

―――――――――

Therefore *C* is *D*

―――――――――

This is called the *modus ponendo ponens*, i.e. in positing the antecedent one posits, by implication, its consequence.

If *A* is *B*, *C* is *D*

C is not *D*

―――――――――

Therefore *A* is not *B*

―――――――――

This is called the *modus tollendo tollens*, i.e. in denying the consequent one is committed to denying the antecedent which implies it.

The following two forms, however, are invalid, i.e. the conclusion is not really implied:

If *A* is *B*, *C* is *D*

A is not *B*

―――――――――

Therefore *C* is not *D*

―――――――――

The fallacy of denying the antecedent is committed here. We have not evidence that *A* being *B* is the only condition under which *C* is *D*; accordingly we are not entitled to argue that since *A* is not *B* then *C* is not *D*; nor would we be entitled to argue that since *C* *is* *D* then it must be a fact that *A* is *B*—this is the fallacy of affirming the consequent:

If *A* is *B*, *C* is *D*

C is *D*

―――――――――

Therefore *A* is *B*

―――――――――

An example of the valid *alternative syllogism* is '*A* is either *b* or *c*, *A* is not *b*, therefore *A* is *c*'. There are two valid forms of the *disjunctive syllogism*: '*A* is either *b* or non-*b*, *A* is *b*, therefore *A* is not non-*b*' and '*A* is either *b* or non-*b*, *A* is not *b*, therefore *A* is non-*b*'. The valid *conjunctive syllogism* reads '*A* is not both *b* and *c*, *A* is *b*, therefore *A* is not *c*'.

The *dilemma* is a syllogism having as major premiss a conditional proposition and as minor premiss an alternative or disjunctive proposition. The conditional premiss must contain at least two antecedents or two consequents.

If *A* is *B*, *C* is *D*; and if *E* is *F*, *G* is *H*

But Either *A* is *B* or *E* is *F*

―――――――――

Therefore Either *C* is *D* or *G* is *H*

―――――――――

The antecedents are called the horns of the dilemma as they face us with a choice between unpleasant consequences. (The figure is taken from bull-fighting.) The choice may be between two, three, four or many consequences, so the analysis of dilemma covers also trilemma, tetralemma, polylemma.

The rules for a valid dilemma are:

(1) The antecedents must involve the consequences attributed to them.
(2) The disjunction in the minor premiss must be complete, i.e. there must not be a third possibility.

To escape from a dilemma one may
(a) *grasp one of the horns*, i.e. deny that an antecedent really entails the consequence attributed to it. One could perhaps grasp both horns in the following dilemma:

> If you take wine, you will gradually becomes intemperate;
> if you don't take wine, you will become dull and anaemic.
> But you must either take wine or not take it.
> ___
> Therefore you will either become intemperate or become dull and anaemic.
> ___

(b) *Escape through the horns*, i.e. assert that there is a further possibility which the minor premiss does not visualize. One could escape through the horns of the following:

> If you advise a person to do what he intends to do, your advice is superfluous; and if you advise him to do what he intends not to do, your advice is useless.
> But you advise a person to do either what he intends to do or what he intends not to do.
> ___
> Therefore your advice is either superfluous or useless.
> ___

Quite clearly the possibility of a person being undecided is not listed.
(c) *Rebut the dilemma*—get another bull to attack it by formulating a second dilemma in which one formulates the same facts from a different (and more pleasant) point of view:

> If you go through the field you will meet the bull, and if you go down the lane you will meet the farmer.
> But you must either go through the field or down the lane.
> ___
> Therefore you will meet the bull or meet the farmer.
> ___

One rebuts this dilemma as follows:

If I go through the field I will not meet the farmer, and if I go down the lane I will not meet the bull.
But I must either go through the field or down the lane.

Therefore I will either not meet the farmer or not meet the bull.

X. Validity and truth in argument

An argument is an implicative statement: it claims that the evidence it brings implies the conclusion it draws. And it claims that the evidence is factually true. Thus there are two kinds of truth claim in an argument—a claim that the physical facts referred to are as they are said to be (natural truth) and a claim that the logical fact of implication is present in the argument as it is said to be by, e.g. the word, *therefore* (logical truth). Validity is really a synonym for logical truth—the truth of words such as 'therefore', 'then', 'as a consequence'; the 'truth' with which it is contrasted is natural truth, not truth in its general sense of conformity to fact of any kind.

When one detects that an argument is invalid one does not thereby learn anything about the truth or falsity of the conclusion. One simply sees that there is no logical sequence or necessitation from evidence to conclusion: implication is not present as it is claimed to be, so that there is a logical falsity about the argument. But the natural facts asserted may or may not be so: some or all of the propositions in the argument may be materially true. It is a mistake, therefore, to infer that because an argument is invalid, its conclusion is a false proposition.

When an argument is seen to be valid we have this guarantee: if its premisses are true propositions, the conclusion is a true proposition also. It is a fascinating fact that we can have such a guarantee about natural truth from the logical form of the argument, i.e. from the presence of implication which is a phenomenon of meaning. When premisses are false propositions, is a valid conclusion from them false also? An example shows that since we are not dealing with facts in the evidence, the presence of implication ensures *consistency of meaning* solely—the conclusion may be true: 'All Roman Emperors were Presidents of U.S.A.; Lincoln was a Roman Emperor, therefore Lincoln was a President of U.S.A.' In this consistent argument the premisses are false but the conclusion states a fact.

XI. Rules of inference

All men are mortal
But the Greeks are men

Therefore the Greeks are mortal

Here we see very easily that the conclusion is implied by the premisses. But what precisely causes the implication? We could answer that there is a principle or canon governing this argument, namely that what is stated or denied about any class in its entire extension (e.g. mankind) is also stated or denied for each member and each species of that class (e.g. the Greeks). (In Aristotelian logic this particular canon is technically called the *Dictum de Omni et Nullo.*)

The rules that govern valid argumentation, giving rise to implications, constitute a very important topic in modern logic. This topic covers every form of argument, not merely the syllogism.

XII. How to analyse an argument

(One should be concerned to observe the argument fully before passing to value judgments about its validity or the truth of the statements in it.)

1. What is the question at issue?
2. What conclusion or conclusions are drawn in the course of the argument?
3. What evidence is presented for each conclusion? Is there any assumption made? What is the nature of the reasoning?
4. With regard to each conclusion and its evidence, note the presence of any or all of the following features in the language:

   (a) Ambiguity in any word or phrase. If the statements are quite clear note that fact.
   (b) Metaphorical words and phrases, i.e. note the presence of picturesque, colourful language.
   (c) Emotive words, i.e. words that are emotionally toned.
   (d) Intimidating words and phrases.
   (e) Prestige words or associations.
   (f) Repetition.

5. Is the reasoning for each conclusion *valid* reasoning? If there is a flaw, point it out.
6. With regard to each of the statements constituting the evidence, a further and separate question is: is it true?

Chapter 3

THE PHENOMENON OF UNREASON: ANTINOMIES (OR PARADOXES) AND FALLACIES

It is a common human experience to be unreasonable and to encounter unreason in other people; one, however, does not expect to encounter unreason as an objective phenomenon within meaning itself. That is what appears to happen in the antinomies—statements whose meaning does not seem amenable to the norms of contradiction; etymologically, they are in opposition (*anti*) to law (*nomos*). Antinomies are of great concern to logicians as, ultimately, they challenge the possibility of sciences of meaning; and the study of them has been an important factor in the development of modern logic.

Historically, antinomies or paradoxes were prominent in early Greek philosophy. Zeno of Elea constructed some in order to argue for the unreality of motion (e.g. the paradox of Achilles and the Tortoise). The Megarians designed the antinomies of the Heap and the Bald man (what number of pebbles make a heap? what number of hairs constitute baldness?) which were really concerned with the possibility of precision. One of the Megarian antinomies, that of the Liar, is of great concern to logic: 'A man says that he is lying. Is what he says true or false?' In being true it seems to be falsified and in being false it seems to be confirmed.

Medieval logicians over two centuries studied this paradox and Paul of Venice in his *Logica Magna* lists about fourteen solutions.

This century has seen the development of new paradoxes, one of the simplest and most important being Russell's: Take the class or set of all objects that are not members of themselves. Is that set a member of itself? If it is, then it is not. If it is not, then it is. Other modern examples are the Burali–Forti paradox, Cantor's, Richard's, the Zermelo–König paradox, Berry's and Grelling's.

Antinomies are important for logic because they challenge current logical intuitions and since they are of various types their solution demands the formulation of an explicit and complete body of logical laws. It is possible to handle individual antinomies in many ways and the literature on them is very great; the best work has consisted not so much in undermining a paradox as in enlarging logical insights as, e.g. in Russell's theory of types and the modern analysis of metalanguage.

The unreason that appears in ourselves and in other people presents itself as an object for scientific study rather than as a challenge to the logical possibility of science. In its intellectual aspect where it consists in the violation of some evident logical rule it is called a fallacy.

A fallacy may be committed outside the context of reasoning. Ambiguity, for instance, is a flaw in our use of words or structuring of sentences. It may arise from the employment of the same word in different senses (*the fallacy of equivocation*), e.g. 'our cheeses are handled by dealers all over the country'; or it may consist in forming a proposition the structure of which makes it ambiguous (*amphibology*, literally: throwing on both sides), e.g. the witch in Henry VI says, ambiguously: 'the Duke yet lives that Henry shall depose'; and the testator was not perfectly clear in stating 'I give and bequeath the sum of £500 to my cousins . . .' Originally, the source of the *fallacy of accent* lay in the fact that Greek words were written without accents and breathings, were capable of varying accentuation and consequently of different meanings. Accents were not employed in Greece until the end of the third century B.C. and the fallacy appears in Aristotle's list with the above meaning. Today the fallacy lies in perverting the original and intended meaning of a statement by false emphasis in speaking or writing. By the use of italics or capitals in writing or tone in speaking or by selecting special passages, one may give a false impression of another's statement. From a logical point of view this is unreasonable and a fallacy; it is interesting to note that, etymologically, an ethical criticism is built into the word, fallacy (*deception*).

The fallacy of many questions (*plures interrogationes*) consists in framing a composite question and demanding a single yes or no answer to it: 'Have you begun paying your debts yet?' One might reply, '*Nego suppositum*—I deny the assumption that I have debts.' In ordinary life when one is asked, 'Isn't it terrible that X did such and such?' one is asked to comment on two things really: is it terrible to do that kind of thing and did X actually do it. *The fallacy of figure of speech* (*figura dictionis*) consists in supposing an undue similarity in meaning between words of similar structure. We might easily suppose from 'visible' and 'audible' that 'desirable' means 'able to be desired', instead of 'able to stimulate desire, worthy to be desired'.

We have already noted fallacies at the level of simple reasoning (within the Square of Opposition; in the operations of conversion, obversion, contraposition, inversion; and in other simple operations) and at the more complex level of syllogistic reasoning. These are called Formal Fallacies because they occur in the basic form of an argument, this form being focused by the use of artificial symbols S, P, a, e, i, o, M.

The remaining fallacies in the traditional (basically Aristotelian) classification are as follows:

1. (A dicto) *secundum quid* (ad dictum simpliciter): The defect here consists in interpreting a qualified statement as if it were unqualified, or in assuming that what holds true in some particular respect, or under special circumstances, will hold true in every respect or under all circumstances. A person commits this fallacy when, having got assent to the statement that it is lawful to take life in a just war, he proceeds to argue as if it had been conceded that it is always lawful to take life. When in 1910 the Liberal Government of Great Britain threatened

to create enough peers to override the veto of the House of Lords, the Conservative press countered by picturing the absurdity of cab-drivers and butlers being lords.

2. *Ignoratio elenchi* (ignorance of the nature of refutation): This fallacy consists in being irrelevant in argument. It is committed when one establishes some point that does not conflict with the view one is attacking. Sidgwick comments on some of the leading varieties of this fallacy: 'Thus mildly denying that a certain thing is absolutely all-important, we are met by arguments to show it has some use; boldly pointing out that something else is altogether valueless, we are met by the answer that we can't expect perfection; asserting that some doctrine lacks arguments to prove its truth, we are referred to excellent reasons for believing in its utility; disputing an argument or an instance, we are supposed flatly to deny the theory in support of which these are brought forward; making some merely tentative suggestion we are asked for definite proofs.' (*Fallacies*, p. 188)

3. Various forms of appeal to feeling or prejudice, etc. presented as if they were logical arguments:

(a) *Argumentum ad populum*: appealing to the emotion and feeling of an audience (instead of setting out a logical argument) in order to gain support for one's view.

(b) *Argumentum ad hominem*: attacking the view of one's opponent by attacking his character or history. A contemporary form is constructing a psychogenetic account of how and why the proponent came to hold his view.

(c) *Argumentum ad baculum*: threat or insinuation of physical force instead of logical argument.

(d) *Argumentum ad ignorantiam*: using an argument the plausibility of which rests on the ignorance of the audience.

(e) *Argumentum ad verecundiam*: urging the dignity of those who hold a particular opinion as an adequate reason for holding the opinion.

(f) *Argumentum ad misericordiam*: seeking to excite sympathy instead of bringing forward relevant arguments.

4. *Petitio principii* (begging the question): This fallacy consists in assuming, to some extent at least, the conclusion which is to be proved. The original meaning of this fallacy was: asking your opponent to concede some fundamental point in your case. The present day meaning is wider. Thus a person commits this fallacy if he claims to prove a conclusion by a premiss that is only verbally different from the conclusion, if he uses as an argument some proposition that requires the conclusion in order to be proved true (circular reasoning) or if (without proof) he uses as an argument some principle which his opponent is not prepared to concede. The assumption may be separated by a great length from the conclusion. Whately comments: 'A very long discussion is one of the most effectual veils of fallacy. Sophistry, like poison, is at once detected and nauseating when presented to us in a concentrated form; but a fallacy which when stated barely, in a few sentences, would not deceive a child, may deceive half the world if diluted in a quarto volume.'

5. *Fallacy of composition*: This consists in assuming that what is true of things taken separately, is true of things taken collectively. 'You can carry this? This? This? Therefore you can carry this plus this plus this.' The capacity of a jury to reach a sound verdict is not measured by the summation of individual capacities. Everywhere in human life and in chemistry, the bonds of society and of organization contribute.

6. *Fallacy of division*: This consists in assuming that what is true of things taken collectively is true of them taken separately.

7. *Non causa pro causa*: This consists in putting forward as proof an argument that is not relevant or not cogent. It differs from *ignoratio elenchi* where you really prove some point, but the point does not conflict with the view you are attacking. This fallacy is committed in *post hoc ergo propter hoc* reasoning. The Latin name of the fallacy can be translated thus: 'to give as a reason that which is not a reason'. A fallacious argument of this kind is sometimes called a *non sequitur*.

8. *Proving too much*: Using an argument which if pressed to its full logical conclusion would entail the truth of some proposition known to be false, or unfavourable to one's own position. That which proves too much proves nothing, e.g. 'It is wrong to deprive oneself of anything one did not give oneself. But to commit suicide is to deprive oneself of something one did not . . . Ergo to commit suicide is wrong.' The conclusion may happen to be true, but the major premiss proves too much—it implies also that it is wrong to dispose of gifts.

The pioneer work on fallacies is Aristotle's *De Sophisticis Elenchis* (Concerning Sophistical Refutations). Francis Bacon gave a psychological classification of subjective factors (or tendencies) which are harmful to reasoning. He called these tendencies *idols*. *Idols of the Tribe* are beliefs which spring from natural tendencies and impair objectivity (he draws attention, e.g. to 'the danger of relying upon appearances, on the untested and uncriticized data of the senses'); *Idols of the Den* are errors arising from individual temperament, education, etc.; *Idols of the Market Place* are the tyranny of freely and frequently used words: unless we are alive to the ways in which a smoothly operating language can mislead us, it will be a barrier to real knowledge; finally *Idols of the Theatre* are philosophic systems that are fashionable but false.

Chapter 4

THE APPLICATION OF LOGIC IN
LIFE AND SCIENCE

Wherever there is an evidence-conclusion structure there is room for some contribution from logic, for it is the business of logic to construct a general theory of implication and to display all the possible forms of implication. Accordingly the primary function of applied logic is to abstract the formal structures of concrete reasoning and to convey what is known about them in Formal Logic, i.e. to service life and science with technical knowledge of the basic forms they are using—whether valid or invalid, etc.

It is possible to misconceive the legitimate role of logic and, e.g. to visualize it as seeking to formalize human life or as seeking to dictate the structure of scientific investigation. Logicians themselves have often been quite unrealistic about their role and have alienated people whose mind and responsibility is severely practical. Mr Baldwin, an English Prime Minister, exemplified this alienation in his last public speech (1937):

> Now I would like, as but an indifferent historical student, to make an observation about our Constitution . . . One of the most interesting features about it historically is that the Constitution was not evolved by logicians. The British Constitution has grown to what it is through the work of men like you and me— just ordinary people who have adapted the government of the country in order to meet the environment of the age in which they lived, and they have always preserved sufficient flexibility to enable that adaptation to be accomplished.
>
> Now that is extremely important, because it seems to me that one of the reasons why our people are alive and flourishing, and have avoided many of the troubles that have fallen less happy nations, is because we have never been guided by logic in anything we have done.
>
> If you will only do what I have done—study the history of the growth of the Constitution from the time of the Civil War until the Hanoverians came to the Throne—you will see what a country can do without the aid of logic, but with the aid of common sense. Therefore, my next point is: Do not let us put any part of our Constitution in a strait waist-coat, because strangulation is the ultimate fate.
>
> And I would say one more thing—don't let us be too keen on definition . . . Politically, if ever a saying was true, it is this: 'The letter killeth, and the spirit giveth life.'

Mr Baldwin feels that a constitution evolved by logicians would be a precise, rigid, inflexible instrument—quite unworkable in real life over any period of time. This must be said however: making constitutions is a political function, not a logical, scientific or artistic one; logic itself is a limited, technical science of forms but that is no reason why logicians should, in personal and social living, become dedicated to formalization.

The view that what is reasonable must not be confused with what the laws of abstract reasoning allow had its greatest advocate, perhaps, in John Henry Newman. He argues that reasoning in concrete matters whether of everyday life or history or law or science or religion cannot be fully formalized. Logic works in an impersonal way and is quite unequal to the task of formulating fully the grounds, the stages and the elements of reasoning that give rise to personal belief. Thus one of the main tasks of his *Essay in aid of a Grammar of Assent* was to explore personal inference which on the one hand could not be completely formalized and yet, on the other hand, could achieve results which passed formal logical tests. It would be difficult to overestimate the contribution which this book has made to the psychology of inference. And although Newman speaks as if his work were, in some way, an indictment of logic, it is at most an indictment of some logicians. For while the science of logic studies forms, of itself it neither prescribes formalization nor attenuates reality to form.

In the logic of science, again there is no reason why the contribution of logic should assume the character of an intrusion. Science, in both its experimental and highly theoretical stages, is the great living context of evidence-conclusion structures. It is of great human importance to examine these structures in their basic forms, to see if they pass formal tests of validity, and if not, to what extent their deficiency is, or can be, counterbalanced. Both the scientist with his experience of the context, and the logician with his knowledge of forms, must co-operate here.

Some of the problems indeed appear quite formidable. The laws of empirical science (e.g. that heavy bodies unsupported in air will fall) are universal propositions formulated on the basis of limited sense experience. There seems to be a process of reasoning here which moves from 'some instances' to 'all instances' and accordingly is an excessive generalization. Certainly in Formal Logic there is no valid form of implication between 'some' and 'all'. Yet from the time of Francis Bacon until the present century, logicians tried to validate as *proof* the inductive reasoning of empirical science. This was the historical problem of induction (induction being the process of generalization from 'some' to 'all'). Today both scientists and logicians are quite clear on the fact that induction does not embody a form of implication and can only establish a probable conclusion.

However, evaluating conclusions in terms of probability creates new problems about the evidence-conclusion structure: What are the rationale and grounds of probability theory itself? Can probability theory be used in science without making prior assumptions about the world, without a 'scientific faith' that the world is amenable to rational enquiry? Or can the probability value of inductive generalizations be validated directly from instances, without any extra-logical assumptions about the world, i.e. is it of formal logical consequence? Modern logicians have made important contributions towards the answering of these questions; their success owes a good deal to the fact that they work under controlling descriptions given by the physicist and mathematician. Logicians like Bacon and Mill, who wrote outside any such control, had been quite unrealistic and were severely criticized by contemporary scientists.

In the theoretical stage of science where laws are co-ordinated under a comprehensive theory, the deduction of implications and verification of them are important procedures. Science demands that every theory be verifiable. Yet while a theory is disproved if its logical consequences, the results it predicts, do not occur, it is not proved by their actual occurrence. For the form in positive verification is 'If A then B; B; therefore A.' Formal Logic does not classify this as a valid form, an embodiment of implication. Translated into a rule, as it is in verification, it is quite fallible. Thus while verification increases the probability of a theory it can never prove it; to claim it could is to commit the fallacy of the consequent.

The end-results of science are theories that grow more and more comprehensive with the advance of science. Resting as they do, for validity, on verification these theories are exceedingly fragile. Indeed the greater the degree of co-ordination they achieve, the more vulnerable are they to small discrepancies.

Modern science recognizes logical limitations in its structure but balances them by the scrupulous and extensive nature of observation and experiment in it, and by being a continuously self-correcting, self-testing enterprise.

Any ultimate clarification of evidence-conclusion structures and problems, in human thinking generally and in science, cannot be achieved by the logician solely. These are dealt with in an (applied) discipline of logic called Methodology which is now written, however, under controlling descriptions and guidance from other sciences.

EXERCISES

Exercises on the general nature and structuring of meaning

1. Compile a general bibliography on the topic, meaning.
2. Write an essay comparing and contrasting the human vehicles of meaning—words (in social life) and ideas (within consciousness).
3. Write out an account of the working of any material object or process—natural or artificial. This account should include some reasoned observations. Then examine the list of sentences you have written. They are true of the material object yet not a facsimile of it. Discuss the kind of features and phenomena present in the sentences and not in the material object (and vice versa).
4. Using as a basis the following statements, suggest what factors in statements tend to stimulate laughter:

> 'I collided with a stationary tramcar coming in the opposite direction.'
> 'To avoid a collision I ran into the other car.'
> 'The car had to turn sharper than was necessary owing to an invisible lorry.'
> 'The accident was due to the road bending.'
> 'If the other driver had stopped a few yards behind himself, it would not have happened.'
> 'I blew my horn but it would not work as it was stolen.'
> 'I consider neither vehicle was to blame but if either was to blame it was the other one.'
> 'I knocked over a man. He admitted it was his fault as he had been knocked over before.'

5. In each of the following groups arrange the terms in the order of increasing connotation:
(a) integer, number, positive integer, prime, rational number, real number.
(b) cheese, dairy product, limburger, milk derivative, soft cheese, strong soft cheese.
6. How far can one get in a definition of the following terms:
'right' (in the context of a 'declaration of human rights'); 'normal' or 'normalcy', and 'proved'?
7. Evaluate the following formulas as definitions:

> A lawyer is a man who defends criminals in court.
> 'Sleep' means a dormant state of the organism.
> War is an armed conflict between nations.
> A king is a person invested with the office of royalty.

8. If Walter Scott is the author of the novel *Waverly*, have the terms 'Walter Scott' and 'the author of *Waverly*' the same sense and reference values?
9. Classify the forms of political government that exist in the world today. Suggest an *a priori* division of 'transport'.

Exercises on the phenomenon of conflict—contradiction and contrariety

Give the contradictory and, where possible, a contrary of the following propositions:

Some mistakes need not be rectified.
Everyone is mistaken sometimes.
That is exactly what I wanted.
If Paul were rich, he would be happy.
Youth is always full of hope.
Half the flock perished of the pest.
It is either unworkable or too expensive.
One thing alone gathers people into seditious assemblies—oppression.
Under certain conditions we can achieve certainty.
Humour is never totally devoid of aggression.
No news is good news.
It is only if *a* is *b* that *c* can be *d*.
Through a point which lies outside a straight line one and only one straight line can be drawn parallel to the given line.
A little learning is a dangerous thing.
A is *b* because *c* is *d*.

Exercises on simple implications

Given a certain proposition is true and asked to test the validity of an inference from it, this is a sound procedure:

Put both propositions into symbolic form and compare them. If the terms S and P reappear in the new proposition and in their original positions, then the new proposition must be a contradictory, contrary, sub-altern or sub-contrary of the original and be true or false accordingly. (The Square of Opposition covers the relationships between propositions with the same S and P.)

Otherwise see if the proposition to be tested has the form of a converse (S and P interchanged), obverse (quality changed with $\bar{P}$ as predicate), contrapositive ($\bar{P}$ as subject) or inverse ($\bar{S}$ as subject). Then get the genuine converse or obverse, etc. (as the case may be) and compare the two propositions. The proposition to be tested may be seen immediately to be valid or invalid. Or a closer comparison may be required (e.g. the proposition to be tested may be the sub-altern, the contradictory or a contrary of the genuine conclusion you have drawn for comparison).

The following are exercises:

1. Granted the truth of the first proposition in this series, designate the succeeding propositions as consequently true, consequently false, or as not being implied by the original:

Every living thing is conscious.
No living thing is conscious.
No living thing is non-conscious.
No non-conscious thing is living.
Some living things are conscious.
Some living things are not non-conscious.
Some conscious things are living.
Every conscious thing is non-living.
Some conscious things are not living.
No conscious thing is living.
Every non-conscious thing is non-living.
Every conscious thing is living.
Some non-conscious things are non-living.
Some non-living things are non-conscious.
Some living things are non-conscious.

2. Granted that every X is Y designate the following propositions as consequently true or false, or as being such that the given proposition does not imply either truth or falsity:

Every X is non-Y
Every Y is X
Every Y is non-X
Every non-X is non-Y
Some Y is non-X
Some non-X is non-Y
Some Y is not X
Some non-Y is not non-X
No Y is X
Every non-X is Y

3. Give, where possible, the converse, obverse, contraposition and inverse of the following:

Some mathematicians are not musical.
All comparisons are odious.
No norm is absolutely valid.
Some temperaments are difficult to control.

4. Given SaP is true, list all propositions which are either consequently true or consequently false. (As a basis use relationships within the Square of Opposition and the operations of conversion, etc.)

5. Given SeP is true, how many propositions are there which are either consequently true or consequently false?

6. Investigate the formal relations between:

    (a) All S is P, and All non-S is P.
    (b) All non-S is P, and All non-P is S.
    (c) All non-S is P, and All S is non-P.

7. Granted that the first proposition in the following series is true, indicate (with reasons) whether each of the other propositions is consequently true, consequently false or simply not implied:
Good men alone are wise.
He who is good is not unwise.
Anyone who is not good is unwise.
No unwise men are good.
Not all good men are wise.
It is false that all unwise men are good.
8. Examine the following simple inferences:
(a) a tortoise is an animal; therefore a swift tortoise is a swift animal.
(b) all German existentialists are German philosophers; therefore, all existentialists are philosophers.

Exercises on the syllogism

1. Prove that O cannot be a premiss at all in Fig. 1, that it cannot be the major premiss in Fig. 2 and that it cannot be the minor premiss in Fig. 3.
2. If the minor premiss of a syllogism be O what is its figure and mood?
3. Determine the figure and mood of a valid syllogism which fulfills these conditions: (a) the major premiss is affirmative; (b) the major term is distributed in the conclusion; (c) the minor term is undistributed in both premiss and conclusion.
4. Granted that the major term is distributed in its premiss and undistributed in the conclusion of a valid syllogism, determine the figure and mood of the syllogism.
5. Given SaP as the conclusion of a valid syllogism, determine the figure and mood of the syllogism.
6. If the minor premiss of a valid syllogism is negative, can you determine the position of the terms in the major premiss?
7. If the conclusion of a syllogism is a universal proposition, the middle term can be distributed only once in the premisses. Explain.
8. Test the following syllogism for validity: 'If some dinosaurs are carnivorous, and if all dinosaurs are extinct, then some extinct animals are carnivorous.'
9. Prove that when the middle term is distributed in both premisses, the conclusion must be particular and the mood is a strengthened mood (i.e. both premisses are universal and the same conclusion could be proved with one of them particular).

10. Prove that if a valid syllogism contains an O premiss its middle term must occupy the same position in both premisses.

11. If the major premiss and the conclusion of a valid syllogism agree in quantity but differ in quality, what further information can you derive about the syllogism?

12. Can you give an instance of an invalid syllogism in which the major premiss is universal negative, the minor premiss affirmative and the conclusion particular negative. If not, why not?

13. Restate each of the following arguments in the form of a categorical syllogism and indicate whether it is valid:

(a) Whenever A has a lecture, B has one; but C has lectures that A has not. Hence C has lectures that B has not.

(b) Of all animals man alone is capable of speech and man alone is rational. Therefore no animals not capable of speech are rational.

(c) Mr X has recently made a telling point in defence of salesmen. He argues that the prejudice against selling is perverse since in everything we do, working or playing, we are selling ourselves.

14. Given the premisses but not the conclusion of a valid syllogism show (a) in what cases it is possible, and (b) in what cases it is impossible, to determine which is the major and which the minor term.

15. Show that the conclusion cannot be an A proposition, if the major term is subject in its premiss.

16 Assuming the general rules of the syllogism, show that the combination OAO is only valid in Fig. 3.

17. Examine the following argument: S is either p or q; either p or q is R; therefore S is R.

18. 'A valid argument may consist entirely of untruths.' Evaluate.

19. Do you think that the following dilemmas could be answered effectively?

(a) If the conclusion of a syllogism goes beyond the premisses, then the inference is invalid; and if the conclusion does not go beyond the premisses then the inference does not yield new knowledge. But the conclusion of a syllogism must either go beyond the premisses or not go beyond them. Therefore the inference in a syllogism must either be invalid or yield no new knowledge.

(b) (This is a summary of the argument used by a Board of Education to support its dismissal of a professor who had invoked the privilege against self-incrimination under the Fifth Amendment. The summary is that of the United States Supreme Court in its decision on the case dated April 9th, 1956.) 'Here the Board in support of its position contends that only two possible inferences flow from the appellant's claim of self-incrimination: (1) that the answering of the question ("Were you a member of the Communist Party during 1940 and 1941?") would tend to prove him guilty of a crime in some way connected with his official conduct; or (2) that in order to avoid answering the question he falsely invoked the privilege by stating that the answer would tend to incriminate him, and thus committed perjury. Either inference, it [the Board] insists, is sufficient to justify the termination of his employment.'

(c) (James Joyce was asked to consent to the expurgation of certain parts of *Ulysses* in order to make its publication possible. This is his reply:) 'To consent would be an admission that the expurgated parts are dispensable. The whole point about them is that they cannot be omitted. Either they are put in gratuitously without reference to my general purpose; or they are an integral part of my book. If they are mere interpolations, my book is inartistic; and if they are strictly in their place, they cannot be left out.'

(d) If men are good, laws are not needed to prevent wrongdoing; if men are bad, laws will not succeed in preventing wrongdoing. Men are either good or bad. Therefore either laws are not needed to prevent wrongdoing or laws will not succeed in preventing wrongdoing.

(e) (An Athenian mother is supposed to have argued, using this 'horned' syllogism, when her son contemplated entering public life:) 'If you say what is just, men will hate you; and if you say what is unjust, the gods will hate you. But you must say either what is just or what is unjust. Therefore either men will hate you or the gods will hate you.'

(f) (In the fifth century B.C., Protagoras trained Euathlus as a lawyer on the understanding that he would receive payment when Euathlus won his first case. When the pupil did not go into practice at all, Protagoras sued for his fee, using this dilemma:) 'If Euathlus loses this case, then he must pay me (by the judgment of the court); if he wins this case, then he must pay me (by the terms of the contract). But he must either lose or win this case. Therefore, he must pay me.'

(g) (Mahomet's successor, Omar, the proverbial fighting Puritan, is supposed to have formulated this dilemma concerning the Library at Alexandria:) 'If its books are in conformity with the Koran, they are superfluous; if they are at variance with it, they are pernicious. But they are either in conformity with it or at variance with it. Therefore they are either superfluous or pernicious.'

(h) Once a crocodile stole a baby from a mother who was washing clothes along the banks of the Ganges. In answer to her pleas, the crocodile promised to return the baby if the mother would give the right answer to this question: is the crocodile going to restore the baby? The mother said: 'The answer is "no". Now you must keep your promise. If the answer is wrong, that must mean you are going to give back the baby anyway; if it is right, you must keep your promise. In either case you must give me back the baby.' But the crocodile answered: 'If "no" is the right answer, what makes it right is that I am not going to give back the baby; if it is the wrong answer, then my promise does not hold. In either case I am not going to restore the baby.'

(i) (Bishop Morton, minister to Henry VII, formulated this dilemma to show that all could pay taxes:) If a man is a sparer, he has money (for he is laying it by); if a man is a spender, he has money (for his way of life shows it). But every man is either a sparer or a spender. Therefore every man has money.

Exercises in analysing vernacular arguments

1. Analyse the following simple disputes:
(a) X: Senator Gray is a fine man and a genuine liberal. He votes for every progressive measure that comes before the legislature.

Y: He is no liberal, in my opinion. He contributes less money to worthy causes than any other man in his income bracket.
(b) X: I see by the financial pages that money is much more plentiful than it was six months ago.

Y: That can't be true. I read a government report just yesterday to the effect that more old currency has been destroyed at the mint during the last half year than has been replaced. Money is therefore less plentiful, not more so.
(c) X: Don't ask your parents about it. You ought to use your own judgment.

Y: I am using my own judgment, and in my judgment I should ask my parents.
2. In what ways is this statement fallacious: 'My client could not have murdered X since, as my witnesses have shown, he did not even know X.'
3. Is the following statement an antinomy: 'It is raining but I don't believe it.'?
4. Analyse the following arguments:
(a) You ask me what I think of life. I am frankly a pessimist. We seek happiness, that is to say health, prosperity, freedom from pain and suffering. At every turn we meet want and pain and suffering. If happiness were unattainable, these would be inevitable. They are inevitable. Therefore happiness is unattainable.
(b) If the object of education were to make pupils think rather than to accept certain conclusions, it would be conducted quite differently; there would be less rapidity of instruction and more discussion, more attempt to make education concern itself with matters in which the pupils feel some interest.
(c) It is wrong for you to become a contemplative, to bury your talents in a monastery. Think of your responsibilities. Were you born into this world to loiter through life, an idle worshipper at the altar of beauty? You will find in the monastery a beautiful corner of the world—that is all very well for you, but how about the rest? How about the millions who are chained to the cities because they must earn their living pittance? You can help them; you should help them. Hide though you may from your responsibilities, the burden of them will lie heavy on your conscience, and discontent will penetrate sometime into your jealously guarded paradise.
(d) In your editorial of last week you stated: 'The infliction of pain upon a man for ill-gotten pleasure is an essential element in punishment. Indeed punishment is primarily retributive in character.' You did not attempt a proof, for the good reason that your position is obviously false and indefensible. Ordinary informed opinion revolts at retribution and insists that punishment must be deterrent and reformatory only. There are but two classes which subscribe to your view: At the one extreme are the unthinking masses, who ingeminate the doctrine that the brute should be given a dose of his own medicine. At the other

extreme are super-subtle philosophers who hold that punishment must be an end in itself, not a means to other worthwhile results. The reasonably reflective middle-brow justifies punishment on the ground that it reforms or at least deters.

(e) In answer to (d) I would like to point out that the 'reasonably reflective middle-brow' is more expiationist than he is apt to suppose. While the word *retribution* is not allowed to soil his lips, the idea lingers on in his bones, informs his conduct and undermines his logic. If anyone questions this he can submit it to a simple test. Suppose that in Utopia (which I must assume for this purpose possesses unlimited public resources) there lives a confirmed burglar. No amount of prison will deter, let alone reform, him. But it is established that he would never again attempt or desire to burgle if, on his latest conviction, he were awarded not prison but a pension of 50,000 dollars a year free of tax. Would anyone defend such an award? Surely not. But if not, why not? Simply, I think, because we all think that the award must not merely deter or reform but must do so by means of its unpleasant or painful character. And what is this but to reintroduce the retributive criterion by a side door alongside the other two?

(f) 'Whenever we find Arctic animals which, from whatever cause, do not require protection by the white colour, then neither the cold nor the snow-glare has any effect upon their coloration. The sable retains its rich brown fur throughout the Siberian winter; but it frequents trees at that season and not only feeds partially on fruits or seeds, but is able to catch birds among the branches of the fir-trees; with the bark of which its colour assimilates ... But the most striking example is that of the common raven, which is a true arctic bird, and is found even in mid-winter as far north as any known bird or mammal. Yet it always retains its black coat, and the reason, from our point of view, is obvious. The raven is a powerful bird and fears no enemy, while, being a carrion-feeder, it has no need for concealment in order to approach its prey. The colours of the sable and of the raven are, therefore, both inconsistent with any other theory than that the white colour of arctic animals has been acquired for concealment, and to that theory both afford a strong support.'

5. Using the following argument as a basis, discuss the validity of a conclusion from circumstantial evidence and why circumstantial evidence is accepted in law:

'It is said that the prisoner had access to the till—so had several others. That he spent money freely soon after the theft was committed—but he may have received funds from a legacy, from winning a bet or from good fortune at cards. That he was being given a second chance after theft on a previous occasion—but remember the proverb "once bitten twice shy". That he was the last to leave the shop the evening before the theft was discovered—but it is not known that the theft was committed that evening.'

Section B: Formal Logic

DETAILED CONTENTS OF SECTION B

Chapter 1

THE LANGUAGE OF FORMAL LOGIC

I. Introduction

The language employed by Formal Logic is a special artificial one. There are many advantages in departing from the use of vernacular languages. The latter are object-languages but logic needs a second-order or meta-language. Again vernacular words are constantly acquiring new nuances of meaning and new idiomatic uses; scientific work requires greater fixity of meaning. Finally built into vernacular words is a whole code of directions for pronunciation; the alphabet is a phonetic code, vernacular words are phonograms or phonographs. Thus a person is able to pronounce a vernacular word before he learns to associate the appropriate meaning with it. It is important that a vernacular language should facilitate oral communication. It is not necessary that a scientific language do so and great economy and conciseness is achieved by devising a language which consists of ideograms, i.e. signs which stand directly for concepts. The mathematical symbol ' $\times$ ' exemplifies this: it stands directly for a mathematical idea, we learn to associate a certain sound or pronunciation with it; on the other hand seeing the corresponding vernacular word, 'multiplied by', we can immediately pronounce it without knowing what meaning to associate with it.

For the purpose of doing complex calculations quickly it is important not only that one's language be non-vernacular, but also that it be very simple visually. A multiplication sum that is simple with Arabic numerals (e.g. 87×96) is very difficult with Roman ones ($\text{LXXXVII} \times \text{XCVI}$). Operations performed in Formal Logic have a great affinity with mathematical calculation; as a consequence the artificial languages developed by logicians have been very simple.

At the present day two important notations used are the Lukasiewicz system and the Peano–Russell system. The former was invented and employed by the Polish logician, Lukasiewicz, since 1929; the latter was a modification by Russell of the symbolism of the Italian logician, Peano, and goes back to 1910 when the *Principia Mathematica* by Bertrand Russell and A. N. Whitehead was published.

At the end of the chapter a table will display and correlate symbols of the main notations. For the present it will be convenient to use the Lukasiewicz system. Like any logical language it can be analysed into variables and constants.

II. The utility of variables

Using variables a logician can isolate, for study, the basic structure of an argument. In other words variables accomplish for him, in the world of meaning, what scientific equipment accomplishes for the physicist or chemist, in the physical world. It was through his invention and use of variables that Aristotle became the founder of Formal Logic.

Take the following argument:

> If all living things can reproduce their kind
> And if the virus is a living thing
> Then the virus can reproduce its kind.

This is an argument in biology. By using the familiar variables M, P, S we can abstract the generic structure of this discourse from its specific context; or, in other words, we can generalize its structure to the utmost as follows:

> If all M is P
> And if all S is M
> Then all S is P.

This generic or generalized structure is still intelligible and meaningful, but its specific content or matter has been emptied out. We are focusing the original discourse on biology in its basic or generic intelligibility, drained of all particular reference; as such it is seen to have a valid structure, to be a syllogism in Barbara.

The variables used here (M, P, S) were substituted for terms, i.e. for the subjects and predicates of the propositions constituting the argument. The section of Formal Logic in which the variables used always stand for terms is called Terminal Logic. In Lukasiewicz's notation, variables are denoted by small latin letters, and the initial ones of the alphabet a, b, c, d ... are used to denote term-variables of the Aristotelian logic: Aab means All A is b; Eab means No a is b; Iab means some a is b; and Oab means some a is not b. (The capital letters A, E, I and O are used in their traditional senses, signifying quantity and quality.) When these symbols are substituted in the above discourse on biology it reads: If Abc and if Aab then Aac.

In the case of some arguments the only way of displaying basic structure is to use variables that stand not for terms but for whole (unanalysed) sentences. A person may reason as follows: 'If the army revolted, there would have been bloodshed; there has not been bloodshed, therefore the army has not revolted.' This argument connects up, conditionally, the sentences 'the army revolted' and 'there has been bloodshed'. The way to display its structure is to substitute variables for these sentences. Lukasiewicz denotes such (sentential) variables by the small letters p, q, r, s, ... Using two of these the generic form of the argument is isolated as follows: 'If p, q; but not q, therefore not p.' The section of Formal Logic in which the variables used always stand for whole sentences or propositions is called Propositional Logic or Sentential Logic (or the Logic of Propositions, the Logic of Sentences). The Stoics founded this section and in modern times Frege is responsible for its immense development.

The logician needs a third kind of variable to deal with arguments that centre around relationships. 'If Smith is the teacher of Jones, then Jones is the pupil of Smith.' To isolate the generic structure of this argument we need to substitute variables not only for Smith and Jones but also for the particular relationship between them: 'If X is R of Y, then Y is R-converse of X.' The section of Formal Logic which studies generic structures of discourse where there are variables standing for relations is called the Logic of Relations. It was pioneered by Augustus de Morgan but nowadays is developed as part of Predicate Logic and Class Calculus. Lukasiewicz's notation does not cover it.

III. Constants

It is a matter of empirical fact not of logic that, e.g. 'animal life depends on oxygen'. But it is a matter of logic, not of empirical fact, that 'if all living things are dependent on oxygen, and if animals are living things, then animals are dependent on oxygen'. If that discourse comes under questioning it won't be relevant to investigate the biological facts (none are asserted) but the significance of the words *If . . . and if . . . then.* These are formative, organizing words with fixed meanings, giving basic structure to the discourse. They are an example of logical *constants* (*operators, functors, connectives* are also used to name these words). Other familiar vernacular constants are: *and*; *either . . . or*; *not both*; *it is not the case that.*

Constants are obviously a very important part of logical language. The particular constants used in any system must be presented and defined very exactly. In Lukasiewicz's system constants are denoted by capital letters—N, K, A, D, C being the main ones used. He says: 'The principle of my notation is to write the functors before the arguments [an argument is an expression determined by a functor, e.g. p is an argument in the expression Np]. In this way I can avoid brackets.' (*Aristotle's Syllogistic*, p. 78)

It is tempting to associate each of these capital letters with a vernacular phrase, e.g. N with 'it is not the case that', K with 'and', A with 'either . . . or', D with 'not both', C with 'if . . . then'. The underlying assumption is that the meanings are identical. This is not always the case and it is an important theoretical fact that the artificial symbols were not created simply to follow directions of reference in the vernacular. Thus it is important to note how each constant is defined. The technique used is a very exact one: it consists in showing the effect or influence a constant or functor has on the propositional variables it modifies or connects. By drawing up truth-tables the variables are seen in all the possible truth-values they can have; the resulting, net, truth-value of the complex expression measures the force of the logical constant in the expression.

Thus take the expression Np which has one variable (N is said to be a monadic functor, having only one argument), p is a propositional variable and has two possible values, true and false. Where p is true, the expression as a whole (Np) is false; where p is false, the expression as a whole is true. These results are determined by the meaning of the logical constant N; they measure and present that meaning very exactly. Thus with the number 1 signifying true, and the number 0 signifying false, Np is defined technically as follows (the value of the whole expression being put under the constant):

$$N\ p$$
$$0\ 1$$
$$1\ 0$$

Obviously N has the very same truth-table as the vernacular negative, 'it is not the case that . . .'

In the expression Kpq, there are two variables and K is said to be a dyadic functor, connecting two arguments. The possible combined values of the variables are

$$p\ q$$
$$1\ 1$$
$$1\ 0$$
$$0\ 1$$
$$0\ 0$$

(These values are given in a standard order: 11, 10, 01, 00). The resulting values of the expression as a whole, given under K, are:

$$K\ p\ q$$
$$1\ 1\ 1$$
$$0\ 1\ 0$$
$$0\ 0\ 1$$
$$0\ 0\ 0$$

The values under K (1000) form the matrix line of the truth-table. Such is the meaning of K that the expression as a whole is true only when p and q are both true. Obviously K has the force of conjunction like the vernacular 'and'. Its technical definition is the matrix line of the truth-table: 1000.

The truth-tables for the other constants are as follows:

A	p	q		D	p	q		C	p	q
1	1	1		0	1	1		1	1	1
1	1	0		1	1	0		0	1	0
1	0	1		1	0	1		1	0	1
0	0	0		1	0	0		1	0	0

It is evident that the constant A (1110) corresponds to the vernacular '*either . . . or*' in the simple alternative force of these words where the alternatives are not presented as mutually exclusive; also that D (0111) corresponds to 'not both'. However, the disadvantages of associating vernacular meanings with the symbols of Formal Logic is brought out in the case of *C*. It is frequently translated as 'if ... then'. Now, a truth table for 'if ... then' would read as follows (with the value of the expression as a whole in the last column):

p q	If *p* then *q*
1 1	1
1 0	0
0 1	here the expression as a whole does not seem to qualify for either value
0 0	„ „ „ „ „ „ „ „ „ „ „ „ „ „

Thus *C* (1011) and 'if ... then' (10——) simply do not have the same truth-tables and are not equivalent.

If one insists on translating *C* as 'if ... then' formidable paradoxes develop. In the truth-table for *C*, whenever *p* has the value 0 (false) the total proposition (*Cpq*) is true; whenever *q* has the value 1 the total proposition is also true. If *p* and *q* are identified as the antecedent and consequent, respectively, of an 'if ... then' proposition then according to our truth table a conditional with a false antecedent is always true as is also any conditional with a true consequent (any sentence, *q*, follows from a false sentence, *p*; and a true sentence *q* follows from any sentence, *p*). Thus the proposition, 'If the moon is made of green cheese then the earth is flat,' is true because the moon is not made of green cheese; and the proposition, 'If 2 + 2 = 4 then today is Monday,' is true when today is Monday, regardless of any other fact.

These are called the paradoxes of material implication (verum sequitur ad quodlibet; ex falso sequitur quodlibet) because the vernacular word, implication, is still frequently retained to denote the significance of *C*, the qualification *material* being added to indicate that the connection asserted between *p* and *q* is not one of consequence but of simple material concurrence —that *C* signifies the lowest common denominator in the various vernacular uses of the words, *if ... then*.

The fundamental solution to the paradoxes lies, however, in pointing out that *C* is a symbol in Formal Logic and is not properly presented as a shorthand equivalent of any vernacular expression. What fact is it employed to signify? It is a binary propositional constant or connective, i.e. it connects two propositional variables (*p* and *q*). Now the possible combined truth-values of these variables are 11, 10, 01, 00; and it is possible to have 16 different connectives each resulting in a different matrix line for the proposition as a whole:

Value of variables		Possible matrix lines (with the symbol defined by each line)														
p	*q*	*V*	*A*	*B*	*C*	*D*	*E*	*F*	*G*	*H*	*I*	*J*	*K*	*L*	*M*	*X*	*O*
1	1	1	1	1	1	0	1	0	0	1	1	0	1	0	0	0	0
1	0	1	1	1	0	1	0	0	1	0	1	1	0	1	0	0	0
0	1	1	1	0	1	1	0	1	0	1	0	1	0	0	1	0	0
0	0	1	0	1	1	1	1	1	1	0	0	0	0	0	0	1	0

From the viewpoint of Formal Logic there are 16 possible logical constants, each exercising a different connecting force on *p* and *q*, as defined in a special matrix line. Since *p* and *q* are variables applicable to any entities which have propositional form, no connection or relevance of meaning is asserted or can be assumed in their joint use—their only known value is that each must be true or false and that together they have a limited combined set of values. With such variables a constant can only construct a truth-functional expression, i.e. one whose meaning is confined to truth-values and whose truth is therefore determined by the particular truth-values of its constituents. In social communication, however, one's connectives are not merely truth-functional: one expects a relevance in meaning between the propositions one connects in, e.g. an 'if . . . then' statement. Such a presumption would not be in keeping with the use of genuine variables whose simple function it is to formalize any and all entities that are propositions.

The symbols *A*, *C*, *D*, *E*, *K* denote constants which are very useful in Formal Logic (*J* is the symbol for the important relation of contradiction). To what extent they may be equivalent to vernacular words is a matter not for Formal Logic but for Applied Logic.

IV. Well-formed formulae (wff's)

There are rules for the formation of complex expressions from variables and constants. The principle of Lukasiewicz's notation is 'to write the functors before the arguments' whether the argument be simply a variable (e.g. *Np*) or variables (e.g. *Cpq*) or an expression consisting of variables and a monadic functor (e.g. *ANpq*) or a complex expression consisting of variables and other functors, monadic or dyadic, etc. (e.g. *CCpqKNqNp*). (We shall see that in working out truth-tables one proceeds leftwards from the variables and simplest arguments to the constant of widest force.)

An expression is a wff in propositional logic if and only if
(1) it is a *p*, *q*, *r* or *s*; *or*
(2) it is a two-unit expression in which the first unit is a monadic functor (in practice *N* is the only one used) and the second unit is a wff; *or*
(3) it is a three-unit expression in which the first unit is a dyadic functor (e.g. *C*, *A*, *K*, *E*, *D*), and the second and third units are wff's.

Thus the expression *p* is a wff; so is the expression *Np*; so therefore are the expressions *NNp* and *NNNp*. We can see whether any complex expression is or is not well-formed by underlining, from the left, every constituent wff that consists of two or more letters; the expression as a whole is a wff if and only if it gets underlined by one line. Thus
NCAKpqrs is a wff.

but

ANCpNqrNs is not a wff: *Ns* is outside the scope of the main functor *A*.

V. Equivalent expressions

Expressions are said to be equivalent when their truth-tables are identical, i.e. when they have the same variables and are true or false together for all the values of these variables. (*E* is the symbol for the constant, equivalence, and the matrix line of *Epq* is 1001.)

The following are examples of equivalent expressions:

C *p* *q*	*A* *N* *p* *q*	*D* *p* *N* *q*
1 1 1	1 0 1 1	1 1 0 1
0 1 0	0 0 1 0	0 1 1 0
1 0 1	1 1 0 1	1 0 0 1
1 0 0	1 1 0 0	1 0 1 0

The matrix line of the two latter expressions, appearing under the dyadic functors *A* and *D*, is the same as that of the first expression (1 0 1 1). Thus these expressions have a common definition; any one of them may be substituted for any other in processes of logical derivation for their value (truth or falsity) is the same.

Theoretically, it would be possible to so translate all expressions in Propositional Logic that besides the variables only one symbol would be needed, *D* (called also Sheffer's functor). But what would be gained by this economy in basic symbols would be lost in the cumbersome lengthy appearance of formulae. Logical language must try to achieve both economy in its symbols and a basic readability in its formulae.

VI. The main notations used in propositional logic

In their *Dictionary of Symbols of Mathematical Logic*, R. Feys and F. B. Fitch correlate (p. 31) the symbols used by Russell in the *Principia Mathematica* (henceforth PM), by Hilbert and Ackermann in *Principles of Mathematical Logic* and Hilbert & Bernays in *Grundlagen der Mathematik* (HA and HB), by Lukasiewicz (L), by Hermes-Scholz (HS) and by some other authors:

English equivalent	PM	HA HB	L	HS	Other notations
not *p*	$\sim p$	$\bar{p}$	Np	$\bar{p}$	$p', -p, \neg p$
p and *q*	$p \cdot q$	$p \& q$	Kpq	$p \wedge q$	
p or *q*	$p \vee q$	$p \vee q$ pq	Apq	$p \vee q$	$p + q$
if *p* then *q*	$p \supset q$	$p \rightarrow q$	Cpq	$p \rightarrow q$	
p if *q*	$p \subset q$		Bpq	$p \leftarrow q$	
p if and only if *q*	$p \equiv q$	$p \sim q$	Epq	$p \leftrightarrow q$	

The authors observe that the notation under HA, HB is used also by Gentzen, while that under HS appears in numerous publications by members of the school of Münster. Polish logicians frequently use Lukasiewicz's notation, of course. 'Notations related to those given under HA and HS are used, e.g. by Tarski, Beth and also by Kleene, but the latter uses Heyting's negation sign' (Ibid., p. 32) (Heyting symbolizes not–p as $\neg p$).

Chapter 2

LOGICAL TRUTH AND METHODS OF DECIDING WHAT IS LOGICALLY TRUE

I. The nature of logical truth

Take this syllogistic sentence: '*If* all men are mortal *and if* Socrates is a man, *then* Socrates is mortal.' To decide whether this sentence is true or false, you do not study the *natural truth* of the constituent propositions. The sentence does not say that these are true; it says that the words 'if and if then' are true. You find that these words are true in virtue of the form of the sentence (it is a first figure form, mood Barbara) and independently of the content.

By using variables let us get rid of any particular content from the above syllogism: *If MaP and if SaM then SaP*. This sentence is true because of its form and independently of any particular content it may have. Such truth is called formal or logical truth. It is concerned with the truth of the words 'if and if then', with the presence of implication which these words signify and which the syllogism claims is present. It must be distinguished from natural truth, which is the truth of statements about natural facts, about the natural world.

When it is *said* that in the syllogism logic is not concerned with truth, what is *meant* is that logic is not concerned with *the natural truth* of the constituent propositions (with the mortality of men, the humanity of Socrates in the example given earlier). It is very much concerned with logical truth (the word *validity* is used as a synonym for logical truth). One and the same sentence may claim to be true both logically and naturally—e.g. 'All men are mortal, but Socrates is a man; therefore Socrates is mortal.' The word, *therefore*, signifies the logical claim that implication is present; but in addition the premises and conclusion are *asserted* to be true. Logic does not deal with propositions as personal assertions. Thus it won't formulate the syllogism as a pattern of personal inference but exclusively as a pattern of implication (*If* all men are mortal *and if* Socrates is a man, *then* Socrates is mortal).

II. Examples of sentences whose claim is to logical truth

Sentences which express valid forms of immediate inference are logical truths, e.g. (a) those based on relationships in the Square of Opposition as: 'If *SaP* then *SiP*' 'If *SoP* is true then *SaP* is false' (b) those expressing converses, obverses, contrapositives and inverses as: 'If *SaP* then *PiS*' 'If *SaP* then *SeP*'.

Coming to mediate inference there are 24 valid moods of *the simple categorical syllogism* (including 4 weakened moods not mentioned in the mnemonic Barbara, Celarent). The 24 sentences which express these moods are true in virtue of their form and express logical truth, e.g. If *PeM* and if *SaM* then *SeP* (Cesare). These 24 sentences do not express any natural truth, they express the fact of implication or involvement.

Similarly, the sentences which express valid forms of other varieties of the syllogism express logical truth.

The above are examples treated already in the preparatory section of this course. They belong to Terminal Logic where the variables signify terms. In Propositional Logic where the variables signify propositions, the following sentence, e.g expresses logical truth: 'If it is the case both that if *p* is true *q* is true and that *p* is true, then *q* is true.' This sentence is true independently of content, of any particular propositions substituted for *p* and *q*. Finally, in Relational Logic, the proposition expressing converse relationships has formal or logical truth, e.g. 'If *X* is *R* of *Y*, then *Y* is *R*—converse of *X*.'

III. On finding a decision procedure for logical truth in propositional logic

We have seen that a sentence may be a statement about natural facts and be either true or false naturally, in virtue of its content. Or it may be a statement about the presence of implication and be true or false logically, in virtue of its form, independently of its content. (It may also be a statement claiming both natural and logical truth.) By what criterion can we determine whether a sentence claiming logical truth is actually true or false, logically? We are concerned at present with sentences whose variables, *pqrs*, stand for propositions.

Wittgenstein used the concept of tautology to clarify the idea of logical truth and through him truth-tables were accepted as an important method (always applicable in propositional logic) for determining logical truth or falsity. The relationship between truth tables and logical truth may be explained as follows:

1. A proposition expressing logical truth is always complex (it must have room for the presence of implication).
2. Given a complex proposition with *n* constituent propositions, if the truth of the complex proposition is completely determined by the truth of the constituent ones, then it is said to be a truth-function of *n* propositions. There is always a rule determining its truth from the truth or falsity of the constituents. The following are examples of truth-functions of two propositions, denoted by the variables *p* and *q*, with their truth-tables (the numerals indicate the order in which the columns should be filled):

3	1	2		7	6	5	1	3	2	4		7	5	1	3	6	2	4
C	p	q		C	K	C	p	q	p	q		K	D	p	q	K	p	q
1	1	1		1	1	1	1	1	1	1		0	0	1	1	1	1	1
0	1	0		1	0	0	1	0	1	0		0	1	1	0	0	1	0
1	0	1		1	0	1	0	1	0	1		0	1	0	1	0	0	1
1	0	0		1	0	1	0	0	0	0		0	1	0	0	0	0	0

The matrix-line in each case is the first column; in the first example it is 1 0 1 1, in the second 1 1 1 1, in the third 0 0 0 0.

3. Among the various truth-functions of the *n* propositions we have referred to, that proposition which has the truth-value 'true' for every possible combination of truth-values in the *n* propositions is said to be the *tautology* of the *n* propositions. It is clear that what it expresses is true independently of the content of its variable constituents; it is a *logical truth* or *logical law*. It is the business of logic to detect tautologies. The second example above (*CKCpqpq*) is a tautology or logical truth, its matrix line being 1 1 1 1. The first example (*Cpq*) is true for some of the combined values of its variables but not for all of them: its matrix line is 1 0 1 1 and it is called a *contingent proposition*. The third example (*KDpqKpq*) is not true for any of the combined values of its variables: its matrix line is 0 0 0 0 and it is described as *logically false or* as a *logical contradiction*.

IV. Drawing up truth-tables: some technical details

The order in which values are given to the variables is governed by rule. According as there are one, two or three variables, the order is as follows:

p	*p*	*q*	*p*	*q*	*r*
1	1	1	1	1	1
0	1	0	1	1	0
	0	1	1	0	1
	0	0	1	0	0
			0	1	1
			0	1	0
			0	0	1
			0	0	0

If there are *n* variables, the column under the *m*th variable should contain 2^{m-1} sets of 2^{n-m} 1's followed by 2^{n-m} 0's (where *m* is the numerical ranking of the variable, first, second or third, etc.). A truth function of *n* variables needs 2^n rows across to provide for all combined values (the 2 denotes the values possible in Two-Value Logic, truth and falsity).

In evaluating the expression as a whole for each of the combined values of the variables, one fills in the values for the most elementary parts first under the relevant constant or functor. In Lukasiewicz's system this means moving from right to left. The table on p. 74 recalls the values of basic expressions.

When one is simply concerned with deciding whether an expression is or is not a logical law, and the number of variables makes the full truth-table procedure too laborious, one may use a shorter, *reductio ad absurdum*, type of procedure. If the expression is a logical law, then the matrix line of its table must be a series of 1's. Making the assumption that an 0 is included in its

Values of Basic Expressions

Expression (the numbers here are the values of the variables)	Value	Expression (the numbers here are the values of the variables)	Value
N 1	0	K 1 1	1
N 0	1	K 1 0	0
A 1 1	1	K 0 1	0
A 1 0	1	K 0 0	0
A 0 1	1	E 1 1	1
A 0 0	0	E 1 0	0
D 1 1	0	E 0 1	0
D 1 0	1	E 0 0	1
D 0 1	1	C 1 1	1
D 0 0	1	C 1 0	0
		C 0 1	1
		C 0 0	1

matrix line and working downwards from this fact to consequent values for the elementary parts of the total expression, we may find that one of these values contradicts the definition of one of the constants (e.g. that C 1 1 would have the value 0). This would show that 0 could not occur in the matrix line and therefore that the expression is a logical law. If, on the other hand, the assumption does not involve the violation of any basic rule or definition, then the matrix line, which has all possible values, must include an 0 and so the expression is not a logical law.

V. Testing the validity of arguments (in propositional logic) by the truth-table method

An argument may be formulated as an 'if ... then' statement, with the cumulative evidence as antecedent and the conclusion as consequent. Testing its validity may be treated as a process of discovering whether the antecedent may be true and yet the conclusion be false. At first sight, it does not seem possible to apply a test based on truth-tables, as an 'if ... then' statement does not seem to qualify for evaluation in the cases where its antecedent is false. However, the vernacular 'if ... then' and the symbol C agree partially in their truth-tables, namely in the cases where the antecedent is true; further a C proposition is never false or invalid (but always true) when its antecedent is false. Thus, since we are simply trying to discover whether the conclusion may be false when the antecedent is true, the extra values in the C-truth-tables would not affect a test for invalidity. This is the pragmatic justification for symbolizing arguments as C statements so as to make them amenble to evaluation by truth-tables. The matrix line of a valid argument should consist of 1's, since only a true antecedent with a false consequent will give rise to an 0.
Example: 'If the cost of living rises or the balance of payments improves, then

salary increases will be granted. But no salary increases will be granted. Therefore the balance of payments will not improve.' Symbolizing 'the cost of living will rise' as *p*, 'the balance of payments will improve' as *q*, and 'salary increases will be granted' as *r*, the total expression may be formulated as: *CKCApqrNrNq*. Its truth table is:

11	10	9	8	1	2	4	7	5	6	3
C	*K*	*C*	*A*	*p*	*q*	*r*	*N*	*r*	*N*	*q*
1	0	1	1	1	1	1	0	1	0	1
1	0	0	1	1	1	0	1	0	0	1
1	0	1	1	1	0	1	0	1	1	0
1	0	0	1	1	0	0	1	0	1	0
1	0	1	1	0	1	1	0	1	0	1
1	0	0	1	0	1	0	1	0	0	1
1	0	1	0	0	0	1	0	1	1	0
1	1	1	0	0	0	0	1	0	1	0

(The numerals indicate the order in which the columns should be filled.) The matrix line (under *C*, on the left) does not include an 0, and so the argument is not invalid.

VI. Decision procedures (for propositional logic) other than that of truth-tables

Truth-tables furnish an effective procedure, in Propositional Logic, for deciding whether any sentence is true or any argument is valid. This decision can be made for a sentence or argument, chosen quite arbitrarily, without the need of relating it to any other proposition or displaying it as deducible from other propositions. In other words, the method is mechanical. There are two other mechanical decision procedures (a) the normal form procedure and (b) the trees procedure. In outlining these procedures it is convenient at times to depart from the Polish notation in using '*V*' instead of '*A*', '.' instead of '*K*', '–' instead of '*N*' and '→' instead of '*C*'.

(a) *The normal form procedure*: This procedure is based on the fact that with regard to two contradictions, *p* and −*p*, both of them can never be true together, and one or other of them must be true. Because of the latter fact a *conjunctive* chain of expressions *each* of which has the form *pV* −*p* (with or without other alternatives) is definitely a tautology; and because of the former fact, a *disjunctive* chain of expressions *each* of which has the form, *p* . −*p* (with or without other conjuncts in the atom), is definitely a chain of propositions none of which can ever be true and so is a logical contradiction.

From this basis it is possible to construct fully a decision procedure. Beginning with definitions:

An *atomic expression* is either a propositional variable or the negation of some propositional variable, e.g. *p*, −*q*.

An *elementary disjunction* is an expression of the form $(A_1 \vee A_2 \vee \ldots A_n)$ where $A_1 \ldots A_n$ are atomic expressions.

An *elementary conjunction* is an expression of the form $(A_1 . A_2 \ldots A_n)$ where $A_1 \ldots A_n$ are atomic expressions.

A *Conjunctive Normal Form* (CNF) is an expression of the form $(B_1 . B_2 \ldots B_n)$ where $B_1 \ldots B_n$ are elementary disjunctions.

A *Disjunctive Normal Form* (DNF) is an expression of the form $(B_1 \vee B_2 \ldots \vee B_n)$ where $B_1 \ldots B_n$ are elementary conjunctions.

Now it is possible to reduce every wff in propositional logic to a CNF and to a DNF. The basic reason is that the constants are a systematic set of symbols and the force of all operators can receive an equivalent expression in CN terms and in DN terms. Thus even in the most complex formula equivalent replacements can be made, systematically, until the whole formula has the required normal format. For such systematic replacements the following equivalences are very useful:

$$EKppp$$
$$EAppp$$
$$EKpqKqp$$
$$EApqAqp$$
$$EKpKqrKKpqr$$
$$EApAqrAApqr$$
$$ENNpp$$
$$ECpqANpq$$
$$EEpqKCpqCqp$$
$$ENKpqANpNq$$
$$ENApqKNpNq$$
$$EApKqrKApqApr$$
$$EKpAqrAKpqKpr$$

When a complex expression is simplified down to a CNF an inspection of the atomic expressions shows whether or not it is a conjunctive chain of elementary disjunctions each of which must always be true (on the basis of containing, among the alternatives, two contradictories). If so it is a tautology. If not it may be a logical contradiction or a contingent proposition. Simplified down to a DNF an inspection of the atomic expressions shows whether or not it is a disjunctive chain of elementary conjunctions none of which can ever be true (on the basis of containing, among the conjuncts, two contradictories). If so it is a logical contradiction. If not (since we already know it is not a tautology) it must be a contingent proposition.

Thus with this method we can decide, independently of truth-tables, whether any given wff in propositional logic is a tautology, a logical contradiction or a contingent proposition.

(b) *The method of truth trees*: It derives from Beth's method of semantic tableaux and Hintikka's method of model sets and is based on the fact that if an argument is valid no case can be cited in which the premisses are true along with the contradictory of the conclusion. By means of branch-lines the method diagrams the various ways in which the constituent propositions of an argument can be made true. As soon as contradictories are discovered on a branch-line it is closed (it cannot be cited in support of a possibility that the premisses and contradictory of the conclusion may be simultaneously true). If all the branch-lines are closed the argument is valid. In *Formal Loic: Its Scope and Limits* Richard Jeffrey gives an excellent presentation.

Applying the method to the simple argument: If $A \to -B$ and if $-C \to A$, then $B \to C$, we first list the premisses and the contradictory of the conclusion. Then we write down the various ways in which the contradictory of the conclusion, i.e.$-(B \to C)$, may be made true namely by B being true or C being false. Next on lines branching from C we put the conditions which can make the first premiss true, namely by A being false or $-B$ being true (i.e. B being false). The diagram now reads:

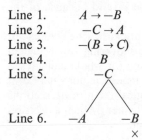

Line 1. $A \to -B$
Line 2. $-C \to A$
Line 3. $-(B \to C)$
Line 4. B
Line 5. $-C$

Line 6. $-A$ $-B$
             $\times$

The branch line with $-B$ can now be closed because it has a contradictory on the main line (i.e. B). Closure is indicated by placing an $\times$ under $-B$. Now on lines branching from $-A$ (which is the only open branch line left) we put the conditions which can make the second premiss true:

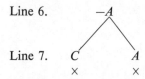

Line 6. $-A$

Line 7. C A
     $\times$ $\times$

Each of these branch lines must be closed because C is in contradiction with $-C$ (Line 5) and A is in contradiction with $-A$ (Line 6).

Thus the diagram displays the fact that no instance can be cited in which the premisses and the contradictory of the conclusion are simultaneously true. Since an argument can always be formulated as a statement of material implication this decision procedure may be described as deciding both the validity of arguments and the logical truth of statements.

VII. Decision procedures in sections of logic other than propositional logic

Propositional Logic is the basic section of Formal Logic: its variables stand for whole sentences and its truth can be used in other sections of Logic where the internal structure of propositions is analysed. Thus the tautology *CKCpqpq* holds no matter what kind of propositions are substituted for *p* and *q*. However, while the truths of Propositional Logic can be imported into e.g. Terminal Logic, the latter discovers logical truths that are quite outside the reach of the former. Thus *CKpqr* is a contingent proposition: if one does not look within the internal structure of three propositions (*p*, *q*, *r*) there is nothing to indicate that a logical truth could have this form. But if the three propositions happen to be internally structured as follows: *MaP*, *SaM*, *SaP*, then the whole expression is seen, in Terminal Logic, to be logically true and is described in traditional terms as a valid syllogism. If the three propositions were structured *MoP*, *SaM*, *SaP*, the whole expression would, logically, be invalid because of the fallacy of an undistributed middle.

Thus other sections of Formal Logic not only use the truths of Propositional Logic but have the function also of discovering other logical truths. The problem is that where variables do not stand for whole unanalysed propositions a truth-table test is not applicable and indeed it does not seem possible to devise a *mechanical* test for displaying logical truth in *all* sections of logic. This problem will arise again at the end of Chapter 5 when a decision procedure for part of Predicate Logic is being provided.

Chapter 3

LOGIC AND DEDUCTIVE SYSTEMS

I. Introduction

Logic is concerned with:
(a) defining the nature, elements and structuring of a deductive system. There are two main types, axiomatic systems and natural deduction systems;
(b) formulating logical truths into a deductive system;
(c) defining the relationship between its own deductive system and others: do the propositions of Logic function elsewhere as, e.g. axioms or rules of inference?

II. The nature of a deductive system

On what general conditions is an explanatory system of concepts and propositions (such as a human science) possible? Aristotle asked that question and answered it as follows: On condition (a) that every term need not be resolved into simpler terms and meanings, i.e. that there are indefinables, primitive terms and concepts in human experience which cannot be humanly defined and need not be defined; (b) that every proposition need not be proved, i.e. that there are propositions which are indemonstrable, whose meaning guarantees their truth, which cannot be proved and need not be proved. Aristotle pointed out that if actually there are not such terms and propositions, then human science as an explanatory system of propositions about the real world is not possible.

We are not concerned here with the empirical value of particular primitive terms and propositions, or with the claim that this or that system of propositions may make to be true knowledge of the world, but with the organizational fact that system is impossible if there is an infinite regress in the certification of meanings and implications.

For about 2000 years Euclid's Geometry was regarded as the model of logical organization, consisting firstly of a set of underived propositions: definitions, postulates and axioms (general and geometrical), and secondly of a systematic series of derived propositions or theorems. However, a rigorous study of Euclid beginning in the last century revealed very important logical deficiencies, such as the following:
(1) Euclid begins with definitions; what one really needs to begin with is indefinables, a geometrical alphabet and rules for constructing definitions from it.

(2) Euclid does not distinguish between the kind of definition which simply says 'this is my name or symbol for this entity' and the kind of formula which gives a description of the entity. The former is an appellation, the latter a description.

(3) Euclid separates postulates and axioms but he does not distinguish between them sharply. Some of his axioms are not really self-evident, and his postulates were generally presented as safe assumptions.

(4) Theorems are supposed to be derived exclusively on the basis of the definitions, postulates and axioms. But in fact that is often not so. Diagrams which appear to be only aids to the imagination may provide spatial intuitions without which one could not be satisfied with the deducibility of the theorem. Thus in the first proposition of Euclid, describing two circles of radius AB, one with A as centre, the other with B, the existence of a point of intersection is exhibited in the diagram, not proved. Again, sometimes a theorem requires a postulate that does not feature in the original set—e.g. the argument for his twenty-ninth proposition assumes that through a point outside a straight line there passes only a single line parallel to that straight line.

This rigorous study of Euclid's Geometry and the desire to perfect its structure gave rise to the broader question: what is required, logically, for any system of propositions to be fully and perfectly organized? At first it was assumed that every system would be axiomatic in character, i.e. that the deductive apparatus must always consist of axioms as well as rules of inference. Indeed the whole study used to be called Axiomatics. But by 1934 Gerhard Gentzen and Stanislaw Jaskowski had developed an alternative procedure to the axiomatic one: it dispenses with axioms, using rules of inference alone, and is known as natural deduction. Thus a general study of deductive systems must take account now not only of axiomatic systems but also of natural deduction systems. Further, it is no longer assumed that the only acceptable way of presenting the propositions of Logic itself is in an axiomatic system. In this respect contemporary Logic seems to be moving away from Frege and Russell in whose systems deductive behaviour was controlled by axioms and rules; many authors hold today that it would be best to concentrate the deductive power of a system in rules alone.

III. The elements and structure of an axiomatic system

In this logical study we are not concerned with the material or natural truth of propositions but with their organization into a system. We are concerned (1) that there be an explicit distinction between expressions and propositions that are underived and those that are derived; (2) that rules for constructing well-formed expressions and propositions be explicit; (3) that rules for deriving propositions be explicit also.

In detail, the following rules must be observed in the construction of an axiomatic system:

1. The primitive language or underived symbols of the system, together with rules for constructing complex expressions from them, must be clearly set out. Expressions that conform to these rules are called well-formed expressions; the rules are called formation rules. Included in the formation rules are rules of definition in virtue of which one can state that an expression is equivalent to some other one.

2. The postulates of the system must be set out clearly and fully. In axiomatics all underived propositions are classified as postulates, i.e. they are not presented as truths, and thus there is not any distinction made between axioms and postulates. The postulates of a system are the propositions from which we deduce the others. An economical selection is called a set. The requirements for a postulate are that it be (a) *coherent*, entirely expressible in the language of the system; (b) *contributive*, i.e. give rise to implications; (c) *consistent*, i.e. not be incompatible with any other proposition of the system; and (d) *independent*, i.e. not be implied by other postulates, jointly or singly taken. A proposition derived within the system is called a theorem.

Thus in an axiomatic system there are no mere facts, i.e. facts which cannot be known from anything else and do not entail anything else.

3. The rules of inference must be set out fully. These are rules which determine when a proposition can be said to be a consequence of other propositions. If the rule relates simply to the mechanical transformation of expressions (e.g. by the substitution of equivalent expressions), the consequence is said to be syntactic; if the rule is based on meaning then the consequence is said to be semantic. These are the rules which determine when a deduction is properly constructed.

4. The definitions or fundamental equivalences used in the system must be set out and accord with the formation rules for expressions.

The rest of the system consists in proceeding by successive stages to all the possible theorems, every step being shown and its validity certified by a reference to the relevant rule of inference used. In modern systems the whole deduction proceeds in a formalistic manner, i.e. the rules of inference are such that attention can be completely focused on the form of the symbols (not on any content of meaning they may have or be given later) and propositions be derived with the eye as in mathematical calculation. When a system is worked out completely, at a syntactic or formalistic level, it may be found applicable to more than one context in life or science. Thus two axiomatic systems dealing with different sets of objects may be isomorphic, i.e. be simply two interpretations of the same primitive language, postulates, rules of inferences and definitions. This is a feature not only of mathematical systems in particular but in general of all axiomatic systems:

'Mathematics is a science in which we never know what we are talking about nor whether what we are saying is true': this well known sally of Russell's which occurred to him in reflecting on axiomatized mathematics, holds equally well for axiomatics in general. Similarly, it is really towards axiomatics that this other sally of Poincaré's is directed: 'Mathematics is the art of giving the same name to different things.' (*Axiomatics* by Robert Blanché, p. 31)

Indeed, formalized logic has been used in areas as distant from argument as electrical switching circuits and computers. It is frequently possible to master a system in itself and to distinguish it from various interpretations or projections of it.

IV. Natural deduction systems

In presenting an organized body of knowledge in any area, the axiomatic approach takes an initial grip on the reality we seek to know. Such a grip is furnished by the axioms or fundamental truths, and from there a theoretic process provides other truths in the form of implications. In contrast, a natural deduction system takes its first grip not on *what* is known, but on the *rational quality* of all human knowledge. It begins by formalizing movement in which reason is acting under the impulse of its own nature. Each of these movements is a natural deduction: its guarantee is the nature of reason and it is presented as acceptable to any person who is not prepared to abdicate his reason.

Any formalization of a natural deduction may be called a logical argument formula (LAF). It is evident that if one can reduce arguments to LAF's one has a method of showing their validity. It will also emerge that one can not only prove the validity of arguments but also the truth of all the propositions that feature in the systems of propositional and predicate logic.

To the ordinary conventional symbols a natural deduction system adds a symbol which indicates, positionally, assumption and derivative. It is of the form, $\vdash$, and is often called 'the therefore indicator'. The assumption(s) may be put to the left of $\vdash$ and the derivative to the right (this has advantages for the printer); or the assumption(s) may be situated above the horizontal line and the derivative beneath. For the moment, we will continue to use the Polish symbols.

The following are the main LAF's. Most of them are named after the connectives *K*, *A*, *C*, *N* according as a connective features in the premiss but not the conclusion (e.g. '*K*-out', '*K* eliminated'), or is introduced by the conclusion (e.g. '*K*-in', '*K* introduced').

Ki (*K-in*)				*Ko* (*K-out*)			
(1)	*p*	*A*		(1)	*Kpq*	*A*	
(2)	*q*	*A*					
				(2)	*p*	1,	*Ko*
(3)	*Kpq*	1, 2, *Ki*					

The right hand column gives the reason for each line: *p* and *q* are assumptions (a rule of assumptions justifies the introduction of any proposition at any stage in a proof); the reasons for line (3), *Kpq*, are the premisses (1) and (2) and a natural deduction formalized as the rule of inference *Ki*.

Ai (A-in)

(1) | *p*   *A*
   —————
(2) | *Apq*   1,   *Ai*

(Given *p*, a proposition combining *p* and any other alternative proposition is derivable.)

Ao (A-out)

(1) | *AKqpKqr*   *A*
(2) | (2.1) | *Kqp*   *A*

   (2.2) | *q*   2.1,   *Ko*
(3) | (3.1) | *Kqr*   *A*

   (3.2) | *q*   3.1,   *Ko*

(4) | *q*   1,   2,   3,   *Ao*

In *Ao*, items (2) and (3) are themselves composite or tail items, sequences. Item (1) is called simply a well formed formula (wff). It is important to note the force of the word, *formula*. One can use symbols as a kind of shorthand to represent sentences; used in this way symbols indicate both content and form. However, when I use a symbol, *p*, to indicate the presence of the kind of entity that has propositional form, then an act of understanding of form underlies my use of the symbol and I am formalizing sentences not merely representing them. In *Ao* the natural deduction is based on the fact that each of the alternatives has the same derivative, *q*.

Ci (C-in)

(1) | (1.1) | *p*   *A*
      —————
   (1.2) | *Apq*   1.1,   *Ai*

(2) | *CpApq*   1,   *Ci*

Co (C-out)

(1) | *Cpq*   *A*
(2) | *p*   *A*
  —————
(3) | *q*   1,   2,   *Co*

In *Ci*, *p* which is an assumption in (1) becomes the antecedent of the wff, *CpApq*. This latter formula does not require *p* as assumption: its truth-table shows that it is true for all values of *p* and *q*. Thus although *CpApq* is reached by a *method* of supposition, any assumption made is discharged in the process and *CpApq* can be asserted, absolutely, as a wff that is true. Thus it is not impossible for the method of natural deduction to establish absolute truth; the only question is the extent of its capacity here.

Ni (N-in)

(1) | (1.1) | *KqKpNp*   *A*
      —————
   (1.2) | *KpNp*   1.1,   *Ko*

(2) | *NKqKpNp*   1,   *Ni*

(1) | (1.1)   *KrKsNr*   *A*
   (1.2)   *r*   1.1,   *Ko*
   (1.3)   *KsNr*   1.1,   *Ko*
   (1.4)   *Nr*   1.3,   *Ko*
   (1.5)   *KrNr*   1.2,   1.4,   *Ki*

(2) | *NKrKsNr*   1,   *Ni*

No (*N-out*)

(1)	(1.1)	$NCKpqp$	A
	(1.2)	(1.2.1) | Kpq	A
		(1.2.2) | p	1.2.1, Ko
	(1.3)	$CKpqp$	1.2, Ci
	(1.4)	$KCKpqpNCKpqp$	1.3, 1.1, Ki
(2)	$CKpqp$		1, No

In these LAF's, an assumption leads to a formal contradiction (the conjunction of a proposition and its negation); thus by natural deduction the negation of the assumption is derivable.

Rep (*Repetition*)   *Double Negation* (*DN*)

(1) | p A	(1) | $KpAsr$ A	(1) | p A	(1) | NNp A
(2) | p 1, rep	(2) | $KpAsr$ 1, rep	(2) | NNp 1, DN	(2) | p 1, DN

The importance of being able to repeat a proposition at various stages in our reasoning, reminds us that circular argumentation is unsound only if it claims to be providing new information and fails to acknowledge the repetition. Repetition can advance a reasoning process: the legitimacy of our repetition of p derives from the fact that it is already a proposition in our system (by assumption or derivation). With regard to negation, a double application of this operation is, intuitively, self-nullifying.

What constitutes proof in a natural deduction system? A proof is a complete sequence of items each of which has a good reason. Items are of two kinds: (1) single wff's and (2) a sequence of items, called a tail item.

(1) With regard to a single wff, it will be either above or below the horizontal line in a ⊢. If it is above, a good reason is that it has the status of an hypothesis (we are assuming it in order to see what is deducible from it: we can write *hyp* or *A* at the right hand side to indicate this). If it is below, then in order to provide a good reason we must be able to present it as the last item in an LAF, indicating two things: firstly, the kind of LAF of which this wff is being thought of as the last item and, secondly, which preceding items are being presented as the preceding items of this LAF. The basis of this is that the LAF's are such that any argument that can be formalized by one of them is a valid argument (the last item, the conclusion, actually does follow from the premises).

(2) With regard to a tail item, it has a good reason if each of its constituent items has a good reason. Some of these constituent items may themselves be sequences, but ultimately all the sequences resolve into items that are wff's. Thus eventually we can always decide whether the whole tail item has a good reason.

Thus in a natural deduction system an argument is valid when it can be formalized by an AF that corresponds to a proof in that system. It is evident that such a system is potentially a rich and powerful source of proof.

What exactly is proved in a natural deduction system? It establishes two kinds of conclusion really: (1) *sequents* (a sequent being a whole complex of items including the assumptions); and (2) *theorems* (*theorem* has a specialised meaning here and connotes the conclusion of a provable sequent which in the process of being reached by the method of supposition becomes logically independent of the actual suppositions. The LAF, *Ci*, is a rich source:

1	1.1	*p*	*hyp*
	1.2	*Apq*	1.1, *Ai*
2	*CpApq*		1, *Ci*

(We may take advantage of theorems and their substitution instances to shorten proofs by a rule for theorem introduction, just as it is practical to have a rule for using sequents already proved.)

Are truth-tables useful in natural deduction systems? As an adequate mechanical decision procedure in propositional logic, the truth-table method reaches the same results as the process of natural deduction or the axiomatic process. The relative simplicity of this area permits a mechanical procedure to be adequate and it can be useful in many ways and equally in all systems. However, natural deduction systems differ in their reliance on truth-tables. One kind relies completely on rules of inference to control the use and behaviour of logical constants. An example is in *Logic: Techniques of Formal Reasoning* by Donald Kalish and Richard Montague (New York, 1964; chs. 1 and 2). The second kind uses truth-table definitions for the connectives and the notion of tautological-implication. An example is in *Introduction to Logic* by Patrick Suppes (Princeton, N.J. 1957; ch. 2).

V. Relating the axiomatic and the natural deduction approaches to the science of logic itself

In 1934 Carnap noted (*Logische Syntax der Sprache*) that for every logical axiom there is an equivalent inference rule and therefore that the choice of formulating a logical fact as an axiom or rule of inference is an issue of practice rather than of principle. Putting the words 'can be asserted' before a law translates it into a rule, i.e. into a declaration of *something that can be done* rather than a declaration of *what is so*. The equivalence of *P* and *Q* can be translated into a rule by saying one can be substituted for the other; the implication of *P* and *Q* is similarly translated by saying that if *Q* is asserted *P* can be asserted. Thus the same logical content and power can be built into both an axiomatic system and a natural deduction one.

Both techniques are frequently used nowadays. It is a matter for metalogic to study their comparative suitability within logic. The following chapters which present a precis of the main sections of formal logic will exemplify both techniques. It is important to remember that formalized logic is unique as a formal system. Every other system (e.g. geometry) presupposes a logic that governs the derivation of its theorems from its axioms; this logic brings to the system not extra premisses but rules of inference. Thus logic is a formalizing principle in other systems.

The main sections of standard two-value logic are Propositional Logic and Predicate Logic. The former is the logic of the interconnection of propositions, the latter is generated from their internal structure. (*Sentence* is the name of the verbal structure; *proposition* is the name of the meaning contained in this structure. In his practical work, which resembles mathematical calculation, the logician is immediately concerned with the verbal structure; accordingly, propositional logic is often called *Sentential Logic*, or *The Logic of Sentences*, or *Sentential Calculus* or *The Calculus of Sentences*. Predicate logic gives rise to a Class Calculus or a Calculus of Classes. Later we shall note the difference between a logic and the calculus associated with it.)

Modal Logic and Many-Valued Logic are sections of logic which are called non-standard because they do not work within the simple true–false framework.

Chapter 4

A PRECIS OF PROPOSITIONAL LOGIC

In Propositional Logic, truth-tables furnish an effective procedure for deciding whether any sentence is true or any argument is valid. Thus it is not necessary to organize this section into a system of propositions: the propositions can be shown, separately, to be tautologies and do not need the credential of deducibility within a system.

This chapter will (1) present a limited, selected list of tautologies in Propositional Logic; (2) indicate how these tautologies can be formalized into an axiomatic system; and (3) survey the classic axiomatic systems that have been constructed.

I. A selected list of tautologies or laws in propositional logic

(a) *First principles of traditional logic*

Epp	(Principle of Identity)
NKpNp or *DpNp*	(Principle of Non-Contradiction)
ApNp	(Principle of Excluded Middle)

(b) *Tautologies in which the variables are equiform*

Epp	Principle of Identity
ENNpp	Principle of Double Negation
ENNNpNp	Principle of Triple Negation
ENpDpp	Reduction of Negation
EAppp	1st law of Tautology
EKppp	2nd law of Tautology

(c) *Tautologies which analyse the meaning of the A functor*

EApqCNpq	
EApqDNpNq	Reduction of Alternation
EApqNKNpNq	De Morgan's 3rd Law
EApqCCpqq	
EApqAqp	Commutative Law of the Sum
EApAqrAApqr	Associative Law of the Sum
EApKqrKApqApr	Distributive Law of the Sum
EApApqApq	1st law of Simplification of the Sum
EApKpqp	2nd law of Simplification of the Sum
ENApqKNpNq	De Morgan's 1st Law

(d) *Tautologies which analyse the meaning of the C functor*

ECpqANpq	
ECpqDpNq	Reduction of Implication
ECpqNKpNq	
ECpqEpKpq	
ECpqEqApq	
ECpqCNqNp	Law of Simple Contraposition
ECpNqCqNp	2nd Law of Simple Contraposition
ECNpqCNqp	3rd Law of Simple Contraposition
ECpCqrCqCpr	Law of Simple Commutation
ECKpqrCpCqr	1st Law of Exportation
ECKpqrCqCpr	2nd Law of Exportation
ECpCpqCpq	
ECKpqrCKNrqNp	1st Law of Syllogistic Contraposition
ECKpqrCKpNrNq	2nd Law of Syllogistic Contraposition
ENCpqKpNq	

(e) *Tautologies which present the C functor in an evidence-conclusion format*

CpCqp	1st Paradoxical law ('Verum sequitur ad quodlibet')
CNpCpq	2nd Paradoxical law ('Ex falso sequitur quodlibet')
CCpNpNp	1st Reductio ad absurdum
CpCNpq	
CKpNpNp	2nd Reductio ad absurdum
CpApq	Law of the new factor
CKpqp	1st law of the *a fortiori*
CKpqq	2nd law of the *a fortiori*
CKpqCpq	
CEpqCpq	

(f) *Tautologies which analyse the meaning of the D functor*

EDpqANpNq	
EDpqCpNq	
EDpqNKpq	
EDpqDqp	Commutation of Exclusion
EDppNp	Reduction of Negation
ENDpqKpq	

(g) *Tautologies which analyse the meaning of the K functor*

EKpqNANpNq	De Morgan's 4th Law
EKpqNCpNq	
EKpqNDpq	Reduction of Conjunction
EKpqKqp	Commutative Law of the Product
EKpKqrKKpqr	Associative Law of the Product

EKpAqrAKpqKpr	Distributive Law of the Product
EKpApqp	1st Law of Simplifying the Product
EKpKpqKpq	2nd Law of Simplifying the Product
ENKpqANpNq	De Morgan's 2nd Law
ENKpqDpq	

(h) *Tautologies which analyse the meaning of the E functor*

EEpqAKpqKNpNq	
EEpqKCpqCqp	
EEpqEqp	Commutative Law of Equivalence
EEpEqrEEpqr	Associative Law of Equivalence
EEpqENpNq	Inversion of Equivalence
EEpqENqNp	1st Contraposition of Equivalence
EENpqENqp	2nd Contraposition of Equivalence
EEpNqEqNp	3rd Contraposition of Equivalence

(i) *Tautologies which have the format of models for general syllogistic inference*

CCqrCCpqCpr
CCpqCCqrCpr
CCpqCCqrCCrsCps
CCpqCCqrCCrsCCstCpt
CKCpqCqrCpr
CKKCpqCqrCrsCps
CKKKCpqCqrCrsCstCpt
CCpqCArpArq

(j) *Tautologies which have the format of models for syllogistic inference of the hypothetical kind*

CpCCpqq	Modus ponendo ponens 1°
CKCpqpq	Modus ponendo ponens 2°
CKCpNqpNq	
CKCNpqNpq	
CKCNpNqNpNq	
CNqCCpqNp	Modus tollendo tollens 1°
CKCpqNqNp	Modus tollendo tollens 2°
CKCpNqqNp	
CKCNpqNqp	
CKCNpNqqp	
CKCpqCprCpKqr	Law of multiplying the consequent
CpCqKpq	
CKCpqCrsCKprKqs	Multiplication of both sides
CKCpqCrsCAprAqs	Addition of both sides
CKCprCqrCApqr	1st constructive dilemma
CKCprCNprr	2nd constructive dilemma
CKNqNrCCpAqrNp	1st destructive dilemma

CKCpKqrKNqNrNp	2nd destructive dilemma
CKCpqCpNqNp	3rd reductio ad absurdum

(k) *Tautologies which have the format of models for syllogistic inference of the disjunctive and copulative kind*

CNpCApqq	Modus tollendo ponens 1°
CNqCApqp	
CKApqNpq	Modus tollendo ponens 2°
CKApqNqp	
CKApNqNpNq	
CKANpqpq	
CKANpNqpNq	
CpCDpqNq	Modus ponendo tollens ˙ °
CqCDpqNp	
CpCNKpqNq	
CKDpqpNq	Modus ponendo tollens 2°
CKDpNqpq	
CKDNpqNpNq	
CKDNpNqNpq	

II. An axiomatic system of the tautologies of propositional logic

The work of formalizing Propositional Logic, begun by Frege & Peano was completed by Russell & Whitehead in the *Principia Mathematica*. Subsequently, the five axioms used in the PM were reduced to four by Hilbert, to three by Lukasiewicz, to one by Nicod. The problem of the 'single, sufficient and shortest' axiom continued to be investigated by Lukasiewicz and his school. In 1925 Alfred Tarski provided a fifty-three lettered axiom; in 1933 Sobocinski provided a twenty-seven letter one; this was shortened soon afterwards by Lukasiewicz to twenty-five letters, and again by Lukasiewicz, in 1936, to twenty-three letters. The shortest one was proposed in 1955 by C. A. Meredith, an Irish associate of Lukasiewicz, and contains 21 letters:

$$CCCCCpqCNrNsrtCCtpCsp$$

The following system is that of Hilbert–Ackerman, as modified by Bochenski through incorporating Lukasiewicz's method of deduction. The proof preceding each theorem is expressed in a single probative verse or derivational line, and it employs special symbolism. Before presenting the system as a whole it may be helpful to anticipate two of the early theorems which will be proved and to analyse the derivational lines which precede them:

1.44 *r/Nr* × 1.23 *p/r, q/p* × 1.23 *p/r* = 1.51
1.51 *CCpqCCrpCrq*

Here the theorem proved is 1.51. The derivational line reads: 'Take the expression 1.44; for "*r*" substitute "*Nr*"; apply the expression 1.23 (a definition) after substituting "*r*" for "*p*" and "*p*" for "*q*"; apply the same definition 1.23 again but this time substitute "*r*" for "*p*"; and one will thus obtain the theorem to be proved 1.51.' (Bochenski's *A Precis of Mathematical Logic*, p. 31).

$$1.51\ p/App,\ q/p,\ r/p = C\ 1.41 - C\ 1.42\ q/p - 1.52$$

1.52 *Cpp*

Here the theorem proved is 1.52. The derivational line reads: 'Take the expression 1.51; for "*p*" substitute "*App*", for "*q*" substitute "*p*", for "*r*" substitute "*p*"; this will result in an expression composed of (1) *C* followed by an expression equiform with 1.41; (2) *C* followed by an expression equiform with 1.42 after "*p*" is substituted for "*q*"; (3) the theorem 1.52 (which by a double application of the rule of detachment can now be stated separately, i.e. since the whole sentence is a law of the system, and 1.41 and 1.42 are also laws, then 1.52 is also a law).'

The foundations and early theorems of Hilbert–Ackerman's system, as modified and presented by Bochenski, are as follows:

1.1 *Primitive Terms, Rule of Definition and Rules of Formation*
1.11 Primitive terms: '*D*'—dyadic functor; '*p*', '*q*', '*r*', '*s*'—sentential variables.
1.12 Rule of Definition: A new term can be introduced into the system by formulating a group of terms, called the 'definition', and consisting of: (1) an expression which contains the new term and in which all the others are terms of the system; (2) '='; (3) an expression which contains only primitive terms or terms already defined.
1.13 Rules of Formation: (1) a variable is a sentence; (2) a group of terms consisting of '*N*' followed by one sentence is a sentence; (3) a group of terms consisting of '*A*', '*C*', '*D*', '*E*' or '*K*' followed by two sentences is a sentence.
1.2 *Definitions*
1.21 $Np = Dpp$
1.22 $Apq = DNpNq$
1.23 $Cpq = ANpq$
1.24 $Kpq = NANpNq$
1.25 $Epq = KCpqCqp$
1.3 *Rules of Deduction*
1.31 Rule of Substitution: A sentence may be substituted for a variable, but the same sentence must be substituted for all equiform occurrences of variables in the expression.
1.32 Rule of substitution by definition: A definition may be substituted for the expression which it defines in a sentence, and reciprocally, without being substituted for all equiform occurrences of that expression.
1.33 Rule of detachment: If a sentence consisting of '*C*' followed by two sentences is a law of the system, and if a sentence equiform with the

first of these sentences is a law of the system, a sentence equiform with
the second can be posited as a law of the system.

1.4 *Axioms*
1.41 *CAppp*
1.42 *CpApq*
1.43 *CApqAqp*
1.44 *CCpqCArpArq*
1.5 *Deduction of Theorems*
      1.44 $r/Nr \times 1.23$ p/r, $q/p \times 1.23$ $p/r = 1.51$
1.51 *CCpqCCrpCrq*
      1.51 p/App, q/p, $r/p = C$ $1.41 - C$ 1.42 $q/p - 1.52$
1.52 *Cpp*
      1.52×1.23 $q/p = 1.53$
1.53 *ANpp*
      1.43 p/Np, $q/p = C$ $1.53 - 1.54$
1.54 *ApNp*
      1.54 $p/Np \times 1.23$ $q/NNp = 1.55$
1.55 *CpNNp*
      1.44 p/Np, $q/NNNp$, $r/p = C$ 1.55 p/Np, $- C$ $1.54 - 1.56$
1.56 *ApNNNp*
      1.43 $q/NNNp \times 1.23$ p/NNp, $q/p = C$ $1.56 - 1.57$
1.57 *CNNpp*
      1.44 q/NNp, $r/Nq = C$ $1.55 - 1.58$
1.58 *CANqpANqNNp*
      1.51 $p/ANqNNp$, $q/ANNpNq$, $r/ANqp = C$ 1.43 p/Nq, $q/NNp - C$
      $1.58 - 1.59$
1.59 *CANqpANNpNq*
      1.59 p/q, $q/p \times 1.23 \times 1.23$ p/Nq, $q/Np = 1.60$
1.60 *CCpqCNqNp*
      1.41 $p/Np \times 1.23$ $q/Np = 1.61$
1.61 *CCpNpNp*
      1.51 p/Apq, q/Aqp, $r/p = C$ $1.43 - C$ $1.42 - 1.62$
1.62 *CpAqp*
      1.62 $q/Nq \times 1.23$ p/q, $q/p = 1.63$
1.63 *CpCqp*
      1.63 $q/Np = 1.64$
1.64 *CpCNpp*
      1.44 p/r, q/Apr, $r/q = C$ 1.62 p/r, $q/p - 1.65$
1.65 *CAqrAqApr*
      1.44 p/Aqr, $q/AqApr$, $r/p = C$ $1.65 - 1.66$
1.66 *CApAqrApAqApr*
      1.51 $p/ApAqApr$, $q/AAqAprp$, $r/ApAqr = C$ 1.43 $q/AqApr - C$ $1.66 -$
      1.67
1.67 *CApAqrAAqAprp*
      1.51 p/Apr, $q/AqApr$, $r/p = C$ 1.62 $p/Apr - C$ 1.42 $q/r - 1.68$

1.68 *CpAqApr*
    1.44 *q/AqApr, r/AqApr* = *C* 1.68 − 1.69
1.69 *CAAqAprpAAqAprAqApr*
    1.51 *p/AAqAprAqApr, q/AqApr, r/AAqAprp* = *C* 1.41 *p/AqApr* − *C*
    1.69 − 1.70
1.70 *CAAqAprpAqApr*
    1.51 *p/AAqAprp, q/AqApr, r/ApAqr* = *C* 1.70 − *C* 1.67 − 1.71
1.71 *CApAqrAqApr*
    1.44 *p/Aqr, q/Arq, r/p* = *C* 1.43 *p/q, q/r* = 1.72
1.72 *CApAqrApArq*
    1.51 *p/ApArq, q/ArApq, r/ApAqr* = *C* 1.71 *q/r, r/q* − *C* 1.72 − 1.73
1.73 *CApAqrArApq*
    1.51 *p/ArApq, q/AApqr, r/ApAqr* = *C* 1.43 *p/r, q/Apq* − *C* 1.73 −
    1.74
1.74 *CApAqrAApqr*
    1.51 *p/AqApr, q/AqArp, r/ApAqr* = *C* 1.72 *p/q, q/p* − *C* 1.71 − 1.75
1.75 *CApAqrAqArp*
    1.51 *p/ArApq, q/ArAqp, r/ApAqr* = *C* 1.72 *p/r, q/p, r/q* − *C* 1.73 −
    1.76
1.76 *CApAqrArAqp*

III. A survey of classic axiomatizations of propositional logic

This survey is based on the detailed systematic presentation in *Notions De Logique Formelle* by Professor Dopp (Appendix 1, p. 261 seq.). The axiomatic systems are classified according to the nature of the functors used in their sets of axioms, and they are further varied according to the number of axioms needed:

1. *Systems using the five operators C, N, K, A, E* (→, ~, ., ∨, ↔ *in the Peano–Russell notation*):
(a) Having 15 axioms:

Hilbert–Bernays, 1934
Hermes–Scholz, 1952

(b) Having 10 axioms:
      Moh Shaw–Kwei, 1957 (two different systems)
(c) Having 9 axioms:

Jaskowski

(d) Having 5 axioms:

Moh Shaw–Kwei, 1957

2. *Systems using the four functors C, N, K, A:*
(a) Having 12 axioms:

Heyting, 1930
S. Kanger, 1955

(b) Having 10 axioms:

Tarski, 1952

3. *Systems using the three functors C, N, K:*
(a) Having 5 axioms:

Porte, 1958 (three different systems)

(b) Having 4 axioms:

Porte, 1958

(c) Having 3 axioms:

Rosser, 1953

4. *Systems using the three functors C, N, A:*
(a) Having 7 axioms:

Jaskowski, 1948

5. *Systems using the two functors C, N:*
(a) Having 7 axioms:

Russell, 1906

(b) Having 6 axioms:

Frege, 1879
Hilbert, 1922
Moh Shaw–Kwei, 1957 (two different systems)

(c) Having 5 axioms:

Curry

(d) Having 4 axioms:

Curry
Tarski, 1930
Porte, 1958

(e) Having 3 axioms

Lukasiewicz, 1924
Lukasiewicz, 1929
Lukasiewicz, 1930
Sobocinski, 1953
Arai, 1965
Mendelson

(f) Having 1 axiom:

Lukasiewicz (two different systems)
Meredith, 1953
Lukasiewicz–Tarski, 1930
Tanaka, 1966

6. *Systems using the two functors C, A:*
(a) Having 6 axioms:

Jaskowski, 1948

(b) Having 5 axioms:

Russell and Whitehead, 1910

(c) Having 4 axioms:

Hilbert–Ackerman, 1928

(d) Having 3 axioms:

Rasiowa, 1949
Meredith, 1951

(e) Having 1 axiom:

Meredith, 1953

7. *Systems using the two functors N, A:*
(a) Having 5 axioms:

Reichenbach, 1953

(b) Having 3 axioms:

Rose, 1949

8. *Systems using the two functors N, K:*
(a) Having 4 axioms:

Sobocinski, 1939
Sobocinski, 1962

9. *Systems using only the functor D:*
(a) Having 1 axiom:

Nicod, 1918
Lukasiewicz, 1925
Wajsberg, 1931
Lukasiewicz, 1931

10. *Systems which include a propositional constant, Λ, which symbolizes a proposition that is (necessarily) false:*
(a) Having 11 axioms:

Schütte, 1960

(b) Having 5 axioms:

Peirce, 1885

(c) Having 4 axioms:

Wajsberg, 1937

(d) Having 3 axioms:

Church, 1951

(e) Having 2 axioms:

Rose, 1951

(f) Having 1 axiom:

Lukasiewicz–Meredith, 1953 (two different axioms, each with 6 variables)

Meredith, 1953 (two different axioms, the first with 5 variables, the second with 6)

Chapter 5

PREDICATE LOGIC

I. Introduction

In propositional logic variables stand for whole, unanalysed propositions; these are the atoms out of which complex, molecular propositions are constructed through the operation of connectives such as K, C, A, etc. A variable such as p, q or r is used to signify any entity that has propositional form, whatever its internal structure. Thus propositional logic is only suited for dealing with arguments whose logical force derives completely from the connectives, K, C, A, etc. It cannot evaluate the following argument, for instance: 'If everything that can reproduce its kind, is living; and if a virus can reproduce its kind; then it follows that a virus is living.' Translated into the language of propositional logic this sequence of three different propositions reads 'If p and if q, then r.' Such a reading does not credit the argument with any logical force. However, if we use the traditional symbols S, P and M for the subject of the conclusion, the predicate of the conclusion and the term common to both premisses we display the basic and compelling force of the argument:

> If all M is P;
> and if all S is M,
> _____
> then all S is P
> _____

Obviously there is room for a section of logic which expresses the internal structure of atomic propositions and studies the operation and the laws of predication. This is broadly the function of Predicate Logic.

II. The language of predicate logic

It consists of
1. *proper names*: frequently the initial letter of the proper name is used, e.g. 'v' for 'Voltaire';
2. *arbitrary names*: they designate individuals also but only those arbitrarily chosen. The letters 'a', 'b', 'c', 'd' will be used for such individuals which are designated not in their individuality but only in so far as they are typical cases;
3. *individual variables*: the letters 'x', 'y', 'z' will be used as variables for the individuals of any universe of discourse;
4. *predicate letters*: the initial capitals of the predicate words will be used as

such letters; otherwise '*F*', '*G*', '*H*', '*I*'. Followed by one name they signify a *property*; followed by two or more names they signify a *relation*. Thus *Fx* signifies that *x* has the property *F*; *Fxy* signifies that *x* has the relation *F* to *y*.

5. *quantifiers*: (*x*) is the symbol of universal quantification; thus (*x*)*Fx* can be read: 'for every value of *x* (or take any object *x*) *x* is *F*.'

(*Ex*) is the existential quantifier and (*Ex*)*Fx* means that 'an object *x* can be found such that *x* is *F*' or 'there exists some object *x* such that *x* is *F*'.

6. *the connectives of propositional logic*: instead of using the Polish notation, we will use a notation that is basically Peano–Russell:

$$
\begin{array}{lll}
\text{'}-\text{'} & \text{instead of} & \text{'}N\text{'} \\
\text{'}\equiv\text{'} & \text{,,} \quad \text{,,} & \text{'}E\text{'} \\
\text{'}\vee\text{'} & \text{,,} \quad \text{,,} & \text{'}A\text{'} \\
\text{'}\rightarrow\text{'} & \text{,,} \quad \text{,,} & \text{'}C\text{'} \\
\text{'}|\text{'} & \text{,,} \quad \text{,,} & \text{'}D\text{'} \\
\text{'}.\text{'} & \text{,,} \quad \text{,,} & \text{'}K\text{'}
\end{array}
$$

7. *A class designating symbol*: '$\hat{x}$' signifies 'the *x*s such that . . .'

8. *A symbol representing identity*: '=' is this symbol; when it is included predicate logic or calculus (PL or PC) is called predicate logic or calculus with identity (PLI or PCI). This symbol is a predicate letter although it has a fixed meaning, and by convention is placed between its terms. It appears in complex expressions in just the way *F* and *G* appear.

The above simple formal language has great expressive power, as can be seen from the following translations:

Voltaire is a Frenchman who smiles: *Fv . Sv*

There is a Frenchman who smiles: (*Ex*) (*Fx . Sx*)

All Frenchmen smile: (*x*) (*Fx → Sx*)

(A universal proposition is expressed in the form of a material implication governed by the universal quantifier: Russell called this formal implication.)

Some Frenchmen smile: (*Ex*) (*Fx . Sx*)

(A particular proposition is expressed in the form of a simple conjunction—not a material implication—governed by the existential quantifier; the truth of an existential proposition is not implied by the truth of the corresponding universal.)

No Frenchmen smile: (*x*) (*Fx → −Sx*)

Some Frenchmen do not smile: (*Ex*) (*Fx . −Sx*)

The class of cats who smile: (*x*) (*Cx . Sx*)

John does not *l*ike any strangers: (*x*) (*Sx → −Ljx*)

*V*alid *c*onclusions are those which are *i*mplied by the premisses: (*x*) (*Cx . Vx → Ix*)

Only valid conclusions are implied by the premisses: (*x*) (*Ix → Cx . Vx*)

Following Euclid if we can prove that an arbitrarily selected triangle has the property *F* (i.e. if we can prove *Fa*), then we can soundly conclude that all triangles have *F* (i.e. that (*x*) *Fx*).

There are exactly two *F*renchmen who *s*mile:

(*Ex*) (*Ey*) [(*Fx . Sx*) . (*Fy . Sy*) . −(*x* = *y*) . (*z*) [(*Fz . Sz*) → ((*z* = *x*) ∨ (*z* = *y*))]]

'There exists an x and there exists a y such that x is a Frenchman and smiles and y is a Frenchman and smiles, and x and y are not the same person; and for every value of z, if z is a Frenchman and smiles he is either x or y.'

Thus through use of the identity symbol we can make exact numerical statements in predicate calculus—'at least one thing', 'at most one thing', 'one thing', 'two things', 'three things' and so on through the number series.

III. Discovering truths in predicate logic

In the section on propositional logic we used the mechanical method of truth-tables to discover the logical truths (tautologies, laws) of that area; in addition, selecting a few of these simple truths as a set of axioms we systematically deduced the rest. We can establish also that our axiomatic system is both consistent and complete (see later section on Metalogic).

Predicate logic does not possess a mechanical decision procedure. On the other hand it has this enormous advantage that for every law of propositional logic one can formulate analogous laws in predicate logic by simply substituting wff's from predicate logic for the propositional variables p, q, r, s, prefixing the universal quantifier if individuals variables are used. Thus from the law $p \equiv p$, one can form the analogous law $(x) Fx \equiv Fx$; we could also form the law $Fa \equiv Fa$, using the individual constant a and omitting the quantifier. One can discover a vast number of logical laws, simple and complex in this way; the only limit is the range of laws within propositional logic itself and the scope of substitution for the propositional variables.

How are the laws which are not analogous discovered and established? Of course both the axiomatic and the natural deduction approach employ procedures which are techniques of discovery. We have seen axiomatic techniques in operation in the area of propositional logic, and one well known axiomatic system of predicate logic is that presented by Hilbert and Ackermann in their *Principles of Mathematical Logic*. Here we will indicate how the same range of logical truth can be discovered from the natural deduction approach.

To the LAF's of propositional logic four further ones are added concerning the quantifiers:

	U-in			U-out	
(1)	Fa	A	(1)	$(x) Fx$	A
(2)	$(x) (Fx)$	1, U-in	(2)	Fa	1, U-out
				('a' being an arbitrary name)	

also

(1)	$(x) Fx$	A
(2)	Fi	1, U-out
	(where 'i' is a proper name)	

U-in is based on the logical force of a typical case having the predicate *F*. It is not because the individual designated by *a* is arbitrarily chosen that we can generalize from it but because it is designated and used not in its individuality but only in so far as it is a typical case. Arbitrary choice as such does not guarantee that the individual chosen will be used only in so far as it is typical; however it is an acknowledgement that *any* individual can be used in this way, and some proofs in Euclidean Geometry are familiar examples of this usage. Formal logic is not concerned with the practical difficulties of defining the typical case but with the fact that on the assumption that a typical case, as such, has a predicate *F*, then it follows by natural deduction that this predicate belongs to every individual of the type. *U*-out accepts that any instantiation of a universal predication holds.

E-in

(1) | *Fa*   *A*

(2) | *(Ex) Fx*   1, *E*-in

E-out

(1) | *Ex (Fx)*   *A*

(2) | 2.1 | *Ga*   *A* (*G* signifies properties that constitute the type.)

2.2 | *P*   *any expression that follows from 2.1.*

(3) | *P*   1, 2, *E*-out

also

(1) | *Fi*   *A*

(2) | *(Ex) Fx*   1, *E*-in

(where '*i*' is a proper name).
E-in accepts that any single case of a predication entitles the derivation of an existential proposition; *E*-out is based on the fact that an existential proposition is a finite or infinite disjunction (A_1 or A_2 or A_3 or A_n has *F*) and what is shown to be true of each and every disjunct or of a typical disjunct, *a*, is therefore derivable from the existential proposition. The fact that *E*-out, like *U*-in, can be based on the logical force of a typical case does not render it redundant: a function of propositional logic is to determine the conditions, if any, on which an existential assumption can give rise to a natural deduction process.

There are two rules concerning identity in proofs: *I*-in allows us to introduce, at any time and as a matter of transparent logical truth not as an assumption, $t = t$; in virtue of the rule *I*-out, given that $t = s$ we are allowed to transform a statement containing occurrences of *t* into a statement which replaces one or more occurrence of *t* by *s*.

Finally to expedite and shorten proof there is a rule of theorem introduction (*TI*), allowing us to introduce, at any stage, a theorem already proved or any substitution instance of it; and there is a rule of sequent introduction (*SI*) enabling us to do the same with regard to sequents and their substitution-instances.

The complete list of LAF's and rules which constitute our apparatus for discovering logical truth is given in the following table. Assumptions are placed for convenience to the left of the therefore indicator ⊢, and the derived propositions to its right; in some cases there are no assumptions for, as we have seen, the method of supposition can lead to a conclusion where truth is displayed as free from the initial suppositions. The LAF's from propositional logic are the same as those formulated in chapter 3 in the Polish notation.

Table of LAF's and rules used in a natural deduction system of Predicate Logic

---

A rule of assumptions (*A*) entitles us to introduce any proposition at any stage in a proof)

1. $p, q \vdash p \cdot q$	Symbolized as *Ki* (*K*-in)
2. $p \cdot q \vdash p$	„ „ *Ko* (*K*-out)
3. $p \vdash p \vee q$	„ „ *Ai*
4. $(q \cdot p) \vee (q \cdot r) \vdash q$	„ „ *Ao*
5. $\vdash p \rightarrow (p \vee q)$	„ „ *Ci*
6. $p \rightarrow q, p \vdash q$	„ „ *Co*
7. $\vdash - (r \cdot (s \cdot - r))$	„ „ *Ni*
8. $\vdash ((p \cdot q) \rightarrow p)$	„ „ *No*
9. $p \vdash p$	„ „ *Rep.* (Repetition)
10. $p \vdash - - p$	„ „ *DN* (double negation)
11. $Fa \vdash (x) Fx$	„ „ *Ui*
12. $x (Fx) \vdash Fa$ also $(x) Fx \vdash Fm$	„ „ *Uo*
13. $Fa \vdash (Ex) Fx$ also $Fm \vdash (Ex) Fx$	„ „ *Ei*
14. $Ex (Fx), Fa \rightarrow P \vdash P$	„ „ *Eo*
15. $t = t$	„ „ *Ii* (Identity appears as a line in the proof)
16. Given that $t = s$, we are allowed to transform a statement containing occurrences of $t [P(t)]$ into a statement which replaces one or more occurrences of t by $s [P(s)]$.	Symblized as *Io* (Identity is used in the production of a line in the proof, and disappears on use).
17. Rule of Theorem Introduction, allowing us to introduce any theorem already proved and any substitution instance of it.	Symbolized as *Ti*
18. Rule of Sequent Introduction, allowing us to introduce any sequent already proved and any substitution instance of it.	„ „ *Si*

This table constitutes an apparatus for discovering proofs (and therefore truths) in predicate logic: we can construct sequences, the last item being a conclusion, the other items the basis on which it is derived and *all* items having a good reason: being justified by a rule such as that of assumptions, or theorem introduction, etc. or by an LAF such as *Ki* or *Ko*, etc. Thus, directly, the table provides us with the means of displaying a fundamental basis on which logical truths or valid sequents can be justified; it does not provide us with a direct means of discovering and displaying invalidity. By contrast the method of truth-tables is a procedure that within propositional logic displays both validity and invalidity and can always be applied.

Truth discovery by natural deduction is a matter of strategy. Can the table of LAF's and rules be used to supply a justification (proof) for saying that this proposition (*p*) is derivable from certain assumptions; or that this other proposition (*q*) can be derived by the method of supposition and also shown to be true independently of any initial supposition made. Through practise and experience one must develop a sensitivity as to what LAF, and rules are likely to be helpful in discovering, constructing and formalizing derivations.

IV. Practice in derivation by the method of supposition—a sampling of logical laws in predicate logic with their proofs

The law is stated first. Each line of the proof is numbered serially; the number is placed to the immediate left of the expression and is in brackets (e.g. (1), (2)). Each line must have a good reason; this reason may be, e.g. the rule of assumptions, or that this line is derivable from earlier ones by one of the LAF rules; whatever the reason be it is given in the column on the right, e.g. *A* (this line is an assumption); 1, 2 *Ki* (this line is derived from 1 and 2 on the basis of the LAF, *Ki*). On the extreme left there is a column giving the assumptions required for each line. If a line is there through use of the rule of assumptions, then it depends on itself as an assumption and accordingly we put its own number in the left-hand column; if it is there by derivation we must pool the assumptions required for its premises (this is easily done as the right-hand column gives us the serial numbers of the premises, and the left-hand column at each number gives us the relevant assumptions). Thus taking the following line

$$1, 2, 3 \ (6) \ P \qquad 2, 3 \ Ko$$

we may read it as follows: the expression, *P*, is line 6 in the proof; it is derived by *Ko* from lines 2 and 3; the assumptions on which it rests are lines 1, 2 and 3. It is well to recall that in the application of *Ci*, the new conditional has as its antecedent an expression which was an assumption; it is not an assumption for the new conditional and does not appear in the column of assumptions for the new conditional; it is called the discharged assumption. Thus in the application of *Ci* the number of assumptions is reduced by one and a *Ci* proposition derived by the method of assumptions may have no assumptions. Such a proposition is called a theorem. A sample example is $\vdash (p \, . \, q) \to p$. Its proof is

$$1 \ (1) \ p \, . \, q \qquad A$$
$$1 \ (2) \ p \qquad 1, Ko$$
$$(3) \ (p \, . \, q) \to p \qquad 1, 2, Ci$$

A similar discharging of assumptions occurs in the application of *Ni* and *No*. If on the assumption of a proposition *p* (positive or negative) a formal contradiction is derived from it then the negation of *p* follows by natural deduction; and −*p* is implied by the formal contradiction not by the proposition *p* which has been used in the *method* of supposition but is now discharged *evidentially* as an assumption. A simple example is $\vdash - (r . (s . - r))$. Its proof is

$$
\begin{array}{lll}
1\,(1)\,r . (s . - r) & & A \\
1\,(2)\,r & & 1, Ko \\
1\,(3)\,s . - r & & 1, Ko \\
1\,(4) - r & & 3, Ko \\
1\,(5)\,r . - r & & 2, 4, Ki \\
1\,(6)\,(r . (s . - r)) \to r . - r & & 1, 5, Ci \\
(7) - (r . (s . - r)) & & 6, Ni
\end{array}
$$

Of course if there are assumptions involved in the derivation of the formal contradiction then the conclusion will rest on these. An example is the proof of the logical law $p \to q, p \to - q \vdash - p$:

$$
\begin{array}{lll}
1\,(1)\,p \to q & & A \\
2\,(2)\,p \to - q & & A \\
3\,(3)\,p & & A \\
1, 3\,(4)\,q & & 1, 3, Co \\
2, 3\,(5) - q & & 2, 3, Co \\
1, 2, 3\,(6)\,q . - q & & 4, 5, Ki \\
1, 2\,(7)\,p \to (q . - q) & & 3, 6, Ci \\
1, 2\,(8) - p & & 7, Ni
\end{array}
$$

−*p* rests on 1 and 2 as assumptions; 3 is discharged as an assumption although its supposition has been useful in the process of discovering 8.

What are basic guidelines in the technique of proof-discovery? The nature of the quantifier (e.g. *U*) and of the main connective (e.g. *C*) in the desired conclusion invite the use of those LAF's which succeed in introducing such a quantifier (e.g. *Ui*) and such a connective (e.g. *Ci*). Similarly the quantifier (e.g. *E*) and the connective (e.g. ∨) in an assumption we are given invite us to consider LAF's which reach derivations on the basis of such a quantifier (e.g. *Eo*) or such a connective (e.g. *Ao*). In the proof of theorems we rely heavily on *Ci*, *Ni* and *No*. At times with the help of *Ni* or *No* it is easiest to reach a desired proposition through the rejection of its contradictory. The repetition of a proposition already in our sequence with a good reason, and the operation of double negation on it, can facilitate proof work; and such work is shortened by use of rules permitting the economy of theorem and sequent introduction. Finally, immense technical advantages are gained by the use of the typical case (symbolized by the arbitrary name) to prove a universal or to replace it; in the latter eventuality one is enabled to use procedures from propositional logic which would be inapplicable with quantifiers present.

The following are examples of proofs for some valid sequents and some true theorems (in these proofs where there is more than one assumption, a comma is used to separate them):

$$Proof\ of\ (x)\ Fx \to Gx,\ (x)\ Gx \to Hx \vdash (x)\ Fx \to Hx$$

1 (1) $(x)\ Fx \to Gx$	A
2 (2) $(x)\ Gx \to Hx$	A
1 (3) $Fa \to Ga$	1, Uo
2 (4) $Ga \to Ha$	2, Uo
(5) $((p \to q) . (q . r)) \to (p \to r)$	SI (from propositional logic)
(6) $((Fa \to Ga) . (Ga \to Ha)) \to (Fa \to Ha)$	5, $p \mid Fa, q \mid Ga, r \mid Ha$
1, 2 (7) $(Fa \to Ga) . (Ga \to Ha)$	3, 4, Ki
1, 2 (8) $Fa \to Ha$	6, 7, Co
1, 2 (9) $(x)\ Fx \to Hx$	8, Ui

$$Proof\ of\ Fm . Gm \vdash Hm \to Gm$$

1 (1) $Fm . Gm$	A
2 (2) Hm	A
1 (3) Gm	1, Ko
1 (4) $Hm \to Gm$	2, 3, Ci

This is one of the paradoxes of material implication: in virtue of the meaning of $\to$, Gm established in the domain of the assumption $Fm . Gm$ is materially implied by any other assumption. There is a good reason for each of the lines (2), (3) and (4) so this sequence constitutes a proof. The more familiar format of the paradox of material implication is, of course, that a true proposition is implied by any proposition.

$$Proof\ of\ Fa \to Ga,\ - Ga \vdash - Fa$$

1 (1) $Fa \to Ga$	A
2 (2) $- Ga$	A
3 (3) Fa	A
1, 3 (4) Ga	1, 3, Co
1, 2, 3 (5) $Ga . - Ga$	4, 2, Ki
1, 2 (6) $Fa \to (Ga . - Ga)$	3, 5, Ci
1, 2 (7) $- Fa$	6, Ni
	(In the domain of the assumptions (1) and (2), Fa involves a formal contradiction and so can be negated by the rule Ni)

$$Proof\ of\ (Fm \to Gm) . Hm,\ - Hm \vdash - p$$

1 (1) $(Fm \to Gm) . Hm$	A
2 (2) $- Hm$	A

$$3\ (3)\ p \qquad\qquad\qquad A$$
$$1\ (4)\ Hm \qquad\qquad\qquad 1, Ko$$
$$1, 2\ (5)\ Hm\ .-Hm \qquad\qquad 4, 2, Ki$$
$$1, 2\ (6)\ p \rightarrow (Hm\ .-Hm) \qquad 3, 5, Ci$$
$$1, 2\ (7)-p \qquad\qquad\qquad 6, Ni$$

The negation of any proposition, p, follows from assumptions that posit both Hm and $-Hm$.

Proof of $-(Fm\ .-Gm) \vdash Fm \rightarrow Gm$

$$1\ (1)-(Fm\ .-Gm) \qquad\qquad\qquad\qquad A$$
$$2\ (2)\ Fm \qquad\qquad\qquad\qquad\qquad\qquad A$$
$$3\ (3)-Gm \qquad\qquad\qquad\qquad\qquad\quad A$$
$$2, 3\ (4)\ Fm\ .-Gm \qquad\qquad\qquad\qquad 2, 3, Ki$$
$$1, 2, 3\ (5)\ (Fm\ .-Gm)\ .-(Fm\ .-Gm) \qquad 4, 1, Ki$$
$$1, 2\ (6)-Gm \rightarrow ((Fm\ .-Gm)\ .-(Fm\ .-Gm)) \qquad 3, 5, Ci$$
$$1, 2\ (7)--Gm \qquad\qquad\qquad\qquad\qquad 6, Ni$$
$$1, 2\ (8)\ Gm \qquad\qquad\qquad\qquad\qquad\quad 7, DN$$
$$1\ (9)\ Fm \rightarrow Gm \qquad\qquad\qquad\qquad\quad 2, 8, Ci$$

Proof of $Fm \rightarrow Gm, Fm \vee (Hm\ .\ Gm) \vdash Gm$

$$1\ (1)\ Fm \rightarrow Gm \qquad\qquad\quad A$$
$$2\ (2)\ Fm \vee (Hm\ .\ Gm) \qquad\quad A$$
$$3\ (3)\ Fm \qquad\qquad\qquad\qquad\quad A$$
$$1, 3\ (4)\ Gm \qquad\qquad\qquad\quad 1, 3, Co$$
$$5\ (5)\ Hm\ .\ Gm \qquad\qquad\qquad A$$
$$5\ (6)\ Gm \qquad\qquad\qquad\qquad 5, Ko$$
$$1\ (7)\ Fm \rightarrow Gm \qquad\qquad 3, 4, Ci$$
$$(8)\ (Hm\ .\ Gm) \rightarrow Gm \qquad 5, 6, Ci$$
$$1, 2\ (9)\ Gm \qquad\qquad\qquad\quad 2, 7, 8, Ao$$

In applying *Ao* to the disjunction assumed at line 2, we take each disjunct in turn and assume it (lines 3 and 5). If the required conclusion can be demonstrated to be derivable from each disjunct then we may present it as derivable from the assumption of the disjunction as a whole. However, any extra assumption used in the course of this demonstration must either be eliminated (the assumption made at line 5 is eliminated at line 8) or be cited among the assumptions on which the final conclusion is based (accordingly, the assumption made at line 1 is requisite).

Proof of $(x)\ Fx \vdash (Ex)\ Fx$

$$1\ (1)\ (x)\ Fx \qquad\quad A$$
$$1\ (2)\ Fa \qquad\qquad\quad 1, Uo$$
$$1\ (3)\ (Ex)\ Fx \qquad\quad 2, Ei$$

Proof of $(x)\ (Fx \rightarrow Gx), (Ex)\ Fx \vdash (Ex)\ Gx$

$$1\ (1)\ (x)\ Fx \to Gx \qquad\qquad A$$
$$2\ (2)\ (Ex)\ Fx \qquad\qquad A$$
$$3\ (3)\ Fa \qquad\qquad A$$
$$1\ (4)\ Fa \to Ga \qquad\qquad 1,\ Uo$$
$$1,\ 3\ (5)\ Ga \qquad\qquad 4,\ 3,\ Co$$
$$1,\ 3\ (6)\ (Ex)\ Gx \qquad\qquad 5,\ Ei$$
$$1,\ 2\ (7)\ (Ex)\ Gx \qquad\qquad 2,\ 3,\ 6,\ Eo$$

The desired conclusion is reached at line (6) but not on the desired assumptions. However, having shown that the conclusion follows from the assumed existence (line 3) of *any* typical demonstration instance with the property F, we know by the rule of Eo that this conclusion is therefore secure provided that *some* object can be found which has F. Thus assumption (3) is discharged and replaced by assumption (2).

Proof of $(x)\ Fx \to Gx \vdash (Ex)\ Fx \to (Ex)\ Gx$

$$1\ (1)\ (x)\ Fx \to Gx \qquad\qquad A$$
$$2\ (2)\ (Ex)\ Fx \qquad\qquad A$$
$$3\ (3)\ Fa \qquad\qquad A$$
$$1\ (4)\ Fa \to Ga \qquad\qquad 1,\ Uo$$
$$1,\ 3\ (5)\ Ga \qquad\qquad 3,\ 4,\ Co$$
$$1,\ 3\ (6)\ (Ex)\ Gx \qquad\qquad 5,\ Ei$$
$$1,\ 2\ (7)\ (Ex)\ Gx \qquad\qquad 2,\ 3,\ 6,\ Eo$$
$$1\ (8)\ (Ex)\ Fx \to (Ex)\ Gx \qquad\qquad 2,\ 7,\ Ci$$

This proof simply needs to conditionalize the previous proof: what was an assumption in the latter has now the role of antecedent in a conclusion.

Proof of $\vdash (x)\ (p\ .\ Fx) \to (p\ .\ (x)\ Fx)$

$$1\ (1)\ (x)\ (p\ .\ Fx) \qquad\qquad A$$
$$1\ (2)\ p\ .\ Fa \qquad\qquad Uo$$
$$1\ (3)\ p \qquad\qquad 2,\ Ko$$
$$1\ (4)\ Fa \qquad\qquad 2,\ Ko$$
$$1\ (5)\ (x)\ Fx \qquad\qquad 4,\ Ui$$
$$1\ (6)\ p\ .\ (x)\ Fx \qquad\qquad 3,\ 5,\ Ki$$
$$(7)\ (x)\ (p\ .\ Fx) \to p\ .\ (x)\ Fx \qquad\qquad 1,\ 6,\ Ci$$

Conditionalizing (6) results in line (1) no longer having the role of an assumption: it appears in line (7) as an antecedent materially implying line (6). Thus line (7) does not depend on any assumption—it is a *theorem* in the distinctive sense this term has in a system of natural deduction.

Proof that $(x)\ (Fx \to Gx) \vdash (x)\ (Ey)\ (Fx\ .\ Hxy) \to (Ey)\ (Gy\ .\ Hxy)$

$$1\ (1)\ (x)\ Fx \to Gx \qquad\qquad\qquad A$$
$$2\ (2)\ (Ey)\ (Fy\ .\ Hay) \qquad\qquad\qquad A$$
$$3\ (3)\ Fb\ .\ Hab \qquad\qquad\qquad A$$

3 (4) *Fb*	3, *Ko*
3 (5) *Hab*	3, *Ko*
1 (6) *Fb → Gb*	1, *Uo*
1, 3 (7) *Gb*	4, 6, *Co*
1, 3 (8) *Gb . Hab*	7, 5, *Ki*
1, 3 (9) *(Ey) (Gy . Hay)*	8, *Ei*
1, 2 (10) *(Ey) (Gy . Hay)*	2, 3, 9, *Eo*
1 (11) *(Ey) (Fy . Hay) → (Ey) (Gy . Hay)*	2, 10, *Ci*
1 (12) *(x) (Ey) (Fy . Hxy) → (Ey) (Gy . Hxy)*	11, *Ui*

Introducing the universal quantifier (x), line (12) simply universalizes line (11).

$$\text{Proof of} \vdash (x) (x = x)$$

(1) $a = a$	*Ii*
(2) $(x) (x = x)$	1, *Ui*

Rule *Ii* permits us to introduce an identity and it does not rest on any assumptions. Thus in this proof there is no column of assumptions.

$$\text{Proof of } (a = b), (b = c) \vdash (a = c)$$

1 (1) $(a = b) . (b = c)$	*A*
1 (2) $a = b$	1, *Ko*
1 (3) $b = c$	1, *Ko*
1 (4) $a = c$	2, 3, *Io*
	(since $a = b$, we can
	substitute a for b in
	(3).)

$$\text{Proof of } Fa \vdash (Ex) (x = a . Fx)$$

1 (1) Fa	*A*
(2) $a = a$	*Ii*
1 (3) $(a = a) . Fa$	1, 2, *Ki*
1 (4) $(Ex) ((x = a) . Fx)$	3, *Ei*

$$\text{Proof of } (Ex) Fx . (Ey) Fy . -(x = y) \vdash - ((Ex) Fx . (Ey) Fy) \to (x = y)$$

1 (1) $(Ex) Fx . (Ey) Fy . - (x = y)$	*A*
1 (2) $(Ex) Fx . (Ey) Fy$	1, *Ko*
1 (3) $- (x = y)$	1, *Ko*
4 (4) $((Ex) Fx . (Ey) Fy) \to (x = y)$	*A*
1, 4 (5) $x = y$	4, 2, *Co*
1, 4 (6) $(x = y) . - (x = y)$	5, 3, *Ki*
1, 4 (7) $((Ex) Fx . (Ey) Fy \to (x = y)) \to (x = y) . - (x = y)$	4, 6, *Ci*
1 (8) $- (((Ex) Fx . (Ey) Fy) \to (x = y))$	7, *Ni*

This law says that if at least two objects have *F*, it is not the case that at most one object has *F*. This indicates how Predicate Calculus with Identity (*PCI*) extends itself naturally into a calculus of numerical quantifiers.

V. The range of logical laws in predicate logic

Some analogous laws

$(x) Fx \vee Fx \vdash (x) Fx$ $[(p \vee p) \rightarrow p]$

$(x) Fx . Gx \vdash (x) Fx$ $[(p . q) \rightarrow p]$

$(Ex) Fx \vdash (Ex) Fx$ $[p \rightarrow p]$

$- (Ex) Fx \vdash - (Ex) (Fx . Gx)$ $[- p \rightarrow - (p . q)]$

$(x) Fx \rightarrow Gx \dashv \vdash - (Ex) (Fx . - Gx)$ $[p \rightarrow q \equiv - (p . -q)]$

$(x) (-Fx . - Gx) \dashv \vdash - (Ex) (Fx \vee Gx)$ $[- p . - q \equiv - (p \vee q)]$

$(x) (-Fx \vee - Gx) \dashv \vdash - (Ex) (Fx . Gx)$ $[- p \vee - q \equiv - (p . q)]$

$(x) Fx . Gx \vdash (x) Fx \vee Gx$ $[(p . q) \rightarrow (p \vee q)]$

$(x) Fx \rightarrow Gx \vdash (x) - Gx \rightarrow - Fx$ $[(p \rightarrow q) \rightarrow (- q \rightarrow - p)]$

$(x) Fx \rightarrow Gx, (x) - Gx \vdash (x) - Fx$ (modus tollendo tollens)

$(x) Fx \rightarrow Gx, (x) Fx \vdash (x) Gx$ (modus ponendo ponens)

$(x) (Fx \rightarrow Gx) . (x) (Fx \rightarrow Hx) \vdash (x) Fx \rightarrow$
$$(Gx . Hx) \; [((p \rightarrow q) . (p \rightarrow r)) \rightarrow p \rightarrow (q . r)]$$

In *Principia Mathematica* the chief purpose of the propositions which are numbered *10 is 'to extend to formal implications (i.e. to propositions of the form $(x) \ldots$) as many as possible of the propositions proved previously for material implications, i.e. for propositions of the form $p \supset q$.' (*Principia Mathematica*, Vol. 1, p. 138)

Some laws governing the movement of quantifiers

$(x) Fx . Gx \dashv \vdash (x) Fx . (x) Gx$

$(Ex) Fx . Gx \vdash (Ex) Fx . (Ex) Gx$ (The converse conditional does not hold.)

$(x) Fx \vee (x) Gx \vdash (x) Fx \vee Gx$

$(Ex) Fx \vee Gx \dashv \vdash (Ex) Fx \vee (Ex) Gx$

$(x) Fx \rightarrow Gx \vdash (x) Fx \rightarrow (x) Gx$

$(x) Fx \rightarrow Gx \vdash (Ex) Fx \rightarrow (Ex) Gx$

$(x) (y) Fxy \dashv \vdash (y) (x) Fxy$ (The order of universal quantifiers does not affect meaning.)

$(Ex) (Ey) Fxy \dashv \vdash (Ey) (Ex) Fxy$ (The order of existential quantifiers does not affect meaning.)

$(Ex) (y) Fxy \vdash (y) (Ex) Fxy$ (Where quantifiers are mixed the order can affect meaning; here the converse conditional does not hold. Taking F as signifying the relation of '*father of*' in the domain of people: if there exists an X such that for every value of Y, X is the father of Y—i.e. X is the father of everybody—then it follows that for every value of Y there exists a person X who is his father. But it does not follow *e converso* that if any person Y is child of *some* father, that there is one person who is father of everybody.)

Some laws expressing the relation between universal and existential quantifiers

$$(x)\ Fx \dashv\vdash - (Ex) - Fx$$
$$(Ex)\ Fx \dashv\vdash - (x) - Fx$$
$$(x) - Fx \dashv\vdash - (Ex)\ Fx$$
$$(Ex) - Fx \dashv\vdash - (x)\ Fx$$

An indefinite number of more complicated laws follow from the above, e.g.:

$$(x) - (Fx\ .\ Gx) \dashv\vdash - (Ex)\ (Fx\ .\ Gx)$$
$$(x) - (Fx \vee Gx) \dashv\vdash - (Ex)\ (Fx \vee Gx)$$
$$(x) - (Fx\ .\ - Gx) \dashv\vdash - (Ex)\ (Fx\ .\ - Gx)$$

The following laws draw our attention to the fact that predicate calculus presupposes that any universe with which it deals is non-empty, i.e. that there is at least one thing in it corresponding to the variable x:

$$(x)\ Fx \rightarrow (Ex)\ Fx$$
$$(x) - Fx \rightarrow (Ex) - Fx$$

However predicate calculus does not presuppose that any *particular predicate* is verified in the universe of discourse, and (as we shall see in discussing the integration of the Aristotelian syllogistic into modern logic) it does not include $(x)\ (Fx \rightarrow Gx) \rightarrow (Ex)\ (Fx\ .\ Gx)$ among its logical truths.

As a calculus of quantifiers there is no essential reason why predicate calculus should restrict itself to the universal and existential quantifiers although it actually does so. It could be extended to include the numerical quantifiers: (there is at least one x such that . . .), (at most one x such that . . .), (exactly one x such that . . .), (at least two x's such that . . .), etc. This possible extension invites consideration of the relationship between logic and mathematics.

Some laws governing multiple quantification:
(While presenting some laws governing the movement of quantifiers it was noted that when all the quantifiers are universal, or all are existential their order does not affect meaning. Where quantifiers are mixed, the order can affect meaning.)

$$(x)\ (y)\ Fxy \dashv\vdash (y)\ (x)\ Fxy$$
$$(Ex)\ (Ey)\ Fxy \dashv\vdash (Ey)\ (Ex)\ Fxy$$

$(Ex)\ (y)\ Fxy \vdash (y)\ (Ex)\ Fxy$ (the converse conditional does not hold)
$(x)\ (y)\ Fxy \vdash (x)\ (Ey)\ Fxy$
$(x)\ (y)\ Fxy \vdash (Ex)\ (Ey)\ Fxy$
$(x)\ (y)\ (Fxy \rightarrow Gxy) \vdash (x)\ (y)\ Fxy \rightarrow (x)\ (y)\ Gxy$
$(x)\ (y)\ (Gxy \rightarrow Hxy),\ (Ex)\ (Ey)\ (Fxy\ .\ Gxy) \vdash (Ex)\ (Ey)\ (Fxy\ .\ Hxy)$
$(x)\ (y)\ Fxy \dashv\vdash - (Ex)\ (Ey) - Fxy$
$(x)\ (y) - Fxy \dashv\vdash - (Ex)\ (Ey)\ Fxy$
$(Ex)\ (Ey)\ Fxy \dashv\vdash - (x)\ (y) - Fxy$
$(Ex)\ (Ey) - Fxy \dashv\vdash - (x)\ (y)\ Fxy$

Some laws governing instantiation

$$(x)\ Fx \dashv\vdash (y)\ Fy$$

(Both sentences express the same proposition, that everything has F. Thus this law makes the point that a universal holds for any instantiation. The instantiation here may be described as ambiguous expressed as it is through the use of a second variable. Similarly, $(Ex)\ Fx \dashv\vdash (Ey)\ Fy$ is a law.)

$$Fm,\ (x)\ Fx \rightarrow Gx \vdash Gm$$
$$- Gm,\ (x)\ Fx \rightarrow Gx \vdash - Fm$$
$$Fm,\ (x)\ Fx \rightarrow - Gx \vdash - Gm$$

(Here m is used as a proper name and the instantiation is singular.)

$$(x)\ Fx \dashv\vdash Fa$$
$$Fa \vdash (Ex)\ Fx$$

(Here a is an arbitrary name and the instantiation is typical. We can argue from the universal to the typical instance, and the typical instance justifies both a universal and an existential derivative.)

Some laws which combine predicate and propositional variables

$$(x)\ p\ .\ Fx \dashv\vdash p\ .\ (x)\ Fx$$
$$(x)\ p \vee Fx \dashv\vdash p \vee (x)\ Fx$$
$$(x)\ p \rightarrow Fx \dashv\vdash p \rightarrow (x)\ Fx$$
$$(Ex)\ p \rightarrow Fx \dashv\vdash p \rightarrow (Ex)\ Fx$$
$$(x)\ (Fx \rightarrow p) \dashv\vdash (Ex)\ Fx \rightarrow p$$

(Note that the quantifier, (x), governs the whole expression while the existential quantifier only governs an antecedent. The law may be read: 'Taking any x, if when x is F the proposition p is the case, then if an object x can be found such that it is F this materially implies that p is the case. And conversely, if an object x can be found which being F this materially implies that p is the case, then for every value of x: when x is F the proposition p is the case.')

$$(Ex)\ (p \rightarrow Fx) \dashv\vdash p \rightarrow (Ex)\ Fx$$

Some laws concerning identity

$$\vdash (x)\,(x = x)$$
$$\vdash (x)\,(y)\,(x = y) \rightarrow (y = x)$$
$$\vdash (x)\,(y)\,(z)\,((x = y\,.\,y = z) \rightarrow (x = z))$$
$$Fa\dashv\vdash (Ex)\,(x = a\,.\,Fx)$$

Some laws presenting expressions that are interderivable (and therefore equivalent)

$$(x)\,Fx \rightarrow Gx \dashv\vdash - (Ex)\,(Fx\,.\,-\,Gx)$$
$$(x)\,Fx \dashv\vdash (y)\,Fy$$
$$(Ex)\,Fx \dashv\vdash (Ey)\,Fy$$
$$(x)\,p \dashv\vdash p$$
$$(Ex)\,p \dashv\vdash p$$
$$(Ex)\,(Ey)\,(Fx\,.\,-\,Fy) \dashv\vdash (Ex)\,Fx\,.\,(Ex) - Fx$$
$$(x)\,(y)\,Fx \rightarrow Fy \dashv\vdash (x)\,Fx \lor (Ey) - Fy$$

VI. The laws of dyadic, triadic ... n-adic predicates interpreted as a logical theory of relations

A propositional form with two free variables, such as $F\,(x,\,y)$, expresses a relation between the things x and y and may be translated explicitly and equivalently into an expression of the form xRy (read 'the thing x has a relation R to the thing y'). The negative $\sim F\,(x,\,y)$ can be similarly translated $\sim xRy$. The above expressions with R may be considered as generalizations of propositional forms with two free variables. Where there are three, four ... n free variables the symbolization is $R\,(x_1,\,x_2,\,x_3)$, $R\,(x_1,\,x_2,\,x_3,\,x_4)$, $R\,(x_1 \ldots x_n)$.

Thus, technically speaking, what is called a logical theory of relations develops simply as the construction, in predicate logic, of complex expressions with more than one free variable or argument place. The tautologies discovered in this way are valued, interpretatively, as a theory of relations. Indeed, since these tautologies are predications made about ordered groups or sets of two, three, four ... n members, it is felt that their predicates are properly and exactly conceived and symbolized as relations which generate and constitute sets of ordered dyads, triads, tetrads, etc. However, one might also argue that the abstract uninterpreted value of this part of predicate logic is being neglected, that this reflects the central position which class and set have occupied in the history of mathematical logic since Boole, and that here there may be a lapse from constructive, formalist logic into the more abstractive approach of earlier logics.

Some of the tautologies in question have already been noted in this chapter in the course of giving a sample of laws governing multiple quantification. Here we will not compile a more extensive list but rather will give such a summary account of the general nature, types and properties of relations, as is useful to the logician in interpreting many-termed predicates as relations. It is clear that such an account will apply to relations of all kinds, both those that are realized in the physical world and those that exist only in the mind, both those that are logical in their nature and those that are not. The terminology used will be rather like that of contemporary mathematics but in some respects will be slightly different; attention will be drawn to differences.

Two-term predicates or dyadic relations. The theory of dyadic relations is the only part of the logic of relations that has been developed. De Morgan and Peirce were pioneers, their calculus of relations being completed by the German logician E. Schröder (1841–1902).

In xRy, x is a predecessor with respect to the dyadic relation R, and y is a successor with respect to R. The class of all predecessors is known as the domain of R, the class of all successors as the counter-domain (converse domain or range). The domain and converse domain together make up the field of a relation. Relations of the First Order are those which hold between individuals; relations of the Second Order are those which hold between classes or between relations of the First Order. The relation of, e.g. membership is mixed since its predecessor is an individual and its successor a class.

A relation R is *reflexive* in the class K if every element of that class has the relation R to itself, i.e. if xRx. If that condition never holds R is *irreflexive*; if it may or may not hold, R is *non-reflexive*. Thus 'equal to' is reflexive; 'taller than' is irreflexive; 'admires' is non-reflexive: it simply allows of the case of self-admirations, aRa.

R is *symmetrical* when it always fulfils the condition: if xRy then yRx; where the condition of symmetry never holds (If xRy then $\sim yRx$, as, e.g. in 'being parent of') the relationship is *asymmetrical*; if it may or may not hold (as, e.g. in 'likes', 'fears') the relation is *non-symmetrical*.

The necessary and sufficient condition for R being transitive is that if xRy and yRz then xRz (as in 'taller', 'older'). An *intransitive* relation does not allow of this condition being fulfilled (e.g. 'father of'); a *non-transitive* relation admits of, but does not require, this transferability (e.g. 'admires'). A transitive relation is such that relating two terms to a mean it also relates these terms to each other. Accordingly it gives rise to important deductive possibilities.

The interdependencies between reflexivity, symmetry and transitivity may be listed as follows (for non-empty relations):
1. If a relation is transitive and symmetrical, it is reflexive.
2. If a relation is transitive and asymmetrical, it is irreflexive.
3. If a relation is transitive and irreflexive, it is asymmetrical.
4. If a relation is asymmetrical, it is irreflexive.
5. If a relation is symmetrical and irreflexive, it is either intransitive or non-transitive.
6. If a relation is symmetrical and reflexive, it is either transitive or non-transitive.

R is said to be *connected* in the class K (i.e. to be a principle of order) if for any two elements x and y in the class, either xRy or yRx. Where both conditions are fulfilled at the same time, the relation is still connected. Connexity is very important in the creation of serial order: any relation that is transitive, asymmetrical and connected is a serial relation (e.g. 'left of' and 'right of' with regard to points on a line are connected relations), and any system ordered by a serial relation is a series, e.g. the system of natural numbers, the calendar. 'Ancestor of' is not a connected relation: the field of this relation is of those who are either ancestors or descendants, and picking any two individuals it is not true that some one of the two must be the ancestor of the other.

The relation of identity is reflexive, symmetrical and transitive; that of diversity is irreflexive, symmetrical, non-transitive and connected. The relation of inclusion between classes is reflexive and transitive; it is non-symmetrical (i.e. neither symmetrical nor asymmetrical) and it is not connected; the relation of membership in a class, on the other hand, is irreflexive, intransitive and asymmetrical. Thus the properties of membership are very different from those of class inclusion.

Some broad categories of relation are as follows:

(a) Relations that have the three properties of being reflexive, symmetrical and transitive are an important category. There is no universally accepted term for this category, 'equivalence' and 'identity' denoting examples rather than the category as such. Mathematicians, however, do designate the category by the term, equivalence relation; identity for them is a particular example of an equivalence relation. Numerous other examples may be cited, e.g. congruence (from Geometry), equally old, synonymous.

(b) Relations that are asymmetrical, transitive, connected (and consequently irreflexive) are a common class also—an example being the relation of 'less than' in the class of distinct numbers. They are often described as 'ordering', i.e. as establishing a serial order in their class. (Mathematicians reserve 'order relation' for a closely allied class of relations typified by 'less than or equal to'.)

(c) Functional relations form a category which consists of relations whose terms fall into a one–one, or one–many correspondence. 'Being a twin brother' is an example of a one–one relation: each person who is a twin of any other person is a twin of no other, and the other has no twin brother but this one— there is a one-to-one correlation between the terms (denoted by the variable x) of the domain of this relation (xRy) and the terms of its converse domain (denoted by the variable y). Thus the necessary and sufficient conditions for a one–one relation are that if xRy and if xRz then $z = y$; and, at the same time, if xRy and if wRy, then $w = x$. A one-many relation holds between a single term in the domain and more than one term in the converse domain; these latter terms are not in the same relationship with any other term of the domain so that if xRy and if wRy, then $w = x$. The relation of a perfect square to its roots is an example of a one–many relation: as a square 9 correlates with both 3 and -3 as roots. (In this context 'many' means simply 'more than one'.)

In a functional relation x is always single-valued. Corresponding to any value for y there is a unique value for x: thus if xRy and if wRy then $w = x$. In the formula xRy, x is said to be the variable for function values, and y the variable for argument values. (Mathematicians, however, use domain for the argument values and the counter domain for the function values.) A unique value of the function corresponds to every value of the argument: this fact is symbolized $x = R\,(y)$ or in familiar mathematical symbols $x = f\,(y)$ which means 'x is that value of the function f which corresponds to (or is correlated with) the argument value y'. It is the defining characteristic of a functional relation that for any value of y it admits of only one value for x. In the vernacular to indicate the functional character of a relation, we insert the word 'the': e.g. we say 'x is the father of y' indicating that for every person y there exists but one person x who is the father of y; the formula $x = f(y)$ has the same force as the word 'the'.

The force of the word *function* in the context of functional relation may be brought out simply as follows: Since $9 = (-3)^2$, it is possible to correlate the value 9 to the value -3, i.e. we can assert in general that 9 is a function of -3, that $9 = f\,(-3)$. Specifically we can go on to say that 9 is predecessor in the relationship of being the square of -3, i.e. that it is the unique domain value of the relation (or function) of 'being square of' with respect to the argument value, -3. The number 9 is also predecessor in the relationship of being the square of 3. This is a one–many relationship therefore. In a one–one relation or biunique function not only is there a unique domain value x correlated to every converse domain value y, but also conversely only one converse domain value y, corresponds to any domain value x.

In elementary and in higher mathematical reasoning functional relations are of great importance; in applied mathematics too one frequently tries to analyse dependencies into functional relations. And in general there is an obvious value in trying to discover functions which establish one-to-one, or one–many, correspondences between the elements of separate classes, i.e. which map one class on another.

Many relations are not functional. Being a subject of the king is a many–one relation; being smaller than is a many–many relation. In neither case is the domain value unique, so the relation is not functional. (There used to be a wider meaning of the term, function: in the formula $x^2 + y^2 = 25$, where $y = 4$ the formula is valid for both $x = 3$ and $x = -3$; thus correlated with one number, y, are two numbers, x; the function was sometimes called a two-valued function and there could be many-valued functions. In the logic of relations, however, the efficacy of a function consists in correlating any argument value with a unique domain value.)

The converse of a one–many relation is many–one, e.g. 'The king rules the people' converts into 'the people are subject to the king'—the converse relation is substituted and domain and converse domain are interchanged. The converse of a one–one relation is one–one, of a many–one is one–many and of a many–many is many–many.

Many-termed predicates (n-adic relations). The most fundamental property of a relation is that of always forming dyads, triads, tetrads, etc. All other properties presuppose this one of degree. As well as two-termed or binary relations one also meets frequently with three-termed (ternary) relations and in general with many-termed ones. Some relations, e.g. 'among' and superlatives like 'least of', 'greatest of' have no definite degree but are simply more than dyadic: they are generally called *polyadic relations* (this term however has more than one usage). In geometry one speaks of a point B lying between A and C; in arithmetic of a number being the sum of two others; in algebra of the ratio $x : y : z : t$. Although many-termed relations play an important part in the various sciences, any detailed study of them has been within the mathematical discipline known as the theory of sets. The logic of relations focuses two-termed relations. However, relations of a higher degree than dyadic can be defined and treated as dyadic—as, e.g. the relation of a dyad to an individual, of a dyad to another dyad, of a triad (already reduced to dyadic form) to an individual, etc. Thus any function of three variables, $T(x, y, z)$ can be treated as a function of two variables, the couple (x, y) and z or the couple (y, z) and x. Hence the theory of dyadic relations is a general theory.

A later chapter will treat of that part of the theory of relations which focuses them in extension as, e.g the class of couples (x, y) such that xRy. This extensional part of the theory (the calculus of relations) is worked out, again, within an extensional study of predicates in general, the class calculus. Thus the logical theory of relations is constructed, intensionally, within Predicate Logic and, extensionally, within Class Calculus; for that reason, it does not feature as prominently or as fundamentally in contemporary formal logic as early mathematical logicians, like De Morgan, felt it would.

VII. Has predicate logic a decision procedure for determining whether any well-formed formula in its language is a tautology

We have seen that the sole assumption made by modern Predicate Logic is that the universe with which it deals is non-empty—it may be finite or infinite but there is at least one individual in it. Thus a decision procedure for the whole of Predicate Logic would be a mechanical and automatic way of deciding, in a finite number of steps, whether any given wff (in the language of Predicate Logic) was true under all interpretations in all non-empty universes, finite or infinite. In 1936, on the basis of the work of Kurt Gödel, Alonzo Church went on to prove the impossibility of discovering such a decision procedure. However, decision procedures have been found for certain fragments of quantificational logic—most importantly various ones have been found (independently, by many authors) for monadic-predicate formulae. The following one combines, in essence, the techniques of the Normal Form and Truth Trees procedures used in Propositional Logic.

It is based on the principle that an argument (expressed in the language of predicate logic) is valid only if the premises and the negation of the conclusion cannot be jointly true in any non-empty universe. A positive search is conducted for a universe of which they could be a joint and true description, on the basis of (a) simplifying the truth functional structure of the argument, making it totally explicit in terms of '−', '∨' and '.'; (b) simplifying the atomic quantificational statements to instantiations that are systematically mapped on to the positive integer series 1, 2, 3 ... When contradictory predications occur among the instantiations, the proof of possibility (for a universe described jointly by the premises and the negation of the conclusion) is said to be blocked; if it is clear that it must always be blocked in the search, then the universe sought is an impossibility and the original argument has been shown to be valid.

A set of rules must be drawn up governing the whole process of simplification and evaluation. In *Modern Deductive Logic*, Robert Ackermann gives the following rules for simplifying truth-functional structure and evaluating arguments in propositional logic:

Rule 1 $p . q \vdash p$	CS_1 (conjunctive simplification$_1$)
Rule 2 $p . q \vdash q$	CS_2 („ simplification$_2$)
Rule 3 $-(-p) \vdash p$	DN (double negation)
Rule 4 $-(p . q) \vdash -p \vee -q$	DM_1 (De Morgan Rules$_1$)
Rule 5 $-(-p . q) \vdash p \vee -q$	DM_2 (De Morgan Rules$_2$)
Rule 6 $-(p . -q) \vdash -p \vee q$	DM_3 („ „ „ $_3$)
Rule 7 $-(-p . -q) \vdash p \vee q$	DM_4 („ „ „ $_4$)
Rule 8 $-(p \vee q) \vdash -p . -q$	DM_5 („ „ „ $_5$)
Rule 9 $-(-p \vee q) \vdash p . -q$	DM_6 („ „ „ $_6$)
Rule 10 $-(p \vee -q) \vdash -p . q$	DM_7 („ „ „ $_7$)
Rule 11 $-(-p \vee -q) \vdash p . q$	DM_8 („ „ „ $_8$)

(By using the 8 De Morgan Rules we can simplify any negation of a conjunctive or disjunctive propositional form.)

Rule 12 $p \vee q, -p \vdash q$	DS_1 (disjunctive syllogism$_1$)
Rule 13 $p \vee q, -q \vdash p$	DS_2 (disjunctive syllogism$_2$)
Rule 14 $-p \vee q, p \vdash q$	DS_3 (disjunctive syllogism$_3$)
Rule 15 $p \vee -q, q \vdash p$	DS_4 (disjunctive syllogism$_4$)

(By application of these rules, any of the two expressions appearing on the left-hand side of a sequence can be simplified into the simple variable on the right-hand side.)

Rules 16 and 17: These are auxiliary rules of proof applying to the case when, with regard to a disjunctive proposition appearing in the argument, we do not know which disjunct is true. They are called auxiliary rules *D* and *DS* and entitle us to try each disjunct in turn to see whether in both cases the proof is blocked or whether in both cases it is not blocked. In the former case it is clear that our search for the possible universe is totally blocked by the disjunctive proposition (we have tried both its disjuncts). In the latter case, it is clear that the disjunctive proposition is not blocking the proof; indeed blocking does not occur if contradiction arises only through one disjunct and not through the other.

Rule D is the rule we cite when we are trying the first disjunct within our proof; the new line of proof is prefixed with an asterisk to remind us that it is a guess. Rule DS is the rule we cite when we are trying the remaining disjunct after the first disjunct has blocked the proof; we draw a line through each of the lines connected with the first disjunct and do not prefix an asterisk to the new line of proof as it expresses the only remaining sense in which the disjunctive proposition has to be considered.

Thus taking an argument which formalizes in propositional logic as $(-p.-q) \lor (p.-q), -p \lor r \vdash -q$, we write down the two premises and the contradictory of the conclusion and proceed to see whether they constitute a description of a possible universe:

(1) $(-p.-q) \lor (p.-q)$
(2) $-p \lor r$
(3) q contradictory of original conclusion.
~~*(4) $-p$~~   ~~(2) D~~
~~*(5) $p.-q$~~   ~~(1) D~~
~~(6) $-q$~~   ~~(5) CS_2~~

(The proof blocks at this stage with $-q$ at (6) contradicting q at (3). Therefore erase lines (5) and (6) and try the remaining disjunct of (1), using the numbers 5 & 6 for the new lines.)

~~(5) $-p.-q$~~   ~~(1) DS~~
~~(6) $-q$~~   ~~(5) CS_2~~

(Again the proof blocks: now we have tried both disjuncts of (1) under the first disjunct of (2). Since the proof blocks we can erase line 4 and all subsequent lines. We must try now the second disjunct of (2) using the number 4 for the new line.)

(4) r (2) DS
~~*(5) $(-p.-q)$~~   ~~(1) D~~
~~(6) $-q$~~   ~~(5) CS_2~~

(The proof blocks here with $-q$ at (6) and q at (3). Erase lines (5) and (6). Try the second disjunct of (1).)

(5) $p.-q$ (1) DS
(6) $-q$ (5) CS_2

(Again the proof blocks and since each of the two disjuncts in (1) has been used with each of the two disjuncts in (2), this final blocking of proof shows that there is no possible universe of which the two premises are true jointly with the contradictory of the original conclusion.)

What extra rules are needed to simplify the atomic quantificational statements so that we can evaluate arguments in the section of Predicate Logic that is confined to monadic predicate formulae? The clue to simplification lies in the fact that a universally quantified one-place predicate expression is a true statement only if *every* instantiation of that one-place predicate expression is true, and an existentially quantified one-place predicate expression is true only if *at least one* instantiation is true. Thus with regard to any monadic predicate formula: either it already links a predicate with *a definite individual* in the universe, or it can be instantiated to *any* individual (if its quantifier is universal) or to *an indefinite individual* (if quantification is existential). This makes it possible for the decision procedure to assume the added form of a search for a universe which could verify all predications contained in the premisses and contradictory of the conclusion, i.e. a universe in which the same individual would not have both a predicate, F, and its negation, $\sim F$. The usual numerals (1, 2, 3 . . .) for the positive integers may be used as constants referring to individuals in this universe.

Ackermann gives the following extra rules for simplifying predicative statements down to predicates linked with positive integers:

Rule 18: This enables us to go through all the predicative expressions replacing the individual constants (a, b, c . . .) by positive integers, the same positive integer being used for each recurrence of the same constant. This gives us expressions like $F1$, $G2$, $G1$ for Fa, Gb, Ga.

Rule 19: 'If any line of a proof is a universally quantified form, a line may be added which is the instantiation of the formal one-place predicate expression following the quantifier in terms of any numeral already appearing in the proof, or of the first numeral not already appearing in the proof. The new line is justified on the far right by citing "U—elimination".'

Obviously the useful instantiations for a decision procedure are those in terms of numerals linked with the same predicate as is in the universal statement.

Rule 20: 'If any line of proof is an existentially quantified form, a line may be added to the proof which is the instantiation of the formal one-place predicate expression following the quantifier in terms of the next numeral appearing in the proof. The new line is justified by citing "E—elimination" on the far right.'

We use a new numeral because the reference in an existential statement is indefinite. Further if there are other existential statements equivalent to the one we have instantiated [e.g. (Ex) (Fx), (Ey) (Fy), (Ez) (Fz) are equivalent] we cross them out, citing 'RED' on the far right as our reason (this is shorthand for 'redundant')—these are simply three different ways of making the same indefinite reference to 'at least one individual' and to instantiate them with separate numerals would be to claim that there was more than one individual with the predicate.

The above 20 rules constitute a complete set for a decision procedure that does not go beyond truth-functional structure and monadic predications. The following test illustrates their use:

(1) $(x)(-Wx \lor Rx)$	First premiss of argument
(2) $(y)(-(-Cy) \lor Wy)$	Second premiss of argument
(3) $(Ez)(-Cz \cdot -Rz)$	Contradictory of original conclusion
(4) $-C1 \cdot -R1$	(3) E—elimination
(5) $-(-C1) \lor W1$	(2) U—elimination
(6) $-W1 \lor R1$	(1) U—elimination
(7) $-R1$	(4) CS_2
(8) $-W1$	(6), (7), DS_2
(9) $-(-C1)$	(5), (8), DS_2
(10) $-C1$	(4), CS_1

With lines (9) and (10) in formal contradiction the proof is blocked, and so the original argument is shown to be valid.

Chapter 6

THE TRADITIONAL THEORY OF THE SYLLOGISM PRESENTED AS A FRAGMENT OF MODERN PREDICATE LOGIC

I. Introduction

In the preparatory section of this book we presented Aristotle's theory of the syllogism substantially as it has been handed down for over 2000 years. It has been of great importance in the history of logic and it is of interest to see how it has been integrated into both axiomatic and natural deduction systems of predicate logic.

II. Axiomatizing the syllogistic

The formal system presented here is that of Lukasiewicz who was the first to axiomatize Aristotle's theory. It does not go beyond the non-modal or assertoric syllogisms, the theory of which is the most important part of the Aristotelian Logic. That is a study of four types of predicative propositions which are distinguished by quantity and quality—*A*, *E*, *I* and *O*. Alternatively we might describe it as the simplest known system of name variables, the constants, *A*, *E*, *I* and *O*, being sentence-forming functors of two-name arguments. Lukasiewicz pointed out (*Aristotle's Syllogistic*, Preface) that until the 1930s there was not a trustworthy exposition of the Aristotelian syllogistic: 'all expositions have been written not by logicians but by philosophers or philologists who either, like Prantl, could not know or, like Maier, did not know modern formal logic. All these expositions are in my opinion wrong. I could not find, for instance, a single author who realized that there is a fundamental difference between the Aristotelian and the traditional syllogism.' (The traditional syllogism *All B is A; All C is B; therefore All C is A* is not Aristotelian; an Aristotelian syllogism is represented in the form of an implication such as *If A is predicated of all B, and B is predicated of all C, then A must be predicated of all C*.) The traditional type of syllogism is encountered for the first time in the works of Alexander, and Lukasiewicz believes that 'this transference of the Aristotelian syllogisms from the implicational form into the inferential is probably due to the influence of the Stoics'. (Ibid., p. 21) Boethius was certainly one of the main figures in the transmission of the tradition.

Towards the end of his life, Lukasiewicz (d. 1956) studied Aristotle's theory of the modal syllogism and he constructed a system of modal logic. The following is his axiomatization of the non-modal syllogisms (the *C–N* system of the theory of deduction being assumed) as presented by him in *Aristotle's Syllogistic*:

1. *Primitive terms:* the constants *A* and *I*.
2. *Definitions:* The constants *E* and *O* are defined by *A* and *I*:

   Df. 1. *Eab* = *NIab*
   Df. 2. *Oab* = *NAab*

3. *Rules of Inference:*
   In order to abbreviate the proofs I shall employ instead of the above definitions the two following rules of inference:

   Rule *RE*: *NI* may be everywhere replaced by *E* and conversely.
   Rule *RO*: *NA* may be everywhere replaced by *O* and conversely.

   Besides the rules *RE* and *RO* I accept the two following rules of inference for the asserted expressions:

   (a) Rule of substitution: If *α* is an asserted expression of the system, then any expression produced from *α* by a valid substitution is also an asserted expression The only valid substitution is to put for term-variables *a*, *b*, *c* other term-variables, e.g. *b* for *a*.
   (b) Rule of detachment: If *C α β* and *α* are asserted expressions of the system, then *β* is an asserted expression.

4. *Axioms:*
   The four theses of the system axiomatically asserted are the two laws of identity and the moods Barbara and Datisi:

   1. *Aaa*;
   2. *Iaa*;
   3. *CKAbcAabAac* (Barbara);
   4. *CKAbcIbaIac* (Datisi).

   As an auxiliary theory I assume the *C-N*-system of the theory of deduction with *K* as a defined functor. For propositional variables propositional expressions of the syllogistic may be substituted, like *Aab*, *Iac*, *KEbcAab*, etc. In all subsequent proofs I shall employ only the following fourteen theses denoted by roman numerals:

I. *CpCqp*	(law of simplification)
II. *CCqrCCpqCpr*	(law of hypothetical syllogism, 2nd form)
III. *CCpCqrCqCpr*	(law of commutation)
IV. *CpCNpq*	(law of Duns Scotus)
V. *CCNppp*	(law of Clavius)
VI. *CCpqCnqNp*	(law of transposition)
VII. *CCKpqrCpCqr*	(law of exportation)
VIII. *CpCCKpqrCqr*	
IX. *CCspCCKpqrCKsqr*	

X. *CCKpqrCCsqCKpsr*
XI. *CCrsCCKpqrCKqps*
XII. *CCKpqrCKpNrNq*
XIII. *CCKpqrCKNrqNp*
XIV. *CCKpNqNrCKprq*

5. *Deduction of Syllogistic theses:*
(In all syllogistic moods the major term is denoted by *c*, the middle term by *b*, and the minor term by *a*. The major premiss is stated first.)

A. THE LAWS OF CONVERSION

VII. *p/Abc, q/Iba, r/Iac* × C4–5

5. *CAbcCIbaIac*

   5. *b/a, c/a, a/b* × C1–6

6. *CIabIba*   (law of conversion of the *I*-premiss)
   III. *p/Abc, q/Iba, r/Iac* × C5–7

7. *CIbaCAbcIac*

   7. *b/a, c/b* × C2–8

8. *CAabIab*   (law of subordination for affirmative premisses)

   II. *q/Iab, r/Iba* × C6–9

9. *CCpIabCpIba*

   9. *p/Aab* × C8–10

10. *CAabIba*   (law of conversion of the *A*-premiss)

   6. *a/b, b/a* × 11

11. *CIbaIab*

   VI. *p/Iba, q/Iab* × C11–12

12. *CNIabNiba*

   12. *RE* × 13

13. *CEabEba*   (law of conversion of the *E*-premiss)

   VI. *p/Aab, q/Iab* × C8–14

14. *CNIabNAab*

   14. *RE, RO* × 15

15. *CEabOab*   (law of subordination for negative premisses)

B. THE AFFIRMATIVE MOODS

X. *p/Abc, q/Iba, r/Iac* × C4–16

16. *CCsIbaCKAbcsIac*

    16. *s/Iab* × C6–17

17. *CKAbcIabIac*   (Darii)

    16. *s/Aab* × C10–18

18. *CKAbcAabIac*   (Barbara)

    8. *a/b, b/a* × 19

19. *CAbaIba*

    16. *s/Aba* × C19–20

20. *CKAbcAbaIac*   (Darapti)

XI. *r/Iba, s/Iab* × C11–21

21. *CCKpqIbaCKqpIab*

    4. *c/a, a/c* × 22

22. *CKAbaIbcIca*

    21. *p/Aba, q/Ibc, b/c* × C22–23

23. *CKIbcAbaIac*   (Disamis)

    17. *c/a, a/c* × 24

24. *CKAbaIcbIca*

    21. *p/Aba, q/Icb, b/c* × C24–25

25. *CKIcbAbaIac*   (Dimaris)

    18. *c/a, a/c* × 26

26. *CKAbaAcbIca*

    21. *p/Aba, q/Acb, b/c* × C26–27

27. *CKAcbAbaIac*   (Bramantip)

C. THE NEGATIVE MOODS

XIII. *p/Ibc, q/Aba, r/Iac* × C23–28

28. *CKNIacAbaNIbc*

    28. *RE* × 29

29. *CKEacAbaEbc*
    29. *a*/*b*, *b*/*a* × 30

30. *CKEbcAabEac*   (Celarent)
    IX. *s*/*Eab*, *p*/*Eba* × *C*13–31

31. *CCKEbaqrCKEabqr*
    31. *a*/*c*, *q*/*Aab*, *r*/*Eac*, × *C*30–32

32. *CKEcbAabEac*
    XI. *r*/*Eab*, *s*/*Eba* × *C*13–33

33. *CCKpqEabCKqpEba*
    32. *c*/*a*, *a*/*c* × 34

34. *CKEabAcbEca*
    33. *p*/*Eab*, *q*/*Acb*, *a*/*c*, *b*/*a* × *C*34–35

35. *CKAcbEabEac*   (Camestres)
    30. *c*/*a*, *a*/*c* × 36

36. *CKEbaAcbEca*
    33. *p*/*Eba*, *q*/*Acb*, *a*/*c*, *b*/*a* × *C*36–37

37. *CKAcbEbaEac*   (Camenes)
    II. *q*/*Eab*, *r*/*Oab* × *C*15–38

38. *CCpEabCpOab*
    38. *p*/*KEbcAab*, *b*/*c* × *C*30–39

39. *CKEbcAabOac*   (Celaront)
    38. *p*/*KEcbAab*, *b*/*c* × *C*32–40

40. *CKEcbAabOac*   (Cesaro)
    38. *p*/*KAcbEab*, *b*/*c* × *C*35–41

41. *CKAcbEabOac*   (Camestrop)
    38. *p*/*KAcbEba*, *b*/*c* × *C*37–42

42. *CKAcbEbaOac*   (Camenop)
    XIII. *p*/*Abc*, *q*/*Iba*, *r*/*Iac* × *C*4–43

43. *CKNIacIbaNAbc*
    43. *RE*, *RO* × 44

44. *CKEacIbaObc*
    44. *a*/*b*, *b*/*a* × 45

45. *CKEbcIabOac*   (Ferio)

31. *a/c, q/Iab, r/Oac* × C45–46

46. *CKEcbIabOac*   (Festino)

X. *p/Ebc, q/Iab, r/Oac* × C45–47

47. *CCsIabCKEbcsOac*

47. *s/Iba* × C11–48

48. *CKEbcIbaOac*   (Ferison)

31. *a/c, q/Iba, r/Oac* × C48–49

49. *CKEcbIbaOac*   (Fresison)

10. *a/b, b/a* × 50

50. *CAbaIab*

47. *s/Aba* × C50–51

51. *CKEbcAbaOac*   (Felapton)

31. *a/c, q/Aba, r/Oac* × C51–52

52. *CKEcbAbaOac*   (Fesapo)

As a result of all these deductions one remarkable fact deserves our attention: it was possible to deduce twenty syllogistic moods without employing axiom 3, the mood Barbara. Even Barbari could be proved without Barbara. Axiom 3 is the most important thesis of the syllogistic, for it is the only syllogism that yields a universal affirmative conclusion, but in the system of simple syllogisms it has an inferior rank, being necessary to prove only two syllogistic moods, Baroco and Bocardo. Here are these two proofs:

XII. *p/Abc, q/Aab, r/Aac* × C3–53

53. *CKAbcNAacNAab*

53. *RO* × 54

54. *CKAbcOacOab*

54. *b/c, c/b* × 55

55. *CKAcbOabOac*   (Baroco)

XIII. *p/Abc, q/Aab, r/Aac* × C3–56

56. *CKNAacAabNAbc*

56. *RO* × 57

57. *CKOacAabObc*

57. *a/b, b/a* × 58

58. *CKObcAbaOac*   (Bocardo)

Aristotle calls first figure syllogisms perfect, self-evident arguments and he devises methods for reducing the syllogisms of other figures to these. It is not unreasonable to interpret this reductionism as a form of axiomatization. Lukasiewicz is quite definite: 'Aristotle reduces the so-called imperfect syllogisms to the perfect, i.e. to the axioms. Reduction here means proof or deduction of a theorem from the axioms.' (*Aristotle's Syllogistic*, p. 74) However, this is an area in which Aristotle's thinking seemed to suffer from an overestimate of the range of application of the syllogism, in which he is not entirely free from obscurity and inconsistency, and in which, at times, principles used intuitively by him are never formulated explicitly. These facts make it quite difficult to evaluate reductionism in Aristotle.

He was indeed the first person to formalize the structure and properties of an axiomatic system. This was the achievement of his chapters on demonstrative science in the *Posterior Analytics*. In his view the syllogism is the only medium of proof, and he defines the deductive sciences as those in which the formal medium of every proof is the syllogism. This is the explicit teaching of the *Prior Analytics* and *Posterior Analytics*. Thus, within this view, proving syllogisms and axiomatizing the syllogistic not only means deriving the imperfect from the perfect first figure syllogisms but using the latter as the medium of derivation. 'The syllogisms should therefore be proved not only *from* but also *by means of* syllogisms.' (Patzig in *Aristotle's Theory of the Syllogism*, p. 133) However, proving a syllogism (which states a relationship between propositions) is quite different from proving the conclusion of a syllogism (where it is terms that are related), and as forms of proof the reductive procedures of Aristotle must draw on principles of propositional logic for their force and credentials. Aristotle used these principles intuitively without ever formally discerning, apparently, the existence of a logical theory more basic than his syllogistic. The net result is that his theory of proof and his practice of it do not coincide here.

This inconsistency which could not be resolved without the formal discovery of propositional logic—a later, Stoic, achievement—explains much of the obscurity in Aristotle's texts where the broad concern seems to be proof but the procedures are frequently presented in the lesser role of 'perfecting', 'transforming' syllogisms that are already intrinsically valid.

Patzig sums up the matter: 'The historical fact that Aristotle, understandably overestimating, not the value, but the range of application of his discovery, believed the syllogism to be the only possible form of proof, explains the difficulty he encountered when he tried to prove the syllogisms themselves. His terminology straddles two different ways of evading this difficulty: on the one hand he assumes the first figure syllogisms as undemonstrable and evident axioms and "reduces" the other moods to them, thus avoiding the word "proof"; on the other, he acknowledges that not all syllogisms can be perfected in this way (notably Baroco and Bocardo) and that their validity must therefore be *proved* . . . The contradictory tendencies of Aristotle's language show that he felt the inconsistency between his theory of proof and his practice [in *Prior*

Analytics] but that he could not steel himself to revise the theory.' (Ibid., p. 136) The central facts are that Aristotle regarded his syllogistic as a deductive system, but that a broader conception of proof than his and a propositional calculus (which he lacked) were necessary to complete the formal task of axiomatization. This, in essence, is Lukasiewicz's view.

III. Proving the syllogistic theses in a natural deduction system

The traditional syllogistic which is traceable mainly to Boethius, although it antedates him, is closer to a natural deduction system than is Aristotle's theory which consists of implicational propositions and lends itself to axiomatization. The contrast is very striking to Lukasiewicz:

> The difference between the Aristotelian and the traditional syllogism is fundamental. The Aristotelian syllogism as an implication is a proposition, and as a proposition must be either true or false. The traditional syllogism is not a proposition, but a set of propositions which are not unified so as to form one single proposition. The two premisses written usually in two different lines are stated without a conjunction, and the connection of these loose premisses with the conclusion by means of 'therefore' does not give a new compound proposition. The famous Cartesian principle, 'Cogito, ergo sum', is not a true principle, because it is not a proposition. It is an inference, or, according to a scholastic terminology, a consequence. Inferences and consequences, not being propositions, are neither true nor false, as truth and falsity belong only to propositions. They may be valid or not. The same has to be said of the traditional syllogism. Not being a proposition the traditional syllogism is neither true nor false; it can be valid or invalid. The traditional syllogism is either an inference, when stated in concrete terms, or a rule of inference, when stated in variables. The sense of such a rule may be explained by the example given above: When you put such values for *A*, *B* and *C* that the premisses 'A belongs to all B' and 'B belongs to all C' are true, then you must accept as true the conclusion 'A belongs to all C'.
>
> If you find a book or an article where no difference is made between the Aristotelian and the traditional syllogism, you may be sure that the author is either ignorant of logic or has never seen the Greek text of the *Organon*. Scholars like Waitz, the modern editor and commentator of the *Organon*, Trendelenburg, the compiler of the *Elementa logices Aristoteleae*, Prantl, the historian of logic, all knew the Greek text of the *Organon* well, but nevertheless they did not see the difference between the Aristotelian and the traditional syllogism. Only Maier seems to have felt for a moment that something is wrong here, when he asks for permission to replace the Aristotelian syllogism by the more familiar and more convenient form of the later logic; immediately afterwards he quotes the mood Barbara in its usual traditional form, neglecting differences he has seen between this form and

that of Aristotle, and does not even say what differences he has seen. When we realize that the difference between a thesis and a rule of inference is from the standpoint of logic a fundamental one, we must agree that an exposition of Aristotelian logic which disregards it cannot be sound. We have to this day no genuine exposition of Aristotelian logic. (*Aristotle's Syllogistic*, pp. 21–2)

In a natural deduction system, proof of Aristotle's syllogistic consists not in deriving each thesis from axioms but in showing that within each the movement from premises, as assumptions, to conclusion, as derivative, is reducible to movements of natural deduction. The process of doing this reveals a presupposition in the Aristotelian theory that is not shared by modern predicate logic, namely that no term is empty, that corresponding to names, individual variables and predicate letters there are always real objects, properties or relations.

Dealing firstly with Aristotle's language, it is quite clear that he chose it very deliberately in order to display as clearly as possible the logical structure of premises, conclusion and relationship of implication. Instead of the conventional scheme, S is P, he generally uses the expressions '. . . belongs/does not belong to all/some . . .' or '. . . is said/is not said of all/some . . .'; in all his expressions the predicate is in the nominative case, the subject in the dative or genitive. Thus his language suggests a process relating subject and predicate rather than an identity, and he looks on this relationship from the direction of the predicate. Linguistically, his approach is remarkably similar to that of modern logic; indeed in the *Prior Analytics* (Book I, 49b 14–31) he formalizes the universal affirmative as 'the A belongs to all to which B belongs' which is very close to $(x)\,(Bx \to Ax)$. Modern formulae for the other simple categorical propositions are $(x)\,(Bx \to -Ax)$ for E, $(Ex)\,(Bx \, . \, Ax)$ for I, and $(Ex)\,(Bx \, . \, -Ax)$ for O.

These formulae map on to the traditional Square of Opposition as follows:

$$(x)\,(Bx \to Ax) \qquad\qquad\qquad\qquad (x)\,(Bx \to -Ax)$$

$$(Ex)\,(Bx \, . \, Ax) \qquad\qquad\qquad\qquad (Ex)\,(Bx \, . \, -Ax)$$

The traditional relationships of contradiction admit of formal proof, e.g. if A is false, O is true; if O is true, A is false; if E is false, I is true; if I is true, E is false.

Example: Proof that if A is true, O is false

1 (1) $(x)\,(Fx \to Gx)$		A
1 (2) $Fa \to Ga$		1, *Uo*
(3) $p \to q \equiv -(p \, . \, -q)$		*TI* (from propositional logic)

$\quad$ (4) $(Fa \rightarrow Ga) \dashv\vdash -(Fa \cdot -Ga)$ $\qquad$ Specialization of 3

1 (5) $-(Fa \cdot -Ga)$ $\qquad$ 4, 2, *Co*

1 (6) $(x) - (Fx \cdot -Gx)$ $\qquad$ 5, *Ui*

1 (7) $-(Ex)(Fx \cdot -Gx)$ $\qquad$ 6, *SI* (i.e. one of the laws, presented earlier, which express relations between universal and existential quantifiers)

However, traditional implications of relationships other than contradiction do not admit of formal proof without an existential assumption. Thus the propositions that contraries (*A* and *E*) are not both true, that one of a pair of subcontraries (*I* and *O*) is true, that *A* implies *I* and *E* implies *O*—these appear in modern logic as conclusions under an existential assumption:

$$(Ex)\ Fx \vdash -((x)(Fx \rightarrow Gx) \cdot (x)(Fx \rightarrow -Gx))$$
$$(Ex)\ Fx \vdash (Ex)(Fx \cdot Gx) \vee (Ex)(Fx \cdot -Gx)$$
$$(Ex).Fx \vdash (x)(Fx \rightarrow Gx) \rightarrow (Ex)(Fx \cdot Gx)$$
$$(Ex)\ Fx \vdash (x)(Fx \rightarrow -Gx) \rightarrow (Ex)(Fx \cdot -Gx)$$

Similarly, while there is formal proof that the converses of *I* and *E* propositions are of logical consequence, the conversion of an *A* proposition, $(x)(Fx \rightarrow Gx)$, into an *I* proposition $(Ex)(Gx \cdot Fx)$ is not, demonstrably, of logical consequence without the presupposition that $(Ex)\ Fx$.

$\quad$ Most of the moods of the syllogism admit of formal proof. The following, e.g. are demonstrably valid sequents:

$$(x)(Fx \rightarrow Gx) \cdot (x)(Hx \rightarrow Fx) \vdash (x)(Hx \rightarrow Gx) \qquad \text{[Barbara]}$$
$$(x)(Fx \rightarrow -Gx) \cdot (x)(Hx \rightarrow Fx) \vdash (x)(Hx \rightarrow -Gx) \qquad \text{[Celarent]}$$
$$(x)(Fx \rightarrow Gx) \cdot (Ex)(Hx \cdot Fx) \vdash (Ex)(Hx \cdot Gx) \qquad \text{[Darii]}$$
$$(x)(Fx \rightarrow -Gx) \cdot (Ex)(Hx \cdot Fx) \vdash (Ex)(Hx \cdot -Gx) \qquad \text{[Ferio]}$$

However, any standard or weakened mood in which the premisses are universal and the conclusion particular requires an existential presupposition and this is included in the modern representation of the mood. Nine of the twenty-four traditional moods require such a (single) presupposition:

$$(Ex)\ Hx \cdot (x)(Fx \rightarrow Gx) \cdot (x)(Hx \rightarrow Fx) \vdash (Ex)(Hx \cdot Gx) \qquad \text{[Barbari]}$$
$$(Ex)\ Hx \cdot (x)(Fx \rightarrow -Gx) \cdot (x)(Hx \rightarrow Fx) \vdash (Ex)(Hx \cdot -Gx) \qquad \text{[Celaront]}$$
$$(Ex)\ Hx \cdot (x)(Gx \rightarrow -Fx) \cdot (x)(Hx \rightarrow Fx) \vdash (Ex)(Hx \cdot -Gx) \qquad \text{[Cesaro]}$$
$$(Ex)(Hx) \cdot (x)(Gx \rightarrow Fx) \cdot (x)(Hx \rightarrow -Fx) \vdash (Ex)(Hx \cdot -Gx) \qquad \text{[Camestros]}$$
$$(Ex)\ Fx \cdot (x)(Fx \rightarrow Gx) \cdot (x)(Fx \rightarrow Hx) \vdash (Ex)(Hx \cdot Gx) \qquad \text{[Darapti]}$$
$$(Ex)\ Fx \cdot (x)(Fx \rightarrow -Gx) \cdot (x)(Fx \rightarrow Hx) \vdash (Ex)(Hx \cdot -Gx) \qquad \text{[Felapton]}$$
$$(Ex)\ Gx \cdot (x)(Gx \rightarrow Fx) \cdot (x)(Fx \rightarrow Hx) \vdash (Ex)(Hx \cdot Gx) \qquad \text{[Bramantip]}$$
$$(Ex)\ Fx \cdot (x)(Gx \rightarrow -Fx) \cdot (x)(Fx \rightarrow Hx) \vdash (Ex)(Hx \cdot -Gx) \qquad \text{[Fesapo]}$$
$$(Ex)\ Hx \cdot (x)(Gx \rightarrow Fx) \cdot (x)(Fx \rightarrow -Hx) \vdash (Ex)(Hx \cdot -Gx) \qquad \text{[Camenos]}$$

IV. Conclusion: Aristotle's syllogistic as a fragment of predicate logic

Modern logic does not invalidate Aristotle's theory: it simply displays its character and its presuppositions very clearly. Aristotle selected four forms of propositions for special study and he presupposed that the terms appearing in these forms are non-empty. These are only some of the forms expressed and studied in modern predicate logic whose scope is not restricted by the assumption that corresponding to its names, individual variables and predicate letters, there are always real objects, properties or relations. Because of this assumption some of the traditional implications in the broader framework of modern logic, and some of the traditional valid syllogistic moods are seen to require, in formal proof, a special single existential presupposition. Thus modern logic has integrated Aristotle's theory, as a fragment, into its predicate logic.

This predicate logic is not entirely free of presuppositions. It has not devised any way for expressing or dealing with the peculiar formal properties of empty universes, and built into its language and rules is the presupposition that there is at least one thing in any universe it deals with. This becomes evident when the following expressions work out as theorems:

$$\vdash (x) Fx \to (Ex) Fx$$
$$\vdash (x) - Fx \to (Ex) - Fx$$
$$\vdash (Ex) \, Fx \lor (Ex) - Fx$$

If there was nothing at all these expressions would be false; they depend, for truth, on interpretation in some non-empty universe of discourse.

Although modern logic presupposes that at least one individual exists in any universe it deals with, it does not presuppose that any particular property is realized there. Thus while $(x) \, Fx \to Gx$ does imply $(Ex) \, Fx \to Gx$, it does not imply $(Ex) (Fx \cdot Gx)$ and it is this latter which is the I proposition of Aristotle's theory. In the modern notation, the universal and existential propositions differ not only in quantification but also in the propositional function quantified ($Fx \to Gx$ on the one hand, $Fx \cdot Gx$ on the other). Thus a universal may be true and the corresponding existential false. This was not possible in the Aristotelian and traditional syllogistic where not only is the universe of discourse non-empty but every term has a real correspondent in it, this being reflected in formalizing A and I propositions as differing only in quantity. The Aristotelian presupposition, natural to a logic that was *abstractive* from living object language, is transcended by modern logic whose point of departure is an artificial logical language and whose method is *constructive*.

Günther Patzig (in *Aristotle's Theory of the Syllogism*) concludes a very thorough exegesis with the observation (p. 193) that 'it is not unaristotelian to consider the logical constants, a, e, i and o as relations between terms' and that from this viewpoint 'Aristotle's syllogistic is the theory of the relative product of these binary relations between terms.' In explanation it should be noted that if R denotes the relation of x to y, and S the relation of y to z then the relative product of these two relations, xRy and ySz, is the relation of x to z and it is symbolized R/S. Thus if R denotes 'husband of' (in xRy) and S denotes 'daughter of' (in ySz), R/S denotes 'son-in-law of', i.e. the relation which exists between the husband (x) and parent (z) of a person (y). For Patzig Aristotle's theory displays the cases in which the relative products of the binary relations, a, e, i and o have the character of being one of these relations; there are procedures for establishing whether a relative product has a definite a, e, i or o value and when it lacks any such definite value. For example with SaM, MaP the relative product S a/a P has the value a (Barbara); with SaM, MeP the relative product S a/e P has the value e (Celarent). In the latter case the relative product lacks a definite a, e, i or o value and tells us nothing logically about its terms; in the former case it does, and the set of three binary relations is called a syllogism. He concludes that Aristotle's theory can be presented as 'a special part of the logic of binary relations'. (Ibid., p. 194)

Chapter 7

CLASS CALCULUS

I. Introduction

Logically (as distinct from psychologically) the concept of class is not generated by a process of collecting and arranging individuals but by the fact that a
propositional form has a field of applicability. Thus it is possible to focus an
expression such as Fx extensionally, in terms of the field of its applicability.
Monadic predicates constitute, indeed, the simplest basis for classification: e.g.
specifying F as 'must die', the propositional form, Fx ('x must die'), may be
said to define the class of mortal beings since it furnishes the criterion for
membership—a member is any true value that can be substituted for the
variable x. A system or calculus in which monadic predicates are focused
extensionally as classes is called a calculus of classes or a class calculus. It may
be described as being parallel to the logic of monadic predicates or as being an
extension of it.

This chapter presents the symbols, classes, statements and inferences that
characterize the calculus; it shows how truth-tables are replaced by a box
diagram of classes and sub-classes as a mechanical decision procedure for
validity, and it includes a formalization of the Boole–Schröder Algebra
(devised by Boole and given its definitive form by Schröder)—interpreted of
course as a class calculus, for this algebra is a highly generalized system patient
of other interpretations, both logical and extralogical, besides the classal one.

II. The symbolism of class calculus

The variables are a, b, c, etc. and they designate classes. The universe of
discourse (the total space containing objects, classes being the collections of
objects) is represented by the number 1, and 0 represents the limiting null class
(containing no objects). Where extension only is taken into consideration there
is no distinction between classes that have identically the same membership.
Thus while the term 'unicorn' and the term 'centaur' have very differen meanings or intensions, the classes of things denoted by them are identical: they are
both the class of nothing existent. Similarly, there is only one class 'nothing'
(the null class or empty class, symbolized 0) and only one class 'everything'
(the universe class, symbolized 1). The term 'universe of discourse' denotes a
device adopted to make the determinateness of the class, a' (the negate of a),
completely unambiguous: the members of a' are outside the class a but within
the same universe of discourse. Thus if one class a (red things) is

given, its negate a', is automatically determined as the things which are not red in the universe of discourse (coloured things).

There are no proper names apart from 1 and 0, except those used for individuals in the context of their being members of a class. In the course of Boolean operations on simple classes (to be discussed in the next section) the basic variables, a, b, c, etc. are used in the construction of complex variables, e.g. ab represents the class of things which belong to both a and b; a' represents the class of things which are not members of a; $a + b$ represents the class of things which belong to a or b or both.

The constants or functors which express relationships between classes are as follows:

$=$ symbolizes identity of membership or material quivalence; $a = b$ is a statement saying that the class a and the class b have identically the same membership; $a \neq b$ denies such an identity or equation of membership: it expresses an inequation.

$\rightarrow$ symbolizes the relation of inclusion; $a \rightarrow b$ is a statement saying that the class a is included in the class b.

$\leftarrow$ symbolizes sub-inclusion; $a \leftarrow b$ states that b is included in a.

$\leftrightarrows$ symbolizes joint inclusion and sub-inclusion; $a \leftrightarrows b$ states that a is included in b, and b in a.

$\wedge$ symbolizes the relation of exclusion; $a \wedge b$ states that a is excluded from b.

$\vee$ symbolizes the relation of sub-contrariety; $a \vee b$ states that the class a is sub-contrary to the class b: this implies that everything is either in a or in b or in both.

$\diamondsuit$ symbolizes the relation of contradiction; $a \diamondsuit b$ states that a is contradictory to b: this implies that everything is either in a or in b and cannot be in both.

$\uparrow$ symbolizes partial inclusion; $a \uparrow b$ states that a is partially included in b.

$\nrightarrow$ symbolizes partial exclusion; $a \nrightarrow b$ states that a is partially excluded from b.

ϵ (the Greek letter epsilon) symbolizes the relationship of membership of a class, $P \epsilon a$ states that the individual, P, is a member of the class a.

Functors expressing relationships between statements about classes are as follows:

$\rightarrow$ will be used to symbolize the relationship of implication; $(a \rightarrow c) \rightarrow (ab \rightarrow c)$ says that the statement, 'the class a is included in c' implies the statement, 'the class ab is included in c'.

$\equiv$ symbolizes equivalence; $(a \uparrow b) \equiv (ab \neq 0)$ says that the statement, 'the class a is partially included in b', is equivalent to the statement, 'the class ab is not identical in membership with the null class'. The equivalence here of course is of truth conditions (it is the connective from propositional logic): each statement is true when the other is true, false when the other is false. It is interesting to note that, with regard to statements about classes, truth-conditions are not displayed in truth-tables but in equations or inequations: thus the essential condition for the statement, $a \to b$, being true is that $ab' = 0$, the condition under which it is false being $ab' \neq 0$; thus we can say simply that $a \to b$ is true if and only if $ab' = 0$.

Quantified predicative statements can be translated into the language of class calculus. A singular statement affirmative or negative formalizes as a statement about class membership (Chicago is a member of the class of ports; it is also a member of the class of non-Asiatic cities). Particular statements ('at least one . . .') are formalized as partial class inclusion or partial class exclusion; and universal statements as total class inclusion or total class exclusion. Thus taking a as the class of things which are A, and b as the class of things which are B:

$\begin{cases} \text{All } A \text{ is } B \text{ is formalized as } a \to b \\ \text{No } A \text{ is } B \text{ is formalized as } a \wedge b \end{cases}$ (equivalent to the equation $ab' = 0$)
(equivalent to the equation $ab = 0$)

$\begin{cases} \text{Some } A \text{ is } B \text{ is formalized as } a \wedge\!\!\!\!/\, b \\ \text{Some } A \text{ is not } B \text{ is formalized as } a +\!\!\!\!/\, b \end{cases}$ (equivalent to the inequation $ab \neq 0$)
(equivalent to the inequation $ab' \neq 0$)

III. Boolean operations generating complex classes from simple ones

Boolean operations are performed on the membership of classes, since the calculus of classes does not deal with what a class means, with the properties or form which define it. Classes are designated by variables which have no specific meaning. The operations performed on these variables designate, unambiguously, all the classes and sub-classes in the universe of discourse. Basic operations are as follows:

(1) *Unary operations*, i.e. operations upon one variable: there is one, negation. Given a class a, by performing this operation on it we get its negate, a' (the class of things that are not a).

(2) *Binary operations*, i.e. operations upon two variables. The operation of conjunction on the classes a and b results in a class (called the conjunct) which comprises things that are members of both a and b. The conjunct is symbolized $a \cap b$ or $a \times b$ (abbreviated often to ab). The operation of disjunction on these classes results in a class (called the disjunct) which comprises things that are members of either a or b. The disjunct is symbolized $a \cup b$ or $a + b$ (which symbolism is used in this chapter). Boole defined his operation of disjunction exclusively (either . . . or . . but not both) but Jevons in England, Peirce in the United States and Schröder in Germany all showed that the inclusive disjunct (either . . . or . . . or both if there are any of both) is more useful and now disjunction is always conceived inclusively. (One of the reasons for this is the usefulness of De Morgan's theorems (*infra*) which will not work if the disjunct is defined exclusively.)

The class ab is a sub-class of a: all its members belong to a; it is also a sub-class of b. The classes a, b and ab are all sub-classes of $a + b$. The negate or complement of ab is $(ab)'$ or $a' + b'$; the complement of $a + b$ is $(a + b)'$.

Several other binary operations are possible but they can all be symbolized in terms of conjunction, disjunction and negation. Thus the operation rejection performed on the classes a and b, resulting in the class of things which are neither members of a nor of b can be symbolized $(a + b)'$, i.e. the negate of the disjunct, or $a' \times b'$, i.e. the conjunct of the negate of a and the negate of b.

Further, any conjunct can be symbolized as a disjunct and vice versa, if the classes are negated in the correct manner. Each term is negated and then the whole is negated: thus the transformation formula for disjunction is $a + b = (a' \times b')'$; for conjunction it is $a \times b = (a' + b')'$. (If a thing belongs to the class of objects that are both P and Q it cannot possibly belong to the class of things that are either P' or Q'. These transformation formulas or equivalences are called *De Morgan's theorems* after their discoverer Augustus De Morgan. Fully listed for classes a, b, a' and b', they are:

$$a \times b = (a' + b')'; \qquad a + b = (a' \times b')'$$
$$a' \times b = (a + b')'; \qquad a' + b = (a \times b')'$$
$$a \times b' = (a' + b)'; \qquad a + b' = (a' \times b)'$$
$$a' \times b' = (a + b)'; \qquad a' + b' = (a \times b)'$$

Reversing the sides of the above equivalences one may state De Morgan's Theorem as follows: The negative of a product, e.g. $(a \times b)'$ is the sum of the negatives of its terms, $a' + b'$; and the negative of a sum, e.g. $(a + b)'$ is the product of the negatives of its terms, $a' \times b'$. The correspondence in Boolean Algebra between principles in terms of $\times$ and principles in terms of $+$, is called the Law of Duality.

Many of these operations follow the same laws or protocol as analogous operations of arithmetic:

(1) Just as $(2 + 3) + 4 = 2 + (3 + 4) = 2 + 3 + 4$ (i.e. the grouping does not affect the final result and need not be indicated) so the class $(a + b) + c = $ (in membership) the class $a + (b + c) = a + b + c$; and as $(2 \times 3) \times 4 = 2 \times (3 \times 4) = 2 \times 3 \times 4$ so $(a \times b) \times c = a \times (b \times c) = a \times b \times c$. These are laws of association and both disjunction and conjunction in Boolean algebra are associative.

(2) Just as $2 + 3 = 3 + 2$ and $2 \times 3 = 3 \times 2$ (i.e. it does not matter in what order the numbers are added or multiplied) so we can commute $a + b$ to $b + a$, and $a \times b$ to $b \times a$ (without affecting the referential value of these class names). These are laws of commutation and both disjunction and conjunction are commutative.

Following the practice of Boole himself, disjunction is often called logical addition and symbolized $+$, the disjunct being called the logical sum. Similarly, conjunction is often called logical multiplication and symbolized $\times$, the conjunct being called the logical product. It is interesting to note that 'in two papers dated 1867 Peirce clearly differentiated between the arithmetical and the logical operation upon classes. This led to a dropping of Boole's division and a reinterpretation of his subtraction.' (Lee's *Symbolic Logic*, p. 8)

IV. A sampling of statements expressing relations between classes

In the calculus of classes which considers extension only, the most basic thing we can say about a class is that it has or has not members. Given this information about the classes of a universe we can define the relationships between them.

For example, if the conjunct $a \times b$ designates an empty or null class then the classes a and b are mutually exclusive. If the class of objects which belong to a but not to b is empty, then a is included in b; if $a \times b'$ has members, then there is a relation of non-inclusion. When $a' \times b' = 0$ (i.e. when there is nothing which is neither a member of a nor a member of b) then the classes, a and b, jointly exhaust their universe. If the classes $a \times b$ and $a' \times b'$ are both empty then the simple classes, a and b are mutually exclusive and collectively exhaustive. There is a relationship of mutual inclusion between a and b when the classes $a \times b'$ and $b \times a'$ are both empty. Finally, a class a is said to be a proper part of the class b when there are no members of a which are not members of b but there are members of b which are not members of a (i.e. when $a \times b'$ is empty while $b \times a'$ has members).

The following is a summary list of formulae expressing the basic Boolean relations with those equivalent expressions which express the essential truth conditions for each formula (Note that '.' symbolizes the propositional connective 'and', and '$\vee$' symbolizes the propositional connective 'either-or'):

Formulae	Relations expressed	Equivalences (expressing truth conditions)
$a \wedge b$	exclusion	$a \times b = 0$
$a \uparrow b$	non-exclusion (or intersection)	$a \times b \neq 0$
$a \rightarrow b$	inclusion	$a \times b' = 0$
$a \nrightarrow b$	non-inclusion (or protrusion)	$a \times b' \neq 0$
$a' \wedge b'$	exhaustion	$a' \times b' = 0$
$a' \uparrow b'$	non-exhauston	$a' \times b' \neq 0$
$a \lozenge b$	mutual exclusion and joint exhaustion	$(a \times b = 0) . (a' \times b' = 0)$
$(a \uparrow b) \vee (a' \uparrow b')$	non-mutual-exclusion-and-joint-exhaustion	$(a \times b \neq 0) \vee (a' \times b' \neq 0)$
$a \leftrightarrows b$	co-extension (mutual inclusion)	$(a \times b' = 0) . (b \times a' = 0)$
$(a \nrightarrow b) \vee (b \nrightarrow a)$	non-co-extension	$(a \times b' \neq 0) \vee (b \times a' \neq 0)$
$(a \rightarrow b) . (b \nrightarrow a)$	proper part	$(a \times b' = 0) . (b \times a' \neq 0)$
$(a \nrightarrow b) \vee (b \rightarrow a)$	non-proper part	$(a \times b' \neq 0) \vee (b \times a' = 0)$

In class calculus a statement is a tautology if its truth condition is self-evidently fulfilled. Thus the statement, $ab \rightarrow a$, has as its essential truth condition that $aba' = 0$; this is self-evidently fulfilled as the logical product of the class a and its complement a' is necessarily empty; similarly, the statements $a' \rightarrow a'$ and $c' \wedge c$ are also tautologies. The denial of $ab \rightarrow a$ is a logical inconsistency as it is equivalent to an assertion that the product of a and a' is non-empty; it is necessarily false not just accidentally so. On the other hand, $ab \rightarrow c$ is a contingent statement: a formal analysis of its truth condition, $abc' = 0$, does not reveal whether it is, or is not, actually fulfilled.

In the Aristotelian class calculus, $a \neq 0$ is a variable mode of expressing the postulate that no simple class is empty; its truth condition is this postulate and so it is a tautology, formally necessitated by the logical system itself. In modern logic, $a \neq 0$ is a contingent statement, as is the statement $a = 0$; consequently $a \wedge a$ is also a contingent statement as its truth condition is that $aa = 0$ (i.e. that the class aa, which is the class a, is empty—a contingent fact in modern logic).

V. Diagramming statements about classes and using such diagrams as a method of displaying the validity or invalidity of arguments

Diagramming statements. If ⬚ is the universe of discourse, the complementary classes a and a' exhaust it thus: ⬚. The two classes are exclusive and exhaustive: every object in the universe belongs to one class and no object belongs to both.

Two sets of complementary classes exhaust their universe thus:

	b	b'
a	ab	ab'
a'	$a'b$	$a'b'$

	b	b'
a		0
a'		

$a \rightarrow b$

	b	b'
a	*	
a'		

$a \nmid b$

	b	b'
a	?	?
a'		

$a \neq 0$

Given that $a \rightarrow b$, then the class ab' is empty ($ab' = 0$ is the essential truth condition of $a \rightarrow b$); we signify this by putting a zero in the upper right-hand box. The essential truth condition of $a \nmid b$ being $ab \neq 0$ (i.e. ab has one member at least) it can be diagrammed by putting an * in the upper left-hand box. Given simply that a has members we put a ? in each of the boxes for the complementary sub-classes ab and ab' until further information reveals membership or emptiness.

Thus what is diagrammed is the essential truth conditions for class statements:

For $a \wedge b$, a zero is put in box ab.
„　$a \leftarrow b$, „　„　„　„　„　„　$a'b$.
„　$a \leftrightarrows b$, zeros are put in ab' and $a'b$.
„　$a \vee b$, a zero is put in $a'b'$.
„　$a \diamond b$, zeros are put in ab and $a'b'$.

„ $a \curlywedge b$, the box *ab* has an asterisk, signifying that the class has at least one member.

„ $a \curlyvee b$, *ab'* has an asterisk.

„ $P \in a$, *P?* is put in each of the boxes *ab* and *ab'* to signify diagrammatic ambiguity as it is not clear to which sub-class *P* belongs.

It is important to note that diagrams do not provide a box for the product of a class and its complement (e.g. for *aa'*): class calculus postulates that such a complex class is empty and diagrams work within this postulate: they are governed by it but do not display it. Thus there is no way of positively diagramming the truth condition (*aa'* = 0) that is fulfilled in a tautology or contradicted in an inconsistency.

Three and four sets of complementary classes exhaust their universes as follows:

	b	*b'*
a C	abc	ab'c
C'	abc'	ab'c'
a' C	a'bc	a'b'c
C'	a'bc'	a'b'c'

	b		*b'*	
	d	*d'*	*d*	*d'*
a C	abcd	abcd'	ab'cd	ab'cd'
C'	abc'd	abc'd'	ab'c'd	ab'c'd'
a' C	a'bcd	a'bcd'	a'b'cd	a'b'cd'
C'	a'bc'd	a'bc'd'	a'b'c'd	a'b'c'd'

The sub-classes are exclusive and exhaustive: every member of the universe belongs to one and only one of these sub-classes. Thus if *a* is the class of black objects, *b* of round objects, *c* of tall objects and *d* of thick objects, and if there is nothing which is white, round, tall and thin, then a zero is put in the square *a'bcd'*. If only tall objects are black, thin and round, a zero is put in the square *abc'd'*.

We have already seen that any statement asserting a relation between classes may be translated into an equivalent claim that certain classes are, or are not, empty (note that universal statements are equivalent to equations and particular statements to inequations):

	Vernacular Equivalent
$a \wedge b \equiv ab = 0$	No *a* is *b*
$a \curlywedge b \equiv ab \neq 0$	Some *a* is *b*
$a \rightarrow b \equiv ab' = 0$	All *a* is *b*
$a \curlyvee b \equiv ab' \neq 0$	Some *a* is not *b*
$a \leftarrow b \equiv a'b = 0$	Only *a* is *b*
$a = b \equiv (ab' = 0) \,.\, (a'b = 0)$	All *a* and only *a* is *b*
$a \vee b \equiv a'b' = 0$	Everything is *a* or *b* or both.
$a \diamondsuit b \equiv (a'b' = 0) \,.\, (ab = 0)$	Everything is *a* or *b* but not both.

The above equivalences can present very clearly and powerfully the truth conditions of vernacular statements. For example 'No one but a very simple person would believe that' translates (with a as the class of simple people and b as the class of people that would believe that) into $a'b = 0$. Again 'The only criticism made referred to style' translates (with a as the class of criticisms made, and b the class of things that referred to style) into $ab' = 0$.

Statements in the above list can be opposed by asserting that a class declared to be empty is non-empty, or one declared non-empty is empty. Thus the range of possible conflict and compatibility can be clearly displayed in a diagram: a statement that is diagrammed as putting a zero in a box is in conflict with a statement diagrammed as putting an * in the same box. Both statements are compatible with any third statement which is diagrammed either as not saying anything about the box in question or as putting a ? in it (i.e. denying neither that it is empty nor that it has members).

It follows that where arguments are analysable into statements of the above kind (as, e.g. in the Aristotelian syllogistic), the evidential force of the premisses can be diagrammed and the diagram inspected to see if the conclusion is really necessitated. In other words, the diagram displays the essential truth condition for each and all the premisses to be true, and we can inspect it to see if, as a consequence, the essential truth condition for the conclusion is fulfilled. This is a powerful method of displaying validity or invalidity, a decision procedure as simple and effective as truth tables in propositional logic.

Table of the valid immediate inferences in class calculus

Conversion (an operation in which subject and predicate classes interchange positions with a new and valid relationship):

Converse	Essential truth conditions for both expressions
$(a \wedge b) \equiv (b \wedge a)$	$ab = 0$
$(a \vee b) \equiv (b \vee a)$	$a'b' = 0$
$(a \mathbin{\vee\!\!\!\wedge} b) \equiv (b \mathbin{\vee\!\!\!\wedge} a)$	$(ab = 0) \,.\, (a'b' = 0)$
$(a \mathbin{\curlywedge} b) \equiv (b \mathbin{\curlywedge} a)$	$ab \neq 0$
$(a = b) \equiv (b = a)$	$(ab' = 0) \,.\, (a'b = 0)$

Obversion (an operation which replaces the predicate class with its complement, expressing the valid class relationship present):

Obverse	Essential truth conditions for both expressions
$(a \wedge b) \equiv (a \rightarrow b')$	$ab = 0$
$(a \mathbin{\curlywedge} b) \equiv (a \mathbin{\nrightarrow} b')$	$ab \neq 0$
$(a \vee b) \equiv (a \leftarrow b')$	$a'b' = 0$
$(a \mathbin{\vee\!\!\!\wedge} b) \equiv (a = b')$	$(ab = 0) \,.\, (a'b' = 0)$

Contraposition (an operation which validly replaces the subject class with the complement of the original predicate class, and the predicate class with the complement of the original subject class):

Contrapositive	Essential truth conditions for both expressions
$(a \rightarrow b) \equiv (b' \rightarrow a')$	$ab' = 0$
$(a \leftarrow b) \equiv (b' \leftarrow a')$	$ba' = 0$
$(a \lozenge b) \equiv (b' \lozenge a')$	$(ab = 0) . (a'b' = 0)$
$(a = b) \equiv (b' = a')$	$(ab' = 0) . (a'b = 0)$
$(a \mathbin{+\!\!\!\!+} b) \equiv (b' \mathbin{+\!\!\!\!+} a')$	$ab' \neq 0$

Inversion (an operation which validly replaces both subject class and predicate class with their complements):

Inverse	Essential truth conditions for both expressions
$(a \wedge b) \equiv a' \vee b'$	$ab = 0$
$a \vee b \equiv a' \wedge b'$	$a'b' = 0$

Diagramming Aristotelian operations of immediate inference displays the fact that some conclusions are valid only on the special Aristotelian postulate that no simple class term is empty (i.e. that none refers to an empty class). Without this postulate, *Some b is a* is not a valid converse of *All a is b*, for the essential truth condition of the latter is $ab' = 0$, and of the former $ba' \neq 0$; the diagram displays these truth conditions as being simply compatible (a zero in box ab', an * in box ab). A similar lack of logical necessitation is shown between *No a is b* and its Aristotelian contrapositive *Some non-b is a* (the truth conditions being, respectively, $ab = 0$ and $b'a \neq 0$); also between *All a is b* and its inverse, *Some non-a is not b* (the truth conditions being $ab' = 0$ and $a'b' \neq 0$).

The validity of inferences based on the traditional Square of Opposition.

A All *a* is *b* $(a \rightarrow b)$	E No *a* is *b* $(a \wedge b)$
Some *a* is *b* $(a \uparrow b)$	Some *a* is not *b* $(a \mathbin{+\!\!\!\!+} b)$
I	O

The A and O propositions are contradictory: from the truth of either we can infer the falsity of the other and vice versa.	Their truth conditions are, respectively, $ab' = 0$ and $ab' \neq 0$.
E and I are also contradictory.	Their truth conditions are $ab = 0$ and $ab \neq 0$.

A and E may not only both be false, they may also both be true if one does not postulate, with Aristotle, that the basic class *a* is non-empty.

Their truth conditions are diferent but compatible, being respectively $ab' = 0$ and $ab = 0$.

The A proposition does not imply the I proposition, sub-alternating it, unless one postulates, with Aristotle, that the simple class *a* cannot be empty.

Their truth conditions are $ab' = 0$ and $ab \neq 0$. Notice that *a* is conjoined here with the complementary classes *b* and *b'*. If *a* has members, and one of these sub-classes is empty, the other must have members.

Similarly, without the Aristotelian postulate that *a* is not empty, *E does not imply O* sub-alternating it.

The truth conditions of *E* and *O* are respectively $ab = 0$ and $ab' \neq 0$.

Logically, *I* and *O* may not only both be true, they may also both be false, except in a system which operates the Aristotelian postulate that no simple class is empty.

Their truth conditions are $ab \neq 0$ and $ab' \neq 0$.

Sample arguments containing statements which have complex subjects or predicates. We have seen that a class calculus which is Aristotelian postulates that every simple class has at least one member, and that some Aristotelian theorems would not hold for a world which did not provide a real correlate for every simple class. However, even Aristotelian calculus does not postulate that a complex class (generated by a Boolean operation on simple classes) has members; e.g. *ab* may be empty, although it is not possible for both *ab* and *ab'* to be empty, since *a* must have members and these classes are the product in turn of *a* and the complementary classes *b* and *b'*. The existential postulate of modern calculus is simply that the universe of discourse is not a totally empty one, and so it accepts that any class, simple or complex, may be empty.

Argument 1: $(a \wedge b) \dashrightarrow (ab \wedge c)$

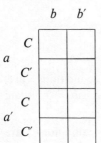

The essential truth condition for $a \wedge b$ is $ab = 0$. This means that $abc = 0$ and $abc' = 0$. The former is the essential truth condition for the consequent, $ab \wedge c$. Thus the argument is valid. However, the converse does not hold, i.e. it is not the case that $(ab \wedge c) \dashrightarrow (a \wedge b)$. The truth conditions demanded by the consequent are more extensive than those fulfilled by the antecedent: although the box *abc* is empty (we are given $ab \wedge c$), *abc'* might not be empty.

Argument 2: $(ab \curlywedge c) \rightarrowtail (a \curlywedge b)$

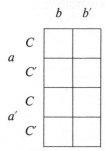

The essential truth condition for $ab \curlywedge c$ is $abc \neq 0$. Since the members of the sub-class abc are also members of the wider class ab this means that the class ab is non-empty. This is the essential truth condition for the conclusion $(ab \neq 0)$. Again the converse, $a \curlywedge b \rightarrowtail (ab \curlywedge c)$, does not hold: given that $ab \neq 0$, it is possible that the members of ab are concentrated in the sub-class abc'; we are not entitled to conclude that abc has members, which is the essential truth condition for the conclusion. Thus granted that some employees pay taxes it does not follow that there are some employees over 60 years of age paying taxes.

Standard forms of syllogistic argument. In seeking valid forms of syllogistic reasoning, the information provided by each premiss can be represented in a box diagram, and the diagram can then be inspected to see if the premisses have furnished the essential truth condition for the conclusion. One has to be clear whether or not we are postulating (with Aristotle) that no basic class is empty; if so then when, e.g. the class ab is empty, the class ab' cannot be empty also.

In modern calculus (where the Aristotelian postulate is not made), the standard form of argument for a universal conclusion is $((a \rightarrow b) . (b \rightarrow c)) \rightarrowtail (a \rightarrow c)$, and the standard form for a particular conclusion is $((a \curlywedge b) . (b \rightarrow c)) \rightarrowtail (a \curlywedge c)$. Any argument in one of these forms or reducible to one of them (by, e.g. obverting, converting premisses or conclusion) is valid.

Proof of standard argument form 1: $((a \rightarrow b) . (b \rightarrow c)) \rightarrowtail (a \rightarrow c)$

		b	b'
a	C		0
	C'	0	0
a'	C		
	C'	0	

The truth condition of the premiss $a \rightarrow b$ is $ab' = 0$; $\therefore ab'c = 0$ and $ab'c' = 0$ (if a class is empty then all its sub-classes are empty).

The truth condition of the premiss $b \rightarrow c$ is $bc' = 0$; $\therefore abc' = 0$ and $a'bc' = 0$.

The truth condition of the conclusion, $a \rightarrow c$, is $ac' = 0$; this is fulfilled if both the sub-classes $ac'b$ and $ac'b'$ are empty (for a class is empty if all its sub-classes are empty). Actually, as we have seen, the first premiss necessitates

$ab'c' = 0$, and the second premiss necessitates $abc' = 0$. Thus the truth of the premisses involves fulfilment of the truth condition for the conclusion.

Proof of standard argument form 2: $((a \curlywedge b) . (b \rightarrow c)) \rightarrow (a \curlywedge c)$.

		b	b'
a	C	?*	
	C'	?0	
a'	C		
	C'	0	

The truth condition of the premiss $a \curlywedge b$ is $ab \neq 0$; $\therefore$ one of the sub-classes abc or abc' has members. (In the diagram a ? is put in each of these boxes.)

The truth condition of the premiss $b \rightarrow c$ is $bc' = 0$; $\therefore abc' = 0$ and $a'bc' = 0$ since sub-classes of an empty class must also be empty. (In the diagram the ? in box abc' is now replaced by a zero, and the ? in box abc is replaced by an *, since we now know that abc must have members.)

The truth condition required for the conclusion, $a \curlywedge c$, is $ac \neq 0$; this is fulfilled if one of its sub-classes acb or acb' is shown to have members. Actually, we have just seen that in the light of the first premiss, the second one necessitates that abc is not empty.

Aristotelian moods, standard or weakened, in which the premisses are universal and the conclusion is particular, cannot be reduced to either of the standard forms in modern class calculus. This draws our attention once more to the existence of a special postulate in Aristotle's calculus permitting the inference of a particular conclusion from universal premisses—the postulate, namely, that simple classes are never empty and that consequently, particular propositions are simply less extensive statements about their membership than universal propositions.

Simple arguments in the vernacular

First argument:

No successful lawyers are dull	$(a \wedge b)$
P is a successful lawyer	$(P \in a)$
$\therefore$ *P is not dull*	$(P \in b')$

$a = $ the class of successful lawyers; $b = $ the class of dull people. The premisses of the above argument may be represented in a box diagram as follows:

$$
\begin{array}{c|c|c}
 & b & b' \\
\hline
a & O & P \\
\hline
a' & & \\
\end{array}
$$

Since the truth condition of the major premiss is that ab is empty, P (a member of a) must be placed in ab'. The truth condition of the conclusion is indeed that P is a member of b'. Thus the argument is valid—the premisses being true necessitate the truth of the conclusion.

Second argument:

'None of the expenses which John cited in his tax claim were for personal expenses or for depreciation in value of property. Now all other relevant claims are acceptable. Therefore John's claims are acceptable.'

Let $a =$ the class of claims John made

$b =$ the class of claims that are for personal expenses

$c =$ the class of claims that are for depreciation in value of property

$d =$ the class of all other claims relevant to John

$e =$ the class of claims that are acceptable

The argument, fully expressed, may be formalized as follows:

$$(a \wedge (b + c)) . (d \to b'c') . (a \to d) . (d \to e)) \to (a \to e).$$

The truth condition of $a \wedge (b + c)$ is $a(b + c) = 0$

,, ,, ,, ,, $d \to b'c'$ is $dbc = 0$

,, ,, ,, ,, $a \to d$ is $ad' = 0$

,, ,, ,, ,, $d \to e$ is $de' = 0$

The force of this evidence may be represented in a box diagram thus:

			b	b	b'	b'
			d	d'	d	d'
a	C	e	0	0	0	0
a	C	e'	0	0	0	0
a	C'	e	0	0		0
a	C'	e'	0	0	0	0
a'	C	e	0			
a'	C	e'	0		0	
a'	C'	e				
a'	C'	e'	0		0	

The truth condition for the conclusion, $a \to e$, is $ae' = 0$. The class space occupied by ae' is represented in the upper half of the diagram by the two rows of boxes designated e'. The premisses have been diagrammed as filling these boxes with zeros. Thus they are displayed as logically necessitating the truth condition of the conclusion ($ae' = 0$), and the argument has been validated.

VI. Axiomatizing the class calculus—a formalization of the Boole–Schröder Algebra of Classes

Different codifications have been worked out by Whitehead, Huntington (who in 1904 and 1933 published five), Sheffer (whose codification in 1913 remains the most concise and simple perhaps), Lewis and Langford, and Eaton. These codifications have exactly the same content and are consequently equivalent— the same elements, operations and relations are organized under varying sets of primitive terms, definitions and postulates. The formal system presented in this chapter is that of Lewis and Langford; in their *Symbolic Logic* (chapter 2) it is completely and meticulously worked out for about one hundred representative theorems. Only the basic structure and some of the theorems (with commentary) are presented here:

Primitive term. Any term of the system, 'a, b, c, etc.', will represent some class of things, named by some logical term.

'$a \times b$' for the class composed of these things which are members of a and members of b, both.

'$-a$' for the negative of a, for the class of all things which are not members of the class a.

'0' for the unique class 'nothing', the 'null class'.

'$a = b$' for the proposition: the terms a and b have the same extension; the class a and the class b have identically the same members.

Definitions
1.01 $1 = -0$

>   That is, 1 represents the class of all things which are not members of the null class; thus 1 represents 'everything' or 'everything being considered' or 'the universe of discourse'.

1.02 $a + b = -(-a \times -b)$ Def.

>   That is, $a + b$ represents the class of things which are either members of a or members of b (or members of both). Since $-a \times -b$ is the class of what is both not-a and not-b (neither a nor b), the negative of this, $-(-a \times -b)$, will be what is either a or b or both.

1.03 $a \subset b$ is equivalent to $a \times b = a$ Def.

>   This is the relation of class-inclusion: $a \subset b$ represents 'a is contained in b' or 'Every a is also a b'. The class 'both men and mortals' is identical with the class 'men' if and only if all men are mortals.

Postulates

1.1 $a \times a = a$.

What is both *a* and *a*, is identical with *a*. Since this law holds, there are no exponents in this algebra.

1.2 $a \times b = b \times a$.

What is both *a* and *b* is the same as what is both *b* and *a*.

1.3 $a \times (b \times c) = (a \times b) \times c$.

Since this law holds, parentheses in 'products' can be omitted.

1.4 $a \times 0 = 0$.

What is both *a* and nothing, is nothing.

1.5 If $a \times -b = 0$, then $a \subset b$.

If nothing is both *a* and not $-b$, then all *a* is *b*.

1.6 If $a \subset b$ and $a \subset -b$, then $a = 0$.

If all *a* is b and all *a* is not $-b$, then *a* is a class which has no members. All the laws of the algebra can be rigorously deduced from these three definitions and six postulates, given above.

Theorems ($\subset$ signifies class inclusion; the symbol $\times$ is generally omitted, e.g. $a \times b$ is abbreviated to *ab*; in some cases it is replaced by ., e.g. instead of $0 \times a$ the symbolism is $0 \cdot a$)

2.1 If $a = b$, then $ac = bc$ and $ca = cb$.

2.12 If $a = b$, then $a + c = b + c$ and $c + a = c + b$.

These two laws follow immediately from the meaning of the relation $=$.

2.2 $a = b$ is equivalent to the pair, $a \subset b$ and $b \subset a$.

If $a = b$, then by def. 1.1, $ab = aa = a$; and $ba = bb = b$.

But by def. 1.03, $ab = a$ is $a \subset b$; and $ba = b$ is $b \subset a$.

Conversely, if $ab = a$ and $ba = b$, then [1.2]
$$a = ab = ba = b.$$

If two classes are identical, then each is contained in the other; and classes such that each is contained in the other are identical.

2.3 $a \subset a$.

This follows from 2.2, since $a = a$. Every class is contained in itself: 'All *a* is *a*' holds for every *a*.

2.4 $ab \subset a$ and $ab \subset b$.

By 1.1, 1.2 and 1.3, $(ab)a = a(ab) = (aa)b = ab$.

And by 1.03, $(ab)a = ab$ is $ab \subset a$.

What is both *a* and *b*, is contained in *a*, and is contained in *b*.

2.5 $a - a = 0 = -aa$.

By 2.4, $a - a \subset a$, and $a - a \subset -a$.

Hence by 1.6, $a - a = 0$.

This theorem states the Law of Contradiction: Nothing is both *a* and not-*a*.

2.6 $0 \subset a$.

By 1.2 and 1.4, $0 \cdot a = a \cdot 0 = 0$.

But [1.03] $0 \cdot a = 0$ is $0 \subset a$.

Theorem 2.6 states the principle that the null class is contained in every class. This follows from the law, $a \times 0 = 0$, together with the definition of the relation $a \subset b$. It expresses an extensional relationship between the memberships of classes and would not hold if the intension or meaning of classes were taken into consideration.

Some other interesting theorems are:

3.5 $a + -a = 1$.

This is the Law of the Excluded Middle Term: Everything is either a or not-a.

3.6 $-a + b = 1$ is equivalent to $a \subset b$.

'Everything is either not-a or b' is equivalent to 'All a is b'.

The next two principles, concerning the relation $\subset$, are of fundamental importance:

3.7   If $a \subset b$ and $b \subset c$, then $a \subset c$.

[1.03]   If $a \subset b$ and $b \subset c$, then $ab = a$ and $bc = b$.

Hence $ac = (ab)c = a(bc) = ab = a$.

But [1.03] $ac = a$ is $a \subset c$.

If all a is b and all b is c, then all a is c: the relation $\subset$ is transitive.

3.8 $a \subset b$ is equivalent to $-b \subset -a$.

[2.8] $a \subset b$ is equivalent to $a - b = 0$.

[2.9] $a - b = -(-a) \cdot -b = -b \cdot -(-a)$.

And [2.8] $-b \cdot -(-a) = 0$ is equivalent to $-b \subset -a$.

'All a is b' is equivalent to 'All not-b is not-a'. The terms of any relation $\subset$ may be transposed by negating both. This is called the Law of Transposition. These last two laws are the fundamental principles underlying the validity of the syllogism. (From *Symbolic Logic* by C. I. Lewis and C. H. Langford, Dover Publications, Inc., New York, 1959. Reprinted through the permission of the publisher.)

VII. Class calculus specified to a calculus of relations

Whatever the adicity of a relation it may always be expressed as a predication: a dyadic relation is a predication made of an ordered couple, a triadic of an ordered triad, etc. The internal order of the dyad, triad, etc. defines each as a group, i.e. the defining function of each such group or class is a relation. Thus the dyad or triad itself is the relation in extension. The extension of a dyadic relation R is focused when we exhibit it as the class of couples (x, y) such that xRy. Common notation is $R = \hat{x}\hat{y}\,(xRy)$, $S = \hat{w}\hat{z}\,(wSz)$—the circumflex has the force of higher abstraction or generalization, i.e. $R = $ the class of x's and y's such that xRy. This notation is simpler and more suggestive than equivalent notation using dyadic functors, e.g. $R = \hat{x}\hat{y}\,[f(x, y)]$. A triadic relation T is symbolized $T = \hat{x}\hat{y}\hat{z}\,[T(x, y, z)]$, i.e. T is the class of triads (x, y, z) for which the propositional form $T(x, y, z)$ is true.

The symbolism represents, quite definitely, the members of, e.g. a dyad (x, y)

or triad (x, y, z), the relations which constitute them as dyads or triads (R, S, T), and the classes of dyads or triads so constituted (the letters R, S, T are again used here, commonly). Boolean operations can be performed on simple classes of dyads, triads, etc. to generate complex classes and the general laws of class calculus can be seen to hold specifically (or analogically) for these classes. Thus a good deal of any present-day calculus of relations is constructed by simply translating laws of general class calculus into the specific concepts and symbols required by an explicit calculus of relations. Many concepts in the latter are simply adaptations of ones in the general calculus; some are proper.

Sample concepts, postulates and theorems of the class calculus specified to a calculus of relations. *Examples of concepts adapted from the general calculus are*:

'Universal' and 'null': the universal relation (symbolized $\vee$) holds between every two individuals in the universe of discourse; the null relation ($\wedge$) does not hold between any two.

'Inclusion': the relation R is said to be included in the relation S if, for any x and y, xRy implies xSy. Thus 'less than' is included in 'unequal to'—whenever x is less than y, x is unequal to y.

'Identity': R and S are identical relations when they are mutually inclusive: xRy implies xSy; and xSy implies xRy.

'Sum' or 'disjunct': the sum or union of two dyadic relations can be symbolized $x(R + S)y$. Two things x and y form an ordered couple of this class if either xRy or xSy.

'Product' or 'conjunct': the product or intersection of two dyadic relations can be symbolized $x(R \times S)y$. Two things x and y form a dyad of this class if both xRy and xSy. Thus if R denotes fatherhood and S denotes motherhood the relation $x(R \times S)y$ is the null relation, for in no couple can one individual be both father and mother of the other.

'Negate' or 'complement': the negate of a relation R is symbolized R' and holds between two things if, and only if, R does not hold between them: $xR'y \equiv \sim(xRy)$.

The following is a sampling of analogous laws, i.e. expressions in the calculus of relations which are analogues of theorems demonstrated in the calculus of classes. (The symbols 0, 1, +, × have different—but analogous—meanings for relations from their meaning for classes.):

$(x, y)[(x, y) \in 1]$: every couple is a member of the universe of couples or has the universal (dyadic) relation.

$(x, y) \sim [(x, y) \in 0]$: no couple has the null relation.

$R \subset 1$ and $0 \subset R$: every class of couples is included in the universe class of couples and the null class of couples is contained in every class of couples. The latter express an extensional relationship and would not hold if intension or meaning were taken into consideration.

$R \subset S = (x, y)[(xRy) \subset (xSy)]$: the class of couples related by R is contained in the class of couples related by S, means that every (x, y) couple related by R is also related by S.

$(R = S) = (x, y)[(xRy) = (xSy)]$: the expression, the class of couples related by R is coextensive with the class related by S, is equivalent to the expression that every couple related by R is also related by S.

$(R \subset S) = (- S \subset - R)$: if R is contained in S then the negate of S is contained in the negate of R.

$[(R \subset S) \times (S \subset T)] \subset (R \subset T)$: the class of couples such that R is contained in S and S in T is itself included in the class of couples in which R is contained in T. This displays the transitivity of inclusion.

$[(R = S) \times (S = T)] \subset (R = T)$: the class of couples such that R is equivalent to S and S to T is included in the class of couples such that R is equivalent to T. This displays the transitivity of equivalence.

If $(R \times -S) = 0$ then $(R \times S) = R$: if the class of couples related by R and the negate of S is the null class of couples, then the class of couples ordered by R and S is equivalent to the class of couples ordered by R.

$(R \subset S) = [(R \times S) = R]$: the class of couples in which R is contained in S is equivalent to a class which fulfills the condition that $(R \times S) = R$, i.e. that the class of couples ordered by both R and S is coextensive with the class ordered by R.

The following are analogues of the postulates used by Lewis and Langford in formalizing the calculus of classes:

$$(R \times R) = R$$
$$(R \times S) = (S \times R)$$
$$(R \times S) \times T = R \times (S \times T)$$
$$(R \times 0) = 0$$
$$\text{If } (R \times -S) = 0 \text{ then } R \subset S$$
$$\text{If } R \subset S \text{ and } R \subset -S \text{ then } R = 0$$

The analogues of De Morgan's theorems are as follows ($-R$ signifying the class of couples not ordered by the relation R):

$$(R \times S) = -(-R + -S)$$
$$(-R \times S) = -(R + -S)$$
$$(R \times -S) = -(-R + S)$$
$$(-R \times -S) = -(R + S)$$
$$(R + S) = -(-R \times -S)$$
$$(-R + S) = -(R \times -S)$$
$$(R + -S) = -(-R \times S)$$
$$(-R + -S) = -(R \times S)$$

Concepts that are not adapted, by analogy, from the calculus of classes. The following are examples of concepts that are proper to the calculus of relations: (a) 'Identity' and 'diversity' between individuals: these relations have special symbols xIy and xDy respectively. (The symbols $=$ and $\neq$ are pre-empted for identity and diversity between relations or classes.)

(b) A special operation performed on the two relations, R and S, yields a third relation which is called the Relative Product or Composition of R and S, and is symbolized R/S. It is the relation which exists between x and z if and only if there is a y such that xRy and ySz. Thus if R denotes 'husband of' and S denotes 'daughter of', R/S denotes 'son-in-law of', i.e. the relation which exists between the husband (x) and parent (z) of a person (y). This concept is very important in the study of series.

(c) A special operation performed on R yields the converse of R (symbolized $\cup R$). The relation $\cup R$ holds between x and y if, and only if, the relation R holds between y and x.

In the early years of modern mathematical logic, Augustus De Morgan believed that any ultimate formal explanation of the syllogism must be in terms of transitive and convertible relations, and he believed that, for logic generally, a theory of relations was of ultimate and fundamental importance. In the event, modern logic has not grown in accordance with such a vision: it has been more concerned with 'relatives' than with 'relations'; its theories have been constructed as extensions and applications of predicate logic and class calculus; and its concepts, distinctions and laws have their individual values (especially in applied logic) without constituting a section of primary explanatory importance.

MODAL LOGIC AND MANY-VALUED LOGIC

I. Introduction

Standard Logic is, historically, the most developed branch of logic; it operates on the principle that a proposition is either true or false (the Law of Bivalence). However, truth and falsity are actually subject to modes; some propositions must be true, others cannot be true, others again may be actually but not necessarily true or false. In ancient logic these modalities were named *alethic modalities*. Again our knowledge of facts is subject to modalities: we grade our assertions in modes of determinancy from certainly true to certainly false and we quantify these modes in a probability calculus. This evident presence of *alethic* and *epistemic* modalities in human speech and thought has been a motivating force in the development of modal and many-valued logics, i.e. logics which, not being restricted to simple true–false evaluations, are called non-standard.

Modal Logic is concerned with modal statements, e.g. *S* is necessarily *P*; it is impossible that *S* is *P*; *S* may or may not be *P*. It studies the modalities or modal functors—necessity, impossibility, possibility and contingency. Not only does it deal with the meaning of these functors, it endeavours also to formalize their logical features into a system of propositions, a calculus. In many-valued logic propositions are abstracted from their traditional epistemological framework, which simply evaluated truth and falsity; they are conceived as entities which can have three, four ... *n* values, and the objective of many-valued logic is (a) to work out tables or calculi for logics of three, four ... infinite propositional values; and (b) to seek for possible interpretations of these values and useful applications of their calculi.

II. Modal logic

The basic history of its development. Aristotle's pioneer work on modal logic was done, as we shall see, in the context of his syllogistic. Modern work is technically quite different and comparatively recent: it began in 1918 with C. I. Lewis's concern that mathematical logic should extend its primitive language (substantially presented in the *Principia Mathematica*) so as to include a symbol for a stronger form of implication than material implication—such a form indeed as would be free from paradox and could be identified as the implication which governs human argumentation when it is perfect. The definition of material implication (called Philonian because it can be traced back to Philo in the third century B.C. when according to Callimachus even the Greek crows cawed about the nature of conditionals) is such that it makes any conditional automatically true if the antecedent is false or the consequent true:

$$p \supset (q \supset p)$$
$$-p \supset (p \supset q)$$

Lewis suggested the introduction into mathematical logic of the type of implication that holds not merely materially but in strict consequence. He used the symbol ⌐3 and suggested as definitions: 'It is necessary that $(p \supset q)$', or 'it is necessary that $(-p \vee q)$', or 'it is not possible that $(p$ and $-q)$'. The alternative definitions are based on the fact that $p \supset q$ is equivalent to $-p \vee q$ and to $-(p . -q)$.

The relationship defined by Lewis and generally called *strict implication* or *entailment* has paradoxes of its own:

(1) If p cannot be true, it is automatically not possible that $(p . -q)$; thus an impossibility strictly implies any proposition, just as in the case of material implication a simply false proposition (p) materially implies any proposition (q).

(2) If q is necessarily true, then it is strictly implied by any proposition, because it is not possible that $(p . -q)$. This paradox is similar to the one of material implication where a simply true proposition (q) is implied by any proposition (p).

Since Lewis's time various systems of modal logic have been constructed.

Basic concepts and definitions in modal logic. The basic concepts of Modal Logic are necessity, possibility, impossibility and contingency. They are expressed, grammatically, by adverbs, auxiliary verbs and verb phrases, e.g. S is necessarily P; it is necessary that S is P; it is necessarily true that S is P; S must be P; it is bound to be the case that S is P; S is possibly P; it could be that S is P; it is possible that S is P. It is not surprising that there are important metalogical problems in interpreting modal statements: are they to be treated as sentences stating necessary, possible, impossible or contingent facts (the modality being predicated *de re*) or as sentences whose truth or falsity is necessary, possible, impossible, contingent (the modality being predicated *de dicto*)? While recognizing that a modality *de re* and a modality *de dicto* differ in meaning, for the moment the simplest procedure is to interpret modalities as being primarily *de re*, and to regard the necessity, etc. of sentences being true or false as derivative and secondary.

Necessity can be taken as an undefined functor and the remaining modalities be defined in terms of it. In the notation of the Polish School:

'Lp' means 'p is necessary' or 'p is necessarily true'.
'Mp' reads 'p is possible' and is equivalent to $NLNp$.
'Up' reads 'p is impossible' and is equivalent to LNp.

'*Zp*' reads '*p* is contingent' (this latter term coming from Marius Victorinus who used it to translate one of Aristotle's meanings of 'possible'— that which is not necessary and the supposed existence of which implies nothing impossible, i.e. that which is neither necessary nor impossible); it is equivalent to *KNLpNUp*.

Possibility could also be taken as the undefined functor with *Lp* defined as *NMNp*, *Up* as *NMp*, and *Zp* in terms of *Lp* and *Up*.

The basic modal equivalences are:

$$Lp = UNp = NMNp$$
$$LNp = Up = NMp$$
$$NLp = NUNp = MNp$$
$$NLNp = NUp = Mp$$

In the above notation *L*, *M*, *U*, *Z* are modal functors with *p* as their argument, i.e. they signify modalities *de dicto*.

Modal laws in the context of Aristotle's syllogistic and the logic of modal syllogisms. Relations displayed within the traditional Square of Opposition and the operations of conversion, etc. give rise to basic modal laws when *A*, *E*, *I* and *O* propositions are arguments of modal functors. For example, the following are laws of Aristotelian logic:

(a) *Modal laws of sub-alternation*:

CLAabLIab	(Law of Sub-alternation of *LI*—premiss)
CMEabMOab	(„ „ „ „ *MO*—premiss)
CLEabLOab	(„ „ „ „ *LO*—premiss)
CMAabMIab	(„ „ „ „ *MI*—premiss)

(b) *Modal Laws of Conversion*:

CLIabLIba	(Law of conversion of *LI*—premiss)
CMEabMEba	(„ „ „ „ *ME*—premiss)
CLEabLEba	(„ „ „ „ *LE*—premiss)
CMIabMIba	(„ „ „ „ *MI*—premiss)
CLAabLIba	(„ „ „ „ *LA*—premiss)
CMAabMIba	(„ „ „ „ *MA*—premiss)

(c) *Laws of Modal Subordination*:

CLAabAab
CLIabIab
CLOabOab
CLEabEab
COabMOab
CEabMEab
CAabMAab
CIabMIab

It would be easy to derive further relations from these, e.g.

> *CNAabNLAab*
> *CNIabNLIab*
> *CNOabNLOab*
> *CIabMIba*
> *CNMIabNIab*

With regard to Aristotle's theory of the syllogism it is not easy to formalize the extension of it to modal propositions and the consistency of Aristotle's own ideas is controverted. In a modal proposition, one at least of the constituent propositions is modal (symbolized *L*, *M*, *U*, *Z* according to the mode it expresses). Since the propositions may also differ in quantity and quality (i.e. be *A*, *E*, *I* or *O*) the number of possible combinations is very great indeed. Thus using *X* to symbolize a categorical proposition and restricting ourselves to *L* and *M* modals, it is clear that there are 27 different general forms of the *L—X—M syllogism*:

> *LLL, LLX, LXL, XLL, LXX, XLX, XXL, XXX,*
> *LLM, LML, MLL, LMM, MLM, MML, MMM,*
> *XXM, XMX, MXX, XMM, MXM, MMX,*
> *LXM, XLM, LMX, MLX, XML, MXL.*

Within each of these modal arrangements propositions can be further varied in quantity and quality. Sifting out the valid moods is made difficult not only by the number of combinations to be considered but also by the problems associated with particular combinations. In his *Aristotle's Modal Syllogisms*, Storrs McCall arrives at the figure 333 for the total number of valid *L—X—M* moods; extending the range of modal propositions to include the contingent type, he arrived at 464 further valid moods—a grand total of 797. In the Middle Ages, Ockham visualized syllogisms in which the mode of one premiss was *de re* and of the other *de dicto*—the number of valid moods in his whole modal syllogistic was about a thousand. (cf. Bochenski's *A History of Formal Logic*, pp. 229–30)

Jan Lukasiewicz was the first to organize modal syllogisms into a complete deductive system. His system was published in 1953; while 'built up upon Aristotle's ideas' it did not attempt to reproduce his modal syllogistic as Lukasiewicz felt that 'in contrast to the assertoric syllogistic which is perfectly clear and nearly free of errors, Aristotle's modal syllogistic is almost incomprehensible because of its many faults and inconsistencies'. (*Aristotle's Syllogistic*, p. 133) As a contrast Storrs McCall presents a formalized system which he believes agrees with Aristotle's at all important points, the agreement being complete with regard to the apodeictic or necessary moods. Nicolas Rescher, however, believes that Aristotle's doctrine does not admit of complete formalization.

Aristotle's own treatment demonstrates the difficulty one may encounter in finding an adequate formal proof of modal moods. In the *Prior Analytics* (his treatment covers chapters 3 and 8–22) he maintains that when there are two necessary premisses, a necessary conclusion follows in exactly those cases in which an assertoric conclusion follows from two assertoric premisses. An example is the first-figure mood with universal affirmative premisses: If all *B* is necessarily *A* and if all *C* is necessarily *B*, then all *C* is necessarily *A*. (This is known as Barbara *LLL*.) Aristotle says: 'There is hardly any difference between syllogisms from necessary premisses and syllogisms from premisses which merely assert. When the terms are put in the same way, whether something belongs or necessarily belongs (or does not belong) to something else, a syllogism will or will not result alike in both cases, the only difference being the addition of the expression "necessarily" to the terms.' (ch. 8, 29b36–30a1 in the Oxford translation) Turning to moods with one necessary and one categorical premiss (chapters 9–11) he holds that a necessary conclusion is valid in the case of Barbara *LXL*: If all *B* is necessarily *A*, and if all *C* is *B*, then all *C* is necessarily *A*. However, a necessary conclusion is not valid in the case of Barbara *XLL*: If all *B* is *A* and if all *C* is necessarily *B*, then all *C* is necessarily *A*.

Since the time of Theophrastus who held that a valid conclusion must always follow the weaker premiss (the order of strength being: necessary, assertoric, possible), Barbara *LXL* and *XLL* have occasioned controversy both as to their validity and as to the cogency of Aristotle's arguments for his rule that in the first figure an apodeictic major and an assertoric minor may yield an apodeictic conclusion, while an assertoric major and an apodeictic minor cannot. Lukasiewicz says: 'The controversy shown by the example of the mood Barbara can be extended to all other moods of this kind.' (*Aristotle's Syllogistic*, p. 188) He believes that Aristotle is wrong in rejecting Barbara *XLL* as invalid and, of course, that Theophrastus is doubly wrong in rejecting both Barbara's.

Modern systems of modal logic. Well-known systems are:

System T: constructed essentially by Kurt Gödel, subsequently named *T* by Robert Feys. It uses *L* as the undefined modal operator (for necessity) along with the language of propositional logic. The definitions for strict entailment and equivalence are:

$$p \dashv q \equiv \text{Df } L(p \to q)$$
$$p \equiv q \equiv \text{Df } (p \dashv q) \cdot (q \dashv p)$$

Its axioms are:
1. $(p \lor p) \to p$
2. $q \to (p \lor q)$
3. $(p \lor q) \to (q \lor p)$
4. $(q \to r) \to ((p \lor q) \to (p \lor r))$
5. $Lp = p$ (axiom of necessity)
6. $L(p \to q) \to (Lp \to Lq)$

There is a special transformation rule, called the rule of necessitation: If *p* is a thesis, then *Lp* is a thesis, i.e. $(\vdash p) \rightarrow (\vdash Lp)$. The basis of this rule is that a thesis being either an axiom or a theorem has a complete guarantee within the system, i.e. the system as such necessitates it.

Systems S1, S2, S3, S4, S5, S6, S7, S8: These were alternative systems constructed by C. I. Lewis. *S*1 and *S*2 are weaker than *T*; *S*4 and *S*5 are stronger; the rest have laws that *T* does not establish and *T* has laws which they do not have.

Using possibility as the undefined modal functor, defining strict implication $(p \dashv q)$ as $-M(p \,. -q)$, and using a set of six axioms each of which expresses a relationship of strict implication, *S*1 derives among its theorems a set of laws from which the whole of Propositional Calculus can be deduced and it derives also the rule of detachment for material implication. Thus *S*1 contains Propositional Calculus.

*S*4 and *S*5 formalize iterated modalities. *S*4 adds to the six axioms of System *T* the axiom, $Lp \rightarrow LLp$ (necessarily *p* is the case materially implies that it is necessary that necessarily *p* is the case). *S*5 adds a different axiom, namely $Mp \rightarrow LMp$ (possibly *p* is the case materially implies that it is necessary that possibly *p* is the case). Since $Lp \rightarrow LLp$ can be proved as a theorem in *S*5, it follows that *S*5 includes *S*4. Some examples of theorems in these systems are:

$$Mp \leftrightarrow MMp$$
$$Lp \equiv LLp$$
$$MLMp \rightarrow Mp$$
$$LMp \leftrightarrow LMLMp$$
$$MLp \equiv MLMLp$$

The operators, $\leftrightarrow$ (biconditional) and $\equiv$ (equivalence), have the same truth conditions.

System M: Constructed by G. H. von Wright and, like Lewis's systems, using *M* as the undefined modal operator, this system is equivalent to *T*.

Systems which include quantifiers and/or postulates about identity: Since the 1940s these more extended systems have been evolving seeking to combine modal logic with quantification theory and the theory of identity. W. V. Quine does not believe that these efforts can have any valid outcome—the formal conditions and meanings of necessity and concrete individual existence have too little in common. The main work has been done by Ruth Barcan Marcus, A. N. Prior, R. A. Bull, S. A. Kripke and Jaakko Hintikka.

Modern modal logic has revived the medieval and Peircean conception of material implication as a limiting case of strict implication: actual states of affairs (the domain of material implication) are a boundary for possible states of affairs (over the entire range of which strict implication operates). Further since modal language is strongly linked with our language of past, present and future time (the impossible, e.g. is that which can never be, the possible that which may have been in the past or may be in the future), modern modal logic has developed an interest in formalizing the conditions and laws which govern tense. For Prior, tense-logic is a genuine modal system: 'if we define *M* (or "Possibly") as "It either is or will be the case that", and *L* (or "Necessarily") as "It is and always will be the case that", these operators will meet Lukasiewicz's conditions for being modal operators and, furthermore, will have all the formal properties of the *M* and *L* of the Lewis system *S*4. "Possibly" and "Necessarily" were used in this sense by the Megarian logician Diodorus, and I have pointed out the resemblance between Diodoran modal logic and *S*4 . . . .' (*Time and Modality*, p. 12)

III. Many-valued logic

The basic history of its development. In Greek and medieval times there was speculation as to whether there might be more than two truth values. This was bound up with philosophical problems posed by propositions which refer to future contingent events. Aristotle speculated on the possibility of some propositions having a neuter value, e.g. on the proposition 'there will be a sea-battle tomorrow' being neither true nor false now (chapter 9 of *On Interpretation*). Many commentators interpret Aristotle as holding that the Principle of Bivalence (*tertium non datur*) does not govern such propositions. It is clear, on the other hand, that Stoic logicians such as Chrysippus, being determinists, insisted on the absolute validity of this principle; for this reason Lukasiewicz referred to systems which do not use a Law of Excluded Middle as non-Chrysippian systems where earlier writers referred to them as non-Aristotelian ones. In medieval times the possibility of a third truth-value had a significant place in debates on the extent of God's foreknowledge. Various logicians, especially Duns Scotus and William of Occam, relied on Aristotle's treatise in arguing for the need of a third, neuter, truth-value to express a truth indeterminancy of future contingent events.

In modern times, the Scot logician Hugh MacColl (1837–1909) constructed a 'logic of three dimensions' in deference to the reality of probabilistic modalities. Every proposition was the bearer of one of three possible values: certainty (necessity), impossibility and variability (contingency). In effect he anticipated the interest of the 1930s in using many-valued logic to formalize probability theory.

By 1909, Charles Sanders Peirce (1839–1914) had achieved a definite conception of a three-valued logic to which the truth-table method would be extended and he had considered some of the special three-valued operators which were later developed by Lukasiewicz, Post, Slupecki, Bochvar and Kleene. In a letter to William James he wrote (1909):

> I have long felt that it is a serious defect in existing logic that it takes no heed of the limit between two realms. I do not say that the Principle of Excluded Middle is downright *false*; but I *do* say that in every field of

thought whatsoever there is an intermediate ground between *positive assertion* and *positive negation* which is just as Real as they. Mathematicians aways recognize this, and seek for that limit as the presumable lair of powerful concepts; while metaphysicians and old-fashioned logicians—the sheep and goat separators—never recognize this. The recognition does not involve any denial of existing logic, but it involves a great addition to it.

The Russian logician, Nikolai A. Vasil'ev (1880–1940) was writing on 'imaginary non-Aristotelian logics' in the 1910s. In his view all Aristotelian systems of logic include principles which are grounded in the laws of the world in which we live. When any of these principles is eliminated we have an 'imaginary logic'; such a logic could visualize any object as having the predicate A, or the negation of this predicate, non-A, or both A and non-A, where the law of excluded middle would allow only two possibilities. The logic of the imaginary world would be three-valued. Vasil'ev, however, did not develop any logical system.

Neither did the American, Edwin Guthrie, who wrote in 1916:

Not only can logic include more than the logic of Aristotle, as the modern logistic does, there might have been non-Aristotelian logics with principles different from the familiar laws of contradiction and excluded middle. What final authority would judge between the ultimate 'correctness' of Aristotle's logic which offers two contradictories, obeying the laws: $x \cdot x' = 0$, $x + x' = 1$, $(x')' = x$, and a logic which would provide three contradictories, obeying the laws: $x \cdot x' \cdot x'' = 0$, $x + x' + x'' = 1$, $(x')' = x''$, $(x'')' = x$? It is true that we can only discuss other logics in terms of one logic, but this is no more a proof that they are therefore unreal than is the fact that an Englishman in discussing German must use English, a proof that English is the *a priori* conditon of communication, valid for all times and all places.

It was the ancient philosophical discussion about propositions concerning the future which stimulated Jan Lukasiewicz. At a meeting of the Polish Philosophical Society held at Lwów in June 1920 he delivered a paper entitled 'On three-valued logic'. He indicated how principles concerning two-values could be supplemented by principles concerning a third value, and he concluded, firstly, that three-valued logic has great theoretical significance in being the first attempt to create a non-Aristotelian logic, and that its practical significance, if any, would depend on the acceptability of an indeterministic view of the world, this being the metaphysical basis of the new logic. In later papers he formalized his three-valued system in detail, generalizing it to the many-valued case and even to the infinite-valued case. In 1931 Mordchaj Wajsberg succeeded in giving L_3 (Lukasiewicz's three-valued system) an elegant axiomatic format—through a set of four axioms together with the rules of inference: modus ponens and substitution.

Independently of Lukasiewicz, the American Emil Leon Post presented a generalization of m-valued truth-tables as part of a doctoral dissertation, for

Columbia University, on a general theory of elementary propositions (completed in 1920, the dissertation was published in 1921). In contrast with Lukasiewicz, Post's interest was almost exclusively mathematical and in the introduction to his paper he notes that this non-Aristotelian logic 'seems to have the same relation to ordinary logic that geometry in a space of an arbitary number of dimensions has to the geometry of Euclid.' Post's treatment was more generalized than Lukasiewicz's in 1920 (he dealt with *n*-values and allowed for an arbitrary number of designated—truth-like—truth values) but he did not produce any further development of his work.

In the past fifty years many-valued logic has become an important branch of logic. The literature on it is very extensive indeed, covering not only developments of the Lukasiewiczian systems by logicians of the Polish school (such as Mordchaj Wajsberg, Jerzy Slupecki, Alfred Tarski, Boleslaw Sobocinski) but also fundamentally new systems such as those of D. A. Bochvar, Stephen C. Kleene, Kurt Gödel and Hans Reichenbach. A good deal of attention has been given to the special operators in many-valued logic above all to its negator (which is not governed by a *tertium non datur* principle); also to adapting quantification theory to it and to systematizing it both on an axiomatic and on a natural-deduction basis. It has been used to formalize modal logic, to provide a logical groundwork for mathematical intuitionism (which does not accept the *tertium non datur* principle), to analyse paradoxes and to formalize probability theory.

Of course it has remained associated with philosophical questions about future contingent events, and recent literature has provided 'tense logics' (from e.g. A. N. Prior) i.e. logical systems in which tense plays an important part in determining the truth-value of propositions. In Physics, quantum theory has presented its need for a logic of indeterminancy and three-valued logic has been applied to this context of indeterminancy situations. Very concretely, many-valued logics are used for the formal analysis of electronic circuitry and for the formalization of switching theory.

Nicholas Rescher points out: 'Many-valued logic is a very new subject whose original development in effect goes back only a single generation . . . It is built up by a great mass of often rather isolated findings resulting from the work of a diverse group of contributors approaching the subject from many different directions. All this makes the task of integration . . . a particularly urgent one.' (*Many-Valued Logic*, p. 15)

Basic observations about values, operators, proofs and theorems in many-valued systems. *Values.* In standard logic the calculation of the truth-value of propositions is a central operation; in the calculi it uses, the range of values assignable to propositional variables is restricted to two, truth and falsity. Many-valued calculi can have a range of values from three to infinity. It is a matter for metalogic (*infra*) to deal with the logical significance of such calculi, i.e. whether or not they can be an integral part of *logical* evaluation. Certainly many of them have been constructed with a built-in semantical interpretation that links them in some way to a general enquiry into truth. Technically, too, many-valued truth-tables, very useful for showing that some formula is not derivable from certain axioms, are used in independence proofs (one axiom being 'independent' of the rest when it cannot be derived from them) and in consistency proofs (it is not the case that every formula is a theorem, p and not-p).

A many-valued system is said to be *normal* when the matrices of two-valued logic extend into it, i.e. for all 0, 1 combinations of values (or the symbolic equivalent) the matrices are the same. The simple three-valued system constructed by Lukasiewicz in 1917 is an extension of the *C–N* tables in two-valued logic. Its primitive symbols are *C*, *N*; all other expressions can be reduced to *C–N* type ones and can be evaluated by the matrix tables for *C* and *N*. The tables are as follows ($1, \frac{1}{2}, 0$, symbolizing the three vaues possible):

pq		Cpq
1	1	1
1	$\frac{1}{2}$	$\frac{1}{2}$
1	0	0
$\frac{1}{2}$	1	1
$\frac{1}{2}$	$\frac{1}{2}$	1
$\frac{1}{2}$	0	$\frac{1}{2}$
0	1	1
0	$\frac{1}{2}$	1
0	0	1

p	Np
1	0
$\frac{1}{2}$	$\frac{1}{2}$
0	1

Lukasiewicz justifies the extra evaluations made as being 'very intuitive'. Since the extremes $C\ 0\ 1$ and $C\ 0\ 0$ have the value 1, it is evident that the intermediate $C\ 0\ \frac{1}{2}$ should be given the same value; as long as q is not less in value than p (as happens in $C\ 1\ 0$) the table gives Cpq the value 1—thus $C\ \frac{1}{2}\ 1$ and $C\ \frac{1}{2}\ \frac{1}{2} = 1$; finally $C\ 1\ \frac{1}{2}$ and $C\ \frac{1}{2}\ 0$ are given the intermediate value $\frac{1}{2}$ between the extremes $C\ 1\ 0$ and $C\ 0\ 0$. In the N table, $N\frac{1}{2}$ has also an intermediate value.

The tables for C and N constitute a matrix. All expressions in Lukasiewicz's system can be reduced to a *C–N* form and can be evaluated by applying these tables. Thus *Apq* is defined as *CCpqq* and *Kpq* is reduced to *NANpNq*. In 1931, Lukasiewicz's student, Mordchaj Wajsberg, axiomatized the system on the basis of the following axioms:

$$CpCqp$$
$$CCpqCCqrCpr$$
$$CCNpNqCqp$$
$$CCCpNppp$$

While every sentence of this three-valued logic is also a sentence of two-valued logic, the converse does not hold. Indeed neither *ApNp* (the law of excluded middle) nor *NKpNp* (the law of contradiction) have the value 1: both are evaluated $\frac{1}{2}$, and thus three-valued logic lacks a law of excluded middle and a law of contradiction. However, no laws of two-valued logic have ever the value 0 in the Lukasiewicz system and many have the value 1. In summary, this three-valued logic is a proper part of two-valued logic: internally consistent and distinct its theses are contained within the other simpler and more extensive logic.

In two-valued logic we are primarily interested in wff's which always have the value 1 no matter what values are assigned to the variables. The set of such wff's is called the *designated* set (1 being the designated value). In many-valued logics, where 0 and 1 are the value limits, 1 is frequently taken as the designated value (and the term, *designated value*, takes on the force of truth-like value). Accordingly, the designated set of wff's contains those wff's which have the value 1 for any and every value assigned to the variables. Since the range of values is greater than two, it follows that while all theorems of many-valued logic are theorems of two-valued logic (they preserve the value 1 over a greater range of values for the variables) the converse does not hold (what holds within a framework of two values for the variables may not hold in a framework of many values). Thus many-valued systems assess fewer arguments as correct than do two-valued ones. This makes it worth while to entertain the possibility that these systems may provide a better grammar of correctness of argument than a two-valued one with its paradoxes of material implication.

It is interesting to note that Stanislaw Jaskowski devised a technique for extending any *n*-valued logic into an $(n + 1)$-valued one. He also devised a way of forming a new many-valued system from any two other systems that have more than one value—the Cartesian product of the two.

The family of Lukasiewicz—Tarski calculi have a good variety of formal systems with {1} as designated set.

Operators: In standard calculi one has basic operators and later one introduces other operators defining the latter in terms of the former. Thus in the *C–N* calculus one introduces *A* and *K* through the definitions

$$Apq = \text{Df. } CNpq$$
$$Kpq = \text{Df. } NCpNq$$

These definitions would not be suitable for introducing *A* and *K* into a *C–N* calculus that was many-valued as the properties of *A* and *K* which are provable in the two-valued calculus cannot be totally preserved in the many-valued one. Thus we must choose and stipulate, from the sum of requirements which 'disjunction' and 'conjunction' meet in standard logic; otherwise our many-valued operators will have no relevance at all to disjunction and conjunction. In Lukasiewiczian systems it is customary to retain the intuitive properties that the value of a disjunction be the maximum value of its disjuncts $(A10 = 1)$ and the value of a conjunction should be the minimum value of its conjuncts $(K10 = 0)$. Suitable definitions for this purpose are:

$$Apq = \text{Df. } CCpqq$$
$$Kpq = \text{Df. } NANpNq$$

Thus we see there is room for variety of definition in introducing many-valued operators that are analogues of two-valued ones.

The negation operator is particularly interesting. In two-valued logic where a designated wff has the value 1 and an undesignated wff has the value 0, the negation of a designated wff is an undesignated wff and vice versa. Taking L_3 (Lukasiewicz's simple three-valued system) we notice that while the negation of a designated (1) wff is undesignated (0), the converse does not hold: $\frac{1}{2}$ is also an undesignated value and the value of Np where $p = \frac{1}{2}$ is itself $\frac{1}{2}$. Thus this three-valued analogue does not meet the stringent requirements of two-valued N. In order to have a negative function, $\bar{p}$, which would reverse the designated or undesignated value of p, Rosser and Turquette introduced J-functions. Taking two-valued negation as primitive, one can introduce the J-functions defining them in terms of it and C and then introduce the new negative function defining it in terms of J-functions.

Thus in many-valued logic, various types of negation are possible according to the kind and number of properties we choose to stipulate. In his systems, Post stipulates for the negator that it make a cyclic shift in the values as the following table shows:

p	not-p
1	2
2	3
3	4
.	.
.	.
.	.
$m-2$	$m-1$
$m-1$	m
m	1

This of course is a radical departure from standard negation.

It is evident that the number of functors possible is considerably greater than in two-valued logic. The number of n-adic truth functors in a logic of m values is $^nm^m$. Thus while only 4 monadic functors are possible in a two-value logic, 27 are possible in a three-valued one and 256 in a four-valued one; the respective figures for dyadic functors are very disparate: 16; 19,683; and 4,294,967,296. In spite of this kind of complexity Lukasiewicz and others have studied infinitely-valued logic which admits an infinity of values instead of just three or four.

Quantification may also feature of course in many-valued systems.

Proof: In two-value logic, the rule of inference, *modus ponens*, is central in proof and meets the two following conditions:

(1) whenever p has the value 1 and Cpq has the value 1 then q has the value 1;
(2) whenever p and Cpq are tautologies, q is a tautology. In many-valued logic

the second condition may be met in circumstances in which the first condition is not met. (In Lukasiewicz's three-valued system, if 1 and $\frac{1}{2}$ are both designated values then $C\frac{1}{2}0$ has the designated value $\frac{1}{2}$ even though q has the value 0.) Thus *modus ponens* is defined precisely there as a rule of inference governing a movement from tautologies to tautology. Of course the fact that it guarantees the tautologous nature of a conclusion that is derived, by it, from tautologies justifies it as a genuine rule of inference.

Again, turning from the axiomatic approach to that of natural deduction, one finds that not all of the primitive logical argument forms hold in a many-valued framework. For instance, due to the fact that $CCpCpqCpq$ is not a theorem in Lukasiewicz's three-value system, we cannot use the argument form: If $p \vdash q$ then $\vdash Cpq$.

Theorems: It is clear that the Principle of Bivalence (the *tertium non datur* principle) cannot be a theorem in many-valued logic. Other versions of the Law of Excluded Middle may be preserved at will, however, as may various possible versions of the Law of Contradiction. The literature includes much precise discussion on possible formulations of these laws.

Examples of theorems in two-valued logic which do not hold in Lukasiewicz's simple three-valued system are:

$$CCNppp$$
$$CCpNpNp$$
$$CCpqCCpNqNp$$
$$CCpKqNqNp$$
$$CCpEqNqNp$$

Theorems may be characterized as such on the basis of truth-table procedure (this is called the matrix-characterization of theorems), or on the basis of being derived either axiomatically or by natural deduction. While the theorems of modal calculi are usually derived by the axiomatic method, those of many-valued calculi are more usually developed by the use of matrix truth-tables. Wajsberg has shown that the systems of Lukasiewicz are finitely axiomatizable, and very elegant axiomatic systems have been constructed. Completeness proofs have been provided by Wajsberg and by Rosser-Turquette.

The main systems of many-valued logic. Nicholas Rescher's book *Many-Valued Logic* provides an excellent survey of these systems and of the literature that has grown up about them. They are:

(a) *The Lukasiewiczian family*
This includes both finite and infinite systems. There are also systems which are radically different from this family and yet are generalizations of Lukasiewicz's three-valued system.

(b) *The three-valued system of Bochnar*
This was published by the Russian logician, D. A. Bochnar in 1939, and

interprets the third value as 'undecidable' (because of being paradoxical or meaningless). Some infinitely-valued systems are based on the guiding principles of this system.

(c) *The three-valued systems of Kleene*

S. C. Kleene's work was published in 1938. His approach is similar to Bochvar's as he interprets the third value in a knowledge-related way as denoting the unknown.

(d) *Other three-valued systems*

These include Reichenbach's Quantum Logic (1946); Slupecki's system (1946) completely axiomatized and with a proof of its truth-functional completeness; Sobocinski's system (1952) also axiomatized.

(e) *The Gödelian family of many-valued systems*

These were the work of Kurt Gödel (published in 1932).

(f) *'Standard systems' of many-valued logic*

These seek to generalize into a many-valued framework a sequence of rules derived from orthodox two-valued logic. They may be symbolized $S_3, S_4 \ldots S_n$ (*n* indicating the number of values involved).

(g) *The Postian family of many-valued systems*

These were the work of Emil L. Post (1921).

(h) *Stanislaw Jaskowski's systems*

These include systems based on his technique for extending any given *n* valued logic into an (*n* + 1)-valued logic, and those based on his method of forming the product of two pluri-valued systems (1936).

(i) *Boolean systems*

These product systems are due mainly to Church (1953) and are based on an *alternative possible worlds* approach with propositions having truth-values with respect to each world.

(j) *Quasi-truth-functional systems*

These systems need not have a single value entry in each place: they permit in any place an alternative indicating entry, e.g. '*T, F*' meaning: 'the truth-value at issue here may be *T* or it may be *F*'.

(k) *Probability logic*

This is a non-truth functional approach assigning likelihood values or probabilities to statements. The development of such systems was begun in the 1930s by Hans Reichenbach and Zygmunt Zawirski. Values are symbolized by the real numbers from 0 to 1 inclusive; it is stipulated that 1 is a designated value thus ensuring the incorporation into the system of the tautologies of two-valued propositional logic. Further designation is left open.

Chapter 9

THE HISTORY OF FORMAL LOGIC:
A SURVEY OF CREATIVE PERIODS

I. Introduction

Formal Logic begins with Aristotle (384–322 B.C.). At the end of an early work on argumentation he points out that his approach is distinctive and original: 'Of this inquiry . . . it was not the case that part of the work had been thoroughly done before, while part had not. Nothing existed at all ... on the subject of Rhetoric there exists much that has been said long ago, whereas on the subject of reasoning we had nothing else of an earlier date to speak of at all, but were kept at work for a long time in experimental researches.' (*De Sophisticis Elenchis*: 183b, 35; 184b, 1) However, it was possible for Aristotle to found the science of Formal Logic mainly because the Greek people were excellent practitioners of logic, highly skilled in analysis, the organization of knowledge and the strategies of argumentation, and interested also in the syntax and semantics of language. Important also were the Platonic concept of universally necessary laws, the Platonic correspondence theory of truth and the demand, in Greek philosophy, for positive proof rather than negative dialectic.

  'Since logic is not simply valid argument but the reflection upon principles of validity, it will arise naturally only when there is already a considerable body of inferential or argumentative material to hand. Not every type of discourse provokes logical inquiry. Pure story-telling or literary discourse, for example, does not provide a sufficient amount of argumentative material. It is those types of discourse or enquiry in which *proof* is sought or demanded that naturally give rise to logical investigation; for to prove a proposition is to infer it validly from true premises. The conditions of proof are two: true premises, or starting points, and valid arguments. It is not easy to tell how soon it was realized that the two conditions are independent, but this was perfectly clear to Aristotle when he drew the distinction between apodeictic and dialectical reasoning [reasoning respectively from what is known to be true and from what is not known to be true] in the *Topics* and again in the *Prior Analytics*.' (*The Development of Logic*, by Kneale, p.1)

II. Aristotelian logic

Focusing inference as such rather than the varied values of the particular premises used, Aristotle consciously looked for basic relationships of dependence that would guarantee the validity of conclusions and thus he originated the idea of a formal logic where truths are independent of subject-matter. Technically, through his use of variables and his sensitivity to logical syntax, he isolated many logical structures or forms and contributed important observations. He axiomatized his logical discoveries although he did not use the method of formalism or distinguish between laws and rules. No contribution to the science of Formal Logic is really comparable to Aristotle's.

His logical works, collectively called the *Organon* (*instrument* or science), are the *Categories*, the *Topics* with its appendix *De Sophisticis Elenchis*, *De Interpretatione*, the *Prior Analytics* and the *Posterior Analytics*. The Organon covers Formal Logic, Metalogic and the logic of science; and in Formal Logic it contains not only Aristotle's major contribution but also a number of laws, rules and observations dealing with areas where development was later—the logic of classes, the theory of identity, the hypothetical syllogistic, the theory of relations, propositional logic and many-valued logic. There are very few questions completely untouched by him. However his major contributions in Formal Logic were to *Syllogistic Logic* and *Modal Logic*. With no more than a simple notation, consisting of a few Greek letters, he made direct, logical observations of methods of proof, classifying them as inductive and deductive; he formulated a complete axiomatized theory of the assertoric syllogism (having as its sub-structure a theory of the functioning of terms, the structure of predicative statements and the laws of opposition both between terms and between sentences—the latter presupposing his theory of quantification) and he made a major contribution to modal logic.

The explicit presentation of the Aristotelian system is to be found in the *De Interpretatione* (in which the formal study of opposition is central) and the *Prior Analytics* (whose theme is the syllogism). In this latter (and principal) work, logical technique makes an enormous advance with the appearance of term-variables (Aristotle simply uses letters as variables); indeed in one passage, formulating what we know now as the principle of contraposition, Aristotle uses propositional variables: 'First then that it is not possible to draw a false conclusion from true premises, is made clear by this consideration. If it is necessary that *B* should be when *A* is, it is necessary that *A* should not be when *B* is not. If then *A* is true, *B* must be true: otherwise it will turn out that the same thing both is and is not at the same time. But this is impossible.' (*Prior Analytics*, Book II, 2, 53^{b}12; Oxford translation) The early work, the *Topics*, is also of great interest to the historian of Formal Logic although ostensibly it is simply a practical handbook on argumentation. For the theory of the predicables (which gives unity to the treatise) is developed from distinctions between necessary and non-necessary predication and between convertible and non-convertible predication; these distinctions suggested many forms of valid argument to Aristotle in the *Topics* and, indeed, in approach and observation this work may be described as a rudimentary form of his system. Centuries later it contributed to the development of the medieval theory of *consequentiae*.

The remaining parts of the *Organon* are the *Categories* (a metaphysical treatise really; its inclusion by the compilers of the *Organon* was unfortunate for the history of formal logic), and the *Posterior Analytics* (a study, in applied logic, of scientific investigation and reasoning).

III. Megarian–Stoic logic

Aristotelian logic continued institutionally, as a school, but uncreatively. New work in logic begun by contemporaries of Aristotle in Megara and developed by the Stoics is the next creative contribution. Even the indirect and fragmentary knowledge we have of this pre-Christian Greek school shows how important it is in the history of all sections of logic. In Formal Logic, it developed propositional logic, making an explicit study of the functors—implication, disjunction, conjunction, equivalence (using not letters but ordinal numbers as propositional variables—an important help in identifying Stoic texts). It distinguished various types of implication and the Megarian, Philo, formally worked out the matrix (truth-table) for our material (their Philonian) implication, the idea of truth-functional dependence being obviously quite clear to Philo. The logic of this school was worked out formalistically and was presented not as a body of laws but as a body of rules of inference schemata—a natural deduction system. The preference for this technique probably stems from the fact that the study of conditional propositions was central in this logic. While there is no complication in expressing a principle of syllogistic in the form of a conditional proposition: If *MaP* and if *SaM*, then *SaP* (this being a statement of what is so, a law), it is easier when dealing with material that is already conditional to list skeleton arguments (formats or schemata) and to say of each whether it is valid or not (this being a statement of what is permitted in one's system, a rule).

It is not possible to distinguish the contributions of the various members of this school (the Megarians, Eubulides, Diodorus Cronus, Philo; the Stoic, Chrysippus). But the Stoic, Chrysippus, seems to be the most important; indeed it was said 'If there were dialectic among the gods, it would be none other than that of Chrysippus.' He practised the *ars combinatoria* working at the number of complex propositions that could be constructed from simple ones. And he seems to have constructed a natural deduction system, with about five inference schemata as basic (indemonstrable) moods and a vast number of theorems. Details of the proofs of two of these theorems are given by Sextus Empiricus.

It is clear that this school developed very systematically the primary section of formal logic—propositional logic. In its work on Modal Logic it had a great advantage over Aristotle. Although in his analysis of modal statements, modal words modify the whole statement to which they are attached, he used his syllogistic as a basis for his investigation of modal reasoning. The Megarian–Stoic school made this investigation from the correct basis of propositional logic, their logic of unanalysed propositions. Unfortunately, only fragments of their work and discussions are extant.

It is quite possible that the hostility between this school and the Aristotelian school arose from claims that their logic was more fundamental than Aristotle's. Certainly, in ancient times the two logics were treated as alternatives, and their complementary character remained unappreciated.

Creative work in logic finished with the Stoic, Chrysippus of Soli (*c.* 279–206 B.C.). From then until the fall of the Roman Empire the literature of logic consists of general handbooks and of commentaries on Aristotle. Galen (A.D. 129–*c.* 199) is one of the best logicians of the period; Alexander of Aphrodisias (*c.* A.D. 200), one of the best commentators on Aristotle, made explicit the distinction between form and matter. The last Roman logician, Boethius (*c.* 480–524) is very important because his works were a primary source of Greek logic for the Middle Ages.

IV. Medieval logic

Since the 1930s it is an accepted fact that in the strictest contemporary sense of *Formal Logic, Metalogic* and *Philosophy of Logic* the medieval period is most important and creative. The research that made this clear and established the shallowness of previous historical accounts of the period, however, confronted historians with a mass of unedited material from the twelfth and later centuries. Thus our survey must begin by noting, with Bochenski, that 'at the present time much less is known about the history of scholastic than of ancient logic ... the present state of research permits no general survey of the sources, growth and details of scholastic logic ... [even] with regard to the list of logicians we hardly ever know whether a logician was original or only a copyist.' (*A History of Formal Logic*: pp. 148–9)

There is satisfactory evidence for the following general observations:

1. The period from 1150 to 1300 is a rich, creative one in logic; from then until the end of the Middle Ages may be described as a period of organisation and elaboration. Peter Abelard (1079–1142) exercised a major influence in the development of this period. Apart from transmitting familiar Aristotelian logic, he discussed and contributed in practically all the areas that were subsequently developed. It is only since the text of his *Dialectica* was printed in full, in 1956, that the magnitude and importance of his work was properly established. The following are some of the medieval logicians:

> Albert the Great (1193–1280)
> Robert Kilwardby (died 1279)
> William of Shyreswood (died 1249)
> Peter of Spain (died 1277) (The best known Scholastic textbook in the later middle ages was his *Summulae Logicales*)
> William of Occam (died 1349/50)
> John Buridan (died about 1358)
> John of Cornubia (Pseudo-Scotus) (wrote possibly during the first half of the fourteenth century)

Walter Burleigh (died about 1343) (His *De puritate artis logicae* is a very
   rich and pure example of metalogic)
Albert of Saxony (1316–1390)
Ralph Strode (wrote about 1370)
Paul of Venice (died about 1429) (His *Logica Magna*, a vast and systematic
   work, indicates the range of Scholastic discussions)
Peter Tartaret (wrote about 1480)
Stephanus de Monte

2. Scholastic logicians worked in the context of ordinary language. Character-
istically, their work tends to be descriptive and metalogical. In the area of
formal logic they have not an elaborate, artificial notation and their work has
not the modern format of a simple *exhibition* of a system of laws or rules. And
working, as they do, with vernacular language the content of the propositions
they cite as examples often proves an unhelpful distraction, logically. However,
their achievements in formal logic are very considerable indeed. They constructed a system of propositional logic that seems superior to the Megarian–
Stoic one; since only fragments of Megarian–Stoic logic were available (transmitted) to them, this was done from the starting point of Aristotelian term-logic
(their theory of consequences covered both propositional and term-logic
consequences).

   With regard to the assertoric syllogistic, the Aristotelian system was very
completely formulated with the addition of mnemonics, a combinatorial technique for determining possible moods, and a formal development of indirect
moods of the first figure (this was their way of treating the fourth figure,
although the thirteenth-century Jewish philosopher Albalag explicitly deals
with it as a separate figure). With regard to the modal syllogistic there is a full
formal development from the starting point of Aristotle's system on the basis of
the distinction between propositions that are modal *de re* and those that are
modal *de dicto*. For every Aristotelian mood Occam has four, according as
both premisses are *de re*, or both *de dicto*, or that there is one of each.
Including the assertoric proposition as a possible premiss, the total number of
valid moods within his stipulations is about a thousand. Scholastics dealt also
with 'oblique syllogisms' where indirect premisses are used (e.g. Every man is
an animal, Socrates sees a man; therefore Socrates sees an animal). And Occam
developed syllogisms with singular terms, equating singular terms with universal ones on the ground that they are names of classes, just like universal terms,
only in this case unit-classes. This was not a question of instantiation, substituting singulars for general values, but was a widening of the Aristotelian syllogistic.

   'We do not know whether the Scholastics were acquainted with a more
comprehensive logic of relations than Aristotle' (Bochenski, ibid., p. 231) but
there is good evidence that they developed a number of logical theories outside
the areas of propositional logic and syllogistic. For example, they dealt with the
correctness of logical operations performed on propositions in the future and

past tense, and on exponible propositions (i.e. propositions that are equivalent to a product or a sum of categoricals).

Thus working in the context of a living (Latin) language, Scholastic logicians achieved a formal knowledge of a wide variety of logical techniques, laws and rules. 'So even in the present incomplete state of knowledge, we can state with safety that in scholastic formal logic we are confronted with a very original and very fine variety of logic.' (Bochenski, ibid., p. 251)

V. From the end of the middle ages to the development of modern mathematical logic—a period that is not creative and in which a distorted version of logic, the so-called 'classical' logic, developed

This (1450–1850) was a period of decline for logic: as part of the medieval tradition it was under attack; it survived only in an elementary form on the curriculum of most universities, and while many textbooks were current the best of them were summaries or commentaries on earlier work. Some of the textbooks studied in this period were: Peter of Spain's *Summulae Logicales*; *Logica Hamburgensis* by Joachim Junge (1638); *Logica Fundamentis Suis a quibus hactenus collapsa fuerat Restituta* by Arnold Geulincx (1662); *La Logique ou l'Art de penser* by Antoine Arnauld and Pierre Nicole (1662)—it is often called the *Port Royal Logic*, its authors being leaders of the Port Royal movement: 'the epistemological interest of the authors is shown by the division of the work into four parts which are said to treat respectively of conception, judgment, reasoning and method . . . the general conception of logic which they expounded in this book was widely accepted and continued to dominate the treatment of logic by most philosophers for the next 200 years.' (Kneale's *Development of Logic*, pp. 316, 320) John of St Thomas' *Ars Logica* is a very fine example of the commentaries on Aristotle and Aquinas written in this period.

Many reasons are given for the decline of logic. Renaissance scholars were repelled by its style and content; the new scientists did not look on logic as an instrument of discovery: indeed the study of formal necessity seemed singularly barren and in general writers such as Descartes and Bacon 'tended to make philosophers neglect formal logic in favour of the new study of heuristic methodology.' (Kneale: ibid., p. 310) Again the new mathematics which developed—algebra and analysis—were conceived as new reckoning procedures, not axiomatic systems governed by logical entailment (such as geometry); thus logic lost the close link with mathematics that was traditional to it and it was not until the nineteenth century, when mathematical methods achieved a high degree of formal abstraction, that mathematicians reestablished the traditional association with logic. The result was the development of modern mathematical logic, including the recovery of the Formal Logic of Aristotle, the Stoics and the medievals.

The four hundred years from 1450–1850 saw not only the decline of formal logic but also the growth of a new, distorted logic, often called the 'classical' logic. The *Port Royal Logic* (1662), J. N. Keynes *Formal Logic* (1906) and Joseph's *Introduction to Logic* are representative in the best possible sense of this classical logic. For in general, as Bochenski notes, it was 'poor in content, devoid of all deep problems, permeated with a whole lot of non-logical philosophical ideas, psychologist in the worst sense'. (*A History of Formal Logic*, p. 258) Although Kant expressed concern for the purity of logic, protesting against the presence of psychological, metaphysical and anthropological chapters in treatises on logic, it was his transcendentalism which 'began the production of the curious mixture of metaphysics and epistemology which was presented as logic by Hegel and the other Idealists of the nineteenth century'. (Kneale: ibid., p. 355)

However there were some mathematicians who concerned themselves with Logic during this period of its general decline—*Leibniz, Saccheri, Lambert, Ploucquet, Euler* (famous as popularizer of 'Leibniz's device of illustrating logical relations by geometrical analogies' [Kneale, p. 349]), *Gergonne* (who developed Euler's work on relations of extension), and *Sir William Hamilton* (who tried to work out a system for the quantification of predicates).

Of these it can be said that Leibniz is out of character with the period in being one of the greatest logicians of all time. This was only realized when the first really substantial catalogue of his writings was made in 1895, and it became clear that this philosopher, for whom Aristotle's syllogistic was 'one of the most beautiful discoveries of the human spirit', had visualized a basic science (neither mathematics nor logic as he knew them) which would be a general theory of structures and whose abstract formality would provide the possibility of various interpretations and isomorphic inferences. Associated, in his mind, with this science, was a scientifically designed symbolism—a *characteristica universalis*—although he never produced any detailed plan of the new ideal language. And a formalistic method must be included also, for he conceived 'the idea of an alphabet of human thought with which all possible thinkables might be constructed by suitable combinations and by which reasoning might be reduced to the quasi-mechanical operation of going through a list. His inspiration came from the *Ars Magna* of Raymond Lull and the *Computatio sive Logica* of Hobbes ... To the end of his life he thought of the theory of combinations as something more fundamental than ordinary logic.' (Kneale, ibid., pp. 325–6) In general indeed he conceived, as a possibility, formal technical procedures which, integrated into scientific investigation, would constitute a powerful logic of discovery.

He wrote in detail only two formal calculi—a geometrical calculus of similarity and congruence, and a calculus of identity and inclusion. Of the latter 'the most interesting feature ... is its abstract formality. What he produced was certainly much less than he hoped to produce ... [But] here for the first time there was an attempt to work out a piece of abstract mathematics, i.e. mathematics that is not specially concerned with space or numbers. The calculus covers in fact part of the field of logic, but it can be manipulated without regard to any interpretation.' (Kneale, ibid., pp. 344–5)

Finally, in this period, apart from philosophers in the Scholastic tradition (such as Cajetan and John of St Thomas) who wrote commentaries, *Bolzano* (1781–1848) interested himself in some of the logic of Leibniz, and John Stuart Mill (as we shall see in the history of metalogic) tried to expound logic as an empirical science, rejecting the whole of the traditional theory of formal logic.

VI. Modern mathematical logic

A broader history will be given later. Here we are concerned, not with reflection on logic but simply with 'doing' logic.

Modern formal logic began with the calculus of classes of Boole; to this a similar calculus of relations was added by De Morgan. Hugh McColl seems to have been the first (1877) to construct a real propositional calculus. Two years later Frege's *Begriffsschrift* appeared and his full formalization has been developed and varied in many rigorous axiomatizations, especially by Russell, Lukasiewicz, Nicod, Wajsberg, Hilbert, Ackermann, Bernays, Meredith, Sobocinski, Jaskowski, Rasiowa, Tarski, Heyting. Many partial systems have been constructed—notably that using equivalence as sole connective by Lesniewski.

The truth-table method is used informally by Frege in his *Begriffsschrift*; in 1885 Peirce presented it as a general decision procedure. Through the work of Lukasiewicz and Post it has been used very extensively since the 1920s. Lukasiewicz was the first to introduce a three-valued propositional calculus. Independently of each other, he and Post generalized this to a many-valued propositional calculus and indeed Lukasiewicz introduced an infinitely many-valued one. Slupecki provided primitive bases for finitely many-valued propositional calculi.

Modern predicate logic began basically with the notion of propositional function and the use of quantifiers: these originated with Frege's *Begriffsschrift* (1879), although quantifiers were later introduced independently by C. S. Peirce who was responsible for the terms 'quantifier' and 'quantification'. Early work on quantification was done by Schröder, Peano and Russell. The axiomatic approach of Frege and Russell has not been developed and varied here to the same extent as in propositional logic and nowadays natural deduction procedures are preferred. The Hilbert–Ackermann axiomatization (1928, modified in 1938) of first order predicate logic is, perhaps, the best known axiomatic system. Many important results, for predicate logic, were achieved by the work of Löwenheim and Skolem.

The development of a natural deduction approach stems from the work of Jaskowski and Gentzen whose pioneer articles were published in 1934. Modern modal logic owes its inception to the concern of C. I. Lewis that strict implication rather than material implication should be central in logic.

Although principally known for his metalogical proofs, Kurt Gödel has made many important contributions to formal logic as indeed (similarly) have Church, Quine, Carnap.

Section C: Metalogic

DETAILED CONTENTS OF SECTION C

Chapter 1

PERSPECTIVE ON METALOGIC

I. Introduction

Broadly speaking, in formal logic one is 'doing' logic, in metalogic one is reflecting on what is already done: (1) making explicit concepts that are operational in formal logic and (2) establishing results or theorems about logical formulas and systems (these theorems being *metatheorems* since they are not reached *within* formal logic but are about it).

II. Making explicit concepts that are operational in formal logic

These concepts fall under two main categories when they are made explicit in metalogic: they are either syntactic or semantic. In classing and establishing expressions as being, e.g. *well-formed*, *derivable*, *provable*, the formal logician works formalistically, i.e. without having to take into account the meaning of the expressions since his rules of operation refer solely to the material shape of symbols as in mathematics. Accordingly the concepts *well-formed*, *derivable*, *provable* are purely syntactic. On the other hand *consistency*, *entailment*, *logical truth* are conceptions which grow out of attention to the meaning of expressions and are called *semantic* notions. It is interesting to note that for finite sets of statements it can be proved that if A is syntactically derivable from S it will also be semantically entailed by S; further that if A is logically true (being entailed by the null set of statements) it will have to be provable also since provable means being derivable from the null set of statements; and finally that the semantic notion of consistency (which is the possibility of an interpretation in which all the statements of a given set are true) has also a syntactic counterpart, syntactic consistency (predicated of a set of statements when no contradiction is derivable from it).

While a certain coincidence in range is expected of syntactic and semantic concepts, it is important to note that a theorem of Church (1936) showed that there can be no purely syntactic (i.e. mechanical, formalistic, automatic) way of determining, for all possible cases, whether the semantic properties of logical truth, entailment or consistency are present. Thus there is not and cannot be a syntactic procedure for the solution of all logical problems.

Modern formal logic operates at the syntactic level to a considerably greater extent than any other historical form of logic. A formalistic method predominates, it being a strict rule of mathematical logic that within the context of proof one must appeal to nothing but the forms of the symbols and the 'formal' rules of inference which apply to such rules. Of course formalism was not absent from earlier logics but mathematical logic is unique in laying it down as a general principle of logical method and in recognizing that its formalism consists essentially in the extension to logic of a method used for centuries in the language of numbers—calculation (so that sections of logic constructed purely syntactically are called calculi).

It has been humorously said that formalism puts us in the position of not knowing what one is saying nor whether what one is saying is true. But as Bochenski notes:

(1) The goal of formalism is always knowledge. A formalistic system only fulfils its task, therefore, if it is ultimately possible to interpret its results eidetically.

(2) The rules governing formalistic operations must make sense eidetically. They prescribe what we are to do and it must be possible to understand them, ultimately.

(3) In practice, formalized systems are nearly always developed by first establishing meaningful signs, then abstracting from their meaning and building up the system formalistically and finally giving a new interpretation to the finished system. (This holds in particular for logic.)

(4) Although it would not be impossible to have a science whose system had no meaning except a syntactic one, this cannot be the case with logic. For logic has to provide rules of deduction for all indirect thinking and if its rules were not eidetically meaningful no deduction could be carried out. Accordingly most contemporary logicians hold that systems which do not permit any known eidetic interpretation are not really logic. (*The Methods of Contemporary Thought*)

Formalism is a very useful method to use in conjunction with other methods, for the following reasons:

(a) in very complicated matters our eidetic understanding may break down and be helped on by formalistic processes;

(b) the use of formalism (which handles signs according to their written shape) helps to exclude tacit presuppositions about objects;

(c) the process of formalistic deduction is suitable for delimiting and clarifying primitive concepts or terms;

(d) a system that is developed purely formalistically may permit of many interpretations and therefore of many uses.

Bochenski points out that the formalism of modern logic is connected with 'a deeper and more revolutionary innovation. All the other varieties of logic known to us make use of an *abstractive* method; the logical theorems are gained by abstraction from ordinary language. Mathematical logicians proceed in just the opposite way, *first constructing* purely formal systems, and later looking for an interpretation in everyday speech. This process is not indeed always purely applied; and it would not be impossible to find something corresponding to it elsewhere. But at least since Boole, the principle of such construction is consciously and openly laid down, and holds sway throughout the realm of mathematical logic.' (*A History of Formal Logic*, p. 266) Model Theory is the modern theory of interpretations of formal systems.

One can see how very important it is to distinguish, in modern times, between a *logic* and the *calculus* which it interprets and manipulates. 'A logic will always depend upon some intuitive techniques, while a calculus will be defined as an axiomatic system whose construction can be made entirely formal. Calculi as such are uninterpreted, but a calculus associated with a logic will always be chosen because it may receive interpretation (or interpretations) useful to the employment of the logic in solving its range of problems.' (Ackerman, *Introduction to Many-Valued Logics*, p. 3) It is of the essence of a logic to know what it is dealing with, taking account of the eidetic meaning of expressions and rules (i.e. what they refer to and express). A logic cannot be constructed like a calculus, purely syntactically, on the basis of operational meaning only (i.e. knowing how to use symbols and how to operate syntactical rules).

III. Establishing metatheorems

The metatheoretic part of reflection on formal logic establishes results or theorems about logical formulas and systems. It is precisely a theory of those sentences, constructed in logical language, which are used to express truths of logic. Thus it requires a special metalanguage which names and talks about the expressions used in formal logic. These expressions 'must be formulas of a *formal language*, i.e. a "language" that can be completely specified without any reference at all, direct or indirect, to the meaning of the formulas of the "language". It was by the insistence on this requirement that the metatheory of logic, after a long and interesting but desultory history of over two thousand years, came in this century to yield exact and new and deep results and to give promise of systematic growth.' (Geoffrey Hunter, *Metalogic: An Introduction to the Metatheory of Standard First-Order Logic*, p. 3)

However, it is important to note that one is using metalanguage when one gives even the simplest explanations, using words such as *term*, *variable*, *proposition*, *predicate*, *rule*, *deduction*, *system*, *syntactic category*, *truth-function*, which are all metalogical in character. Thus it is useful to distinguish a general (vernacular) discussion of concepts and principles that are operational in logic, from a technical, formalized presentation of metatheorems. Both use metalanguage (whether by adapting English, e.g. or by inventing a special symbolism), both reach results (which may be called metatheorems) and both attempt to validate these results (giving proofs). But the mode of procedure and communication is so different that one can very profitably use the word *metalogic* for the whole section of logic and *metatheory* for its highly formalized study of properties of logical systems, in particular of their deductive apparatus. The metatheory of predicate logic is considerably more complex than that of sentential logic and, of course, beyond these sections of elementary logic there lie the highly technical fields of, e.g. higher-order predicate calculi and various non-standard logics.

The most basic metatheoretic work is concerned with whether sections of logic are essentially consistent (not admitting of internal contradictions), complete (containing all the truths of their domain) and decidable (possessing a mechanical decision procedure for discriminating truth and falsity). Metatheoretic proofs involve reasoning that is not exemplified within formal logic itself, for while a proof *within* a formal system satisfies purely syntactic requirements a proof *about* a formal system must be a meaningful justification of a true statement about the system. Here Gödel's methods are the best known.

IV. Perspective on metalogic

'Logic from Aristotle to Gödel has had three ends in view. The first is to explicate in precise terms various intuitive notions of "logical truth". The second is to codify, with the aid of formal systems and other devices, those statements or formulas that are to count as logical truths. The third is to apply these systems and devices as a means of testing the formal validity of certain arguments and inferences in the sciences and in everyday life.

'Modern logic, since Frege, has sought to achieve these ends by exploiting a variety of mathematical methods and notions, in particular that of formal system. The creation of the formal disciplines of syntax and semantics by Carnap and Tarski added new tools and sharpened older ones. The syntactical notions—formal system, consistency, deducibility and theorem—on which the original systematization of modern logic by Frege and Russell primarily relied have now been paired with their semantical counterparts; interpretation (simultaneous), satisfiability, consequence and validity. The combined use of syntactical and semantical characterizations has resulted in a clearer view of logic itself and of its role in formalizing mathematical and other types of theories.' (Albert Blumberg, article on Modern Logic, *Encyclopedia of Philosophy*, vol. 5, p. 32)

This 'clearer view of logic' must be built up at two levels of reflection, that of metalogic and that of a philosophy of logic. In the latter one seeks to form an ultimate definition of logic and to situate it precisely in the corpus of human science and wisdom. In the former one seeks the kind of clarification that does not commit one to extra-logical, philosophical positions and remains closer to the experience of actually doing logic. This experience brings logic into view as a system which is both syntactical and semantic in character, which pervades every other system of thought as inference rules, and which has unique properties and problems. In our treatment of metalogic we will be concerned to explicate the technical details of this experience, presenting (a) the main concepts and principles that are operational in formal logic, paying particular attention to its concepts of formal language, paradox, meaning, truth, derivability, system, class, predication and the logistic concept of mathematics; (b) the fundamental metatheorems which are concerned with consistency, completeness and decidability. These metatheorems are conveniently presented in an examination of the rigour and range of proof in elementary formal logic.

Our first concern, however, is to present the reader with a survey of the actual development, historically, of self-reflective logic. The position at present is that while there is reasonably exact and complete information on the deliberations, problems and conclusions of modern mathematical logicians, there is not comparable information with regard to the Greek or medieval logicians. We have already seen however that the formal logics of the modern and earlier periods correspond substantially and that the 'classical' logic current from 1500–1900 is alien not only to modern mathematical logic but equally to the logic of the earlier periods. It seems best then to make an historical survey by beginning with the perspective of modern mathematical logicians, then integrating our fragmentary knowledge of the earlier periods within the modern framework of metalogical ideas.

Chapter 2

AN HISTORICAL SURVEY

Modern mathematical logic in perspective

The development of this logic and the endeavour to set it in perspective may be substantially presented through the work of Boole, Frege, Russell and Wittgenstein.

I. George Boole (1815–64). This English mathematician and logician made his contribution in *The Mathematical Analysis of Logic, being an Essay towards a Calculus of Deductive Reasoning* (1847). An article by him entitled 'The Calculus of Logic' appeared, the following year, in the *Cambridge and Dublin Mathematical Journal* and is valuable in being less technical and in underlining the human perspective of his work. His later book, *An Investigation of the Laws of Thought in which are founded the Mathematical Theories of Logic and Probability* (1859) is often described as the authoritative statement of his system; however while his treatment of probability is a new application of his system, there is no new development of its formal character.

Boole saw that the force of argument in any particular context derived partly from the particular concepts involved, but that it was also true that argument in all contexts subserved a common higher logic. His work was directed towards disengaging this logic, formalizing the principles of operation of the human mind, the subjective aspect of human rationality. He believed that these principles are as rigorously mathematical as are the laws which govern particular quantitative conceptions such as those of number and magnitude:

> It appeared to me that, although Logic might be viewed with reference to the idea of quantity, it had also another and a deeper system of relations. If it was lawful to regard it from *without*, as connecting itself through the medium of Number with the intuitions of Space and Time, it was lawful also to regard it from *within*, as based upon facts of another order which have their abode in the constitution of the Mind. (*The Mathematical Analysis of Logic*, Preface)
>
> In one respect, the science of Logic differs from all others; the perfection of its method is chiefly valuable as an evidence of the speculative truth of its principles. (Ibid.)

Boole perceived an analogy between the operations of logic and those of algebra. Using the symbolism of algebra he developed a formal system on the basis of laws which governed the combination of these symbols and not any content they might have. The argumentative processes of the system were disengaged from particular contexts and he showed how the system could be interpreted as a class logic, a propositional logic or a calculus of probabilities. He says:

> They who are acquainted with the present state of the theory of Symbolical Algebra, are aware, that the validity of the process of analysis does not depend upon the interpretation of the symbols which are employed, but solely upon the laws of their combination. Every system of interpretation which does not affect the truth of the relations supposed, is equally admissible, and it is thus that the same process may, under one scheme of interpretation, represent the solution of a question on the properties of numbers, under another, that of a geometrical problem, and under a third, that of a problem of dynamics or optics ... But the full recognition of the consequences of this important doctrine has been, in some measure, retarded by accidental circumstances ... The expression of magnitude, or of operations on magnitude, has been the express object for which the symbols of Analysis have been invented, and for which their laws have been investigated. Thus the abstractions of the modern Analysis, not less than the ostensive diagrams of the ancient Geometry, have encouraged the notion, that Mathematics are essentially, as well as actually, the Science of Magnitude ... That to the existing forms of Analysis a quantitative interpretation is assigned, is the result of the circumstances by which these forms were determined, and is not to be construed into a universal condition of Analysis. It is upon the foundation of this general principle, that I propose to establish the Calculus of Logic and that I claim for it a place among the acknowledged forms of Mathematical Analysis, regardless that in its object and in its instruments it must at present stand alone ... The laws we have to examine are the laws of one of the most important of our mental faculties. The mathematics we have to construct are the mathematics of the human intellect. (Ibid., Introduction)

Thus the essence of his contribution was to conceive a method of deriving consequences which did not draw argumentative force from a context and to conceive a formal system, then, as being constructed, rather than abstracted from a context. In papers from his later life he speaks of revising his book, *An investigation of the Laws of Thought* and in one paper distinguishes his Calculus of Logic from a higher logic which would be 'the Philosophy of *all* thought that is expressible in signs, whatever the object of that thought'. Kneale (*The Development of Logic*, p. 407) says: 'he was on a wrong track when he began to look for the basis of logic in the constitution of the human intellect ... (indeed) it was Boole's work which showed clearly by example that logic could be studied profitably without any references to the processes of our mind. He believed no doubt that he was dealing with laws of thought in some psychological sense of that ambiguous expression, but he was in fact dealing with some of the most general laws of thinkables.' However, 'thinkable' is a bipolar word and seems to include a reference to a subjective aspect of some kind. Boole's actual work, so original in formalistic method, and his use of the words 'constitution of the human mind', provide strong support for the view that he is not psychologistic, that the subjective depth of his reference, left undefined, is below the level of phenomenal, psychic thinking.

II. Gottlob Frege (1848–1925). The most important date in the history of modern mathematical logic is 1879, when his *Begriffsschrift*—'concept writing' (Austin's translation), 'ideography' (Jourdain's translation)—was published. The book itself was neither widely read nor appreciated at the time and the ideas in it came to be known and understood only after many years and piecemeal through the writings of others. Bertrand Russell noted (*Introduction to Mathematical Philosophy*, 1919, p. 25): 'In spite of the great value of this work, I was, I believe, the first person who ever read it—more than twenty years after its publication.'

It was an influential work in philosophy generally, again very indirectly because, apart from Husserl, Russell and Wittgenstein, for most of this century philosophers simply have not been acquainted with Frege. But Frege made a very modern and important departure from Cartesian tradition. For him Philosophy does not begin with a theory of knowledge and with a methodic demolition of scepticism. It begins with logic. If we construct our logic properly, its language and rigour of proof will ramify, controlling and guaranteeing every other discipline.

Logic is something that is constructed. It begins in the Fregean sense when you say: I must construct a language able to signify, exclusively, the forms (simple, complex and systematic) of thought—where thought denotes not thinking (thought as a psychic vitality) but that which is signified by, or contained in, thought. Frege rejected psychologism: logic is not concerned with the mental ideas and images which words may arouse in the mind of a speaker, hearer, writer or reader; it is not concerned with the elements, organization or alteration of consciousness, and psychic realities should not enter basically into any precise and adequate theory of meaning. A logic-language will symbolize precisely what is germane to exact proof, to the inferential sequence as such; it will process conceptual content rather than formalize personal thinking.

Frege felt that meaning (e.g. of a remark or thought) is best handled as an entity which is neither psychic nor physical; similar to both in being factual it is different from both in being timeless. Sentences in many languages may have the same sense. 'And the sense is properly just that which matters to us. The sentence has a value for us through the sense which we apprehend in it, and which we recognize as the same in the translation too. This sense I call "thought" (*Gedanke*). What we prove is not the sentence but the thought. And it makes no difference what language we use for that purpose.' (*Uber Logik und Mathematik*, 1914) 'The thought belongs neither to my inner world as an idea nor yet to the outer world of material, perceptible things ... Thoughts are by no means unreal but their reality is of quite a different kind from that of things ... A property of a thought will be called inessential which consists in, or follows from the fact that, it is apprehended by a thinker.' (*The Thought: A Logical Inquiry*) Here we have meaning as something independent of any particular language and of any particular mind; it can be called thought not in the sense of that which is produced by this or that mind, but in the sense of that which can be understood by any mind and is the same for every mind—it may be named 'objective thought' and it is the *lekton* of Stoic doctrine.

Whatever we may feel about Frege's three-level semantic approach to language (in which there were three elements, the world we speak about, our language and objective meanings), it is quite clear that his conception of logic included a complete rejection of psychologism and implied that the most basic need of logic is a language of objective thought, able to symbolize all those things and only those things that are germane to exact proof. He devised a language consisting of a few primitives and a simple grammar and in his system demonstrated its expressive power, range and flexibility.

The symbolism was two-dimensional and would have the following appearance for the expression, *It is not the case that for every value of x, if fx then gx*:

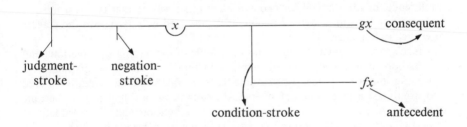

The primitive symbols were:
1. Symbols to designate objects. Roman letters in Roman and Gothic script were used. These symbols covered both individual constants and individual variables.
2. Symbols to express concepts, i.e. symbols that were a formalized expression of concepts. Greek letters were generally used.
3. A symbol expressing the concept of negation—the negation stroke.
4. Variable notation for expressing generality—i.e. quantifier-variable notation. The symbol was a concavity —⌣ x ⌐— containing the variable.
5. A symbol to express the antecedent—consequence sequence in proof. The symbol was the condition stroke.
6. A symbol to express the activity of asserting that the thought expressed is true. This is an element conveyed in language, a force it has as an utterance. It does not affect the truth-conditions of the sentence: it is something *done* with a sentence. We may use a sentence otherwise, e.g. to give a definition,

ask a question. Assertion is symbolized by the judgment stroke (definition by $\Vdash$).

Frege's grammar is very simple. The formation of an expression is such that some symbols can be replaced by others. The 'part of the expression that shows itself invariant under such replacement is called the function; and the replaceable part, the argument of the function'. (*Begriffsschrift*) The part of the expression that is the function may be, e.g. a predicate or a relational expression and it may require one place or many places for arguments. Each place or gap is marked by brackets and a variable or constant appears within the brackets to complete a sentence. With the quantifying symbolism attached to it this function-argument grammar is very powerful and flexible for formalizing propositions.

At this point three observations may be made:

1. Frege's work in constructing a language for logic created in him a basic distruct of natural vernacular language. He saw that power and flexibility of expression did not involve (as was commonly supposed) the kind of complexity that vernacular languages have. Further, where logicians before him had failed to solve the problem of expressing generality by studying the devices of everyday language, he had succeeded by freeing himself from such guidance. Thus the fact that in everyday language one could form a proper name without a reference, or utter a well-formed expression that was neither true nor false—this was not for him a logical problem; it indicated how basic are the defects of everyday language.

2. Frege's next step was to apply his technique of expressing propositions and his method of proof and systematization to the important area of numerical reasoning in Mathematics. (From some basic postulates he had already derived and organized a large number of logical principles.) In doing this he became convinced that there are no basic notions or axioms peculiar to arithmetic—concepts and principles within logic are sufficient to generate it. Subsequently, his main works were devoted to giving an account of this logistic view both without the use of his symbolic language (in *Die Grundlagen der Arithmetik*, 1884) and through the construction of a strict formal system (in *Die Grundgesetze der Arithmetik*: vol. 1, 1893; vol. 2, 1903). The preface to this latter work is a very precise statement of Frege's logic. Its second volume was published in 1903, ten years after the first. While it was in the press, Frege received a letter from Russell informing him of contradiction in his system. Frege modified an axiom as an *ad hoc* device without being satisfied with his system. In 1923, two years before his death, he was quite convinced that his logistic approach had been a mistake, that he and others had been over-influenced and misled by the theory of classes. He conceived the possibility that geometry was fundamental in mathematics.

3. Frege's formula language gave rise to some very interesting and fundamental problems. In the course of dealing with them he developed important metalogical theories:

(a) His theory of object (the correlate of proper name) and concept (the correlate of the functional feature of an expression). This will be discussed in the treatment of predication.

(b) His theory of the meaning of words: 'it is only in the context of a sentence that a word has meaning'. (*Grundlagen*) This appears in Wittgenstein as the principle that it is only in the utterance of a sentence that we make 'a move in the language-game'. The meaning of a word consists in its contribution to this linguistic act, to determining the truth-conditions of the sentence.

(c) His theory of sense and reference which plays an important role in modern semantics and in contemporary logical and philosophical discussion of intension and extension. A remarkable feature of this theory, which focuses what an expression designates and what it expresses, is that it identifies the reference of a *sentence* with its truth-value. The theory will be discussed in the chapter on the nature of a proposition.

(d) His theory of assertion as the force carried by an utterance.

All the essentials of modern metalogic are in Frege. His basic contribution was the theory and practice of concept-writing, the idea and the model of primary logical language and of exact logical proof. The best measure of this contribution is the logistic use of it in *Die Grundlagen der Arithmetik* and *Die Grundgesetze der Arithmetik*, and in the *Principia Mathematica* of Russell and Whitehead.

III. Bertrand Russell (1872–1970). In his autobiography Russell describes how about 1898 'I was beginning to emerge from the bath of German idealism in which I had been plunged by McTaggart and Stout [at Cambridge]. I was very much assisted in this process by Moore, of whom at that time I saw a great deal. It was an intense excitement, after having supposed the sensible world unreal, to be able to believe again that there really were such things as tables and chairs. But the most interesting aspect to me was the logical aspect. I was glad to think that relations are real, and I was interested to discover the dire effect upon metaphysics of the belief that all propositions are of the subject-predicate form.' (*Autobiography*, vol. I, pp. 134–5) Ever afterwards he was strongly realist: it is the business of philosophy to deal with the world of fact, to say what there is in the world, what it is like. There are direct relations of the knowing subject to objects, providing basic knowledge by acquaintance. With regard to Russell's logic, Gödel observes: 'What strikes me as surprising in this field is Russell's pronouncedly realistic attitude, which manifests itself in many passages of his writings. "Logic is concerned with the real world just as truly as Zoology, though with its more abstract and general features," he says in his *Introduction to Mathematical Philosophy* (edition of 1920, p. 169). It is true, however, that this attitude has been gradually decreasing in the course of time and also that it always was stronger in theory than in practice.'

We have seen Frege's objective of inventing a primary language processing, precisely, objective thought. Both he and Frege believed that a logical calculus constructed from such a language would do for theoretical mathematics what the decimal system of numbers had done for numerical computation. Their belief echoed the expectations of Leibniz: he says he had developed his calculus of reasoning to a large extent and that in time a few select scientists would be able to so develop it that 'humanity would have a new kind of an instrument increasing the powers of reason far more than any optical instrument has ever aided the power of vision'. Frege indeed uses the same metaphor: 'I believe that I can best make the relation of my ideography to ordinary language clear if I compare it to that which the microscope has to the eye. Because of the range of its possible uses and the versatility with which it can adapt to the most diverse circumstances, the eye is far superior to the microscope ... But, as soon as scientific goals demand great sharpness of resolution, the eye proves to be insufficient. The microscope, on the other hand, is perfectly suited to precisely such goals, but that is just why it is useless for all others.' (Preface to *Begriffsschrift*) We have seen Frege *use* his language to express, prove and systematize the propositions of two basic sciences—logic and mathematics.

Russell was with Frege in departing from the abstractive tradition of logic: the best logic would be a constructed logic. Both Russell and the early Wittgenstein have been criticized as being preoccupied with the theory of a perfect language. It is certainly true that a great deal of attention was devoted by both to problems of a primary language and to a philosophy of it (variously called 'philosophical grammar', 'clarification of language'). Russell's search for the perfect and minimal language followed from his constructionist method. The kind of Russellian analysis called reduction aims at reducing the number of terms in scientific philosophizing to a minimum. Only those things with which we have immediate experience (by sense or introspection) are to be named by primitive terms. And we should not be trying to systematically infer the existence of entities not directly experienced; instead we should construct classes of the genuinely primitive entities and develop a system accordingly. 'The supreme maxim in scientific philosophizing,' he said (1918), 'is this: whenever possible, logical constructions are to be substituted for inferred entities.' In constructional systems the language has to be carefully and logically structured so that its primitive and class levels are clearly distinguished and that all sentences can be translated into primitive symbolism.

Thus in various areas in which Russell makes contributions in philosophy, logic and mathematics you tend to get not ordinary argumentation but *carefully built up language-systems*—'constructional systems'—which are empirical also in that their basic terms refer only to immediately experienced entities. This empirical data is provided by careful analytical procedures. His objective always is to construct a system based on a union, at the level of basic atomic propositions, between empirical data and logical form; the development thereafter of the system is extremely logical.

With regard to his own primary language, the problems he worked on and his philosophical grammar:

1. Russell is clear on the fact that constructing a language involves one in *ontological commitments*. These are presented in presuppositions we have to make about the world and in our criteria for an ideal language. For him the

most important requirement for an ideal language is an empirical one, for-mulated in 'the principle of acquaintance': Every proposition which we can understand must be composed wholly of constituents with which we are acquainted. Nothing is said or spoken in his language by any expression which cannot be reduced or brought back to such a proposition.

2. For Russell, Logic is essentially concerned with *implication*, the objective involvement of evidence and conclusion which justifies inference: 'Where we validly infer one proposition from another we do so in virtue of a relation which holds between the two propositions whether we perceive it or not: the mind, in fact, is as purely receptive in inference as common sense supposes it to be in perception of sensible objects.' (*Principles of Mathematics*, 1903) Implication and the correlates of other primitive symbols in logic are indefin-able. The discussion of these indefinables is the chief part of philosophical logic, this discussion being 'the endeavour to see clearly and to make others see clearly, the entities concerned, in order that the mind may have that kind of acquaintance with them which it has with redness or the taste of a pineapple'. (*Principles of Mathematics*) Later he preferred to become acquainted with implication through defining it as 'Either not p or q' or, like Sheffer and Nicod, in terms of the stroke functor.

3. In summary his logical grammar is: Sentences are built up (a) through functors that form sentences from names—*fa*. Here f is formative; a, the individual constant, is logically structureless: its function is to pick out an individual, that is all; (b) through functors that form sentences from verbs—quantifiers: $(x) fx$; (c) through functors that form sentences from sentences—$p \supset q$; $(x) fx \supset \sim (Ex) \sim fx$. There can be indefinite development of sentences from functors that already form sentences.

4. Quantification is the logical beginning of the number series. Quantifiers are functors of functors-that-form-sentences-out-of-names, and numbers are im-plicit components of such functors. For $\sim (Ex)$ (x is a man) we could write 'For no x is x a man': $(0x)$ (x is a man). And we can continue the series. 'At least one x is a man' $[(Ex)$ (x is a man)$]$ combined with 'At most one x is a man' [For some x: for any y, if y is human, y is identical with x] translates into 'Exactly one thing is a man': $(1x)$ (x is a man). Similarly, 'At least two things are men' (For some x and for some y, x is a man, y is a man and x is not identical with y) combined with 'At most two things are men' (For some x and for some y, for any z if z is a man z is either identical with x or identical with y) translates into $(2x)$ (x is a man)—for exactly $2x$'s, x is a man, exactly two things are men. This is a very natural translation and analysis of the number series. Unfortunately before he deals with arithmetic in his system, Russell has added to his primary language a secondary 'class-langue' of devices used in common speech. This language obscures the basic naturalness of his analysis of number. Gödel notes that the concept of class needs to be made very much clearer in mathematical logic; Frege came to regret its dominant position in modern logic.

5. We have seen that Russell had to be concerned with the indefinables of his system. In his language there is no way of constructing *names* precisely

because, logically, they are structureless. A genuine proper name (Russell usually takes the demonstrative 'this' as an example) contributes nothing to the meaning of a sentence except the identification of some individual as subject. It picks out an individual; it does not contribute to what is being said: it is logically structureless. But in natural language we seem to construct proper names out of concept words in descriptive phrases like 'the golden mountain', 'the present King of France' (which have no reference value), and 'the author of *Waverly*'. Russell's theory of descriptions makes the point that when translated into primary language such phrases are seen not to be proper names at all. The sentences with such phrases have not any subject: they are statements not about individuals but about functions. Thus 'the golden mountain does not exist' translates into 'For all values of x, the propositional function "x is golden and a mountain" is false.' 'Scott is the author of *Waverly*' translates into 'For all values of x, the propositional function "x wrote *Waverly*" is equivalent to the propositional function "x is Scott".'

6. Russell's theory of types was designed to explain paradoxes as being rooted in the permissiveness of natural language grammar, and to prevent, in his language system, the possibility of well-formed expressions being logically meaningless (neither true nor false). Gödel notes that the reason given by Russell 'is very similar to Frege's, who, in his system, already had assumed the theory of simple types for functions, but failed to avoid the paradoxes, because he operated with classes (or rather functions in extension) without any restriction. This reason is that (owing to the variable it contains) a propositional function is something ambiguous (or, as Frege says, something unsaturated, wanting supplementation) and therefore can occur in a meaningful proposition only in such a way that this ambiguity is eliminated (e.g. by substituting a constant for the variable or applying quantification to it). The consequences are that a function cannot replace an individual in a proposition, because the latter has no ambiguity to be removed, and that functions with different kinds of arguments (i.e. different ambiguities) cannot replace each other; which is the essence of the theory of simple types.' The same point is made from a more nominalistic viewpoint in the second edition of *Principia Mathematica* and in *Meaning and Truth*: propositional functions are presented as constructed out of sentences by leaving one or more constituents undetermined. They can be combined in forming propositions 'only if they "fit together", i.e. if they are of appropriate types'.

Russell's isomorphism (theory of a picture relationship between sentence and fact) got a classic presentation and complete analysis in Wittgenstein's *Tractatus*.

In the historic *Principia Mathematica* he effected, more satisfactorily than Frege, the reduction of mathematics to logic. With the help of A. N. Whitehead in Cambridge he worked on this book over a period of about ten years. His Theory of Descriptions (1905) and Theory of Types (1906) were important moments of progress in dealing with baffling difficulties. 'I worked at ... [the mechanical job of writing the book out] from ten to twelve hours a day for about eight months in the year, from 1907 to 1910. The manuscript became more and more vast, and every time that I went out for a walk I used to be afraid that the house would catch fire and the manuscript get burnt up. It was not, of course, the sort of manuscript that could be typed or even copied ... The strain of unhappiness combined with very severe intellectual work, in the years from 1902 till 1910, was very great ... In the end the work was finished but my intellect never quite recovered from the strain. I have been ever since definitely less capable of dealing with difficult abstractions than I was before.' (*Autobiography*, pp. 152–3) The development and powerful use of primary logical language in the *Principia* is such that Russell must be ranked with Frege as a founder of modern mathematical logic.

Russell describes his philosophical development as 'a gradual retreat from Pythagoras', from the world of mathematical truth which has sustained him in fervor, exultation and peace for much of his early life. Turning more and more to the world of human problems he carried everywhere, however, his realist, constructionist and primary language approach. His thought moved powerfully, utilizing logical technique and syntax, always seeking answers that had the quality of science. He was a humane representative of our scientific and computer culture which owes so much to the development of mathematical logic.

IV. Ludwig Wittgenstein (1889–1951). Russell said of him: 'His thought had an almost incredible degree of passionately intense penetration, to which I gave whole hearted admiration.' Bearing in mind this unique quality of his thought, it is no small thing to say (yet it is perfectly true), that the core of his life's work—both scientific and positivist in spirit—was to study what exactly is *given* in language and in thought. A remark in the early part of his life (*Notebooks* 1914–1916) is apt: 'My whole task consists in explaining the nature of sentences—how is it that a combination of words succeeds in *saying* something, in *telling someone* something; what is *saying*, what exactly is *said*?'

Only his *Tractatus Logico-Philosophicus* (80 pages long) (1921) and a short paper 'Some remarks on Logical Form' were published in his lifetime. Although so much of his philosophical and logical work was done at Cambridge, only two collections of lecture notes, the one in a blue folder, the other in a brown (published accordingly as *The Blue and Brown Books*), are without a German original. The main work of his later life is *Philosophical Investigations*.

The development from the logic of the *Tractatus* to the logic of the *Philosophical Investigations* involves a distinct change in the direction and climate of his thinking. One might say in summary that with the later Wittgenstein the whole development of mathematical logic is seen, philosophically and humanly, in perspective.

The following is a systematic presentation, first of his early work, then of the development of his later thought:

1.1: *Wittgenstein's early work* (the *Tractatus*):

1.11: *The logic of speech*

1.111: In investigating and understanding the logic of speech one is also investigating and understanding the logic of the world and of thought. All three occupy the same logical space, are governed by the same logical conditions and possibilities. 'The limits of my language mean the limits of my world.' (*Tractatus*, 5.61) It is logically meaningless to question the correspondence between language, thought and the world: we can never get into a position outside logical space from which to ask if all three have the same logical space.

Thus the logical structure of language provides the complete set of possibilities for the world: what actually occurs in the world is given only in experience of course. Logical possibilities together with everything that is the case and everything that is not the case set boundaries to the real world. Linguistically, therefore, the logical operator, *negation*, and the predicate, *true*, play a large part in showing boundaries. 'The comparison of language and reality is like that of a retinal image and visual image: to the blind spot nothing in the visual image seems to correspond, and thereby the boundaries of the blind spot determine the visual image—just as true negations of atomic propositions determine reality.' (*Notebooks*, p. 95)

1.112: Wittgenstein is concerned with what is *given* in *language*; accordingly he presents the world as made up not of elements and things but of facts. A fact is what is the case, i.e. that which verifies or falsifies a proposition. There must be something in the world in terms of which a given proposition is either true or false—this is 'fact' for him, and the world as it enters into this philosophy is factual reality and not the substantialist world of traditional philosophy. Each fact is the occurrence or non-occurrence of a state of affairs. The latter is the primary datum of language: it is a combination of objects but, in factual reality, objects never occur except as constituents of states of affairs. Similarly a name occurs meaningfully only in a sentence construct which is the simplest linguistic act.

1.113: A sentence is a picture: it shows its sense. A true sentence shows how things are: what the picture elements stand for are related in the same way as those elements: they have *form* in common since the sentence is a true picture. All sentences—true or false—have logical form and show the form of reality, that which the plan of reality allows.

Not everything can be pictured, not everything therefore can be said. It would be necessary to get to a view-point outside language in order to discuss, e.g. the model character of language or its logical form.

The cardinal problem in philosophy is finding out what can be said in propositions—i.e. in language—and what cannot be said but can only be shown. Thus the agreement of a statement with reality is not logically demonstrable; it is seen, it manifests itself. 'A proposition *shows* its sense. A proposition *shows* how things stand *if* it is true. And it says *that* they do so stand.' (*Tractatus*, 4.022)

1.114: Reality is mirrored, depicted, most clearly in logically formed language. It is the business of logic to provide the rules by which what can be said is said clearly. What is given in everyday language is actual situations; these are very complicated and the everyday use of words is impure, so very often the real situation seems opaque or is not properly seen. What is given in logical language is not the factual occurrence of a situation but the possibilities of a situation actually occurring. While the variable signs in logical notation represent things and facts, logical constants have no referential meaning; their meaning is logical consisting in their possibilities of being true and false, truth-tables being an appropriate technique for their definition. Logical truths do not share in the uncertainties of reality and do not give us an experience of, or information about, the actual and thus contingent states of affairs. Again, every deduction proceeds by logical rule unaffected by real situations. Thus while logical language achieves clarification, the formal systems it builds up represent possible rather than actual reality. 'Logic must look after itself.' (*Tractatus*, 5.473)

There are no logical rules for verifying statements about actual states of affairs. There are only practical directions and the verified statements fall within natural science. If a verifying test cannot *in principle* be carried out, there are no truth possibilities and the statement accordingly is void of sense.

1.115: In determining the *limits* of what can be thought or said, in defining what *can* be 'given' in thought or speech, one indicates or shows what cannot be said. He uses the word *mystical* for that which manifests itself in and through the logical exposure that nothing can be said about it.

The mystical is not something in addition to other things but the bounded nature of thought and language which gives the limits also of what cannot be thought or said. Thus it becomes apparent in clear thinking and meaningful language without falling within the bounds of either.

The mystical is a solution to the riddle of life in a unique sense of the word *solution*. Neither question nor answer about the meaning of life and of the universe can be genuine since they cannot occur within the bounds of language and thought. The mystical is not given within these bounds either to raise an intelligible problem or to clarify or prove something factual. But it shows itself, is manifested through the logical awareness that nothing can be said about it.

When we view the world as a whole, we reach beyond its bounded nature, but we cannot move logically or linguistically. Logical thought and mystic vision can never form one perspective.

1.116: Philosophy is an activity not a system of doctrine. It is a clarification of language with a view to determining what can be said (the tautologies of logic and mathematics, combined with the verified statements of natural science) and what cannot be said. 'What we cannot speak about we must pass over in silence.' (*Tractatus*, 7)—his metaphysics consists of a silent pointing towards what cannot be said.

1.2: *His later work* (from 1929 when he returned to Cambridge)

1.21: He no longer conceives language as being always descriptive (specifically a reflection of things), or measures it in terms of a logical model, or believes that there is a uniform structure in every language. He came to appreciate more and more the many ways in which language serves human life and the limitations of logical language which lacks points of contact and friction with actual situations. To use language in only one way is to let our minds become held and set in one position. 'Philosophy is a battle against the bewitchment of our intelligence by means of language.' (*Philosophical Investigations*, § 109) It is 'to show the fly the way out of the fly-bottle'. (Ibid.) He came to see how absolute and extreme has been his confidence in the notation and rules of logic for understanding language and determining meaning.

1.22: Holding now that the viewpoint of logic is only one viewpoint from which to study language, he proposes to teach not a theory but a skill in probing the depth grammar of language uses. His treatment of language-games constitutes a critique of his earlier logical period. He explains his use of the word language-game for any particular language-system or language-usage: 'Here the term "language-*game*" is meant to bring into prominence the fact that the *speaking* of language is part of an activity, or of a form of life ... It is interesting to compare the multiplicity of kinds of word and sentence, with what logicians have said about the structure of language. (Including the author of the *Tractatus Logico-Philosophicus*.)' (*Philosophical Investigations*, § 23) He presents the following basic insights:

1.23: Language *does* something. The action of ordinary language effects more contact with reality than the mirroring of logical language. With his gift of speech man involves himself with the world, acts on it and creates pathways through social life.

1.24: Words are a boxful of tools with a great diversity of possible uses in real life. The meaning of words is precisely the use we make of them; words have meaning only in the context of their use, and the rules governing a context are public. Every meaning has a background of social convention and is acquired by practising the language-game. Wittgenstein rejects the view that meaning is naming, and also the view that it consists of thoughts or feelings. An entire social convention provides both the meanings of the words and the depth grammar of each language-game.

1.25: It is the business of philosophy to analyse and clarify all forms of language; not to solve problems but to give a clear view, in language, of them. Since he now conceives language to be so flexible and diverse, the distinction between what can be said and what cannot be said is no longer sharp—although it is still present.

1.26: What is the relation between language and reality? He no longer conceives language as being real because, like a mirror, it reflects what is real; but as a form of living with the real. In this interaction it both corresponds to the experienced world and transforms it. The correspondence is clear because it functions in, and belongs to, a real situation and so cannot be arbitrary. Transformation is there also, for reality is plastic: it is affected by the manner in which it is measured and approached and can be remoulded by language and thought. Thus any use of language expresses a decision to take a certain path in life, to interact with reality through the concepts and proofs of a particular language-game; our vision, experience and life is reorganized, given new dimensions, new directions. Wittgenstein says more than once 'The limit of the empirical is concept-formation.' (*Foundations of Mathematics*)

Thus behind our languages and thought today, and expressed in them, lies the history of the forms of life of our people.

1.27: We are back full-circle to the question that constitutes the core of Wittgenstein's life-work: what is *given* in language? The answer is not now: a picture of things, ideally clear if the language is logical. The new answer is: what is brought into view by probing is human vitality. 'What has to be accepted, the given, is—so one could say—forms of life.' (*Philosophical Investigations*)

One can distil from the immensely technical work of Wittgenstein the human point that primary logical language is only one usage of language, that mathematical logic channels the vitality of formalization and clarification, and that in helping to provide our times with the formal efficiency of a computer-culture it must also endeavour to point the way towards maintaining flexibility, variety and human proportion in life. With Wittgenstein modern mathematical logic was seen, from within, in human and philosophic perspective.

A broad survey of metalogical problems and interests in antiquity, the middle ages and in modern and contemporary times

I. Introduction. Any second-order discussion of an operation, structure, system, theory or calculus occurring in formal logic belongs to Metalogic. When such a discussion is completely formalized a special metalogical language is devised the signs of which refer to *terms* of the system under examination and any metalogical theory developed, therefore, systematizes the names of expressions, not their content.

II. Aristotle. Some fundamentals of a metalogical system are in Aristotle and many metalogical observations. He formally classified methods of proof into induction and the syllogism, and he described his syllogistic metalogically, i.e. he explained its mechanism in terms of general rules. Basic to his syllogistic were theories concerning the functioning of terms, the structure of predicative statements and quantification. With regard to predication he does not seem alive to the complexity of general statements: 'In order to justify Aristotle's doctrine as a whole it is necessary to suppose that he assumed application for all the general terms with which he dealt. To a modern logician this seems a rather curious restriction of the scope of logic.' (Kneale, *The Development of Logic*, p. 60) But he is keenly alert about a distinction between the logical phenomenon of predication and the grammatical, and about the need to free predication from its association with a verb of existence. Indeed in the *Prior Analytics* four forms are used interchangeably to express predication: *A is predicated of B*, *A belongs to B*, *B is A*, *B is in A as in a whole*. Finally, the outlines of axiomatics are clear in Aristotle; he initiated the study of necessity, impossibility, compatibility, opposition; and his study of 'there will be a sea-battle tomorrow' opened up the topic of bivalency in logic.

III. Megarian–Stoic logic. Metalogic made an important advance with this school which maintained that formal logic has a unique subject—the *lecta* of expressions, i.e. it deals neither with words nor with psychic ideas but with what is objectively meant by words—*conceptus objectivus* (to anticipate Scholastic language), their *sense* (to anticipate Frege). *Lecta* are divided into deficient and complete; deficient are the lecta of subjects and predicates; complete are the lecta of assertions, questions, enquiries, commands, oaths, prayers, suppositions and addresses. It is lecta that are properly true or false, complete lecta of course.

Another major contribution of this school was an explicit discussion of implication—its nature and types. It seemed to equate the truth and force of implication with the truth and force of a conditional statement. (This outlook was transmitted to the Middle Ages by Boethius in his treatment of *consequentia.*)

Technically, this school advanced Aristotle's conception of system, being very formalistic and clear on the distinction between law and rule. And the interest of the Megarians in paradox produced *The Liar* ('A man says that he is lying. Is what he says true or false?') and demonstrated the strange results that follow when one interprets a statement as saying something about its own truth or falsity.

In the period before the fall of the Roman Empire, two interesting metalogical contributions were made by Alexander Aphrodisias: he was the first, it seems, to make the explicit distinction between form and matter, and came close to an explicit definition of variable.

IV. Medieval logic. Medieval logic has a rich metalogical content: 'in the later period there is nothing but metalogic, i.e. formulae are not exhibited but described, so that in many works, e.g. in the *De puritate artis logicae* of Burleigh not a single variable of the object language is to be found'. (Bochenski, *A History of Formal Logic*, p. 152)

Working in the context of the Latin language they built up a very general semantics and syntax. In their doctrine of the properties of terms they very carefully examined the manifold functions of vernacular words and phrases when they are terms of propositions. Before the time of Occam it was held that basic in every term was its *signification*, its function of conveying a form; based on this was *suppositio* (the function of 'standing for', 'referring to', 'representing' things), *appelatio* (the function of naming) and *ampliatio* (the function of extending the supposition of the subject term which certain terms exercise, e.g. 'possibly', 'can', adjectives, verbs in the past, present or future tense). Occam however rejected *significatio*, making supposition basic: there is nothing else real, nothing else in the world to signify, than individual things. For him a general term is shorthand for a list of proper names. This conception of language as nomenclature was to get its classical presentation and analysis in Wittgenstein's *Tractatus.*

In general the medieval doctrine of properties of terms, had the limitation of covering topics as diverse as meaning and reference on the one hand and inference based on quantification on the other hand; it was also bound up with peculiarities of the Latin language (e.g. its lack of an indefinite article). Thus it could never be incorporated as such into modern logic whose strength lies very much in the careful discriminations made by exact symbolization.

The peculiar problems associated with a proposition about the future were widely discussed in the context of divine foreknowledge, as was also the timeless quality of truth. Some accepted Aristotle's view in the *De Interpretatione* that a proposition about, e.g. a sea-battle tomorrow is neither determinately true nor determinately false even though the disjunction of that proposition and its contradictory is true. But the discussions did not lead to anyone conceiving a three-valued logic.

Antinomies or *insolubilia* (to use the medieval term) were very extensively treated. Paul of Venice lists fifteen solutions, the modern distinction of language and meta-language being used in some of them. He defines an *insolubile* as a 'propositio habens super se reflexionem suae falsitatis aut se non esse veram totaliter vel partialiter illativa', focusing self-reference as a defining feature.

Scholasticism has a very clear doctrine of logical constants (*syncategoremata*) as being the formative elements in expressions. Some logicians indeed were content to say that these words were the subject matter of logic. Others pointed out that words express thought so that it is the *lekta* (*sense*) of these words which are absolutely and basically formative. In this second view logical form is defined as having its being primarily, basically, in thought although, as with the Stoics, it is nothing psychical but something objective. These two views (locating the subject matter of logic in 'syncategoremata' or in 'second intentions' of the mind) were not regarded as conflicting but as complementary, and within both the practice of logic was the same.

Scholastic logicians analysed the structure and sense of propositions very well, their analysis of predication being particularly penetrating. They achieved a quite modern analysis of the quantifiers, 'every' and 'some', and in this context used propositional logic as the basis of term-logic. They also analysed the community of reference in analogous terms and the significance of this for inference by analogy, this being the first known formulation of the notion of *isomorphy.*

Finally, the Scholastic theory of consequences is a major contribution covering, in area, both propositional and term logic. Technically excellent, it describes a wide variety of argument structures metalogically with their rules. The modern paradoxes of material implication were exhibited and analysed, and a distinction between a material truth-functional connection and a strict formal connection in meaning was drawn. The meaning of entailment was explored (the Pseudo-Scotus gives three definitions; Paul of Venice gives ten different interpretations) and it is clear that some logicians were concerned to root the validity of an argument in propositional contents rather than in the correlations of propositional truth-values.

The following text from Albert of Saxony is an example of the formal excellence of Scholastic description:

> Eighth rule: every consequence of this kind is formal: 'Socrates exists, and Socrates does not exist, therefore a stick stands in the corner'. Proof: By formal consequence it follows: 'Socrates exists and Socrates does not exist, therefore Socrates exists', from a complete copulative proposition to one of its parts. Further it follows: 'Socrates exists and Socrates does not exist, therefore Socrates does not exist' by the same rule. And it further follows: 'Socrates exists, therefore either Socrates exists or a stick stands in the corner'. The consequence holds, since from every categorical proposition a disjunctive proposition is deducible (*infert*) of which it is a part. And then again: 'Socrates exists and Socrates does not exist; therefore (by the second part of this copulative proposition): Socrates does not exist; therefore a stick stands in the corner'. The consequence holds since the consequence is formal from a disjunctive with the denial (*destructio*) of one of its parts to the other. And so every proposition similar in form to this would be a valid consequence if it were formed. This rule is usually expressed in the following words: 'from every copulative consisting of contradictorily opposed parts, there follows any other (proposition by) formal consequence'. (*Logica Albertucii Perutilis Logica*: IV, 2, 24 vb–25 ra)

V. From the end of the middle ages to the development of modern mathematical logic. In our survey of the history of formal logic we have seen that this period (of about 400 years) was not a creative one and that a distorted version of logic, the so-called 'classical' logic (permeated with non-logical topics, problems and ideas) developed. In general, apart from the work of Leibniz, logical writings were mainly summary textbooks and commentaries and contributed nothing new to metalogic. As we saw, Leibniz conceived the kind of development that has actually taken place with modern mathematical logic. Thus his work, mainly descriptive and visionary in character, is in effect a primary draft covering some very fundamental elements of modern metalogic. It would be impossible to overestimate this as a personal achievement. Within the Scholastic tradition, commentaries such as those by Cajetan and John of St Thomas have the importance of transmitting a good deal of medieval metalogic.

At the level of detail, two interesting points may be noted. Firstly, for Leibniz every true statement has, on ultimate analysis, a subject-predicate structure—ascribes an attribute to a subject. Thus 'to prove a proposition is to show that its predicate concept is contained in its subject concept, and for this purpose we must analyse the two concepts far enough to make their relations clear ... Discovery consists in the marshalling of chains of definitions, or, at a more fundamental level, in the survey of possible combinations of predicates. This account of demonstration is unsatisfactory because it is based on the assumption that in every affirmative truth *predicatum inest subjecto.* As always Leibniz is thinking of complexity as arising solely from the conjunction of attributes.' (Kneale, op. cit., pp. 332–3) It is interesting to see the philosophers, Bolzano and Mill, also assuming that ultimately all propositions have a subject-predicate structure.

A second interesting detail is the growing interest in relations of extension. It is exemplified in the work of Euler and Gergonne and in the attempt by Hamilton to enlarge Aristotle's syllogistic by including provision for the quantification of predicates. This interest undoubtedly influenced and facilitated the work of Boole.

VI. Modern and contemporary metalogical problems and interests presented as a function of the development of mathematical logic. In this history Boole and Frege are central; Leibniz and Peirce are individualistic. Frege is the dominating figure: both in its ideas and in its deductive system his *Begriffsschrift* (1879) contains all the essentials of modern formal logic, metalogic and philosophy of logic.

6.1: *Boole*: The essence of his contribution was to conceive a method of deriving consequences in completely abstract fashion, i.e. without regard to interpretation. He thought of a formal system as being constructed rather than abstracted, and going to Mathematics for a model to imitate in the construction of a logical system, he wrote the classical description of calculation as formalism and he presented algebra as an abstract calculus capable of various interpretations.

6.2: *Frege*: The essence of his contribution was a comprehension of the structure and divisions of the science of logic; a freeing of logic from undue attachment to the grammar of ordinary language and to the psychology of personal thinking; the construction of a formalized language which processed conceptual content exclusively and was characterized, technically, by the use of quantifiers which made it superior to symbolism of the algebraic type used by Boole and by the central position of function; a sharpening of Euclidean and Aristotelian concepts of axiomatic system, and also of Boolean and contemporary concepts of formal rigour in proof; an excellent presentation of logic as a system, displaying the great variety of thought-forms it accommodates and providing an exact and explicit system of proof for theorems; a philosophy of logic in which it was conceived as the most general of all sciences about reality, the *doctrina formarum* of Leibniz.

6.3: The place of Frege in the history of mathematical logic is such that this history can be conveniently mapped in relation to his work:

6.31: *Developments after Frege in the area of logical symbolism*: Improvements and extensions in symbolism; problems of symbolism and their solutions; theories of language, meaning and logical necessity:

(a) *Triumph of linear symbolism* (Peano, Russell, Lukasiewicz).

(b) *Refinements of notation*, e.g. for expression and for designation (Russell's theory of description); notation for class and function abstractors; Schönfinkel's elimination of variables (combinatory logic); many sorted quantification (where variables of mixed types are used).

(c) *Intensional and extensional language*: An extension is either an individual, a class or a truth-value; an intension is either a concept, a propositional function or a proposition. A language is said to be intensional when it is able to designate intensions and so can be a medium for discussing intensions. The Thesis of Extensionality says that every intensional utterance can be translated without loss into extensional language. The second edition (1925) of *Principia Mathematica* accepts this; also Carnap in his *Logical Syntax of Language* (1934). It is generally easier to work technically with extension rather than intension; e.g. Frege found it easier to deal with the range of values of a function rather than with the function itself, and notation for the former was an important innovation in his later work.

(d) *Paradoxes*: Logical, mathematical and semantical. Russell's theory of types as a solution for the logical, mathematical ones; Tarski's doctrine of metalanguage as a solution for semantical ones.

(e) *The development of a two-level semantics* which excluded subjective psychological concepts and the objective meaning of words and focused the direct relationship between signs and what they stand for. As a result the relation of representation was studied in general, and in particular the relation of representation of predicate signs (giving the traditional problem of universals a new dimension). Important contributions were made by Russell, Wittgenstein, Tarski, Carnap, Lesniewski, Quine and Goodman.

(f) *Meaning*: the meaning of words and of sentences; of variables and of operators; naming and propositioning. The distinction of two modes of meaning, characteristic respectively of subject and predicate terms, as part of logical tradition. Theories of meaning: *de facto* and *de jure* types.

(g) *The nature of logical operators*: The work of symbolizing logical operators, representing them and formalizing them with technical precision, is the *way* we isolate phenomena we study in logic. The more technically precise is our symbolization, the more presentable are our phenomena, the *lekta* of the Stoics. In his syllogistic Aristotle showed that reason is bound by operators in a wholly objective way. Logical operators are not psychic processes or psychic facts. For Wittgenstein one gets a better grasp of them by seeing how they govern and exhaust logical space (the relevant sphere of possibilities). The nature of the predicative operator is intimately connected with the nature of the proposition as such.

(h) *Logical necessity and language*: Since the time of the *Tractatus* a conventionalist theory of necessity has been adopted by many philosophers (cf. the view of Tarski, the thinking of Quine).

6.32: *Developments after Frege in the area of formalization*: These developments were threefold (a) improvements and developments of Boole's and Frege's formal systems; development of other formal systems both standard and non-standard; (b) studies of the process of formalization and of the nature of formal system as such; (c) the development of techniques and theorems related to many problems that were raised about formal systems.

(a) With the development, after the *Principia Mathematica*, of many systems in the various areas of standard logic, and with the work of Hilbert and Bernays in the theory of proof or metamathematics, *a great deal of study has been devoted to axiomatized systems generally*, to methods of proving consistency, independence and completeness of axioms, to the nature and form of exact proof, to the distinction between theorems and rules of inference, to a comparison between the formalized concept of the consequence relation and the ordinary sense of this relation, to the notions of truth and provability, to the problem of priority as between meaning and extension, etc. The Polish School, especially Tarski, has been strongly associated with the study of deductive theory.

(b) Up to 1918 mathematical logicians used only one notion of implication, the Philonian or material one. Thus logic was exclusively assertoric, a logic without modalities, a two-value logic. (The only exception was the system of McColl). For Lewis, *strict entailment* was the heart of logic. He used modalities to formalize it. With Lukasiewicz, Post and Wajsberg there was the development of *many-valued logic*, with the attendant metalogical question: what is the meaning of value here and is many-valued logic simply the application of a calculus—mathematics rather than logic?

(c) The development, through Gentzen and Jaskowski, of *natural deduction systems* was an important contribution to the theory of proof and to the comparative study of axioms and rules in logic. It also raises the question of the relationship between deducibility and implication.

(d) After the time of Boole efforts were made to work out *a logic of relations in an algebraic form* similar to the logic of classes. (De Morgan and Peirce were pioneers here). Some logicians now doubt the value of presenting the theory of relations as an algebra. (Today the term 'algebra of logic' frequently denotes that part of logic which can be presented without the use of quantifiers).

(e) A proof of completeness for a system of general logic was first published by Gödel in 1930. This is *Gödel's completeness theorem*: every valid formula in the predicate calculus of first order is provable. In 1931 the theorem relating to formally undecidable propositions and generally known as *Gödel's Theorem* was published—in any formal system adequate for number theory there is an undecidable proposition, that is, a proposition such that neither the proposition itself nor its negation is provable in the system. Gödel's results by showing that mathematics cannot be completely and consistently formalized in one system raised questions about the value of formalization in mathematics and generally. They also brought general logic and mathematics into contrast.

(f) The impossibility of a *universal decision procedure* for general logic and for many formal systems has been established through the work of Church, Tarski, Mostowski and Robinson. Thus there is not and cannot be a method for the solution of all mathematical or all logical problems. To many (e.g. Wittgenstein) it was a normal expectancy that the truisms of logic would be certifiable as such by some simple procedure.

6.33: *Developments after Frege concerning the question of the boundaries of logic, situating it in the corpus of the sciences*:

(a) *Logic's connection with inference*: In the corpus of logical tradition everything has a connection with the enterprise of classifying and articulating the principles of formally valid inference. Some (e.g. Lewis) would like to see strict entailment, that which governs and guarantees inference, central in logic. Contemporary developments such as many-valued logic seem to move logic in a different direction.

(b) *Logic's connection with language and grammar*: there is great contemporary interest in the relationship of logical language to ordinary language, and in the question whether *a priori* truth and logical necessity are determined by language.

(c) *Logic's connection with mathematics*: The development of formalism and formal systems gave rise to the controversy in this area: can all mathematical terms be defined by logical ones and all mathematical theorems be deduced from logical axioms (*the logistic position*—Frege, Russell)? Do mathematics and logic constitute a single system of symbols (*the position of formalism*—Hilbert)? In contrast to logic has mathematics empirical roots, in the intuition of time, so that it does not presuppose a system of logic (indeed the technique of formalization is to be distrusted), logic being a study of regularities abstracted from mathematical systems (*the position of intuitionism*—Brouwer and Heyting)?

(d) *Logic's connection with technology*: Can a formal system be always used as a computer device? What is the significance of an affirmative answer?

VII. Conclusion. It is clear that basic studies in metalogic have been concerned with language, meaning, truth, proof, generality, classal thought, paradox, the nature of logical principles and logic's connection with mathematics. These topics will be treated in the following chapters.

Chapter 3

LANGUAGE AND LOGIC

I. The complexity of vernacular language systems

What does it mean to *say* something in a vernacular language such as English, 'to sound right' and 'to make sense'? It is important to deal with language in general and with vernacular languages before proceeding to such metalogical questions as: what does it mean to say something in *logical* language? what is the specific character of this language, and what are the main problems associated, historically, with its construction?

One of the most remarkable things in the life of the one-year-old baby is the development of speech. 'The newborn baby and his mother often seem to have a feeling of complete wordless communication through the touch of their skin and the gaze of their eyes. The mother at moments may share the baby's "belief" that they are actually a part of each other. However, as the baby grows up he learns to see his mother as an individual separate from himself. Weaning forces him to accept the fact of the distance between them. The early unspoken physical communication is replaced by a developing means of communication —of sounds, gestures, facial expressions. But sometimes to the baby it can seem very frustrating that he has to learn to tell his mother his needs and wishes in this way. The period after weaning can be one in which the baby is not only sad at the loss of close contact with his mother but also irritable or even angry with her for the distance she has put between them. However, as he learns to use words, this feeling of frustration goes. Through words he can communicate with his mother on a new more mature level, and he delights in this skill, which makes him more like his parents.' (Tavistock series on Child Development published by Corgi)

To a one-year-old language comes as a glorious *bridge* to mother after a growing awareness of separation. 'Bridge'—this is not a bad description: language has a referential force bending the attention of the hearer and a sense carrying the thought or feeling of the speaker. Once we know a language then any hearing of sentences in that language spans the distance between us and the speaker: an invisible network of social conventions and shared understandings bind us to him in the very act of hearing.

The science of linguistics contributes substantially to our understanding of language, its most basic sections being concerned with speech rather than writing. Speech is language in its primary form for the written word 'remains, for the most part, a substitute for speech, with logical and stylistic peculiarities best understood as efforts to overcome obstacles arising from the hearer's absence'. (Max Black, *The Labyrinth of Language*, p. 7) From linguistics we can construct the following schematic picture of the speech situation, this picture being of fundamental value for answering the question: what does it mean to say that a person's use of a particular language sounds right?

The existence of speech 'depends, in the last resort, on the trained capacity of human beings to produce distinctive sounds immediately recognizable by themselves and others'. (Ibid., p. 11) A normal four-year-old has the fundamentals of this skill and with increasing control of his articulatory muscles, he plays his vocal tract—a much more difficult skill than playing an artificial wind instrument. *Articulatory phonetics* describes our 'vocal repertoire—providing a verbal score, one might say, for the vocal tract's performances. Its distinctive vocabulary of labials and dentals, fricatives, liquids and the like, typically identifies vocal features in terms of the muscular adjustments ("articulations") needed to produce them.' But speech requires also that it be *heard* as such. How do we recognize and identify sounds as speech? To take a single detail, how is it that we hear the same word whether the speaker speaks quickly or slowly, calmly or excitedly, in this individual accent or that? Quite clearly, hearing is an active, skilful, abstracting process, drawing selectively on various physical and contextual clues. And natural language must facilitate this process, enabling the speaker to provide, with skill, a reasonable redundancy of clues. However, the process of hearing, so remarkable in what it achieves, remains mysterious in its own nature, although it is believed that to some extent the hearer relies on knowing where and how a speech-sound would be produced in his own speech tract.

It is evident that, physically, each language uses a definite set of sounds, i.e. it has a definite stock of phonemes or minimal units of sound-in-speech, phoneme being a category word under each of which is grouped sounds which are physically and functionally similar. Thus each language is a distinct phonemic or phonological system and is studied as such in the section of linguistics called *phonemics* or *phonology*. In any given language only certain combinations of phonemes sound right and this fact is a constant source of clues which we use for anticipating and identifying what a person is saying.

Speech as an acoustical event, uttered and heard, calls for an analysis which is physical, but much more than physical also, for speech is an intelligible utterance which 'makes sense'. We hear it as words and sentences in our language and such 'hearing' is a highly systematic, selective reaction to sound. Correspondingly, a special section of the science of linguistics studies the superordinate system of rules or syntax to which the basic phonological system of a language is subject for the purpose of achieving intelligible utterance. In this superordinate system or syntax, morphemes are the smallest units referred to, a morpheme being a minimal unit of meaning. Thus as well as simple words being morphemes, even a letter like 's' (which forms a plural or present tense) is a morpheme as is, e.g. the adjectival ending 'al'. 'S' and 'al', however, are bound morphemes as they can only occur in combination with at least one other morpheme, whereas a simple word is a free morpheme, because it can occur alone. Morphemes are the building blocks of complex words, phrases, clauses and sentences; and grammar is the principal set of rules governing the structuring.

Of primary importance is the grammarian's grouping of words into categories on the basis of similar function, so that a word can always be substituted for any other word from the same category, without a sentence degenerating thereby into nonsense.

Thus, whether true or untrue, 'John is smoking a pipe' is as meaningful as 'Peter is smoking a pipe'—'John' and 'Peter' belonging to the same form-class, can be substituted, grammatically, for each other in any context. A special discipline, *Morphology*, is devoted to the construction and study of form-classes, organizing vocabulary (the material collection of individual words) on this basis. Grammar goes on next to the study of how words are systematically modified by prefixes and suffixes and how such modifications give rise to systematic variations of meaning. Finally it gives a precise formalization of acceptable structuring of phrases, clauses and sentences. Some of the requirements for acceptability may have become quite pointless as, e.g. rules for the gender of nouns and for the declension of adjectives according to gender, nevertheless grammar is a set of rules the penalty for not observing which is loss of speech—that we don't succeed in *saying* anything in the medium of the particular language. Essentially, these rules help to bring into existence a social medium both for expressing thought and for receiving directed thought.

Intelligible utterance cannot fail to bring into operation, in however limited an extent, the whole language system—phonological and grammatical. Words function as elements of the system. Thus when we speak intelligibly it is not single words we use but the system; again what we hear and understand are systems of words rather than single words.

II. Logical language

Logical language, like natural language, is an institution requiring social initiation. But it is designed for a far more restricted use, for what, in fact, is called a cognitive use: it is exclusively concerned with processing thought, whether formally as truth-claims (in standard logic) or otherwise (in many-valued logic). Since thought content (of any sentence or judgment) that is necessarily either true or false is called a proposition, and since well-formed expressions in any system of many-valued logic are also patient of evaluation in bivalent terms of truth and falsity, logical language is said to be designed precisely and exclusively for propositional use.

Further it is essentially a written language (the use of letters from known alphabets is incidental); thus it is not a phonemic or phonological system. Its symbols are ideographs standing directly for ideas and not in any way containing a code for pronunciation. In sum, it is a precision instrument for the writing of thought, designed to facilitate both the exact expression, and (to use the basic image in the technical term *implication*) the systematic unfolding, of thought content (the *lekton* of the Stoics). And its economy and power are both very striking: with a small number of primitive symbols and a minimal grammar governing formation and transformation (in proof) of expressions, it presents itself as an open system capable of generating an immense, systematic, range of rule-governed statements. And it has a great advantage over vernacular languages in that it need not be *redundant*: in everyday speech many clues converge to help the hearer interpret both sound and sense; in logical language one has not to compensate for the swift disappearance of sound-signals, and there is no indulgence to over-determination of meaning. As Wittgenstein reminds us, vernacular languages grow out of ordinary life and serve it, concretely, with a multiplicity of tools and of ways in which they are used:

> But how many kinds of sentence are there? Say assertion, question and command?—There are *countless* kinds: countless different kinds of use of what we call 'symbols', 'words', 'sentences'. And this multiplicity is not something fixed, given once for all; but new types of language, new language-games, as we may say, come into existence, and others become obsolete and get forgotten ... Here the term 'language-*game*' is meant to bring into prominence the fact that the *speaking* of language is part of an activity, or of a form of life.
>
> *(Philosophical Investigations, § 23)*

Vernacular language must take into account, express and serve the speaker's living situation and like the speaker, it is in abrasive reactive contact with concrete life; logical language, however, has not the function of ministering to intersubjective, psychic encounters between people, but simply and impersonally of presenting forms of thought.

III. The limitations and capabilities of logical language

The stipulated objectives that are built into the design of logical language increase its specific efficiency, but they also militate against the claim that the thought content of natural language can *always* be perfectly translated into logical language and that an *essential* function of logical language is to legislate and to judge clarity in other media, clarifying and remedying vernacular expression. The *a priori* uneasiness about such claims is justified when one comes to the difficulties which Predicate Logic has in dealing with statements about the beliefs of a person and with statements that have dependent predicates.

In the medium of logical language since any wff is patient of being evaluated as either true or false and since the truth value of a complex expression is a function of the values of the constituent wff's, one can always substitute an equivalent wff for any of the constituent ones without altering the value of the expression as a whole. Taking *CKCpqpq* one can substitute *ANpq* for *Cpq* since they fulfil the same truth conditions; the result is *CKANpqpq* which is guaranteed to have the same truth value as the original from which it is derived. The rule of substitution is an inference license of the utmost importance in logical derivation and every application of it is intuitively valid in systems of logic where thought is processed *impersonally* as truth-claims, not *personally* as, e.g. a belief. In the latter case the rule of substitution cannot be applied: it is not valid to derive '*X* believes that the Tower of Pisa is not at an angle of 90° to the ground' from '*X* believes that the Tower of Pisa is leaning somewhat': *X* may not know anything about angles and degrees and therefore one cannot, with truth, describe his belief in those terms. The impersonal equivalence between 'The Tower of Pisa is not at an angle of 90° to the ground' and 'The Tower of Pisa is leaning somewhat' is not paralleled by an equivalence within the context of belief.

Logic is concerned with thought-content in the *formalized, impersonal,* context of truth-claim, assertion. It is not concerned with psychological conditions of belief, a conscious psychic event. It does not map thought content on to psychic, conscious attitudes; thus its equivalences and discriminations are not at all mental. The result is that if one wants to formalize statements in natural language about beliefs one simply finds that the language and procedures of logic can deal impersonally with the content of a belief but that the psychic aspects and parameters of belief escape its net. *Psychically* one cannot believe that a tower is or is not at an angle of 90° without knowing something of angles and degrees, but *implicitly*, in the content of sheer thought content, one is accepting the geometrical equivalent when one believes that the tower is leaning.

The difficulty involved in formalizing statements with dependent predicates arises from the fact that logic treats predicates as though they were independent of one another just as it treats propositions as being so. Thus while the argument, *Brutus murdered Caesar with a knife, therefore Brutus murdered Caesar*, is simple and seen, intuitively, to be valid it is not easy to formalize it in the medium of logical symbolism. Robert Ackermann points out:

> any attempt to abstract this argument . . . results either in an assessment of the argument as invalid, or in some PL forms which are clearly not appropriate. About the best attempt to obtain a most sophisticated PL argument consistency form which will show the argument to be valid depends on constructing some predicate expressions so as to produce this:
>
> (1) *Mbcd*
> (2) $(\forall x)(Mbcx)$

To obtain this we have to take 'Brutus murdered Caesar' as equivalent to 'Brutus murdered Caesar with something', an intuition that is not easily extended beyond this argument. If Brutus is direct, strangling Caesar with his bare hands, or suitably inventive, sending Caesar off on a doomed mission, we would need to locate some other equivalence to effect an abstraction. It seems doubtful that an appropriate abstraction can be found to conclude that Caesar was murdered by Brutus from any statement of his having been murdered by some means or other, or in some place or other, or in some manner. (*Modern Deductive Logic: an Introduction to its Techniques and to its Significance*, pp. 159–60)

Although logical language is not a criterion of what all languages should be, viewed directly in itself it is a medium of formalization in the most exacting sense that is humanly possible. This is made evident by two facts:

(a) its use of variables to free it from reference (as distinct from application) to particular contexts. Since the time of Boole it has been explicitly and emphatically the aim of logic to write in a way that transcends contexts and is thereby *interpretable* for an indefinite range of contexts. Frege has been the great modern technician for this kind of concept-writing.

(b) by the problems that have arisen, historically, in the designing of modern logical notation. Basic problems were encountered by Russell over the ten years devoted to writing the *Principia Mathematica* and gave rise to his important theories of (1) proper names, (2) definite descriptions and (3) levels or orders of languages. Discussion, even controversy, about these theories makes it clear that it is the function of logical language to formalize in a way that is both exact and ultimate. We shall briefly review these theories.

IV. Russell's theory of proper names and his theory of definite descriptions

For Russell the function of a proper name is simply to pick out an individual; there is no structure to its significance: it simply picks out. The function of naming cannot be exercised if the individual does not exist, so a symbol is not really a proper name if the individual it purports to name does not exist. Further, an existential expression of the type 'Patrick Jones exists' is not a genuine statement at all: the word 'exists' only appears to be a predicate, it does not perform any function that is not already performed by 'Patrick Jones' which picks out the existent individual. Russell indeed emphasizes that in having a category of symbols that are proper names, Predicate Logic is making a certain ontological presupposition, namely that the world it is dealing with is a world of individuals. Technically of course the proofs of predicate logic presuppose that there is at least one individual in the world.

Natural languages do not seem to conform, however, to Russell's theory of proper names. They seem to frequently discharge the function of naming through definite descriptions which (1) can have a rich structured significance, as, e.g. 'The present President of the United States of America'; and (2) may have no real individual corresponding to the description even though it is perfectly intelligible, as, e.g. occurs in 'The King of France'. In Russell's theory the presence of a definite description in a statement means that we are not naming any individual, we are not talking about a subject but about a linguistic expression. Thus properly formalized the vernacular sentence 'The King of France is bald' would read: For all values of x and y the following expressions (propositional functions) are true: 'If x is the King of France x is bald' and 'If y is the King of France, y is identical with x'. For Russell this formalization is the only acceptable way of reconciling the fact that the original statement is meaningful and yet that there is not any King of France. And when we use the word 'exists' with a definite description we are really talking about an expression and saying that there is at least one value of the variable in it for which it will be true.

Taking the three sentences:
(1) The King of France is bald;
(2) The golden mountain does not exist;
(3) Scott is the author of *Waverly*;
their formalizations are:
(1) $(x)(Fx \rightarrow Bx) . (y) Fy \rightarrow x = y$;
(2) $(x) - (Mx . Gx)$;
(3) $(x)(Sx \equiv Wx)$, i.e. x is Scott $\equiv x$ wrote *Waverly*.
It is useful to note that in dealing with a vernacular argument which contains a definite description, whether or not one needs to analyse it in Russellian fashion depends simply on what is necessary to display the force of the argument. The importance of Russell's theory lies in its insight into the design and presuppositions of logical language.

V. Russell's theory of types

In 1903 Russell wrote that a doctrine of types afforded a possible solution to his famous Paradox of Classes. After trying to solve the various paradoxes by other means he developed a theory which became known later as the Ramified Theory of Logical Types and he incorporated this in the *Principia Mathematica*. In the 1920s Ramsey's work on the paradoxes made possible a great simplification of the theory of types. At that time the simpler form became known as the Simple Theory of Types (and was often identified with Russell's 1903 version to which it is quite similar), and the complicated version in *Principia Mathematica* was called the 'Ramified' or 'Branch' theory.

According to Russell, if language is to be immune to paradox it must obey an inbuilt type-theory according to which its parts of speech form a hierarchy, falling into separate categories (e.g. names and predicates) with no element ever performing the function of an element from another category, and some elements not being predicable of others. This is fundamentally the Simple Theory of Types.

Further, in the Ramified Theory, propositions must be seen to form a hierarchy, the basic or first order propositions being those which are not themselves about propositions; the next (second) order of propositions are about the first order ones, and the nth + 1 tier is about propositions of the nth order. In *Principia Mathematica* (p. 42) it is pointed out that 'the words "true" and "false" have many different meanings, according to the type of proposition to which they are applied'.

This hierarchy of propositions does render language immune to the liar paradox but not to others. As a solution to these the Ramified Theory provides a complicated hierarchy of propositional functions. 'One dimension of this ramified hierarchy of functions divides propositional functions into functions of individuals (functions of type 1), functions of functions of individuals (functions of type 2) and so on. When functions of more than one argument are considered, this one dimension of the hierarchy becomes quite complicated itself . . . The other dimension . . . cuts right across the Simple Type Theory. For each type, the functions of that type are divided further into infinitely many *orders.*' (Irving Copi, *The Theory of Logical Types*, pp. 82–3)

Russell's theory was so restrictive that it jeopardized the derivation of a great deal of classical mathematics. To safeguard this derivation he introduced an axiom of reducibility which asserts that to any function of any type, any order and any number of arguments there corresponds a predicative function (i.e. a function of the first order) that is formally equivalent to it—the same in type and holding for exactly the same arguments. However neither the Ramified Theory nor the axiom were ever generally accepted.

It is important indeed not to see the theory as either descriptive or prescriptive with regard to natural languages but as recommendations for the designing of a special artificial language which will render it immune to paradox and will further the specific objectives of mathematical logic. Bar-Hillel comments:

> The attempt to impose a type hierarchy upon natural languages seems misguided and linguistically pointless. The concerns of Russell and other authors about how to formulate the theory of types in English (or any other natural language) without violating the theory in its very formulation (e.g. by speaking of all types) are now no more than interesting curiosities. (*Encyclopedia of Philosophy*, vol. 8, article on Theory of Types, p. 171)

Today an idea suggested by Russell in 1922 has been developed into a doctrine of levels of language—language, metalanguage, metametalanguage, etc.—which is very useful for handling paradoxes. In his introduction to the *Tractatus* of Wittgenstein he said:

> These difficulties suggest to my mind some such possibility as this; that every language has, as Mr Wittgenstein says, a structure concerning which, *in the language*, nothing can be said, but that there may be another language dealing with the structure of the first language, and having itself a new structure, and that to this hierarchy of languages there may be no limit.

This levels of language doctrine which received an important technical presentation from Tarski, has a good deal of affinity with the Ramified Theory but possesses none of its negative effects on mathematical derivations.

VI. Conclusion

Logical language is a medium for *formal presentation* of thought content (the Stoic *lekta*) rather than for *personal expression.* It is designed to facilitate rigorously exact and explicit proof; to exclude paradox; and to express laws that transcend particular contexts and are thus patient of unlimited interpretation.

Chapter 4

TWO BASIC CONCEPTS: MEANING AND TRUTH

I. Language as meaningful

It is expected that when a language system is used properly it 'makes sense' and is not 'meaningless'. Linguistic utterance or writing is intelligible: it can be understood no matter what level of life or science it relates to. Bohr used the striking metaphor: we humans live suspended in language. At this point we are going to focus the medium of language as a constructed, coherent, understandable entity; we are not dealing at all with its truth or falsity and in so far as the concept of meaning or meaningful is used we must be quite sure that it is disengaged from the concept of truth.

In the case of logical language rules for constructing wff's constitute an adequate source and criterion of its intelligibility. A logical expression has *form* or *intelligibility* when it is grammatical. By the use of variables (i.e. blanks) logic transcends contexts instead of setting contexts by rich object words, and thus accord with grammatical rules achieves intelligibility (i.e. the intelligibility that is natural to logical statements) in a way that is fully defined and is patient of exact application. Within logic, therefore, problems of discriminating between meaningful and meaningless statements are solved by referring to the notation and formation rules of the language used. Further the transformation rules must be such that correct use of them guarantees that any theorem generated from wff's will itself be a wff.

Indeed in working out to the full any particular system, modern logicians apply both formation and transformation rules in a purely formalistic way, confident in a resultant coherent intelligibility.

The constitutors of logical meaning (i.e. of the form of intelligibility that is natural to logical statements) are the operators. In propositional logic we have *N*-statements, *C*-statements, *A*-, *K*-, *E*-, *D*-statements, whose intelligibility is truth-functional in definition; in predicate logic the intelligibility is forms of attribution general and existential; in modal logic the intelligibility is forms of necessitation, possibility, impossibility and contingency. Later we shall discuss in detail the nature and functioning of logical operators; at the moment we are concerned in a general way, with the contrast between logical and natural language.

In his introduction to Wittgenstein's *Tractatus Logico-Philosophicus*, Russell said:

> ... logic has two problems to deal with in regard to Symbolism: (1) the conditions for sense rather than nonsense in combinations of symbols; (2)

the conditions for uniqueness of meaning or reference in symbols or combinations of symbols. A logically perfect language has rules of syntax which prevent nonsense, and has single symbols which always have a definite and unique meaning. Mr Wittgenstein is concerned with the conditions for a logically perfect language—not that any language is logically perfect, or that we believe ourselves capable, here and now, of constructing a logically perfect language, but that the whole function of language is to have meaning, and it only fulfills this function in proportion as it approaches to the ideal language which we postulate.

This passage brings out the fact that modern logic begins by designing as perfect a language (for its purposes) as possible, where 'meaningfulness' and 'grammaticality' coincide, and it expresses the view that, ideally, the same coincidence should be true of natural languages.

Turning to natural languages does the 'meaningfulness', 'intelligibility', 'acceptability' of speech and writing coincide with their grammaticality? From the beginning of this century, with the work of Russell on paradoxes and the revival by Husserl of belief in a universal grammar, attempts were made to devise a system of rules acceptable and powerful enough to decide, with respect to any expression of everyday speech, whether it were meaningful or meaningless. The works of Rudolf Carnap are a *locus classicus* for the view that such a system of rules can be discovered for each language. He did not believe in a single, universal grammar; indeed he opposed such a concept with a 'principle of tolerance' towards conventional variety of linguistic forms. But he believed that a syntactical method for detecting pseudo-statements could be worked out in each language:

> ... the whole theory of language structure and its possible applications in philosophy came to me like a vision during a sleepless night in January 1931, when I was ill. On the following day, still in bed with a fever, I wrote down my ideas on forty-four pages under the title 'Attempt at a metalogic' ... At that time I defined the term 'metalogic' as the theory of the forms of the expressions of a language. Later I used the term 'syntax' instead of 'metalogic', or in distinction to syntax as part of linguistics, 'logical syntax'. [In other words his specific interest in syntax was in its capacity to generate and to decide intelligibility—that is the force of the word 'logical' rather than any suggestion that it was a syntax of an ideal logical language.] These shorthand notes were the first version of my book *Logical Syntax of Language* (1943–6). ('Intellectual Autobiography' by Rudolf Carnap, pp. 53 and 54 of *The Philosophy of Rudolf Carnap* edited by Paul Arthur Schilpp)

Later Carnap concluded that a purely syntactical theory of a language was not sufficient for his purpose; its metatheory must include semantics and pragmatics. Noam Chomsky was a pupil of Carnap and his work in linguistics has been very much influenced by Carnap.

The substance of a metatheory of language and meaningfulness may be presented, simply, against the background of specific problems and paradoxes posed by the following sentences:

> Socrates is redness.
> Socrates redness internationally.
> Colourless green ideas sleep furiously.
> Saturday is in bed.
> Today is Monday but I don't believe it.
> This statement is false.

Let us use the term theory of a given language to signify the formulation of its notation together with a set of rules that will generate all the possible meaningful statements in that language, and only meaningful statements. This set of rules will consist of:

(a) syntactical rules which, independently of the meaning of words, govern their proper combination. A passage from Chomsky provides a good example: '... given an appropriate rule, it can be proved that the word-series "Pirots karulize elatically" is a sentence, provided only that "Pirots" is known to be a substantive (in the plural), "karulize" a verb (in the third person plural), and "elatically" an adverb ... The meaning of the words is quite inessential to the purpose, and need not be known.' ('Systems of Syntactic Analysis', *Journal of Symbolic Logic*, 1953)

The two sentences 'Socrates is redness' and 'Socrates redness internationally' violate syntactical rules of the English language.

(b) lexical rules which are concerned with the word stock (vocabulary) of a language and determine for each item other words with which it may combine and words with which it may not combine. When words go together in definable combinations (e.g. 'night' and 'black'; 'coloured' and 'green') they are said to *collocate*. Collocations are part of the total meaning of a word and words cannot be used outside the range of their collocations without a loss of meaning.

The sentences 'Colourless green ideas sleep furiously' (Chomsky) and 'Saturday is in bed' (from Ryle) violate lexical rules.

(c) pragmatic rules which govern those aspects of linguistic form that derive from the user. Thus a statement is formally an assertion and a truth-claim. Pragmatic rules don't allow us to build into an assertion a denial that it is an assertion, or into a truth-claim a claim of falsity.

The sentences 'Today is Monday but I don't believe it' and 'This statement is false' violate pragmatic rules.

Wittgenstein showed that it was wrong to regard logical language as an underlying infra structure present, to some extent, in every natural language. Indeed in his later life he did not think of language in terms of an underlying system of forms. It was Chomsky's achievement to go outside formal logic in providing such a system, combining Carnap's formation and transformation rules with Wittgenstein's deep and surface structures.

Chomsky envisaged a limited Phrase Structure Grammar which would produce a number of terminal strings to be called the *kernels* of a language. All other sentences of the language would then be produced by the operation of transformations upon these kernels. A phonetic representation of each sentence would be produced by the operation of morphophonemic rules upon these transformationally derived sentence forms. A listing of the phrase structure and transformational rules used in the derivation of a sentence would constitute its *structural representation.* Chomsky often refers to the structure of a kernel as the 'deep structure' of *any sentence derived from it*; and the representation of the same sentence that a phrase-structure grammar would give, he calls, by contrast, its 'surface structure'. Both transformations and kernels are to be thought of as finite inventories, presumably stored in the memory of some computer or other device. (Yorick Alexander Wilks, *Grammar, meaning and the machine analysis of language*, published by Routledge and Kegan Paul, pp. 60–1) [Instead of 'kernels' Chomsky speaks now of the 'base component' of the whole grammar.]

There are three ways in which Chomsky views a transformational generative grammar: (i) as a model for sentence production; (ii) as a model for a brain mechanism; and (iii) as a model for what people say about the grammatical structure of their language ... It is the last of these that Chomsky has in mind when he speaks of competence ... Chomsky thinks that performance models (models of what people actually say and write) are too difficult to construct, and also that grammaticality is *not appropriate* to performance. The appropriate notion there, he says, is 'acceptability'. (Ibid., p. 69)

I claim that there can only be performance models, and that when Chomsky talks of competence models he is necessarily talking about models for certain selections from among possible performances. (Ibid., p. 70)

II. The formation, specifically, of logical meaning: logical operations

Our metalogical discussion is concerned with the formation of meaning in the sign medium of logical notation. Every well-formed formula achieves meaning or intelligibility; it expresses and processes thought-content that is relevant to the science of logic. However, in itself, each formula is a *sign construct* and must be studied as such before, humanly, we can speak in general of the constitution of *logical meaning* or of *logical thought-content.* The present discussion will include some treatment of the terms *proposition* and *logical operations*; these and other elements will reappear at the philosophical level of reflection appropriate to the later section on the philosophy of logic.

The whole function of language is to have meaning, and the grammatical use of logical notation produces statements that have logical form or intelligibility, that make logical sense. Logical operations are varieties of ways in which we achieve meaning by the use of logical notation. The sign constructs indicate this variety of meaning: pq; $ECpqANpq$; Fa; $Fabc$; $(x)Fx$; $(Ex)Fx$; $(x)(y)Fxy$; $(x)(y)(z)Fxyz$; $(Ex)(y)Fx \rightarrow Fy$; Lp; Mp (or $NLNp$); Up (or LNp); Zp (or NLp or $KMpMNp$); $a = b \equiv (ab' = 0) . (a'b = 0)$; $a + b = -(-a \times -b)$. It is clear that in each case meaning is a function of the sign-construct as a whole and as a unit, even though in the process of sign-construction we may look on the variables as devices for transcending particular reference and on the constants (or functors) as specific determinants of sense. Indeed constants are often called operators. One must remember, however, that the metaphor, *operation*, is best linked with the fact that meaning is a function of the sign-construct as a complete whole: indeed the sign-construct *is* a whole and not merely a sum of symbols: its constituents signify only in relation to one another as a totality. And instead of speaking of logical operations we could equally well speak of 'making logical sense', 'bringing into existence logical meanings, logical intelligibilities'. However, the metaphor operation does draw attention to the fact that the sign-construct has its meaning only in *use*, i.e. as *thought* by writer or reader.

The various sections of logic are characterized by differing types of sense. In propositional logic meaning is presented in terms of the force it exercises when propositions are subjected to truth–falsity evaluation. The kind of intelligibility that is brought into existence by the use of p, N, C, K, etc. is truth-functional, i.e. such that the truth or falsity of every wff is determined, functionally, according to the truth or falsity of its constituent propositions. Thus N, C, K, etc. are called truth functors and are defined by truth-tables. Similarly the meanings of N-statements, C-statements, K-statements, etc. are discriminated by the matrix lines of their truth-tables.

It is important that when we speak of N as the negator, C as the implication sign, K as the conjunction sign, etc. our mode of speech does not obscure the fact that what has meaning is the sign-construct as a whole. This is particularly important in dealing with negation as a logical operation: being negative or positive is a feature of meaning; negative meaning is achieved by a particular type of use of logical notation. Thus the function of negation is performed by the total sign-construct, not by N which exists only in the totality. Further, as Wittgenstein pointed out, both p and Np lead us back to the same state of affairs which either verifies or falsifies our positive and negative meanings. In dealing with the concept of truth it will become quite clear that being negative or positive is a feature of *meaning*, where being true or false is a feature of *correspondence* between our meanings and the facts.

Predicate logic 'makes sense' in a way quite different to propositional logic: an identification is made of an individual, a dyad, triad, etc. and an attribution is made. Predication admits not only of a referential force that is individual but also of one that is systematic. The latter poses the problem of achieving generality of meaning. Modern logic does so by the use of individual variables and by quantifying their variability. Thus when one uses a universal quantifier one signifies that the range of predication is no less than the whole scope of the variable; when one uses an existential quantifier one signifies that the predication holds for some (indefinite) individual in the world we are talking about. It is a feature of predicate logic, of course, that it cannot speak of a world completely empty of individuals.

Eliminating the verb of existence modern logical notation has achieved a clear simplicity in the representation of predication (e.g. *Fa*) and of generality within predication (e.g. $(x)Fx$, $(Ex)Fx$). There is a welcome departure from grammatical symbolism (the *S* and *P* of traditional presentations) and generality is displayed as formation, the function *Fx* being incomplete potential material for the generalization $(x)Fx$. This quantifier-functor-argument structure also displays the logically heterogeneous nature of identification and attribution which are both necessary for predication but require, graphically, the use of symbols that belong to absolutely different categories (x, F). It is to Frege and Russell that we owe the insistence that the relation of a name to the thing named, and the relation of a predicate to what it is true of, are quite distinct and that the distinction must appear in the notation we use to achieve predicative meaning.

Finally, for a person who uses any of the well-known languages of the world, nothing could be more familiar than the subject-predicate mode of speech. It is important to note that linguistic scholars are by no means sure that all peoples do use natural language to make sense in this type of way.

In class calculus sign-constructs fall, simply, into two main categories: (a) *names* of complex classes generated by Boolean operations on simple classes (e.g. $a + b$; $a \times b$); (b) *statements* which chart the intelligibility of class space by expressing laws governing possible relationships between classes, e.g. $a \neq o \equiv (Ex)(x \in a)$. The meaning of these statements has always a truth-functional or predicative *form*; what is new in this extensional study of predicates is the objects referred to: classes, their equalities and inequalities, class inclusion, class membership.

Modal logic brings us to the spectrum of logical options in the certification of truth-claims. *Lp* is a simple construct but very rich in its signification and implications: the meaning (or thought-content) *as truth claim* is certified as being necessitated. Other certifications may be simply compatible with truth (*Mp*) or be incompatible with truth (*Up*) or be that of falling neither under necessitation nor impossibility (*Zp*). In every case the notation is so used that what is processed through the meaning is a modal claim to truth. The modality of this claim is a function of the sign construct as a whole; it is *meant* and requires a special use of notation to achieve the formation of this meaning. The meaning or thought-content, modal in form, is either true or false, i.e. one can always say of a modal statement: if this is what is meant then it is true or false to say this.

Of course the introduction of the concept of modification and range as inherent possibilities for truth claims involves, *for calculation purposes* (if for no other reason), the setting up of many-valued tables in order to be able to operate a complete truth-calculus. Thus many-valued logic can begin, quite naturally, as a calculus for modal logic.

III. '*What is said*' as distinct from the 'saying'

When the *saying* of something is distinguished from *what is said* we describe it as grammatical, clear, polished, idiomatic, spoken with a good accent, loud, excited, nervous, blurted out ... etc. We are dealing with the qualitative use that is made of the medium; we are evaluating (e.g.) English sentences not that which is said by them and could be said also in German, Irish, Chinese, etc. Proposition is the technical word used for something I say; the same proposition can be expressed in different sentences (German, English, Chinese, etc.) and the same sentence can express different propositions (e.g. 'I was born in China') according as various people use this sentence. It is the proposition that is properly true or false not the sentence, and again it is what is said (the proposition) that is properly described as provable, derivable, exaggerated, implausible, etc. Frege put it as follows: 'The sentence has a value for us through the sense that we apprehend in it, and which we recognize as the same in the translation too. This sense I call "thought" (Gedanke). What we prove is not the sentence but the thought. And it makes no difference what language we use for that purpose.' (*Uber Logik und Mathematik*, 1914) It was to express this fact that Frege prefixed a $\vdash$ to every sentence in logical language when he was formulating propositions or deriving theorems.

It is interesting to note that the most fundamental section of formal logic is propositional logic where one begins with the simplest formulation of what is said—the propositional variables p, q, r, s, t. (Frege would prefix $\vdash$.) The tautologies of this section are needed for proofs in predicate logic where the formalization is more complex being in terms of individual variables, quantifiers and predicate letters.

A natural language pre-exists any particular use we make of it as a brain skill possessed by many people, as a mental competency, a vocabulary and a grammar. When these are brought into use in a normal way, meaningful speech is generated. But it is important to note that when we focus speech as meaningful, intelligible, understandable, we are not examining what is said but the quality of our use of the medium in saying what we do say. It is the constructed sentence as such that is meaningful and we speak of the meaning as being clear or ambiguous, controversial or indisputable, etc. On a last analysis while our saying must 'sound right' and must 'make sense' it is precisely what we say that is alone true or false.

IV. The function of a concept of truth within logic

Logic is not concerned with all forms of meaning, e.g. with those that constitute prayers, commands, exclamations, but with those only that have the property of being appraisable as either true or false. Indeed the term proposition is very accurately described as meaning or thought-content which has the property of having to be either true or false. Thus logic is concerned basically with the fact that, in our speech and in our thought, we can achieve an intelligibility which, through having its being in a sign-context of speech and thought, is also, in some way, appraisable in relation to facts. The notation of logic is such that every logical operation is of its nature the processing of a potential truth claim, and in every section logic evaluates its propositions, seeking to sift, derive and organize those that are always true and so construct the body of logical truth.

Thus, a concept of truth is called for both in philosophy of logic (elucidating the nature of propositions as potential truth-claims) and in metalogic. Here in metalogic our concern is to make explicit such concepts as are operational in formal logic especially the concept of proposition as distinct from sentence and the kind of concept of truth that, technically, is necessary and sufficient for the problems and processes of formal logic.

V. A concept of truth sufficient for metalogic

Since the time of Frege logical notations have been chosen as simple and powerful media for propositional use in two senses of these words: (1) with regard to any wff, *what it says* is said in an eminently clear and economic way: thus the *propositions* which logic discovers and proves are presented in almost ideal sentences; (2) their symbols are predominantly concerned with formalizing entities that are either propositions or are constitutive of propositions. Even in class calculus one's long-term objective is to discover (indirectly) truths about predicative propositions; in many-valued logic we are evaluating propositions although we are not concerned to do so in a framework of truth and falsity; and, of course, in standard logic (outside class calculus) we are directly and explicitly concerned with propositions as entities which are essentially and properly truth-claims. Since it is what is said that is essentially and properly a truth-claim, logic may be described as the formal study of what is said. (In the psychic medium of thought what is *judged* is a truth-claim.)

Since the time of Frege there has been a thorough-going rejection of Psychologism in modern logic, a rejection that is implicitly emphasized by the strictly formal character and formalistic method of mathematical logic.

However, with regard to the concept of truth whose philosophical elaboration has been attended, throughout history, with difficulty and controversy, a notable effort has been made to develop a philosophically neutral theory by disengaging truth from the context of propositions, treating 'true' as a predicate of sentences. This effort culminated in the classical paper of Alfred Tarski in the 1930s, *The Concept of Truth in Formalized Languages*. It crystallized two significant processes within Polish philosophy of the 1920s: (1) an acceptance of the classical concept of truth as conformity of thought with reality, the defence of this concept being sustained over many years by Twardowski, Lesniewski, Lukasiewicz, Ajdukiewicz and Kotarbinski; and (2) concern for semantic analyses, a systematic study of philosophical semantics being due mainly to Lesniewski.

Church interprets Tarski's definition of truth very exactly:

As appears from the work of Tarski, there is a sense in which semantics can be reduced to syntax. Tarski has emphasized especially the possibility of finding, for a given formalized language, a purely syntactical property of the well-formed formulas which coincides in extension with the semantical property of being a true sentence. And in Tarski's *Wahrheitsbegriff* [this German translation had an important appendix to the Polish paper and is the basis of the standard English version] the problem of finding such a syntactical property is solved for various particular formalized languages [including the language of standard mathematical logic]. (*Introduction to Mathematical Logic*, vol. 1, p. 65)

Professor Skolimowski comments:

Church's is perhaps the most accurate and proper interpretation. Tarski's definition of truth, considered as finding a purely syntactical property of the sort specified by Church, is without question the task which he set for himself. (*Polish Analytical Philosophy*, p. 48)

Other evaluations emphasize either a philosophical neutrality in Tarski's work or the view that underlying its formal, syntactical character there is an acceptance of the classical concept of truth. Thus Max Black says:

The neutrality of Tarski's definition with respect to the competing philosophical theories of truth is sufficient to demonstrate its lack of philosophical relevance [because] neither this, nor any formal definition of truth, goes to the heart of the difficulties which are at the root of the so-called philosophical problem of truth. ('The Semantic Concept of Truth', *Analysis*, March 1948, p. 61)

For Karl Popper, however, Tarski's work enabled exact scientists and philosophers of science to openly adhere, in their work, to a correspondence theory of truth:

... before I became acquainted with Tarski's theory of truth, it appeared to me safer to discuss the criterion of progress without getting too deeply involved in the highly controversial problem connected with the use of the word 'true'. My attitude at the time was this: although I accepted, as almost everybody does, the objective or absolute or correspondence theory of truth—truth as correspondence with the facts—I preferred to avoid the topic. For it appeared to me hopeless to try to understand clearly this strangely elusive idea of a correspondence between a statement and a fact ... ... All this was changed by Tarski's theory of truth and of the correspondence of a statement with the facts. Tarski's greatest achievement, and the real significance of his theory for the philosophy of the empirical sciences, is that he rehabilitated the correspondence theory of absolute or objective truth which had become suspect. He vindicated the free use of the intuitive idea of truth as correspondence to the facts. (*Conjectures and Refutations*, p. 223)

In other words, Tarski's work was not a philosophical enquiry into the nature of truth but he accepted the classic concept of correspondence as a basis and although he did not examine, explain or justify the concept on philosophical grounds, nevertheless it possessed form, precision and validity in his work.

In Tarski's paper one encounters both the power of a deceptively simple discovery and, to use the words of A. N. Prior an 'extraordinary precision, elegance and thoroughness' of elaboration which makes the paper one of the classics of modern logic.

The simple basic discovery is that to talk about the truth of a sentence one must construct and use a metalanguage which can speak about both the sentences of the language in question and about the facts to which they refer. Such a metalanguage is described as 'semantical' by Tarski; a metalanguage which can speak about sentences but not about the facts referred to is called 'syntactical'. The need and use of a semantical metalanguage may be exemplified as follows: *the sentence 'Snow is white' corresponds to the facts (i.e. is true) only if snow is white*. However, here the only metalinguistic sign drawing our attention to the fact that we are speaking in a metalanguage is the use of single quotation marks: these are used to signify that we are naming (mentioning) a sentence in the English language; the English language itself is retained as a proper part of the metalanguage to speak of the facts, i.e. of that which will verify the sentence. In a perfect metalanguage every category or level of reference would have a special symbolism and this happens, of course, in metalanguages for formal logic.

Tarski works out the definition of a true sentence in the language L. This specific, rigorous and difficult part of his paper brings out two essential points: firstly, for Tarski a definition of truth is relativized to a particular language and cannot be extended as a formulation for true sentences of other languages; secondly, a definition can be worked out only for sentences of a formalized language, i.e. of a language whose elements and structure are specified in a full and exact way. Formal logic provides an example of such a language, and, e.g. for the section, propositional logic, a semantic definition of truth can be precisely elaborated (in metalanguage) by a recursive statement of the truth-conditions for sentences in this section. By contrast, a semantic definition of truth cannot be constructed for the sentences of an everyday language; such a language is too 'rich' and 'untidy' and is subject to paradoxes like that of the Liar, the reason being that it is semantically closed containing within itself names of its own expressions and semantic notions such as 'true'.

Tarski's work is certainly valid as a metalogical description and formulation of the concept of truth that is *operational* in formal logic. It does not deal, however, with the nature of truth or with the ultimate reality of correspondence. Thus it is left to the philosophy of logic to move from the level of sentences to that of propositions, and to elucidate truth in the personal contexts of speech and knowledge.

Chapter 5

THE RIGOUR AND RANGE OF PROOF IN
FORMAL LOGIC

I. Introduction: the significance of Gödel's theorem; evaluating formal logic as a body of truths

In his historic paper, *On Formally Undecidable Propositions of Principia Mathematica and Related Systems* Kurt Gödel wrote:

> The development of mathematics in the direction of greater exactness has—as is well known—led to large tracts of it becoming formalized, so that proofs can be carried out according to a few mechanical rules. The most comprehensive formal systems yet set up are, on the one hand, the system of Principia Mathematica (PM) and, on the other, the axiom theory for set theory of Zermelo-Fraenkl (later extended by J. v. Neumann). These two systems are so extensive that all methods of proof used in mathematics today have been formalized in them, i.e. reduced to a few axioms and rules of inference. It may therefore be surmised that these axioms and rules of inference are also sufficient to decide *all* mathematical questions which can in any way at all be expressed formally in the systems concerned. It is shown below that this is not the case, and that in both the systems mentioned there are in fact relatively simple problems in the theory of ordinary whole numbers which cannot be decided from the axioms. This situation is not due in some way to the special nature of the systems set up but holds for a very extensive class of formal systems, including, in particular, all those arising from the addition of a finite number of axioms to the two systems mentioned . . .' (pp. 37–8 in Meltzer's translation; published by Oliver & Boyd, Edinburgh and London, 1962)

The discovery by the young Austrian mathematician that there are arithmetical propositions which are neither provable nor disprovable within their arithmetical system, was announced by him to the Vienna Academy of Sciences in 1930, and published in 1931. 'A relation (class) is called arithmetical,' he says, 'if it can be defined solely by means of the concepts $+$, $.$ [addition and multiplication applied to natural numbers] and the logical constants $\vee$, $-$, (x), $=$, where (x) and $=$ are to relate only to natural numbers. The concept of "arithmetical proposition" is defined in a corresponding way.' (Ibid., p. 63) The theorem belongs to metamathematics (Hilbert's name for the study of rigorous proof in mathematics and mathematical logic) and shows that there is an inherent characteristic incompleteness in formal mathematics.

In the light of this limitation of mathematics one can appreciate, properly, the fact that in metalogic one assesses formal logic with regard to possession of the following three qualities:

(1) the quality of neither containing nor admitting of inconsistency among its theses;

(2) the quality that every tautology expressible in its language can be brought into a relation of deducibility from its principles, i.e. from the axioms and rules of inference when logic is given an axiomatized format; from the Logical Argument Formulae when it is constructed on a natural deduction basis;

(3) the quality of being able to decide, with regard to every expression in its language, whether or not it is a tautology (or a logical contradiction or a contingent proposition).

A separate assessment is made of the two main sections of logic—propositional logic and predicate logic.

II. Assessing the consistency, completeness and decidability of propositional logic

(a) *Our modern logic of propositions is a consistent system.*
It is consistent in the strongest possible way because every proposition derived in it is inescapably a tautology. Thus not only are contradictions absent in it but minor inconsistencies and contingent propositions have not any place either. This can be easily shown because of the fact that a certain type of proof, explicit in its sequence, is demanded for every proposition that is derived.

In a natural deduction system proof is begun with an application (or applications) of the Rule of Assumptions. Formalized as a line of proof, such an application reads

$$1 \qquad (1)\, p \qquad A$$

i.e. on the assumption that p is true, it follows that p is true. Formalized for truth-table testing this is the obvious tautology, $p \vdash p$, or Cpp. Any other stage in the proof consists of the application of some LAF and can be formalized, for truth-table testing, as a conditional proposition whose truth-value is guaranteed by the fact that it does not express anything new other than what is contained in a movement of natural deduction which can never give rise to a false consequent from true antecedents. Thus the sequence of proof is at every stage tautology-preserving. (One could take each natural deduction movement in turn —each LAF—and display its tautology-preserving character).

With regard to modern axiomatic systems of propositional logic, a proof of consistency is in principle the same. Any proposition is derived ultimately from axioms (truth-tabled tautologies) on the basis of explicit, simple, rules of inference: the tautologous quality of each minute derivation is evidenced by the simple, explicit, nature of the rule applied.

(b) *Our modern logic of propositions is a complete system.*
In, e.g. physical science, the prevailing theory which co-ordinates and organizes physical knowledge into a deductive system (e.g. relativity theory, today)
is subject to the following assessment when a new discovery in physics is made:
is the explanatory power of the theory such that the new discovery of law
(made independently of the theory perhaps) can be presented as an implication
of the theory—not only compatible with it but also deducible from it. If
physical theory were able to guarantee that it could situate, within itself, any
new discovery as simply another deducible proposition then it would be a
complete system. (The reliability of the discovery is not at issue in this context
of completeness.)

To say that our modern logic of propositions is complete is to say that it can
provide a proof for every wff (in the language of propositional logic) which is
genuinely tautologous—all such tautologies can be derived from the LAF's of
a natural deduction format, and from the rules and axioms of an axiomatic
format. (How one discovers the genuine tautologies is not at issue here.)

The technique of proof consists in trying to achieve, in the format of a thesis,
that which is displayed, mechanically, in each line of a truth-table. If one takes
the truth-table of any tautology, each line provides a particular set of values for
the variables and displays at the matrix point of the line that the expression as a
whole has the value 1. Does this truth-table characteristic of a tautology enable
us to capture for every tautology, the logical content of every line in its truth-
table so that we can express and prove that content in the language and by the
rules of our system? If so we can provide a proof for every tautology.

1. Let P be a metalogical variable used to express our problem: can
propositional logic prove any tautology, P?
2. Let $p, q, r, s, t \ldots$ be the propositional variables in P. Any assignment of
values for p, q, r, s, t enables one to write down a set of propositions that (under
the assignment made) are all true. Thus if $p = 0, q = 0, r = 1, s = 1, t = 0$, then
a set of true propositions are $-p, -q, r, s, -t$ and I can symbolize this set $w_1 w_2$
$w_3 w_4 w_5$.
3. Now under this assignment of values, the total proposition P is either true or
false. If true then (under the given assignment of values), $w_1 w_2 w_3 w_4 w_5$ imply
it. If false then $w_1 w_2 w_3 w_4 w_5$ imply $-P$. Where P is a tautology it always has
the value 1, under all assignments of values for the variables.
4. Thus the logical force or content of each line in the truth-table for a genuine
tautology can be formalized as a sequent: $w_1 \ldots w_n \vdash P$. There can be 2^n
sequents of the same pattern developed simply and solely from the range of
truth possibilities that the variables in P have.

Each sequent comes into existence with its validity guaranteed by two simple
facts: (1) the wff's on the left of the therefore-indicator, $\vdash$, are simply and
validly derived from some particular assignment of values to the variables (i.e.
any assignment enables one to determine, immediately, a set of true wff's,
$w_1 \ldots w_n$); (2) the wff on the right of the therefore-indicator is the tautology

presented, and as a tautology is, of course, true under all assignments of values to the variables in it. Since each sequent corresponds to a different set of values for the variables and since the 2^n sequents completely map the range of possible assignments, it follows that in guaranteeing that these sequents are all true we are situating within our system of deductions not only P but also the tautologous quality of P.

(c) *Our modern logic of propositions contains decision procedures for determining whether any given well-formed formula in its language is a tautology, a logical contradiction or a contingent proposition.*

These procedures are:
(1) the truth-tables procedure;
(2) the normal forms procedure;
(3) the truth trees procedure.

We have seen in chapter 2 that each of these procedures is quite adequate for the function of decision. Accordingly, the system, propositional logic, is said to be *decidable*.

Conclusion. The rigour and range of proof in propositional logic is seen, on assessment, to be quite remarkable. This section of formal logic is a complete corpus of established truths: it possesses all those truths that are expressible in the language of propositional variables; only truths can feature as theses in it; and it has a decision procedure for determining with regard to any expression in its language, whether it is a tautology, a logical contradiction or a contingent proposition. It therefore provides a finished grammar of connectivity.

III. Assessing the consistency, completeness and decidability of predicate logic

The same type of proof is available for the *consistency* of predicate logic as for that of propositional logic. In its natural deduction format its theses are generated entirely from LAF's and inherit a logical soundness from nature; in its axiomatic format the simple rules of inference which determine derivations preserve the truth quality of axioms.

We have seen however that while *decision procedures* have been found for certain fragments of predicate logic, the system as a whole is not decidable. This does not merely signify that a decision procedure has not actually been found for it—in 1936 Alonzo Church proved that such a procedure could never be devised. This technical result is not surprising, humanly: in effect a decision procedure in predicate logic would trace out systematically every consequence of the assumption that the premises and the contradictory of the conclusion are jointly consistent. If they are not, at least two of these consequences must be inconsistent, and must show up in the systematic unfolding of implications as two lines, one of which is the negation of the other. For if the proof can develop without terminating by inconsistency, there is a domain (D_w) (i.e. a domain which has a denumerable, or enumerably infinite number of members) in which a possible world can be described satisfying the assumption that the premises and the contradictory of the conclusion are jointly consistent. However even when the systematic unfolding of implications is proceeding indefinitely, there may be no indication, mathematical or otherwise, about the indefinite process that inconsistency *cannot* appear. Thus in predicate logic where infinite instantiation is possible, while one could expect a decision procedure which would display *any valid* argument as being *valid*, one could not expect a general decision procedure which would display *any invalid* argument as *invalid*.

What is technically called the philosophy of conservatism emphasizes that the important quality of both logical proofs and decision procedures is that they conserve the quality of truth and validity, that they will never assess an invalid argument as valid. It is important to note also that a pragmatic response to Church's result has been the working out of decision procedures for various special cases in predicate logic. Some are, technically, of substantial interest and there are good lists given by W. Ackermann in his *Solvable Cases of the Decision Problem* (1954) and by A. Church in *Introduction to Mathematical Logic* (1956).

The absence of a mechanical decision procedure makes it more difficult to devise a proof for the *completeness* of predicate logic than for that of propositional logic (where the truth table test is basic to the method of proving completeness). Kurt Gödel was the first to devise one (1930) and his method can be extended to both axiomatic and natural deduction presentations. The distinction between weak and strong completeness may be defined as follows in the context of axiomatization: a system is said to be weakly complete if its axiomatic basis is sufficient for the generation of the set of all its valid wff's; it is said to be strongly complete if its axiomatic basis cannot be made more powerful without inconsistency resulting.

Of course no system actually proves all the sequents and theorems that can be proved, for an indefinite number of substitutions is possible for variables and each selection could be proved and given a theorem or sequent number. In practice a system confines itself to the generalizations which are basic to all possible substitution work, adding only theorems and sequents which are of special metalogical interest. It is clear that a proof is not changed in sequence, structure or in grounds cited, when it is repeated for some substitution instance.

The assessment, then, of modern predicate logic shows it to be a consistent and complete system, lacking however a general decision procedure.

IV. A summary assessment of logic in general

Both propositional and predicate logic have the characteristic of being consistent and complete systems. Thus they are completely competent to present logical truths in the format of deducibility. Since the system of predicate logic is not decidable, it follows that deducibility rather than decidability is the primary form of logical certification.

In *The Development of Logic*, the authors (W. and M. Kneale) make the following observation:

> Under the influence of mistaken theories of logic philosophers have sometimes assumed that truisms of logic must all be certifiable as such by a simple procedure. Wittgenstein, for example, wrote:
>
>> 'Our fundamental principle is that every question which can be decided at all by logic can be decided off-hand . . . It is possible . . . to give at the outset a description of all "true" logical propositions. Hence there can *never* be surprises in logic . . . Proof in logic is only a mechanical expedient to facilitate the recognition of tautology, where it is complicated.' (*Tractatus Logico-Philosophicus*, 5.511, 6.125, 6.1251, 6.1262)
>
> And mathematicians for their part have sometimes thought that Frege's theory must be wrong because the problems of number theory are not all soluble by rules of thumb such as should in their opinion be sufficient for the settlement of all logical questions. In the paper in which he proved the incompletability of formal arithmetic Gödel made clear for the first time that discovery of a universal decision procedure for general logic would be sufficient for a solution of some famous unsolved problems of number theory . . . In the context in which it was written this remark was not intended to suggest the unplausibility of finding a universal decision procedure for general logic. Within a few years the impossibility of such a discovery was proved by a development of Gödel's own technique. (p. 729)

V. The concept of proof in logic

The concept of *proof of A* which is operational in logical systems identifies it with a sequence of wff's the last of which is *A* and each of which is either a principle of the system (an axiom or a LAF) or derivable from previous wff's of the sequence according to the rules of inference of the system. In two-valued logic the process of derivation or deduction is presented in specific terms of preserving the value of truth: if the previous wff's of a sequence are true what is *proved* from them is also true; the truth of a conclusion is seen (evidenced) and necessitated by the pervasive presence of truth in the proof. The process of proof has the characteristic of preserving values of rationality, truth and tautologousness during the development of logical systems.

Chapter 6

A DISCUSSION OF RUSSELL'S PARADOX AND OF THE GROUNDS FOR CLASSAL THOUGHT AND FOR CALCULI OF CLASSES

I. Russell's paradox

To fall under a concept or defining property, to belong to a class, to be part of a concept's extension—these seem to be identical.

Take the concept, *class that does not belong to itself*. Examine the content and extension of this concept. Its extension is the class of those classes that do not belong to themselves. This itself is a class (a class of classes). Does it belong to itself or not? If it does, then it does not fall under the concept whose extension it is, i.e. the concept, *class that does not belong to itself*. If it does not belong to itself, then it falls under the concept, *class that does not belong to itself*, while not being part of the concept's extension. The alternatives are exhaustive and the outcome in each case seems to be a contradiction (or to run counter to the expectancy of natural thought).

Russell describes, very simply, the development of the paradox: 'it seemed to me that a class sometimes is, and sometimes is not, a member of itself. The class of teaspoons, for example, is not another teaspoon, but the class of things that are not teaspoons, is one of the things that are not teaspoons. There seemed to be instances which are not negative: for example the class of all classes is a class. The application of Cantor's argument [that there is no greatest cardinal number] led me to consider the classes that are not members of themselves; and these, it seemed, must form a class. I asked myself whether this class is a member of itself or not. If it is a member of itself, it must possess the defining property of the class, which is to be not a member of itself. If it is not a member of itself, it must not possess the defining property of the class, and therefore must be a member of itself. Thus each alternative leads to its opposite and there is a contradiction.

'At first I thought there must be some trivial error in my reasoning. I inspected each step under a logical microscope, but I could not discover anything wrong.' (*My Philosophical Development*, p. 76)

II. The impact of Russell's paradox on Frege's system of logic and mathematics

A primary aim of Frege's was to construct a language able to signify, exclusively, the forms (simple, complex and systematic) of thought—where thought denotes not psychic vitality but that which is signified by, or contained in, thought. This language would symbolize precisely that which is germane to exact proof, to the inferential process as such, for what we prove is not a sentence or the judgment it expresses but the thought content of these, i.e. that in them which can be understood by any mind and is the same for every mind—'objective thought'. He was not interested in concepts of particular objects or in proofs of particular empirical propositions, but wanted to formalize depth structures and depth processes of objective thought in a language that would disengage them from particular contexts and from the particular argumentative forces and consequences of object-language. While having no particular reference, the variables and constants of his language were able to determine definitely the truth conditions of all statements made in the language, so that these statements had two reference values, the True and the False. The true statements constituted Logic, the depth science of objective thought. With his language, syntax and grammar he was able to discover and formalize, substantially, both propositional and predicate logic.

In studying the foundations of Arithmetic (for him the theory of natural and real numbers), Frege came to believe that Arithmetic is reducible to Logic, that the very nature of conceptual thought gives rise to our thinking numerically as it does to our thinking logically; in present-day terms we might say that it lies totally within the impulse of conceptual thought and of natural deduction to think and reason numerically.

Frege's belief may be studied, philosophically, in the light of key concepts which appear in the arithmetical expansion of logical thought—'number', 'class', 'extension'. (In this study the significance of Russell's paradox can be very starkly appreciated); and technically, in the light of his formalization of Arithmetic:

For Frege, a concept symbolized in logic as a propositional function, gives rise to the notion of class, i.e. the set of things realizing this concept, possessing this defining property. A class can be fully described in the logical notation of predicate logic with identity. Classes are similar or dissimilar: two classes are similar if there is a way of coupling all the objects in one with all the objects in the other, one to one. The concept of number arises in response to the question: how many?—no matter what particular form an answer may take its basic conceptual content is 'just as many as are in this similar class'. How many people are there in the auditorium? 'Just as many as there are seats' answers the question numerically, i.e. by coupling the audience with a similar class. If I want to give the number more absolutely I will couple the audience with the set of *all* similar classes: this is what I do when I use a numeral (e.g. 1000) which names the set in question. *Numerals* then are class names; the cardinal *numbers*, designated by numerals, are classes—equivalence classes of concepts generated by the equivalence relation 'just as many as': the number of F's is, in definition, the class of concepts G such that there are as many F's as G's.

Thus number is a property of classes; class and extension are an objective dimension of every concept; numbers can be apprehended as logical objects through the fact that whatever falls under a concept and therefore possesses the defining property of a class must be a member of that class, so that we can pass from a concept to its extension; numerical thought is constitutionally logical, i.e. in content, form and grammar it is totally logical; and any logical formalization of thought is implicitly numerical, for the extension of a concept is so necessarily linked with its intension that whatever object falls under a concept must be part of its extension.

Technically, Frege offered confirmation for this philosophical position by presenting Arithmetic as an axiomatic theory whose notions and laws were entirely reducible to logical ones. (It is important to note that Frege did not hold the logistic thesis for the whole of mathematics but only for the theory of natural and real numbers: for him geometry was founded on synthetic *a priori* truths that could not be reduced to logic. And he did succeed in deriving, on the basis of his definitions, all the Peano axioms for the natural numbers and therefore in showing that all those arithmetical statements are analytic which do not require that every natural number has an immediate successor—i.e. that the number series be infinite.)

It is clear that Russell's paradox affected not only Frege's particular formalization of Arithmetic ('It is a matter of my Axiom (V). I have never disguised from myself its lack of the self-evidence that belongs to the other axioms and that must properly be demanded of a logical law'—Appendix to *Grundgesetze der Arithmetik*), not only his belief that 'The basis of arithmetic lies deeper, it seems, than that of any of the empirical sciences, and even that of geometry' (*Grundlagen*, pp. 20–1), but also his whole philosophical conception of numerical thought. It was just before the publication of the second volume of the *Grundgesetze* (in 1903) that Russell communicated his paradox, and in the Preface Frege had written:

> The whole of the second part is really a test of my logical convictions. It is improbable that such an edifice could be erected on an unsound base ... As a proof of the contrary, I can only admit the production by someone of an actual demonstration that upon other fundamental convictions a better and more durable edifice can be erected, or the demonstration by someone that my premises lead to manifestly false conclusions. But nobody will be able to do that. (p. 147)

In his appendix on the paradox Frege immediately acknowledges its seriousness: 'Hardly anything more unfortunate can befall a scientific writer than to have one of the foundations of his edifice shaken after the work is finished.'

In the event, Frege was content with a technical escape from the paradox by stating a new criterion for equality in extension, modifying his fifth law to read 'Two concepts have equal extensions if and only if any object, which is not the extension of one of them, falls under one if and only if it falls under both.' It is likely that he came to see that with this weakened law the crucial theorem that the series of natural numbers is infinite was no longer valid in his axiomatization of arithmetic; and after his death Stanislaw Lesniewski showed that the modified law gave rise, itself, to contradiction. However, in his late years he seems to have reached the conclusion that he had been mistaken in principle concerning the nature of numerical thought: 'In 1923 he became convinced that the whole project of founding arithmetic on logic was in error and that the theory of classes constituted the nub of the error: set theory was an intellectual aberration which had led him and others astray. Since mathematics still needed to be unified, geometry would have to be taken as the fundamental mathematical theory and analysis and even number theory derived from it: all mathematical truth was thus synthetic *a priori*. Frege began some work expounding this new philosophy of mathematics but he was unable to carry it far and published none of it.' (Article by Michael Dummett on Frege in *The Encyclopedia of Philosophy*, vol. 3, p. 227)

III. The developmental influence of Russell's paradox within his own system

Frege exemplifies a three-level semantic approach to meaning, dealing with it in co-ordinated terms of thought-language-reality. For him, object and concept (real 'thereness' and intelligible content) were fundamental terms for language analysis and for the exact expression or interpretation of logical and mathematical statements. The impact of Russell's paradox within the context of a two-level semantics (where it is the truth of *sentences, their* correspondence with reality that is *solely* focused) is very different and Russell himself exemplifies this difference. He also exemplified a belief in analysis which he described in later life as the strongest and most unshakeable prejudice in his philosophical method. The outcome of this dual commitment (to a two-level semantics and to analysis) was a kind of Russellian analysis called reduction which sought, by means of a strict linguistic rectitude, to eliminate paradoxes and to reach truth and certainty as an impersonal correspondence between what we say and the facts.

This meant, in the first place, reducing the number of primitive terms to a minimum, eliminating inferred entities and oblique talk. As a case in point, number is not a primitive term. Numbers, as Frege had shown, can be defined as classes of classes: 0 as the class of all empty classes; 1 as the class of all classes each of which is such that any member is identical with every other member; 2 as the class of all classes each of which is such that it includes a member not identical with another member and such that any member is identical with one or other of these. Russell comments (in *My Philosophical Development*, p. 71) that thus 'we get rid of numbers as metaphysical entities. They become, in fact, merely linguistic conveniences with no more substantiality than belongs to "etc." or "i.e.". Kronecker, in philosophizing about mathematics, said that "God made the integers and the mathematicians made the rest of the mathematical apparatus." By this he meant that each integer had to have an independent being, but other kinds of numbers need not have. With the above definition of numbers this prerogative of the integers disappears and the primitive apparatus of the mathematician is reduced to such purely logical terms as *or*, *not*, *all* and *some*. This was my first experience of the usefulness of Occam's razor in diminishing the number of undefined terms and unproved propositions required in a given body of knowledge.' (Alan Wood points out that 'Russell's use of Occam's Razor was not only a means to an end but part of something which was a motive in itself, a passion which had almost as much force in Russell's mind as his passion for impersonal truth ... it might variously be described as love of aesthetic elegance, love of unity, love of system, or profundity'. It was part of the inmost essence of his intellectual impulse.)

Another case in point of genuine primitive terms is the category of words that have the straightforward meaning of pointing to an object. These must be carefully distinguished from other words. In his theory of descriptions, he points out that the only primitive terms which have this straightforward meaning are names: these are logically structureless: they simply pick out what we are making predications about; they are significant only because there is something they refer to and if there were not this something they would be empty noises, not words. The man who substitutes a description (e.g. 'the only satellite of the earth' for a name ('the moon') is no longer, linguistically, in direct contact with the world, he is speaking about a complex of concepts and a missing *referent* cannot be replaced by the *sense* of concepts. Fully analysed, the sentence *'the golden mountain does not exist'* is seen to be without a logical subject: it concerns the propositional function 'X is golden and a mountain' and says that this is false for all values of X. Thus the paradox of talking about a golden mountain although no golden mountain exists disappears when we see that while a name cannot occur significantly in a proposition unless there is something that it names, a description may contribute to the meaning of a sentence without having any meaning at all in isolation—it is an incomplete symbol whose use is defined within the context of the entire sentence.

From the very beginning Russell felt that the source of his paradox lay in treating 'class' as the name of an object. It is interesting to recall here Wittgenstein's last meeting with Frege: 'as we were waiting at the station for my train, I said to him "Don't you ever find any difficulty in your theory that numbers are objects?" He replied "Sometimes I *seem* to see a difficulty—but then again I *don't* see it." ' Russell, however, came to the conclusion that classes are merely a convenience in discourse. In *My Philosophical Development* he explains the development of his view:

> Let us start with a homely illustration [of what is meant by 'class']. Suppose, at the end of dinner, your host offers you a choice of three different sweets, urging you to have any one or two or all three, as you may wish. How many courses of conduct are open to you? You may refuse all of them. That is one choice. You may take one of them. This is possible in three different ways and therefore gives you three more choices. You may choose two of them. This again is possible in three ways. Or you may choose all

three, which gives you one final possibility. The total number of possibilities is thus eight, i.e. 2^3. It is easy to generalize this procedure. Suppose you have n objects before you and you wish to know how many ways there are of choosing none or some or all of the n. You will find that the number of ways is 2^n. To put it in logical language: a class of n terms has 2^n sub-classes. This proposition is still true when n is infinite. What Cantor proved was that even in this case, 2^n is greater than n. Applying this, as I did, to all the things in the universe, one arrives at the conclusion that there are more classes of things than there are things. It follows that classes are not 'things'. But, as no one quite knows what the word 'thing' means in this statement, it is not very easy to state at all exactly what it is that has been proved . . .

I should now phrase the matter somewhat differently. I should say that, given any propositional function, say fx, there is a certain range of values of x for which this function is 'significant'—i.e. either true or false. If a is in this range, then fa is a proposition which is either true or false. In addition to substituting a constant for the variable x, there are two other things that may be done with a propositional function: one is to assert that it is always true; and the other that it is sometimes true. The propositional function, 'if x is human, x is mortal' is always true; the propositional function 'x is human' is sometimes true. There are thus three things that can be done with a propositional function: the first is to substitute a constant for the variable; the second is to assert all values of the function; and the third is to assert some values or at least one value. The propositional function itself is only an expression. It does not assert or deny anything. A class, equally, is only an expression. It is only a convenient way of talking about the values of the variable for which the function is true. (pp. 81–2)

Russell believed that his paradox had arisen precisely because classes and individuals had been put on the one level and remained wholly convinced all his life that some form of a doctrine of types was essential to a solution. The basic idea of such a doctrine would be to distinguish various levels of predicates. A predicate holds for individuals, but we cannot meaningfully assert that a predicate of predicates does or does not hold for an individual. In terms of functions, his hierarchy of types was 'individuals, one-place functions of individuals (that correspond to properties), two-place functions of individuals (that correspond to two-term relations) . . . functions of functions of individuals . . . and so on'. (Ibid., p. 77) He realized later that in his early theory of types he was defining categories of entities not syntactical categories of signs, and, indeed, 'a consistently formulated doctrine of syntactical categories was first worked out by Lesniewski and the Polish logistic school'. (Ibid., p. 79) But it is quite clear that his theory provided, in principle, a rule and a reason which eliminated a major cause of paradoxes. Further, as a ground for condemning the kind of reflexive self-reference that is in such paradoxes as The Liar, he introduced a distinction of orders within each type thus obtaining what came to be known as the ramified theory of types.

Reviewing in 1959 the development of his thought, Russell noted that he had come to conceive the science of logic as being grounded in language: 'I no longer think that the laws of logic are laws of things; on the contrary, I now regard them as purely linguistic.' (*My Philosophical Development*, p. 102)

IV. Class terms in the history of traditional philosophy and logic—the problem of universals

To describe our world and our life we use terms such as wood, glass, steel, sky, sea, air, large, small, coloured, black, hot, cold, hard, soft; living, dead, growing, eating, running; angry, pleasant, intelligent, conscientious, etc. We feel that these physical, biological and psychological words are true of individual things and people, but they also have distinctive properties of their own: they are, themselves, classal and universal in meaning and are applied indefinitely to vast ranges of individuals. The question arises: what (if anything) corresponds in reality to the classal, universal features of words? This is the traditional problem of universals.

In its basic formulation it is mainly a logical problem, but it opens on to three departments of philosophy—Metaphysics, Psychology and Epistemology. It leads directly to the more particular and metaphysical question: what precisely is the structure of reality? and rival metaphysical systems have often tested their strength on the general problem of universals. It gives rise also to a psychological question: is there really a universal idea, a unit of cognition higher than sense? We speak of concepts and ideas, and describe them as universal and abstract, but on empirical enquiry are they reducible to sense-impressions and sense-imagery? Finally, an epistemological question emerges: concepts are supposed to disclose and signify real objects: how can universal concepts constitute objective knowledge of individual things?

The problem of universals has been discussed in various ways throughout the history of Western philosophy. A classic text in Porphyry's third-century *Introduction to the Categories of Aristotle* formulated the Greek problem for medieval logicians (Boethius' sixth-century translation of Porphyry being one of the main logical works in early medieval libraries).

Mox de generibus ac speciebus illud, sive subsistant, sive in solis nudisque intellectibus posita sint, sive subsistentia corporalia sint an incorporalia, et utrum separata a sensibilibus an in sensibilibus posita et circa haec consistentia sint, dicere recusabo; altissimum enim negotium est hujusmodi et majoris egens inquisitionis.

As for genus and species, I beg to be excused from discussing at present the question whether they exist in reality or have their place simply and solely in thoughts, and if they exist, whether they are corporeal or incorporeal, and whether they are separable or exist only in sensible things and dependent upon them. For such a study is very deep and requires another and larger inquiry. (As translated in Kneale's *The Development of Logic*, p. 196)

The universal term is *unum—versus—alia*, 'one related to many', a term that can be predicated of many subjects. Porphyry does not speak of universals as such but of 'genera' and 'species' these being the two main members of the predicables, the traditional five-fold division of universal predicate terms— genus, species, differentia, proprium, accident. His choice brings out the fact that the traditional problem was to a great extent a problem of the structure of reality: do essences, natures, types exist? have these words a foundation in reality and if so what is the foundation? His choice also reminds us that traditional philosophy has debated the logical problem mainly in the context of predication rather than in the logico-mathematical context where the issue is the validity of class as such, and of names for collectivities. It is this latter issue which is the more central since the time of Russell's paradox.

The various traditional theories are as follows:

Nominalism: For the nominalist the general term or class name is a purely linguistic phenomenon. It does not derive from a higher level of cognition than sense and it is not founded on the reality of types or essences in nature. Thinking of, and referring to, things in groups or bundles is completely reducible to a skill in the use of linguistic signs for individuals.

In general, nominalists have tended to operate a two-level semantics and, philosophically, a Sensist approach, eliminating belief in genuinely abstract ideas and in a distinctive knowledge and higher insight given by the processes of human understanding. Berkeley and Hume exemplify the traditional nominalist rejection of abstract ideas. Selecting Locke as a typical exponent and defender of them, Berkeley argues that it is psychologically impossible to frame an abstract idea:

> To be plain, I own myself able to abstract in one sense, as when I consider some particular parts or qualities separated from others, with which though they are united in some object, yet it is possible they may really exist without them. But I deny that I can abstract one from another, or conceive separately, those qualities which it is impossible should exist so separated; or that I can frame a general notion by abstracting from particulars in the manner aforesaid [i.e. Lockean]. (*Treatise Concerning the Principles of Human Knowledge*, para. 10)
>
> ... the idea of man that I frame to myself, must be either of a white, or a black, or a tawny, a straight or a crooked, a tall, or a low, or a middle-sized man. I cannot by any effort of thought conceive the abstract idea above described ...
>
> ... wherein 'tis true, there's included colour, because there is no man but has some colour, but then it can be neither white, nor black, nor any particular colour; because there is no one particular colour wherein all men partake. So likewise there is included stature, but then 'tis neither tall stature

nor low stature, nor yet middle stature, but something abstracted from all these . . . (Ibid., paras. 10 and 9)

The so-called abstract idea is really a particular idea used by the mind 'to represent or stand for all other particular ideas of the same sort.' (Ibid., para. 12) Hume carries Berkeley's theory further, explaining how a particular idea 'is applied beyond the limits of its real nature as if it were universal':

> Abstract ideas are therefore in themselves individual, however they may become general in their representation. The image in the mind is only that of a particular object, though the application of it in our reasoning be the same, as if it were universal . . . The word raises up an individual idea, along with a certain custom; and that custom produces any other individual one, for which we may have occasion . . . For this is one of the most extraordinary circumstances in the present affair, that after the mind has produced an individual idea, upon which we reason, the attendant custom, revived by the general or abstract term, readily suggests any other individual, if by chance we form any reasoning, that agrees not with it. Thus should we mention the word, triangle, and form the idea of a particular equilateral one to correspond to it, and should we afterwards assert, *that the three angles of a triangle are equal to each other*, the other individuals of a scalenum and isoceles, which we overlooked at first, immediately crowd in upon us, and make us perceive the falsehood of this proposition, though it be true with relation to that idea, which we had formed. (*Treatise of Human Nature*, Book I, Part 1, § 7)

In so far as a nominalist holds that generality attaches to words he is vulnerable to the type-token distinction. All occurrences of the word 'man' are individual and in speaking of the *same* word we are moving from tokens to types; there seems no reason why generality should not be extended to other categories besides words. On a last analysis, traditional nominalism tends to analyse generality linguistically and on the basis of a skill we develop in dealing with a world of individuals. It adheres strictly (and in a doctrinaire fashion) to a two-level semantic approach.

Conceptualism: For the conceptualist, human thought is a higher level of cognition than sense and is constituted by ideas with a genuinely general signification. Abstraction is a phenomenon of thought and universal, classal ideas are natural mental facts, anterior to, and independent of, conventional verbal expression. This reduction of the universal to thought is total (as the reduction to language was total for the nominalist): to exist outside the mind is to be singular, and the classal, universal properties of ideas are not realized in singular things.

In the Platonic dialogue, *Parmenides*, Socrates appears as a very young man expounding to the great Parmenides and Zeno his theory that individual sensible things participate in *forms*. Parmenides is critical and Socrates is led to make various suggestions as to the nature of the forms. One suggestion is that a form is really a thought and therefore is not in things at all, but in our minds.

Parmenides replies that thought is always a thought of some extramental object, and further if forms are thoughts the things that participate in them must be thoughts also. Thus for the first time in history something like a doctrine of conceptualism was formulated only to be promptly rejected.

It is the medieval philosopher and logician, William of Occam, who gives the most complete version of this view (his school were later called nominalists, terminists, moderns because they were following a new modern and anti-realist way of interpreting Aristotle). For him any form of *concrete* universality, of *concrete* classal stratification, is unthinkable; 'every positive thing existing outside the soul is by that very fact singular'. Universality is a phenomenon of signification *only*; the universal is a predicate or meaning self-producing in thought under the natural action of similar objects on sense and a community of sense-intuitions; it is necessary for thought and communication: 'the intellection, by which I understand man, is the natural sign of man, just as groaning is the sign of sickness, of sadness or of pain, and such a sign can stand for men in mental propositions, just as a word can stand for things in vocal propositions'. (*Summa Logicae*, 1, 15 Böhner's edition, p. 48) Occam feels that he was the first philosopher who did not attribute *any reality at all* to universality in things. (*Sentences*, I, 2, 7, B)

Realism: Forms of realism go beyond both nominalism and conceptualism in asserting some kind of formal correspondence between what is *meant*, in language and thought, and what really *is* so.

In the Ultra-realism of Plato there is a world directly and formally corresponding to the nature and properties of thought; logical properties are also properties of things; the *modus mentis* and *modus rei* are identical in a World of Ideas in comparison with which our present sensible environment is a shadow, opaque, world.

In the Middle Ages the theory of Ultra-realism was widely held in various technical forms from the ninth to the twelfth century, e.g. by Adelhard of Bath, William of Champeaux, William of Auvergne. Moderate Realism slowly took shape with growing opposition to Ultra-realism but it was not formally propounded until the middle of the twelfth century. With Abelard (1079–1142) it was firmly established and became incorporated into Scholasticism. Contact with the works of Aristotle and with his Arabian commentator, Avicenna (980–1037), led to the full development of the theory in the following century. Thomas Aquinas gave it a full exposition mainly in his De Ente et Essentia.

Any statement of Moderate Realism amounts to a commentary on the medieval formula: *Universalia sunt formaliter in mente. fundamentaliter autem in rebus ipsis* (Universals exist formally only in the mind, but they have a foundation in reality itself). There are as many human natures (e.g.) as there are individual men. In each individual, human nature is individualized and therefore rendered exclusive and incommunicable; it exists in reality only as that which a particular unique individual is. But one and the same concept is knowledge of all these individuals; through the concept we grasp the essence not only of the individual present here and now, but of every individual of his class. Thus while human nature exists in reality individualized and therefore incommunicable, it exists in the mind unindividualized, as the content of a concept, as that which a concept means. As abstracted the essence is not characterized by the incommunicability and exclusiveness of the individual; universality is a characteristic of it and it is predicable of many.

A material thing is a complex, sensible, intelligible entity. Intelligible aspects (e.g. being of this or that type) are just as real and as factual as sensible aspects (e.g. shape, size, movement). Thus in virtue of a common intelligibility, individual men and animals are in real relations of specific or generic identity. Confined to the intelligible aspects of things, concepts cannot provide a knowledge of singular objects in their singularity but they do provide a synthetic knowledge of a theoretically indefinite range of objects.

Moderate realism naturally tends to make predication a central topic (how universal meanings can be properly referred to real individuals). Medieval theory provides a complete doctrine here: The subject-term is simply spoken of as designating the object about which we are making the predication. This object is called the supposit of predication. Thus in the sentence: men are mortal, *men* is the subject-term, the supposit of predication are the real men signified by the term. It is the logical function of a subject-term to designate the supposit of predication. This may be done by means of a term like 'this' or 'that' accompanied by a gesture (e.g. this is a hospital) or by means of a term which classifies the supposit (e.g. hospitals are necessary) or which connotes some of its attributes (the very young patients are difficult). In the first case the supposit is taken at the level of perception without any formal conceptualization; in the other cases what before were predicates are used as explanatory and descriptive features of the supposit. In some sentences it may be quite difficult to determine the supposit, e.g. in impersonal statements such as: it is fine.

The predicate term is spoken of as signifying the nature or a less fundamental feature attributed to the subject. It signifies this nature or quality in a state of total abstraction. That is to say (1) it does *not* signify the nature or quality in a state of formal abstraction, as isolated from supposits. We do not say 'Socrates is redness' or 'Socrates is humanity'. A term cannot function as predicate if it connotes a formality, i.e. a form considered in isolation and independence of supposits. (2) It signifies a nature or quality as realized in supposits which however are left undetermined. This state of abstraction is called total abstraction. The nature or quality is thought of not in isolation but as characterizing a concrete whole or *totum* (which, however, is not in any way determined). In English, adjectives like *red, human* and substantives *man, horse*, fulfil this logical requirement for the predicate-term. Both are abstract terms by total abstraction, strictly speaking, although they are often described as concrete to contrast them with terms like *redness, humanity*, which are abstract terms by formal abstraction.

The medieval analysis of predication itself distinguishes an *identity* that is affirmed and an *attribution* that is thereby made. In 'Socrates is a red thing' the copula ('is') identifies the being concretely designated by the subject-term

('Socrates') as a supposit indeterminately referred to by the predicate (which in traditional logic, as we have seen, signifies a quality, e.g. red, as realized in supposits which however are left undetermined).

In and through that identification an attribution is also made. Aquinas says that it is the *natura absoluta* which is attributed. This is a very technical term and doctrine which Aquinas derived from Avicenna (the Arabian translator and commentator of Aristotle) through Albertus Magnus. He distinguishes three ways in which an essence or intelligible structure can be considered or attributed. It can be considered as individualized *hic et nunc* (determinately therefore); and it can be considered as conceptualized. In predication it is not attributed in either of these two ways. When I say Socrates is a man I do not *attribute* to Socrates anything that accrues to human nature from its being individualized in him. If I did so, that which I attribute to him could not be attributed to other individuals—the predicate *man* would be exclusive to him. Neither do I attribute to Socrates anything that accrues to human nature from its conceptual mode of existence. If I did so, the individual Socrates would be declared to be the species man, to have the *ratio speciei*.

What is *attributed* therefore to the supposit is neither the essence (i.e. intelligible structure) as conceptualized nor as determinately individualized, but according to its content or constitutive notes viewed absolutely or *secundem se*. The essence so taken is termed the *natura absoluta*. Aquinas says (*De Ente et Essentia*, ch. IV): 'Haec natura est quae praedicatur de omnibus individuis.'

Summary statement concerning the traditional theories, Nominalism, Conceptualism and Realism. It is evident that in the traditional problem of universals, the problem of generality is restricted predominantly to the names of objects and their qualities. Through Wittgenstein's advocacy of 'family resemblance' instead of 'something in common', and through the development of semantics (pointing out, e.g. the generality that words like 'and', 'if . . . then', 'either . . . or', etc. have through syntactical function) the terms and scope of the problem have changed considerably today.

V. Perspective on Russell's paradox

The role and use of the concept, class, in contemporary mathematics. It is generally accepted in mathematics that the term, *set*, is an undefined term, the concept of set being one of the most primitive and fundamental concepts underlying mathematical structures.

Russell's paradox and others—the Cantor, Burali–Forti and Zermelo–König ones—concern the possibility of certain questionable sets; they showed that not only is an intuitive notion of set not precise enough for use in strict logical derivation but that, also, it is open to these paradoxes. While Russell's theory of types made a contribution to fundamental logical theory providing a new, refined, logical intuition, Zermelo attempted simply to give better 'definition' to set by subjecting it to axioms which do not allow the introduction of the paradoxical sets. The aim of this approach, technically described as axiomatic set theory, is to provide a derivation for all the theorems that mathematicians need. 'Admittedly, the consistency of the system remains unproved, and a new paradox may crop up in the theory. We can only check that the arguments leading to the known paradoxes cannot be reproduced in the system. In view of Gödel's theorem (1931), the very notion of consistency proof for set theory raises profound difficulties. After Zermelo, axiomatic set theory was developed by A. A. Fraenkel, Thoralf Skolem, and John von Neumann in the 1920s, by Paul Bernays and Kurt Gödel in the late 1930s, and by many others since then. It has become a lively and wide domain of investigation, and a return to a naive, intuitive view of sets seems impossible.' (*Encyclopedia of Philosophy*, vol. 5; article on Logical Paradoxes by John van Heijenoort, p. 49)

In subjecting the notion of set to the control of axioms on the basis of our experience of paradox and impossibility, axiomatic set theory seems to agree, in principle, with traditional moderate realism that universals have a foundation in reality and their extensive use in theory must therefore be guided by reality testing. Reality controls deemed necessary to govern classal thought may be formally embodied either in axioms or in a 'definition' of set.

Stanislaw Lesniewski (1886–1939) and mereology, the theory of concrete totalities. Professor Lejewski of Manchester (a disciple of Lesniewski) writes:

Lesniewski's discovery in 1911 of Jan Lukasiewicz's monograph on the principle of contradiction in Aristotle . . . was a turning point in his philosophical career. From this book Lesniewski first learned of symbolic logic, of Bertrand Russell's work and of the antinomy of the class of all classes that are not elements of themselves. The problem of antinomies immediately fascinated him and for many years absorbed a large part of his interest. His persistent efforts to solve this problem eventually resulted in the construction of a system of the foundations of mathematics distinguished by originality, comprehensiveness and elegance.

Analysis of the Russellian antinomy convinced Lesniewski that we should distinguish between the distributive and the collective interpretations of class expressions. The expression 'A is an element of the class of b's' in which the term 'element of' and 'the class of' are used distributively, means simply that A is a b. If, however, we interpret the terms 'element of' and the 'class of' collectively [i.e. as concrete totalities], then our original expression means that A is a part (proper or improper) of the whole consisting of b's, that is, that A is part of the object that has the following two properties: (1) every b is a part of it, and (2) every part of it has a common part with a b. According to Lesniewski the presuppositions of the Russellian antinomy appear to be true because we fail to distinguish between the distributive and collective interpretations. Once the distinction is made it is evident that on either interpretation some of the presuppositions on which the antinomy hinges turn out to be false. Lesniewski developed his ideas concerning the collective interpretation of class expressions by constructing a deductive theory, first outlined in Polish in 1916. At that time Lesniewski mistrusted symbolic language and formulated his theorems and gave proofs of them in ordinary language. Thus, his theory, which he subsequently termed 'mereology' ... does not resemble a formal calculus but reads rather like Euclid. Among the various systems of mereology [after the Greek word for 'part': *meros*] the one based on 'element of' as the only undefined term, with 'the class of' introduced by definition, appears to have been most popular with Lesniewski and his pupils. (*Encyclopedia of Philosophy*, vol. 4, p. 441)

No antinomies occur in this theory and it can in many cases be applied in place of the traditional calculus of classes. Lesniewski uses the word class but the word refers not to abstract classes but to concrete collective totalities ('concrete heaps' Quine called them); it is not only material things that form a mereological whole: if there are purely spiritual beings they too form a concrete collective totality and may be designated as one object. Lesniewski's theory describes objects in terms of the concepts, *part* and *whole*, and he referred to it himself as a doctrine of part-whole relations.

Guido Küng points out:

In 1926 Tarski drew Lesniewski's attention to the similarity existing between his mereology and Whitehead's theory of events. Whitehead too refers to part-relations; one event can be part of another; two events can overlap. In the United States, mereology is known as the 'calculus of individuals'—a designation that is etymologically somewhat paradoxical, since the objects of mereology are anything but indivisible *individua*. It was developed there independently of Lesniewski by N. Goodman and H. S. Leonard around 1930. [It is possible that Whitehead's ideas partly inspired the work: he was teaching at Harvard at the time, with Leonard working under him.] J. H. Woodger, the English biologist, constructed his own, similar theory and applied it to biology ... It is not surprising that interest in mereology should have developed independently in different parts of the world. This is readily explained by the nominalistic trend in contemporary philosophy [the theory of classes makes explicit reference to abstract objects] ... Unfortunately Lesniewski's work, the first in the field of mereology and the most detailed and precise, remained largely unknown outside Poland until 1937, when Tarski brought it to a wider public. Lesniewski's theory is being developed further by B. Sobocinski and C. Lejewski. (*Ontology and the Logistic Analysis of Language*, p. 107)

It is relevant to note that for Lesniewski a theory should develop and formalize knowledge of the truth. Its axioms should be true propositions and its rules of inference should be intuitively valid ones. 'He consequently described himself as a confirmed intuitionist who at the same time was a radical formalist

[insisting on subjecting any intuitively sound theory to the process of for-
malization] and a better characterization of his standpoint could hardly be
given.' (C. Lejewski in an article, 'On Lesniewski's Ontology', *Ratio*, vol. 1, no.
2, December 1958) Thus his mereology, even more than axiomatic set theory,
subjects itself to the control of experience.

It may be helpful to remark here on Geach's work, *Reference and
Generality*. It discusses various kinds of expressions with which, it seems, we
can refer to any given individual: a proper name, a general term, a many-
worded description, a phrase with 'some' or 'every', an indefinite pronoun like
'something', 'everything' or 'the same', or a pronoun looking back to an
antecedent of one of these kinds. In discussing the claims of these expressions
to be referring expressions, he notes that there are two quite distinct relations
which are frequently not grasped as distinct, namely the relation of a name to
the thing named and the relation of a predicate to what it is true of. Lesniewski
had noted, similarly, that class or set terminology (generated by the operation
of an abstraction or collective functor) was needed to name any collection
as a concrete individual, whereas such terminology used distributively in
predication was dispensable: the distributive use could be expressed without
abstraction (collective) operators by means of the copula together with other
functors and defined constants. Accordingly, he emphasized the distinction
between the distributive and collective use of class expressions.

For Frege, Russell and most modern logicians, class terms like 'man' are not
in the syntactic category of names. It is interesting to hear Geach who favours
the opposite ('simple and natural view' of Aristotle) say:

> ... thanks to Russell and Frege, most of the logical insights that were lost
> by Aristotle's Fall have been recovered; but not, to my mind, quite all of
> them ... What we still have not got is a formal theory that recognizes the
> status of some general terms as names without blurring the distinction
> between names and predicables. Success in stating such a theory would be
> Paradise Regained. (*A History of the Corruptions of Logic*: an inaugural
> lecture delivered before the University of Leeds, January 1968)

Formal solutions to the paradoxes. In his *Foundations of Mathematics* (1925),
F. P. Ramsay divided paradoxes into two groups: syntactic paradoxes (e.g.
those of Russell and Burali–Forti) involve only syntactic and mathematical
notions; semantic paradoxes (e.g. the Liar paradox, and those of Berry and
Richard) are not due to any fault in logic but to a vagueness, ambiguity or
confusion that centres on the distinction between a word or phrase and its
meaning. Such a fundamental division, widely used for many years, is no
longer acceptable.

It is true to say that, in practice, paradoxes which cannot be handled by a
simple theory of types (assuming a hierarchy of parts of speech in one's basic
language) are now generally dealt with by assuming a hierarchy of languages—
a basic language, a metalanguage for describing and evaluating the meaning
and truth of expressions in our basic language, a metametalanguage for discuss-

ing expressions in our metalanguage and so on. In general the nonsense of paradoxes is traced to some failure in linguistic rectitude which demands that we acknowledge the natural stratifications within language and between languages. John van Heijenoort sums up the situation: ¸

Any given paradox rests on a number of definitions, assumptions and arguments, and we can solve it by questioning any of these. That is why the literature on paradoxes is so rich and abounds with so many solutions. That is also why there is no one problem of the paradoxes. For the important paradoxes, the question is not of solving them by any means but of solving them by means that enlarge and strengthen our logical intuitions. It is to find, among the sometimes too numerous solutions, the one that fits our logic most smoothly and perhaps, to some extent, to adapt our logic to this solution. (*Encyclopedia of Philosophy*, vol. 5, p. 51)

The history of paradoxes and of their solutions underlines the value, for logic, of a distinction between expressive and descriptive thought. There is a distinction between *meaning* and *intelligibility*. Physical things (e.g. the table) are intelligible. So are the ink marks on this page but they also *say* something, are meaningful, significant; so also as I think about the world, not only am I informed but I judge and assert it to be as I think it—I *know* it: my thought is knowledge. Paradox is always possible in the media of meaningful speech, writing and thought for these are humanly constituted. It has always been an objective and function of logic to be so developed that paradoxes would be logically ungrammatical.

However, there are many forms of thought. In thought, in writing, in speech we may be expressive rather than descriptive or objective—e.g. we may express questions, commands, prayers, exhortations; we may express classes that cannot possibly be—whether classes that do not belong to themselves or classes that do belong to themselves. Logic, however, has shown itself to be concerned not with what reason *can express* but with what reason *must accept* as being possible. It is concerned with what can be *said* as distinct from what can be expressed; its contexts are language and thought as mediating knowledge.

Traditional logic was an abstractive logic and its theory of universals was a theory of descriptive universals (its universals are the universals of a ver nacular object-language). Modern logic is constructive and a distinction between expressive and descriptive universals is demanded in the practice and in the definition of this purer kind of logic. Russell's paradox shows this.

It is interesting to note that modern logic is not an absolutely pure logic: while propositional logic gives *a priori* laws of all possible worlds, predicate logic provides only the depth grammar of thought about a universe with at least one individual in it. Such thought is, of its objective nature, classal and numerical and so the calculus of classes and arithmetic seem to qualify, with predicate logic, to be part of its depth grammar. Thus it is possible to argue that the logistic thesis is correct only because logic as yet is not pure enough.

Chapter 7

THE PRINCIPLES OF LOGIC AND MATHEMATICS

I. The principles of logic: axioms or rules?

Before the 1930s it was taken for granted that any body of established truths must be a development from fundamental truths and any system of theorems (if one desisted from a truth-claim) must develop out of postulates. In both cases the initial principles are axioms in the sense that they state that something is so (on the basis of intuition or as a free choice) and that they are used to derive all other statements. An essential feature of an axiom is that it takes a grip on reality. What is held in this grip will vary from science to science because the difference in subject-matter between sciences will appear in their sets of axioms. But, as axioms, the initial principles always have in common that they are an apprehension—through intuition or postulation—or what is so.

Curiously enough the suitability of axiomatization for logic itself has been called in question although mathematical logic, since the time of Boole, has been perfecting the general study of axiomatics, and since the time of Frege has been perfecting the specific application of the method to logic. Kneale points out:

> It must be confessed, however, that there is something strange in talk about axioms of logic, whether these are supposed to be few, as in Frege's system, or infinitely many, as in von Neumann's. Before Frege's day logicians thought it their business to consider how theorems followed from axioms in studies such as geometry, but they did not commonly try to present logic itself as a deductive system with axioms and theorems. Frege was not, of course, the first to maintain that some logical principles could be derived from others. For Aristotle reduced all valid syllogisms to *Barbara* or *Celarent*, and Chrysippus deduced complex moods from his indemonstrables. But Frege, following some suggestions of Leibniz and Boole, offered a system in which the axioms and theorems are not truths about what follows from what but logical truisms of the same status as the law of non-contradiction and the law of excluded middle. (*The Development of Logic*, p. 530)

Frege's deductive system of logic had many lineal descendants, notably that of Russell and Whitehead in the *Principia Mathematica* and those in Polish logic, before the question was asked: why should logic be conceived as having axioms at all?

It was quite natural that Frege and other mathematicians would extend to the codification and certification of logical truths a method that was very successful in mathematics. It was doubly natural that Frege and Russell would suppose that since (as they thought) arithmetic is conceptually a part of logic, there must be some fundamental logical axioms through which arithmetic merges as a deductive system, into logic. However, with the work of Wittgenstein and Post in 1921, it became clear that in propositional logic, since logical truths coincide with the tautologies certified by truth tables, axiomatization is rendered unnecessary. More importantly it has been seen to be misleading:

> This became apparent in the 1930's, as a result of the pioneering work of Rudolf Carnap in formal syntax and Tarski in formal semantics. Their studies served, among other things, to clarify the distinctions between a theory and the logic in which it is formalized and between the syntactical and the semantical characterizations of logic. The danger is that the axiomatization of logic tends to create the presumption that logic is merely another theory to be axiomatized, like a geometry or an algebra. This, of course, is not so. The axiomatization of a geometry pre-supposes a logic that governs the deducing of theorems from geometrical axioms. This logic, when made explicit, is found to consist of *inference rules*: 'logical axioms', unlike the 'proper axioms' of the axiomatized (mathematical) theories, do not in fact enter as premises in any of the deductions in these systems. (Albert E. Blumberg: article on Modern Logic, *Encyclopedia of Philosophy*, vol. 5, pp. 24–5)

Logic is not simply one system of knowledge that can be brought into co-ordinate and cumulative relationships with other systems. Its principles pervade all other systems, are indeed formalizations of the rational deductive processes they observe. And for this reason most contemporary logicians feel that logic receives its full and proper characterization only when it is given a natural deduction format. A theory of logic, on this view, is an attempt to identify the deep dynamisms which determine our deductions of what is true in everyday life and in science.

In the natural deduction approach a primary grip is taken not on the world but on rationality: what are initially formalized are natural deduction movements, deep movements of reason under the impulse of nature. A logic developed from such principles presents itself as an intensive analysis of rationality, a detailed elaboration of rational dynamisms. Such a logic does not provide extra axioms or truisms for other systems but it can be said to pervade all other systems in so far as they have a rational deductive character, logic being a grammar of their rationality.

It is not an unreasonable tribute to Boole to say that the natural deduction format of logic achieved an objective towards which he was groping although he misconceived it as a higher mathematics. In *The Mathematical Analysis of Logic* he emphasized the need for a contextless calculus, a calculus of deductive reasoning elaborated in abstraction from all contexts, and he expressed the view that the principles of such a calculus would formalize laws to which mental operations as human deductive processes are subject and thus would be revealing the constitution of the human mind:

> They who are acquainted with the present state of the theory of Symbolical Algebra, are aware, that the validity of the processes of analysis does not depend upon the interpretation of the symbols which are employed, but solely upon the laws of their combination. Every system of interpretation which does not affect the truth of the relations supposed, is equally admissible, and it is thus that the same process may, under one scheme of interpretation, represent the solution of a question on the properties of numbers, under another, that of a geometrical problem, and under a third, that of a problem of dynamics or optics. This principle is indeed of fundamental importance ... But the full recognition of the consequences of this important doctrine has been, in some measure, retarded by accidental circumstances ... Thus the abstractions of the modern Analysis, not less than the ostensive diagrams of the ancient Geometry, have encouraged the notion, that Mathematics are essentially, as well as actually, the Science of Magnitude ... That to the existing forms of Analysis a quantitative interpretation is assigned, is the result of the circumstances by which those forms were determined, and is not to be construed into a universal condition of Analysis. It is upon the foundation of this general principle, that I purpose to establish the Calculus of Logic, and that I claim for it a place among the acknowledged forms of Mathematical Analysis, regardless that in its object and in its instruments it must at present stand alone. (Introduction, pp. 3–4)
>
> It appeared to me that although Logic might be viewed with reference to the idea of quantity, it had also another and a deeper system of relations. If it was lawful to regard it from *without*, as connecting itself through the medium of Number with the intuitions of Space and Time, it was lawful also to regard it from *within*, as based upon facts of another order which have their abode in the constitution of the Mind ... The laws we have to examine are the laws of one of the most important of our mental faculties. The mathematics we have to construct are the mathematics of the human intellect. ... Nor will it lessen the interest of this study to reflect that every peculiarity which they will notice in the form of the Calculus represents a corresponding feature in the constitution of their own minds. (Preface, p. 1; Introduction, p. 7)

Of course the language of Boole does remind us at times of Psychologism, a general attitude and detailed doctrine prevalent in the last century and quite alien to the spirit of the new mathematical logic. The general attitude had indeed dominated Europe since 1600 and helped to create the so-called classical logic of the period, 1600–1900. This logic functioned as a science of mental operations in much the same way as latin grammar was a science of latin sentences: it presented itself as a normative science or art of thinking and its natural fruit was better thinking. At the beginning of the nineteenth century a general philosophical position developed which regarded psychology as the fundamental philosophical discipline and identified philosophic method with self-observation: when the laws of the development of the human soul are understood with certainty and clarity, then also a clear and full knowledge of philosophic disciplines is achieved. In Germany the term, *Psychologism*, came to be used in reference to this philosophy. Indeed two of its strongest and most explicit advocates were the German philosophers Jakob Friedrich Fries and Friedrich Eduardo Beneke, who presented it as a radical departure from Kantian doctrine. Towards the middle of the century the philosophy was applied to both logic and mathematics reducing their content to psychic elements of subjective experience. Many logicians accepted this reduction of their discipline and not only on the Continent of Europe but also in England (strongly in the logic of Bradley and Bosanquet, more ambivalently in that of Mill) the logical tradition was anti-mathematical.

At the same time, the modern renaissance of logic as an exact science beginning with Boole continued without interruption, and towards the end of the century the Neo-Kantian opposition to psychologism was developed systematically. Thus refutations of psychologism were written by both philosophers and logicians, the classic ones being by Lotze, Frege and Husserl:

> The psychological act of thinking is, according to Lotze, completely distinct from the content of thought. The psychological act exists only as a determinate temporal phenomenon, whereas the content has another mode of being—validity. A decade later Gottlob Frege defended the same point of view . . .: 'Never take a description of the origin of an idea for a definition, or an account of the mental and physical conditions through which we become conscious of a proposition for a proof of it. A proposition may be thought, and again it may be true; never confuse these two things. We must remind ourselves, it seems, that a proposition no more ceases to be true when I cease to think of it than the sun ceases to exist when I shut my eyes.' (*Die Grundlagen der Arithmetik*, Introduction) The systematic critique of psychologism in the fields of logic and mathematics is an important part of Husserl's *Logische Untersuchungen* . . . Later in his career Husserl wrote, in terms very close to Frege's 'To refer to it [a number] as a mental construct is an absurdity, an offence against the perfectly clear meaning of arithmetical discourse, which can at any time be perceived as valid, and precedes all theories concerning it.' (*Ideen*, Sec. 22) He warned against the tendency to 'psychologize the eidetic'—that is, to identify essences, which are the authentic objects of knowledge, with the simultaneous consciousness of these essences. (Ibid., Sec. 61) (Nicola Abbagnano: article on Psychologism in *The Encyclopedia of Philosophy*, vol. 6)

In retrospect one can see that the early mathematical logicians were at a disadvantage in having to refute Psychologism: they developed logic on the basis of its affinity to mathematics but did not discover and utilize broader possibilities of development. The natural deduction approach has corrected this limitation, making explicit links logic has with philosophy and psychology. It is an authentic development of mathematical logic which is quite alien to the excesses of Psychologism. Its LAF's are no more mental entities than propositions are linguistic sentences: they formalize natural rule content as propositions formalize thought content. The formalized rules are intuitively rational and since they are rationality-preserving they can be operated purely syntactically with the guarantee that what is, syntactically, a correct theorem will also be, semantically, a valid implication.

Thus the natural deduction approach presents rationality as the essential preoccupation of logic. It presents logical truth in the form of consequence, as an expression and working out of rationality rather than as a correspondence with fact. In this presentation, the corpus of logical truth is both a deductive system and a network of paradigms for deductions in all other systems. It is a grammar of proof and as Boole said: 'In one respect, the science of Logic differs from all others; the perfection of its method is chiefly valuable as an evidence of the speculative truth of its principles.' (*The Mathematical Analysis of Logic*, Preface)

In summary it is fair to say that the concept of rule has come to have a central place in metalogic. The concept of logical necessitation has been enriched by formalizing it as an inescapable expression of rationality. The causality operating in cogent reasoning has been clarified by demonstrating the intrinsic power of natural deduction movements to evolve into whole deductive systems. And in general, logicians believe that appropriate principles for logic are rules: in this format logic (1) presents itself as a science certified, ultimately, by the nature of reason; (2) explains how, as a deductive system evolved from rules, it can pervade all reasoning situations in life and in science as the authority for inference-licenses. However, it will be a matter for philosophy of logic to explore how and in what ultimate sense logic not only expresses rationality but also achieves truth, i.e. conforms to fact. The axiomatization of logic which has been systematically perfected in modern times leaves one in no doubt that logic cannot be completely understood except as a corpus of truth.

II. Can a line be drawn between logic and mathematics?

Perhaps the most striking feature of mathematics as an intellectual discipline is the enormous variety of the problems with which it deals ... This variety, coupled with a lack of clear-cut criteria for what forms the subject matter of mathematics, makes large-scale syntheses and unifications extremely difficult to achieve. One must also beware of unifications of such exalted generality as to be trivial and avoid syntheses so rigid that they constrain future growth and developments. It should be noted that the only serious attempt in recent years to present the whole of mathematics from a unified point of view, that of the Bourbaki group, was criticized on *both* of these grounds. (*Mathematics and Logic* by Mark Kac and Stanislaw Ulam, p. 108)

During the last century mathematicians turned their attention to the problem of synthesis and to the foundations of mathematics. The amount of mathematical material in existence was vast and there was a great variety of mathematical notions, nevertheless over centuries the method of proof and the format of organization had hardly changed. There was still the selection of axioms and the repeated application of well-defined rules with a consequent array of theorems describing properties and relations of the mathematical objects that were being studied. Becoming increasingly committed to the ideal of rigour in the construction of proofs and more reliant on logical analysis, mathematicians subjected traditional axiomatics to exhaustive logical analysis and made it more and more efficient and perfect. As a consequence axiomatic thinking was employed in all parts of mathematics with new interest, power and scope. The elegance and success of the results provided both experience and encouragement for attempts to axiomatize the whole of mathematics.

This work on the axiomatization of mathematics coupled with interest in its foundations was the occasion of the origin, with Frege, of *Logicism*. This was the view that mathematics is a branch of logic and it received its best known exposition in the detailed reduction achieved by Russell and Whitehead in their *Principia Mathematica*. In his *Principles of Mathematics* Russell summed up the logistic thesis as follows:

> Pure Mathematics is the class of all propositions of the form 'p implies q' where p and q are propositions containing one or more variables, the same in the two propositions, and neither p nor q contains any constants except logical constants. And logical constants are all notions definable in terms of the following: implication, the relation of a term to a class of which it is a member, the notion of *such that*, the notion of relation, and such further notions as may be involved in the general notion of propositions of the above form. In addition to these mathematics *uses* a notion which is not a constituent of the propositions which it considers, namely the notion of truth. (p. 3)

In other words the whole of classical mathematics can be systematized *within* a logical calculus: the axioms of mathematics leading us back to those of the logical calculus, the truth conditions of the mathematical system to the truth conditions of the primitive logical signs, all mathematical concepts to purely logical ones—so that it becomes impossible to say where logic ends and mathematics begins; indeed it becomes clear that it is merely practical convenience which maintains any distinction between these two subjects.

Before Frege, mathematics had discovered that all mathematical signs can be defined on the basis of the signs of the theory of natural number, and for Frege numbers are logical entities which we can find by correlating the extensions of concepts: if correlation reveals concepts which are similar in extension these concepts may be said to have the same number. It is true that number is not a property of external things; it is 'independent of our sensation, intuition and imagination and of all construction of mental pictures and of memories of earlier sensations' (*Grundlagen*, 36ᵉ); but it is *given to reason* as a set of all similar classes and sheer rationality forces us to accept statements expressing laws of number. It is because numerical thinking is a pure exercise of rational insight that it is essentially logical.

Such a view relies, of course, on the concept of class being so rational as to be immune to paradox. In our treatment of Russell's paradox of classes we have seen that this is not so, that throughout history philosophers and logicians have disputed the grounds of classal thinking, and that set theory in particular has had to defend itself from paradox by special axioms rather than to present itself as self-guaranteeing through the inherent rationality of the concept, *set*.

Commenting in general on the logistic approach, Mostowski says:

> This seemed to be an excellent program, but when it was put into effect, it turned out that there is simply no logic strong enough to encompass the whole of mathematics. Thus what remained from this program is a reduction of mathematics to set theory. This can hardly be said to be a satisfactory solution of the problem of foundations of mathematics since among all mathematical theories it is just the theory of sets that requires clarification more than any other. (*Thirty years of Foundational Studies*, Introduction)

It is important to remember that the study of the foundations of mathematics as a whole is so general and so much concerned with the process of deduction rather than with its fruits, that it has not had a profound effect on the main body of mathematics. The discovery of non-Euclidean geometries and the study of the foundations of geometry has played a more vital part in modern mathematics and in science generally.

Opposing Logicism, Hilbert and Bernays proposed to systematize classical mathematics as a mere calculus and not to involve mathematics with ideas of logic in a framework of truth and falsehood. Their view is called *Formalism* and the resulting calculus is called metamathematics. It is purely syntactic in character, a theory of mathematics solely as a formal system, and, while not denying that a fuller presentation of the foundations of mathematics would involve considerations of truth and falsity, they are concerned with proof of consistency and even regard this as the main task of metamathematics. Of course in providing a proof of consistency one shows that a true interpretation and application of a calculus is logically possible. However, so far a proof has been provided for only a certain part of arithmetic. In their proofs formalists are Boolean in spirit, insisting on the value and power of a consistent, foolproof symbolism and on the sufficiency of combinatorial processes of thought no more complicated than that involved in seeing that two things and two things make four things.

Evaluating this view, Mostowski says:

the formalism of Hilbert set up a program which required, first that the whole of mathematics be axiomatized and, secondly, that these axiomatic theories be then proved consistent by using very simple combinatorial arguments. As it has turned out, this program is not realizable; and even if it were, it would hardly satisfy philosophically minded mathematicians because of the inevitable arbitrariness of the axioms. (Ibid.)

The final view is that of *Intuitionism* which originated with Brouwer (1912). There is room for this kind of approach once one asks the question: as an interpreted system is mathematics simply an instrument of deduction within fields of empirical knowledge, or is it a system of knowledge, of information, of sentences with factual content. For the intuitionist the latter is emphatically the case. As a system mathematics symbolizes mathematical thought, i.e. thought 'by which individuals organize phenomena in their most general aspect to satisfy their needs. Hence it is not enough to have a symbolism for mathematical thoughts; they are independent of the particular language used to express them. What is absolutely necessary is that the language should significantly express thoughts. We must be able to stop at every point in mathematics and see the state of affairs which is expressed as clearly as we can see the fact that to a heap of objects, no matter how many, it would always be possible to add one more and again one more in a never-ending process. Knowledge of this particular process, the possibility of indefinitely extending a series of objects by the addition of extra members, which may be expressed alternatively with sufficient precision for present purposes as direct knowledge of the sequence of the natural numbers, is termed "Urintuition" (basic intuition) by Brouwer; it is fundamental and irreducible in his philosophy.' (Max Black: *The Nature of Mathematics*, p. 10)

Only propositions with a clear intuitive meaning are admissible into mathematics; general propositions which cannot be tested for truth by any known procedure are simply not admissible. Presumably, on this basis, computerization can vastly extend the body of mathematical knowledge but the latter will always be traceable ultimately to pure intuition and mathematics must always be regarded as a special field of mental activities. Mostowski comments as follows:

[intuitionism] views mathematics in isolation from other branches of science and insists on restricting the notions and methods used in mathematics to the most elementary and intuitive ones. For these reasons, few mathematicians have joined the intuitionistic school. (Ibid.)

How can one sum up the *status quaestionis* at this point of time? A significant development has happened within logic since the 1930s: it is generally held now that a natural deduction format displays the character of logic most properly and fully: logic is essentially semantic, an evolution and formalization of rationality; it is a science generated from rules, unique in being free of axiomatic boundaries. The contention of Logicism can be evaluated now by the criterion: can mathematical material be entirely organized within the natural deduction format? We have seen that a long history of controversy about the key concept, class, seems to imply that it simply could not situate mathematical material within the purely rule-governed system of logic: it seems to require stipulated conditions or axiomatic control to be rendered immune to paradox. The other two foundational approaches, Formalism and Intuitionism, do not contend that logic and mathematics are a continuum in form and content. Formalism works within mathematics at its syntactic organization, without prejudging the nature or extent of isomorphism with logic; Intuitionism accepts a dividing line between mathematics and all other disciplines, and seeks to explain it in terms of unique empirical foundations.

As long as systematization and axiomatization coincided it was impossible to draw a line between logic and mathematics: they are so alike in rigour, clarity, simplicity and in the use of a formalistic method. But once logic presents itself as a purely rule-governed system a line appears and mathematics shows itself as a body of essentially axiomatic disciplines which *uses* rules and paradigms of logic, although it does so in a more immediate, general and aesthetic way than other sciences. To use a modern metaphor, sciences are deductive and probative in character because they are programmed to be so: the true source of this programme is in logic.

Section D: Philosophy of Logic

DETAILED CONTENTS OF SECTION D

Chapter 1

A HISTORY OF THE PHILOSOPHY OF LOGIC

I. Introduction

Metalogic is a level of reflection on Formal Logic which remains close to the experience of actually doing logic; its topics and problems are basically technical and their clarification does not commit one to extra-logical philosophical positions. There is room for a further kind of reflection which seeks more ultimate clarification of the nature of logic in general, of logical entities in particular, and of its situation within the corpus of human wisdom. This kind of reflection gives rise to topics and problems which, in this textbook, are collectively named Philosophy of Logic.

There are two other usages of the name, Philosophy of Logic (or Philosophical Logic). The first does not discriminate types of reflection on formal logic and includes any topic or problem arising at a *meta*-reflective level; in practice it deals predominantly with topics and problems that can be treated and solved, in principle, within logic although the relevant writings of, e.g. Quine (*Philosophy of Logic*) and Strawson (*Philosophical Logic*, which he edited and prefaced) do have important philosophical content. In its second usage the term denotes philosophical applications of logic. Thus, introducing his book *Logic, Language-Games and Information: Kantian Themes in the Philosophy of Logic* Jaakko Hintikka says:

> In this book, the consequences of certain logical insights for philosophical problems will be studied. This kind of enterprise has been given different names: philosophy of logic, philosophical logic, logical analysis in philosophy and so on ... In a rough and ready way, one can ... make a distinction between problems which are studied, at the present moment at least, primarily because of their significance for mathematical logic itself or for the foundations of mathematics, and problems which do not have much of this kind of interest (or not as much as some other subjects) but which are nevertheless of a genuine philosophical interest ... Although many concepts studied in the more technical parts of present-day logic have a clear-cut intuitive content, they are often fairly complicated and soon lead to considerable technical problems ... Nevertheless there are, it seems to me, certain concepts which have a great deal of philosophical interest but which can be explicated without too great technical difficulties. In this book, our attention will be focused on a few such relatively non-technical concepts. They belong to the metatheory (syntax, semantics and pragmatics) of first-order logic (quantification theory). (pp. 1–3)

In *Topics in Philosophical Logic*, Nicholas Rescher interprets philosophical logic as branches of logical theory developed specifically with philosophical applications in mind and he analyses its contemporary content as ethical applications, metaphysical applications, epistemological applications with some specific uses made of inductive logic.

The view adopted in this textbook is that there is need of a section in the science which, seeking to bring ultimate clarifications to logic, is open to extra-logical considerations. These in practice will be mainly philosophical, and the section of logic, which is quite distinct from metalogic and applied logic, is suitably called Philosophy of Logic. The existence of such a section will preserve the clear-cut distinctions of formal logic, levels of reflection on formal logic (metalogical and philosophical), and applications of logic (collectively called Applied Logic). It will also help to preserve something that Rescher felt might be jeopardized by the notable contemporary development of philosophical applications—the aspect which logic has of being 'a unified discipline, exhibiting, across the whole of its great extent, a tight integrative cohesion'. (Topics in Philosophical Logic, p. 5)

Studying the mainstream of logical thought from the Greeks, through medieval Arabian and European logic, on through shallow presentations by post-Renaissance logicians, through the development of modern mathematical logic and its emergence in the form of our contemporary science—one is immediately struck by the fact that self-reflection of an ultimate kind is (relatively to other parts of logic) unextensive in content, indefinite in framework and insecure in quality. The Cartesian experiment, mixing mathematical thinking and philosophical explanation has been a special discouragement, perhaps, in modern times.

The other two traditions in logic—the Indian and the Chinese—have not been more forthcoming. The former seems, most of all, to embody dedication to the purpose of developing a formal apparatus for writing on philosophy, grammar, ritual and science generally. (Of course Indian logic, covering twenty-three centuries, is only superficially known today and only a minute portion of its literature is edited.) Chinese thought, consistently moral and practical in quality, produced a logical tradition devoid of much formal system or abstract speculation and centred on the nature, use and problems of names. (It is surmised that the Chinese language was not one to promote a simultaneous growth of grammar and logic; that as speech with uninflected words it produced lexicographers rather than grammarians.)

II. The Greek period

Principles of the general philosophy of Aristotle are undoubtedly relevant to the discussions in this section of logic but it is clear that he did not conceive the need of a philosophy of logic for situating logical knowledge within a plan of general human knowledge, or for explaining its ultimate reference, scope and value. For Aristotle and his school, apparently, logic was essentially a tool (*organon*) of science.

The Megarian-Stoic school, however, regarded it as a main branch of philosophy. The fragmentary knowledge we have does not include any indication that they had a philosophical doctrine about *lekton*. The fact that the Stoics were, in general, materialists and that their logic was closely associated with their theory of language would not tend to promote a *metaphysic* of lekton.

Thus Greece, so important for the development of Formal Logic, Metalogic and Applied Logic, did not achieve a Philosophy of Logic.

III. The medieval period

It is not surprising that medieval logic—so metalogical in character, so clear about logical form and about the complementary nature of syncategorematic words and second intentions of the mind, so interested in the problem of universals—should have discussed the ultimate reference value of propositional expressions. Such discussions were salient in the fifteenth century. The state of research in this period (as on medieval logic generally) does not provide documentation of the discussion but, e.g. a text from Paul of Venice indicates the type of opinions current. He lists four: the significate of a true proposition is (1) a physical reality; (2) a psychical reality; (3) an objective meaning (the Stoic *lekton*); (4) a complex of the significates of its parts, there being nothing real corresponding to this total as such. The text is as follows:

About the essence of the proposition . . . there are many opinions.

The first is that the significate of a true proposition is a circumstance (*modus*) of the thing and not the thing itself . . .

The second opinion is that the significate of a true proposition is a composition of the mind (*mentis*) or of the intellect which compounds or divides . . .

The third opinion, commonly received among the doctors of my (Augustinian) Order, in particular by Master Gregory of Rimini, is that the significate of a proposition is whatever in any way exists as a signifiable complex. And when it is asked whether such a signifiable is something or nothing, he answers that the name 'something' and its synonyms 'thing' and 'being' can be understood in three ways. (1) First in the widest sense, according to which everything signifiable, with or without complexity, truly or falsely, is called 'thing' and 'something' . . . (2) In a second way these (names) are taken for whatever is signifiable, with or without complexity, but truly, . . . (3) In a third way the aforesaid names are taken in such wise that they signify some existent essence or entity, and in this way, what does not exist is called 'nothing' . . . So this opinion says that the significate of a proposition is something, if one takes the aforementioned terms in the first or second way . . .

The fourth opinion posits some theses. (1) The first is this: that no thing is the adequate or total significate of a mental proposition properly so called; since every such (proposition) signifies a variety of mutually distinct things, by reason of its parts to which it is equivalent in its signifying. And this is evident to everyone who examines the matter. Hence there is no total or adequate significate of such a proposition. (2) The second thesis: whatever is signified by a mental proposition properly so called according to its total signification is also signified by any of its parts ... (3) Third thesis: no dictum corresponding to a mental proposition properly so called, e.g. an expression in the infinitive mood taken as significant, supposes for any thing. For instance, if the dictum, i.e. the expression in the infinitive mood, 'that man is an animal', corresponding to the proposition 'man is an animal', is taken materially it stands for some thing, namely for the proposition to which it corresponds; but if it be taken significatively, i.e. personally, then according to the fourth opinion it stands for no thing. This is evident, since such an expression, so taken, signifies a number of things, viz. all those signified by the corresponding proposition, and so there would be no reason for it to suppose for one of its significates rather than another; hence (it supposes) either for each or for none. But nobody would say for each, since the expression 'that man is an animal' would signify an ass or suppose for an ass. Therefore for none. And what is said of that instance, holds for any other. (*Logica Magna*, II II, 162ra–163rb)

The practice of the whole scholastic tradition sharply distinguished logic from ontology. For one school (represented, e.g. by Thomas Aquinas) it functioned as a science of second intentions; for a second school (represented, e.g. by John Buridan) it was a science of syncategorematic terms (logical constants) and its truths were formulated not in an object-language but in a metalanguage. Both schools regarded logic as being concerned with *discourse* about reality. The old theory of three kinds of discourse, written, spoken and mental had been revitalized by the Aristotelian doctrine that we become aware of things by receiving their forms into the soul; thought was portrayed as consisting of *propositiones mentales* formed from natural signs in the soul. Some indeed—e.g. Pierre D'Ailly (1350–1425)—conceived thought to have a grammar analogous to that of spoken and written sentences. As Bochenski notes:

... in the Middle Ages we find essentially only *one* logic. Exceptions only occur where epistemological or ontological problems exert an influence, as in the determination of the notion of logic itself, and in the assigning of denotations. Everywhere else we find a unified logic, developing organically. The very multiplicity of medieval views about extra-logical matters supports the thesis that formal logic is independent of any special philosophical position on the part of individual logicians. (*A History of Formal Logic*, p. 115)

In general, differences and divisions in philosophical opinions did not carry into the logic of the period. Thus no definite philosophy of logic was constructed. Yet, in the problem of universals, so widely and profoundly discussed in the Middle Ages, potential foundations were laid for investigating the nature of logical entities and the ultimate concern of logic itself. Further the nature of logical form was expressly explained as that which is determined by the syncategorematic terms. Thus a text of John Buridan says:

> When form and matter are here spoken of, by the matter of a proposition or consequence is understood merely the categorematic terms, i.e. the subject and predicate, to the exclusion of the syncategorematic ones attached to them, by which they are restricted, negated, or divided and given (*trahuntur*) a determinate kind of supposition. All else, we say, belongs to the form. Hence we say that the copula, both of the categorical and of the hypothetical proposition belongs to the form of the proposition, as also negations, signs, the number both of propositions and terms, as well as the mutual ordering of all the aforesaid, and the interconnections of relative terms and the ways of signifying (*modos significandi*) which relate to the quantity of the proposition, such as discreteness, universality, etc. . . .
>
> E.g. . . . Since modals have subordinate copulas and so differ from assertoric propositions, these differ in form; and by reason of the negations and signs (*signa*) affirmatives are of another form than negatives, and universals than particulars; and by reason of the universality and discreteness of their terms singular propositions are of another form than indefinites . . . (*Tractatus consequentiarum magistri*, cap. 7)

Medieval Arabic logic was very western and while Latin logic owed many of its formal and metalogical ideas to it, Arabian logicians (in Spain and also in the Middle East) confined themselves to a retrieval and reconstruction of Greek logic.

IV. Post-Renaissance logicians

We have already seen in surveys of the history of formal logic and metalogic that the period after the Middle Ages until the development of modern mathematical logic was not a creative one. As Kneale notes: 'From the 400 years between the middle of the fifteenth and the middle of the nineteenth century we have in consequence scores of textbooks but very few works that contain anything at once new and good.' (*The Development of Logic*, p. 298) Indeed there arose a distorted version of logic, the so-called 'classical' logic which in content was poor, logically, and confused metaphysical, psychological and logical ideas.

Leibniz was a remarkable exception in this period being one of the greatest formal logicians and metalogicians of all time. But he did not contribute to the philosophy of logic. He saw it as a calculus, a formal apparatus which would provide the syntax for his alphabet of symbols signifying the ultimate unanalysable notions, so that the correctness of all reasoning performed grammatically in the language would be made inevitable:

> If we had a body of signs that were right for the purpose of our talking about all our ideas as clearly and in as true and as detailed a way as numbers are talked about in Arithmetic or lines are talked about in the Geometry of Analysis, we would be able to do for every question, in so far as it is under the control of reasoning, all that one is able to do in Arithmetic and Geometry. All work in the sciences which is dependent on reasoning would be done by the changing and exchanging of signs and by a sort of Algebra; an effect of this is that the discovery of facts of great interest and attraction would become quite straightforward. It would not be necessary for our heads to be broken in hard work as much as they are now and we would certainly be able to get all the knowledge possible from the material given. In addition, we would have everyone in agreement about whatever would have been worked out, because it would be simple to have the working gone into by doing it again or by attempting tests like that of 'putting out nines' in Arithmetic. And if anyone had doubts of one of my statements I would say to him: let us do the question by using numbers, and in this way, taking pen and ink, we would quickly come to an answer. (*The Development of Mathematical Logic* by P. H. Nidditch. Published by Routledge and Kegan Paul, p. 20)

This vision, realized so greatly in modern logic and computerization, would indeed have made Leibniz the founder, historically, of mathematical logic if his writings had been published and they had become a force in time and place. The vision of logic, however, was not philosophical in character.

Since the time of Boole one can identify an historical mainstream of logical thought, in the form of mathematical logic. Outside it there were logicians who (like Hamilton) did or (like Whately and Mill) did not enlarge the common traditional logic; there were other logicians like J. N. Keynes and W. E. Johnson who had a logical style reflecting influence from both tradition and the new mathematical logicians. Their logical problems were not philosophical. The main one concerned whether they should be antimathematical, antitechnical: the tradition from Kant and Hegel was antimathematical (in combination with Kant's overestimate of Aristotle's logic).

John Stuart Mill is of special interest in that his *System of Logic* is in opposition to the whole traditional theory of formal logic, treating it as an empirical science. Following the extreme empiricist view—that only empirical statements can give any information about reality—he holds that the principle of non-contradiction must be seen to be a generalization from experience, and that the syllogism must be interpreted as representing inference from particulars to particulars if it is to escape the unanswerable objection of begging the question:

It must be granted that in every syllogism, considered as an argument to prove the conclusion, there is a petitio principii. When we say, *All men are mortal, Socrates is a man, therefore Socrates is mortal*, it is unanswerably urged by the adversaries of the syllogistic theory, that the proposition, *Socrates is mortal*, is presupposed in the more general assumption, *All men are mortal* . . .

All inference is from particulars to particulars. General propositions are merely registers of such inferences already made, and short formulae for making more. The major premise of a syllogism, consequently, is a formula of this description; and the conclusion is not an inference drawn *from* the formula, but an inference drawn *according* to the formula; the real logical antecedent or premise being the particular facts from which the general proposition was collected by induction. Those facts and the individual instances which supplied them, may have been forgotten; but a record remains, not indeed descriptive of the facts themselves, but showing how these cases may be distinguished, respecting which, the facts, when known, were considered to warrant a given inference. According to the indications of this record we draw our conclusion; which is, to all intents and purposes, a conclusion from the forgotten facts. For this it is essential that we should read the record correctly; and the rules of the syllogism are a set of precautions to ensure our doing so. (*System of Logic*, Bk. II, iii. 2 and 4)

The main difficulty encountered in interpreting Mill's *System of Logic* is its inconsistency. The analysis of the syllogism in Book Two is that of an extreme empiricist for whom a universal proposition is really a number of particular propositions formulated in shorthand form, and for whom validity is a derivative of experience not of form. The analysis of induction in Book Three is, on the other hand, that of a utilitarian for whom a machinelike reality underlies experience, the business of an inductive logic being 'to provide rules and models to which if inductive arguments conform these arguments are conclusive and not otherwise'. Thus, paradoxically, there is a stronger basis for valid conclusions in applied logic than within formal logic itself.

It is clear from Mill's work that there is no room within a philosophy of extreme empiricism for logic as a study of form and a science of formal necessity. In treating logic as an empirical science one distances oneself from the historical achievements of formal logic.

V. The period of modern and contemporary mathematical logic

In discriminating between metalogic and philosophy of logic and conceiving the latter as the level of reflection in which one seeks ultimate clarifications about logic and logical entities and in which one must take cognizance of extra-logical, philosophical, ideas—one finds, naturally, that most modern logicians are formal logicians and metalogicians rather than philosophers of logic.

Charles Sanders Peirce (1839–1924) is a case in point. One of the great logicians of all time, with an unusual comprehension of ancient, medieval and modern logic, he was, above all else, a master of logical technique and an innovator whose works are full of original technical suggestions. But he did not devote himself at all to a philosophy of logic. There are logicians who are important through establishing historic theorems within formal logic, e.g. Kurt Gödel (b. 1906), Leopold Löwenheim (b. 1878), Alonzo Church (b. 1903), Thoralf Skolem (1887–1963), Jacques Herbrand (1903–31). Others are famous for developing significant technical innovations, e.g. Gerhard Gentzen (1909–45), Stanislaw Jaskowski, Moses Schönfinkel, Haskell B. Curry (b. 1900), Willard Van Orman Quine (b. 1908).

As a group from a single nation, Polish logicians are uniquely great in modern history as formal logicians, metalogicians and philosophers of mathematics including, as they do, Kazimierz Twardowski, Jan Lukasiewicz, Stanislaw Lesniewski, Tadeusz Kotarbinski, Kazimierz Ajdukiewicz, Alfred Tarski, Mordchaj Wajsberg, Stanislaw Jaskowski, Leon Chwistek, Andrzej Mostowski, Czeslaw Lejewski and Boleslaw Sobocinski. But as Kotarbinski points out about the leading figure, Jan Lukasiewicz (1878–1956), Polish logic was conducted 'in a technological spirit independent of any general philosophical preconceptions'; indeed he comments on 'how wide was the range of the general philosophical attitudes of the various members of a group, who were still all agreed on the importance of mathematical logic as the only adequately scientific modern form of formal logic'. (*Polish Logic 1920–1939*, edited by Storrs McCall, Introduction, p. 12) Thus, in terms of the distinction we have drawn between philosophy of logic and metalogic, Polish logic focused on the latter and not on the former.

Unquestionably it is Wittgenstein who, among modern thinkers, has made the deepest and widest contribution to a philosophy of logic. His writings on the nature of logic, logical space, the proposition and logical operators are of fundamental importance, and the development of his thought which occurred between the time of the *Tractatus* and that of the *Investigations* gives basic guidance to any exploration of the relationship between logic and subjectivity. The influence of Frege, explicit in formal logic and metalogic, is of course implicitly great in philosophical reflection. *Mutatis mutandis* this is also true of Bertrand Russell an important figure in both the history of logic and of philosophy who, however, formulated few positions in philosophy of logic (as it is specified here). A general implicit influence from metalogic must be taken for granted and indeed be emphasized in respect of the Polish logicians. Some, like Carnap and Quine, contributed predominantly to metalogic but also to philosophy of logic.

The only philosophical question to be so extensively discussed over the last fifty years as to give rise to schools of thought is whether an ontological theory is built into logical language. In his paper 'Ontological commitment' Alonso Church shows how, in philosophical discussions, theses put forward can be at variance with an ontological model presupposed by the very language used. He concludes: 'No discussion of an ontological question, in particular of the issue between nominalism and realism, can be regarded as intelligible unless it obeys a definite criterion of ontological commitment.' I.e. one must work out the kind of features in our language (e.g. analytic propositions, quantifiers) which implicitly carry assertions about reality.

To what extent does modern logical language commit logic to an ontological theory? The language of propositional logic does not carry with it any commitment about one world more than any other possible one, for it expresses the logical connectivity of propositions irrespective of content. However, in the logic of monadic predicates and relations one uses individual constants, individual variables, proper names, predicate letters and quantifiers; if, in the pursuit of logical truth, logic uses such notation, does it not presuppose the reality of individuals, properties and relations? What, in this area of logic, is the minimum ontological commitment that must be made? What theory of logical language is implicit in this limited commitment? (Outside modern standard logic one has a logic devised by the Polish logician, Lesniewski, which makes no ontological presupposition.)

In his *A History of the Corruptions of Logic* Peter Geach notes:

> Aristotle's first logical ideas can be described with reasonable certainty. Aristotle's logic, from first to last, was mainly a theory of the subject-predicate relation; and the view of predication he began with was a development of one sketched by Plato in the *Sophist*. Plato there put forward the view that the simplest form of proposition is composed of two heterogeneous elements, a noun (*onoma*) and a verb (*rhema*); for example, 'Man walks', 'Theaetetus flies'. A string of nouns, like 'man lion', or of verbs, like 'runs walks', is on the other hand not intelligible discourse at all . . . Unfortunately . . . Aristotle lost the Platonic insight that any predicative proposition splits up into two logically heterogeneous parts; instead, he treats predication as an attachment of one term (*horos*) to another term. Whereas the *rhema* was regarded as essentially predicative, 'always a sign of what is said of something else', it is impossible on the new doctrine for any term to be essentially predicative; on the contrary, any term that occurs in a proposition predicatively may be made into the subject-term of another predication. I shall call this 'Aristotle's thesis of interchangeability'; his adoption of it marks a transition from the original name-and-predicable theory to a *two-term* theory . . . Aristotle's going over to the two-term theory was a disaster . . .
>
> The restitution of genuine logic is due to two men above all: Bertrand Russell and Gottlob Frege. To Frege we owe it that modern logicians almost universally accept an absolute category-difference between names and predicables; this comes out graphically in the choice of letters from different founts of type for the schematic letters or variables answering to these two categories. Bertrand Russell re-emphasized this point; and he added a denial that significantly many-worded expressions can ever have the logical role of naming; Frege had still allowed many-worded names. (pp. 1, 4, 19)

As a result of a two-level semantics which excludes both subjective concepts and objective meanings, the relationships between names and reality, and between predicables and reality have been directly examined. This correlation has led, naturally, to various theories of representation, to Tarski's development of a theory of the truth of *sentences*, and also to problems of what exactly is real.

It is not controverted that individuals exist, that implicit in the use of names is a belief in the reality of individuals and that logic is consequently committed to this belief. The specific form of the belief is open. In *Individuals* Peter Strawson argues (on the side of Aristotle) that the basic objects of reference are spatio-temporal particulars of a pretty substantial sort—material bodies and persons, the latter being thought of as essentially, though not only, corporeal beings. Here Strawson opposes the classical British empiricism in which particular sense impressions are the basic particulars. Bertrand Russell's final view was as follows:

> I have maintained a principle, which still seems to me completely valid, to the effect that, if we can understand what a sentence means, it must be composed entirely of words denoting things with which we are acquainted or definable in terms of such words ... The subject in psychology, and the particle of matter in physics, if they are to be intelligible, must both be regarded either as bundles of experienced qualities and relations or as related to such bundles by relations known to experience. The fundamental apparatus out of which ordinary proper names are manufactured must, according to the above theory, be composed of what would ordinarily be regarded as qualities rather than substances—e.g. red and blue and hard and soft and pleasant and unpleasant ... We may perhaps define the 'stuff' of the world as what is designated by words which, when correctly used, occur as subjects of predicates or terms of relations. In that sense, I should say that the stuff of the world consists of things like whiteness, rather than of objects having the property of being white ... The importance of the conclusion lies in the fact that it involves the rejection of minds and bits of matter as the stuff out of which the world is built ...
>
> This whole subject [the correlation of language and reality] is discussed in the last chapter of my *Inquiry into Meaning and Truth*. I have nothing to add to what I said there: 'We have arrived in this chapter, at a result which has been, in a sense, the goal of all our discussions. The result I have in mind is this: that complete metaphysical agnosticism is not compatible with the maintainance of linguistic propositions. Some modern philosophers hold that we know much about language, but nothing about anything else. This view forgets that language is an empirical phenomenon like another, and that a man who is metaphysically agnostic must deny that he knows when he uses a word. For my part, I believe that, partly by means of the study of syntax, we can arrive at considerable knowledge concerning the structure of the world.' (*My Philosophical Development*, pp. 169–71, 173)

A really divisive problem concerns the predicate signs: have they real reference? A platonistic language is committed to an ontological model or universe containing not only individuals but classes of individuals; it determines the well-foundedness of predicate signs according to this model. The entities presupposed by a nominalistic language, on the other hand, are individuals: there are no classes. While every platonistic language contains a sub-language which is nominalistic, it also admits quantification over predicate signs whereas in the sub-language quantification extends univocally over a range of individuals only (predicate expressions are admissible only in so far as they are syncategorematic, i.e. in so far as they correspond in function to a name, being the sign of that which is true of individuals). There are, naturally, many problems and opinions concerning what precisely count as individuals or as abstract entities. Within mathematics, from which the designations 'platonism' and 'nominalism' have become widespread, a language of moderate platonism seems to be indispensable: as Guido Küng points out (*Ontology and the Logistic Analysis of Language*, p. 154) a 'decisive drawback of nominalism seems to be that it can interpret mathematics only as an abacus'.

Is there a criterion for determining when language is explicitly assuming existence? Quine says:

> There are those who feel that our ability to understand general terms, and to see one concrete object as resembling another, would be inexplicable unless there were universals as objects of apprehension. And there are those who fail to detect, in such appeal to a realm of entities over and above the concrete objects in space and time, any explanatory value. Without settling that issue, it should still be possible to point to certain forms of discourse as *explicitly* presupposing entities of one or another given kind, say universals, and purporting to treat of them; and it should be possible to point to other forms of discourse as not explicitly presupposing these entities. Some criterion to this purpose, some standard of ontological commitment, is needed if we are ever to say meaningfully that a given theory depends on or dispenses with the assumption of such and such objects ... In general, *entities of a given sort are assumed by a theory if and only if some of them must be counted among the values of the variables in order that the statements affirmed in the theory be true.* (*From a Logical Point of View*, pp. 102–3)

Language, then, explicitly assumes the existence of any value that can be substituted for a variable in true statements. Quine's best-known formulation of this conclusion and the consequent criterion goes back to 1939:

> Here, then, are five ways of saying the same thing: 'There is such a thing as appendicitis'; 'The word "appendicitis" designates'; 'The word "appendicitis" is a name'; 'The word "appendicitis" is a substituent for a variable'; 'The disease "appendicitis" is a value of a variable.' The universe of entities is the range of values of variables. *To be is to be the value of a variable.* ('Designation and existence', *Journal of Philosophy*, 36, p. 708)

Thus by examining a language for the quantified variables in it we can determine the ontological model or universe it is presupposing. Quine's criterion has been generally accepted, e.g. by Alonso Church, a platonist, and by Nelson Goodman, a nominalist. He himself takes the view that language should be as nominalist as possible but cannot be completely so: quantification over mathematical entities is indispensable for science, both formal and physical; accepting such quantification we must accept the existence of the mathematical entities.

He emphasizes that the problem of ontological commitment concerns logical language rather than ordinary language:

> The philosophical devotees of ordinary language are right in doubting the final adequacy of any criterion of the ontological presuppositions of ordinary language, but they are wrong in supposing that there is no more to be said on the philosophical question of ontological presuppositions. In a loose way we often can speak of ontological presuppositions at the level of ordinary language, but this makes sense just in so far as we have in mind some likeliest, most obvious way of schematizing the discourse in question along quantificational lines ... And it is only in this spirit, in reference to one or another real or imagined logical schematization of one or another part or all of science, that we can with full propriety inquire into ontological presuppositions. (*From a Logical Point of View*, pp. 106–7)

Rudolf Carnap has always maintained that predicate notation represents something, and he has also been slow to accept abstract entities. His final view which has gradually developed in the course of his work on the logistic formulation of scientific theories is as follows: language must have two levels, an observational one which is nominalistic and expresses the actual data of experience (*Tatbestand der Erfahrung*), and a theoretical one which is platonistic and expresses a freely chosen form (*wahlbestimmte Form*); the latter represents a heuristic, subjective, pragmatic approach to the world and carries no commitment to an ontological model. In 1934 Carnap had formulated his *thesis of extensionality* which states that any system expressed in intensional language can always be translated into an extensional system, i.e. that no statement can be ultimately resistant to translation into extensional language—on the presupposition that any two predicates which agree extensionally (i.e. are true of the same objects) can be interchanged *salva veritate*. However, the thesis has not been established and even if it were that would not decide the relative merits of the ontological models presupposed by nominalistic and platonistic languages.

VI. Conclusion

We have seen that in modern times the question, whether the use of logical language carries with it an ontological commitment, has been very fully discussed and indeed has given rise to two schools of thought. Other philosophical questions have not the benefit, however, of such organized treatment and settled opinions.

The following chapters will offer a survey and definite philosophical viewpoint on the following topics: the definition of logic; the nature of logical space, of the proposition and of logical operators; logic and subjectivity; logic and the ideal rational life. In this way a philosophic treatment will be provided of what is intrinsic to the science of logic (its matter and form), of its origin and of a valuable perspective it brings to human rational living. In other words, the four causal aspects, which the Greeks required for a complete treatment of any topic, will be covered.

Chapter 2

A DEFINITION OF LOGIC

I. Introduction

Ultimately, what is the concern of logic? How does one define it? What precisely is its position in the corpus of human sciences? The present chapter presents two complementary descriptions ('logic is the depth grammar of human rationality'; 'logic is the ontology of the possible') as developing naturally from any substantial experience of formal logic and metalogic, and a third description ('logic is the science of formal truth') which integrates the first two in a single viewpoint.

II. Logic as a depth grammar of human rationality

The metaphorical phrase, *depth grammar*, being spatial and linguistic in its root force, requires an interpretation that is exactly suited to the context of logic.

The image of a grammar and of rules can be a significant model for many contexts. We can conceive processes as regular, as actively conforming to rules in the fullest sense of this word, and can endeavour to formulate a set of rules with maximum explanatory power. This is true even of unconscious processes. In *Man on his Nature*, Sir Charles Sherrington writes on the development of a whole human body from a single cell and describes in some detail the coming into existence of a human eye:

> The eye's parts are familiar even apart from technical knowledge and have evident fitness for their special uses. The likeness to an optical camera is plain beyond seeking. If a craftsman sought to construct an optical camera, let us say for photography, he would turn for his materials to wood and metal and glass. He would not expect to have to provide the actual motor power adjusting the focal length or the size of the aperture admitting light. He would leave the motor power out. If told to relinquish wood and metal and glass and use instead some albumen, salt and water, he certainly would not proceed even to begin. Yet this is what that little pin's-head bud of multiplying cells, the starting embryo, proceeds to do. And in a number of weeks it will have all ready ... There are not many anatomical organs where exact shape counts for so much as with the eye. Light which will enter the eye will traverse a lens placed in the right position there. *Will* traverse; all this making of the eye which *will* see in the light is carried out in the dark ...

And the whole structure, with its prescience and all its efficiency, is produced by and out of specks of granular slime arranging themselves as of their own accord in sheets and layers, and acting seemingly on an agreed plan. (pp. 105–7)

The eye has a predetermined structure or form. So too the *visual life* that is mediated by eye and brain has a form definable in advance of the baby's birth. Seeing is a constitutional aspect of human vitality paced into being by a growing nervous system interacting with its environment. Mysteriously, the brains and retinal systems of human beings receive and actively translate patterns of light and shade so that they see, in common, objects and characteristics of the physical world. Metaphorically we may speak of the human brain observing innate rules for ordering retinal patterns in terms of objects and thus we may speak of a grammar of vision. This draws attention to the complex skilful activity involved in actually seeing (over and above our constitutional competence) and to the fact that visual experience has a uniform structure however unique particular experiences may be.

When the words, *grammar* and *rules*, are used in reference to unconscious psycho-physiological processes their primary sense must be modified of course. In using 'depth grammar' one is choosing a phrase which is strongly associated with a special linguistic theory of Noam Chomsky. In the course of presenting the primary sense of 'depth grammar' Chomsky clarifies the general concept of grammar also:

A distinction must be made between what the speaker of a language knows implicitly (what we may call his *competence*) and what he does (his *performance*). A grammar, in the traditional view, is an account of competence. It describes and attempts to account for the ability of a speaker to understand an arbitrary sentence of his language and to produce an appropriate sentence on a given occasion. If it is a pedagogic grammar, it attempts to provide the student with this ability; if a linguistic grammar, it aims to discover and exhibit the mechanisms that make this achievement possible. The competence of the speaker–hearer can, ideally, be expressed as a system of rules that relate signals to semantic interpretations of these signals. The problem for the grammarian is to discover this system of rules; the problem for linguistic theory is to discover general properties of any system of rules that may serve as the basis for a human language, that is, to elaborate in detail what we may call, in traditional terms, the general *form of language* that underlies each particular realization, each particular natural language.

Performance provides evidence for the investigation of competence. At the same time, a primary interest in competence entails no disregard for the facts of performance and the problem of explaining these facts. On the contrary, it is difficult to see how performance can be seriously studied except on the basis of an explicit theory of the competence that underlies it, and, in fact, contributions to the understanding of performance have largely been by-products of the study of grammars that represent competence. (*Topics in the Theory of Generative Grammar*, p. 73)

The traditional aim of a grammar is to specify the class of properly formed sentences and to assign to each what we may call a *structural description*— that is, an account of the units of which the sentence is composed, the manner of their combination, the formal relations of the sentence to other sentences, and so on. If we hope to go beyond traditional grammar in some significant way, it is essential to give a precise formulation of the notion *structural description of a sentence* and a precise account of the manner in which structural descriptions are assigned to sentences by *grammatical rules*. The rules contained in a traditional grammar are of widely diversified kinds, and there is no clear indication of what is to be the exact nature of a structural description. Modern linguistics has devoted a great deal of attention to clarifying the latter question, but has not considered with any seriousness the notion *grammatical rule*. Inattention to the process by which structural descriptions are generated and assigned to sentences leaves a serious gap in linguistic theory, however, and leaves open to serious doubt particular decisions about the inventory of elements in actual descriptive studies, since clearly such choices should not be independent of the complexity of the system of rules by which the structural description of each sentence is specified. In any event, it seems that a really insightful formulation of linguistic theory will have to begin by a determination of the kinds of permitted grammatical rules and an exact specification of their form and the manner in which they impose structural descriptions on each of an infinite set of grammatical sentences. (*On the Notion 'Rule of Grammar'*, p. 119)

There is a suitability in describing logic as a depth grammar. It is not concerned with performance. Psychologism distorted logic in trying to anchor it to concrete psychic life. Newman also failed to see that the claim of logic is not that it is a grammar of assent, a grammar of actual inference, but that it is a grammar of rationality. What it deals with is not how, psychically, we do think or should think but rather the quality of rationality and the nature of processes that are rationality-preserving. In this way it does reveal something of the constitutional competence that is exercised in every performance that has a rational character. Boole put it that it reveals something of the constitution of the human mind: one feels that he would have found the phrase, depth grammar, very acceptable and forceful.

Basically, it is the development (since 1930) of a natural deduction format for logic that has endered *grammar* and *depth grammar* extremely suitable images for depicting logic. As we have seen in metalogic, this is arguably the format which most properly displays the character of logical truth and logical processes. It takes the medium of logical language (which since the time of Frege is not simply a set of symbols but the essential design and theory of any medium for processing rationality) and formulating natural deduction movements as rules it evolves from them the standard content of logical truth. Thus it purports to give a combined presentation of the proper medium for expressing logical truth (logical space as Wittgenstein would term this medium) and the proper format for its principles. This format is linguistic—rule, logical argument formula (LAF), schema—but there is a reality signified, namely human vitality in its aspect or quality of being rational, the ultimate ground and justification of logic. What is given in logical language, in logical principles and in logical systems is a *form* of life—the rational form. And the rules are not merely 'regulative' in type, the prescriptions for a higher quality or standard of rational life but are 'constitutive'—they express and interpret in symbols something of the essence of rationality, of basic rational competence.

While using the conceptual models of grammar and rule it is of the utmost importance to be alive to the essential difference that obtains between grammar and logic, grammatical structure and logical structure, grammatical rule and logical rule. Generative grammar has rendered obsolete many comparisons which totally relativized grammar to actual language and has established itself as a fundamental study of a human competence. This is the competence to create a medium of life that 'sounds right', and 'makes sense', grammar being the study of this medium of language as a constructed, coherent, understandable entity. This medium, however, is simply a context in which the reality and phenomena studied by logic are present, and indeed it is not the only context: in the psychic medium of thought the quality of rationality is also present and rational competence exercised. It follows that a grammatical study of the medium of language is not a study of logical realities that can exist in that medium: it is the *saying* that is polished and grammatical, it is *what is said* (the thought content, the Stoic *lekton*) that is formally valid or invalid. And if logic designs a special language for itself it is precisely as a *means* to process thought content more clearly. To take a particular example, while in ordinary life language mediates a great deal of argumentation and discussion, grammar does not study the phenomenon of implication and yet this phenomenon has been so central in the history of logic that some (e.g. Kneale) would be prepared to define logic as the pure science of principles of involvement. Similarly, where grammatical rules guide us to a proper *use* of language and, more fundamentally, formalize our innate language competence, logical rules are concerned rather with the rationality that is mediated by language (and indeed may not be confined to this medium).

Of course speech and thought are in actual fact more unified than can be represented in the sciences which are inevitably highly selective in their concerns. It is interesting to note that in tradition there have been two recurring views. One links speech and thought merely by association: meaning is associated with words; words are loaded with meaning, and language is a public transport system. In the second view speech and thought are much more unified: thought is internal speech, and speech is verbal thought—an externation and elaboration of internal speech: 'I have drawn from the well of language thoughts I had not.' The practice of medieval logicians was to describe logic, in terms of its dual context—thought and language—as a science of discourse, mental and verbal. Without rejecting this practice two medieval schools of thought grew apart through emphasis on one or other context. For one school, thought is the primary locus of logical entities and phenomena; depicting thought through the metaphor of stretching the bow and aiming the arrow in archery, a distinction was made between the first stretching (*intention*) of our minds which is to our environment (disclosing objects of the world and their attributes and expressing this disclosure through object-language) and its second-level activity or intention (focusing the conditions of being known or thinkable, the properties and features which things have when they are conceived by a mind or spoken). Second intentionality gives rise to the distinction between real and logical properties. In its first intention the mind is dealing with objects which *are* this or that; in its second intention it is dealing with signs which *mean* this or that—its disclosures are of sign reality, and the properties and structures it discovers belong to signs which are constituted by people in the process of thinking or saying something. These properties and structures are logical and the distinction between them and real properties is basic in both Greek and medieval logical theory. Thus the first medieval view (associated with, e.g. Aquinas and strongly advocated in recent years by Veatch's *Intentional Logic*) defines logic as a science of second intentions, a study of thought not, of course, in its psychic, entitative existence but in its aspect of disclosing and signifying, of being meaningful and intentional.

The second medieval view, associated with, e.g. Occam and Buridan, sees the overt, linguistic character of logic as paramount, defining logic as a science constructed throughout in a metalanguage and dealing with syncategorematic terms. It became customary to speak of these terms (our modern logical constants) as determining the form of propositions, where categorematic terms (which functioned as subjects and predicates) constituted their matter or particular reference. Bochenski comments:

> Expressed in modern terms, the difference between the two conceptions of logic that have been exemplified, is that the first is semantic, the second syntactical: for the first uses the idea of reference, the second determines logical form in a purely structural way. According to the second the *logical constants* are the subject-matter of logic, while on the view of Thomas [Aquinas] this object is their *sense*. On either view Scholasticism achieved a very clear idea of logical form and so of logic itself. (*A History of Formal Logic*, p. 159)

The controversy was valuable in separating and exploring the two loci of logical phenomena, although it did not explain their unity as a dual context. Some aspects of this unity are clarified in the conception of logic as a depth grammar of rationality. Logical experience is not an experience of thought as such, or of speech as such: it is an analytic experience of rational content and rational structure. Reaching to the basics and the building blocks in meaningful thought and expression, it may be described, procedurally, as a microscopic and genetic type of experience. Since the time of Leibniz and Frege, indeed, logicians have felt themselves in such basic contact with meaning, that they have confidently discarded the imperfect tools of vernacular languages and have created a logical language for mediating the constitution and complexification of meaning. Bertrand Russell has expressed his vivid sense of the potency of symbols, axioms and rules that are very simple and very few. In modern times this experience has been made operational: logicians have engaged in reducing areas of human enquiry and activity to simple beginnings; their experience and their projects have been foundational with regard to modern computerization. One might sum up by saying that logic has displayed systematic thought and speech as the evolution of an initial input of rationality and it has become conscious of itself as a grammar governing such evolutions.

This has tended to make the logician very much aware that one's system of thought in any context is, to an important extent, a function of elementary beliefs, schemas of reasoning and modes of expression. They may be there by choice or be assimilated culturally; they may be articulated or not, be in the focus of consciousness or never more than tacitly known. But wherever there is system, it can be displayed, analytically, as an evolution from genetic rationality.

III. Logic as an ontology of the possible

A tautology is such that it is unconditionally true, e.g. *ApNp*. Such statements are built up from variables, they do not bear a reference restriction to any particular world and their formality guarantees their truth in every context. Propositional Logic is a body of tautologies. A reference restriction governs the laws of Standard Predicate Logic, however, as it presupposes that it is dealing with a non-empty world, i.e. that at least one individual exists; accordingly some of its theorems can be proved true only conditionally on the presupposition being true. Thus not all truths of standard logic are tautologies. The tendency of logic is, of course, to transcend contexts rather than to prescribe their nature in any way however general. Lesniewski indeed has devised a system contrasting with Standard Predicate Logic in not assuming the existence of any object and in being valid for an empty universe.

The concern of logic is to analyse rationality, not to tell us about a particular existing world: it does not seek to be informative in this latter sense. What ontological content then has a depth grammar of rationality? Ontological content arises from two basic facts:

Firstly, the rational *can be* real, i.e. that which in thought is not characterized by unreason can be an actual fact. Taking 'state of affairs' as any item that can be expressed in a proposition, a state of affairs is possible when, being conceptualized or linguistically described, there is no formal inconsistency, no self-contradiction, present either explicitly or implicitly. One can analyse this understanding of possibility more basically by reference to the modal notion of necessity, equiparating 'It is possible that this state of affairs be actual' to 'It is not necessary that this state of affairs be not actual'. Real possibility is decided, then, by the presence or absence of unreason. This approach of Aristotle (in *On Interpretation*, xiii, 22b) has been the most prominent one in history down to contemporary times. It is not at all the psychologistic one of Descartes who identifies the possible with that which, psychically, is clearly and distinctly conceivable.

Secondly, the real *must be* rational. This operates as an assumption in ordinary life and in science; there are systems of metaphysics, traditional and contemporary, in which it is axiomatic; it certainly constitutes part of a faith implicit in rational living. In theoretical science, indeed, this assumption is strengthened to the point that the more rationally aesthetic a theory is the more it is favoured as giving the best understanding of facts. Dirac puts it: 'It seems to be one of the fundamental features of nature that fundamental physical laws are described in terms of a mathematical theory of great beauty and power, needing quite a high standard of mathematics for one to understand it ... The research worker, in his efforts to express the fundamental laws of Nature in mathematical form, should strive mainly for mathematical beauty.' ('The Evolution of the Physicist's Picture of Nature'; and 'The Relation between Mathematics and Physics': for full details see Bibliography, p. 417 below.)

It follows that

(a) No existing world can be in conflict with the corpus of logical truth or with any fragment of it. If a world is rational it fulfils the exigencies of pure rationality (e.g. *ApNp*); if an expression is a logical truth then no genuine instantiation of it can be false.

(b) Every existing world instantiates logical laws that have absolutely no reference restriction. These are the type of laws that logic seeks to discover: as a grammar of rationality it seeks to be free of presuppositions about existence.

Thus logic has ontological content. In being a depth grammar of rationality it is positively a science of the conditions of possibility and thereby provides insight into the limits of our existing world. It is described here as an ontology of the possible, rather than as a metaphysics, to stress the fact that its knowledge is evolved not from the experience of actual being and from an analysis of the *concept of being* as, traditionally, in metaphysics but from an analysis of the quality, rationality. Guido Küng notes and follows this distinction in usage: 'We prefer to use the terms "ontology" and "metaphysics" in the sense in which metaphysics is the science making existential assertions about the different kinds of entities which ontology merely describes without deciding whether they actually exist.' (*Ontology and the Logistic Analysis of Language*, p. 9, n. 30)

Celebrated passages from Wittgenstein's *Tractatus* come to mind supporting the conception of logic as an ontology of the possible:

4.461 Propositions show what they say: tautologies and contradictions show that they say nothing.

A tautology has no truth conditions, since it is unconditionally true: and a contradiction is true on no condition.

Tautologies and contradictions lack sense.

4.4611 Tautologies and contradictions are not, however, non-sensical. They are part of the symbolism, just as 'O' is part of the symbolism of arithmetic.

(It is emphasized here that tautologies do not provide a new experience or particular information about the world. There is nothing extrinsic to the symbolism of a tautology conditioning its truth-value. It fulfils logical syntax but it does not have a sense referring to an actual condition of the world.)

6.112 The correct explanation of the propositions of logic must assign to them a unique status among all propositions.

6.113 It is the peculiar mark of logical propositions that one can recognize that they are true from the symbol alone, and this fact contains in itself the whole philosophy of logic. And so too it is a very important fact that the truth or falsity of non-logical propositions *cannot* be recognized from the propositions alone.

6.1222 ... logical propositions cannot be confirmed by experience any more than they can be refuted by it. Not only must a proposition of logic be irrefutable by any possible experience, but it must also be unconfirmable by any possible experience.

(The propositions of logic simply do not deal with the particular world in which we live and it is not meaningful to describe our experience as evidence for or against them.)

The penetrating thought of the *Tractatus* is narrowed beyond simple acceptance, however, not only by the fact that it must be interpreted in terms of the Picture Theory, but also by Wittgenstein's passionate assumption of an unchanging *a priori* order in the world and by his unsubstantiated identification of logical propositions with tautologies ('The propositions of logic are tautologies. Therefore the propositions of logic say nothing.'—6.1 and 6.11). In his *Investigations*, Wittgenstein recalls, very beautifully, the earlier constricting assumption:

Thought is surrounded by a halo. Its essence, logic, presents an order, in fact the *a priori* order of the world: that is, the order of *possibilities*, which must be common to both world and thought. But this order, it seems, must be *utterly simple*. It is *prior* to all experience, must run through all experience; no empirical cloudiness or uncertainty can be allowed to affect it—it must rather be of the purest crystal. (§ 97)

Noting, in his *A Companion to Wittgenstein's Tractatus*, that Wittgenstein's identification of logical propositions with tautologies is unsubstantiated and indeed inaccurate, Max Black adds:

...the need for known decision procedures for checking on putative logical truths is an integral and indispensable feature of Wittgenstein's philosophy of logic. For he would find it intolerable that we might understand a proposition without knowing in advance how to find out whether it was a tautology or a contradiction; he could never admit that the tautological character of a proposition might reveal itself by accident, as it were, after we had stumbled upon a proof of it. But subsequent research in logic has shown that a universal decision procedure is impossible, even in the relatively simple case of the predicate calculus. This result is fatal to Wittgenstein's philosophy of logic. It shows that any adequate account of the nature of logical truth must be more complex and more sophisticated than that contained in the *Tractatus*. (p. 319)

Finally, an ontology of the possible can appear trivial only to one who conceives reality and life in a static way and is content with a purely observer-culture. To one who conceives the world as evolving and who believes that in the calendar of evolution a new critical phase has arrived calling for more human control and an actively humanizing culture, this ontology of limits is of fundamental importance both in content and in the orientation and discipline it provides for thought.

IV. Logic as the science of formal truth

This description integrates the two previous ones of logic (as a depth grammar of rationality and an ontology of the possible). It requires a richly philosophical interpretation of the term 'formal' which goes back to Aristotle substantially but avoids an essential narrowness inculcated by the Greek theory of knowledge.

For Aristotle, any intelligible aspect of a thing is a form, and intelligibility is exemplified not only in physical things but also in the process of understanding them. As we sense things higher processes of cognition are brought into play. Firstly there is an act in virtue of which the object sensed appears in an intelligible perspective. This activity may be called insight. It is not the act of knowledge itself, but an activity in virtue of which the object is present intelligibly. Secondly, the mind reacts to this presence: it conceives, produces within itself, the meaning displayed in the sense-data. Actually, the mind may need many concepts to express adequately the meaning present to it in a single insight.

This mental conceiving constitutes the simplest activity of intellectual awareness: it does no include a recognition that the intelligibility conceived is that of a real object. The conscious reification of meaning, the conscious identification of intelligibility and object, is accomplished in the act of judging, the personal assertion or denial. This is a more complex act than conception but it is the simplest act that is capable of being true or false.

Conceiving and judging develop into a more complex movement of thought—inference. Structurally, inference is a movement from evidence to conclusion, a movement of the mind to new knowledge through the impetus of implication.

Thus the higher thought processes are insight, conception, judgment and reasoning. Through these processes we become *informed* about the world. They constitute a reactive vitality through which an intelligibility that is in things is duplicated mentally. An inherent narrowness in this psychological theory was that it did not explain and analyse the distinction between thought that apprehends, reactively, forms of actually existing things and thought that expresses forms but does so endogenously, i.e. with independence of what may or may not exist. It was this narrowness which stirred and shaped the modern Cartesian controversy of how to prove that there is really, as we think, a world external to us. More significantly in post-Kantian times there has been a reduction of the exaggerated hellenic dichotomy in the subject–object relationship; this has meant an acceptance of an essential relativization attaching to what is denoted by the terms, *knowledge* and *existence*, and an explicit study of the bipolar nature of each.

The narrowness of the mirror theory of knowledge confines Aristotle's philosophy of form to the range of abstracted forms but does not otherwise diminish its validity. For him (in the reactive context of knowing actual things as they are) one and the same intelligibility (form) is in an external thing, materially, and in an understanding person, mentally. It is in the thing as that which it is; it is in the person as the content, the meaning, of his idea. A form or plan which is materialized, in, e.g. this individual Ford motor-car, has been conceived mentally in the mind of a trained mechanic: the real metal object *is* a Ford motor-car; the consciousness of the mechanic *discloses* to him all that is intelligible about such a car; the Ford Manual of Instructions makes the same disclosure available to the reading public.

In reactive conception not only is there formal identity, there is knowledge also, i.e. not only is the mental form one which is also real, it is essentially a disclosure of the real form: it means it, signifies it. The idea of a Ford car is not itself a Ford car, rather it is a disclosure of what a Ford car is. In the judgment indeed one proceeds to state that the real is as one conceives it to be and accordingly the values true or false may be put on one's judgment.

In contrast with reactive thought, a natural deduction system is worked out without reference to any particular world. It is endogenous rather than reactive in character: it is the most generalized reaction to facticity; it seeks to discover and to follow the evolution of principles of rationality; the type of truth it reaches is not what *is so actually* in our world but what *cannot be otherwise in any world.* Its forms are forms of the possible. Mapping them on to reality we may say that they are the logical scaffolding of the real world in respect to the conditions of possibility that are relevant to it and which it, accordingly, fulfils.

Ideally, logic probes the most universal laws of intelligibility and these laws apply to every rational world as formal truths of it. Humanly, of course, sections and systems of logic may make some ontological commitments, however general, and so their laws are formal truths not of any world as rational but of a type of world. The limiting description may be wide and generic, such as modern Predicate Logic's commitment to deal only with a non-empty world, a world with at least one individual in it. On the other hand it may be quite narrowing as in the abstractive logic of Aristotle. However, the tendency of logic is to discover such formal truths as evolve from principles of reason. Ontological commitment is kept at the minimum that is technically possible at a particular time, technical possibilities being determined by the design of the language used and the range of operations available. The freer a system is from ontological presupposition the more perfectly formal are its truths. It is an accurate summary of the history of logic to say that it has always been tending towards the objective of being a corpus of perfectly formal truths, i.e. of propositions which are such that what they say is so and can be seen to be so purely on the basis of principles that govern intelligibility.

In the *Tractatus* Wittgenstein gives a penetrating analysis of how tautologies are formal truths:

6.113 It is the peculiar mark of logical propositions that one can recognize that they are true from the symbol alone, and this fact contains in itself the whole philosophy of logic. And so too it is a very important fact that the truth or falsity of non-logical propositions *cannot* be recognized from the propositions alone.
6.12 The fact that the propositions of logic are tautologies shows the formal—logical—properties of language and the world.

(The tautological character of given combinations of symbols shows that reality—what is so—is being known in formal aspects which belong to it.)

6.124 The propositions of logic describe the scaffolding of the world, or rather they represent it. They have no 'subject-matter' ... It is clear that something about the world must be indicated by the fact that certain combinations of symbols—whose essence involves the possession of a determinate character—are tautologies. This contains the decisive point. We have said that some things are arbitrary in the symbols that we use and that some things are not. In logic it is only the latter that express: but that means that logic is not a field in which *we* express what we wish with the help of signs, but rather one in which the nature of the natural and inevitable signs speaks for itself. If we know the logical syntax of any sign-language, then we have aready been given all the propositions of logic.
6.1251 Hence there can *never* be surprises in logic.

Thus given as contingent facts that we *think* things and *say* things, and given the tautological possibilities of thought and language it is clear that what-is-so (reality) has formal aspects and that the limits of our knowledge of these aspects derives from the limits of the language we use. Max Black sums up Wittgenstein's position:

The 'connexion' of logic with the world is an identity of logical form, and has nothing to do with the contingent features distinguishing the actual world from the other possible worlds that might have existed in its place. That is why *we* do not express anything by means of logical propositions: the substance of the world shows *itself* through them (6.124 g). And that is why there can be no surprises in logic (6.1251); for in order to be surprised, we must entertain suppositions that *turn out* to be false. The language of 'surprise' and 'discovery' is appropriate in the natural sciences, where contingent falsifications sometimes clash with reasonable expectations; in logic there is nothing to be expected and nothing to cause disappointment or produce gratification. (*A Companion to Wittgenstein's Tractatus*, p. 330)

It is an index of the rich philosophy of form in Aristotle that we find in it a philosophic counterpart to Gödel's demonstration that arithmetic, and any formal system which requires it, is necessarily incomplete. For Aristotle only a system confining itself to formal aspects of reality can be complete: a formal system cannot deal with the material quantitative as such and be complete. The reason is that material things are not totally formal; we cannot conceive and duplicate in our minds the basic individuality of anything for this individuality is unique and incommunicable while a concept has a universal meaning and is applicable to many. Material reality is not completely conceptualizable there-fore; it is not totally formal. Thus no corpus of formal truth can contain complete knowledge of it. It is the core of Aristotle's Hylomorphic (Matter–Form) Theory that each material extended thing has two irreducible aspects: (1) the aspect of being this individual which one can designate by pointing or by the pronoun 'it' (considered exclusively in this aspect a material thing is named Primary Matter by him); (2) the aspect of being intelligible in ways that are common to other things (considered exclusively in this aspect a material thing is a complex of forms, its basic intelligibility being named its essence).

The data investigated by logic is form—not as materially existent in individuals but in its generalized state as content of thought and language. In this generalized state form is properly described as rationality. The truths logic reaches evolve from principles that govern intelligibility; accordingly they refer to what can be, what cannot be otherwise rather than what actually is unless (as, e.g. in predicate logic) it confines itself, in however general a manner, to our particular world.

Not only is logic a corpus of formal truths, these truths at the same time elucidate the principles and evolution of such truth. As Boole notes: 'In one respect, the science of Logic differs from all others; the perfection of its method is chiefly valuable as an evidence of the speculative truth of its principles.' (Preface to *The Mathematical Analysis of Logic*) Thus logical truths permeate every other discipline and science as rules of general intelligibility by which movements are made from evidence to conclusion in particular contexts; they govern implication, conflict, compatibility and subordination of meaning every-where.

We find in the human vitality of thought not simply the power to be intelligible but the power to conform, in its intelligibility, to what can be, what cannot be otherwise, and what is. This is a power consciously exercised, possessing the quality of commitment and assertion, and so patient of the values, true and false. Humanly, it is the function of logic to exercise this vitality in the context of general intelligibility and in accordance with its principles: it is the science of formal truth.

Chapter 3

THE NATURE OF LOGICAL SPACE, OF THE PROPOSITION AND OF LOGICAL OPERATORS

I. The nature of logical space

In its primary sense the word, space, is grounded in the fact that material things are extended, spread out, and that the total extension of the universe may be *viewed, mentally,* as forming a container for the individual objects. The force of the word consists not in conveying that there is anything over and above individual objects and their quantities but in fashioning a medium in which we can talk and reason about various interrelationships, of, e.g. place and magnitude. One might reasonably interpret the word as expressing the set of possibilities of such interrelationships.

The phrase, logical space, maintains contact with the primary sense of the word, space. It denotes a medium brought into existence by rational thought and by logical language which is specially designed to mediate the systematic presence of thought content. It is only thought content that can be expressed and brought into this medium and the interrelationships in which it stands there are all logical ones.

Together, Frege and Wittgenstein provide a clear general idea of the genesis and nature of logical space. In introducing his special logical notation Frege says:

> The most reliable way of carrying out a proof, obviously, is to follow pure logic, a way that, disregarding the particular characteristics of objects, depends solely on those laws upon which all knowledge rests. Accordingly, we divide all truths that require justification into two kinds, those for which the proof can be carried out purely by means of logic and those for which it must be supported by facts of experience ... Now when I came to consider the question to which of these two kinds the judgments of arithmetic belong, I first had to ascertain how far one could proceed in arithmetic by means of inferences alone, with the sole support of those laws of thought that transcend all particulars. My initial step was to attempt to reduce the concept of ordering in a sequence to that of *logical* consequence, so as to proceed from there to the concept of number. To prevent anything intuitive [*Anschauliches*] from penetrating here unnoticed, I had to bend every effort to keep the chain of inferences free of gaps. In attempting to comply with this requirement in the strictest possible way I found the inadequacy of language to be an obstacle; no matter how unwieldy the expressions I was ready to accept, I was less and less able, as the relationships became more

and more complex, to attain the precision that my purpose required. This deficiency led me to the idea of the present ideography. Its first purpose, therefore, is to provide us with the most reliable test of the validity of a chain of inferences and to point out every presupposition that tries to sneak in unnoticed, so that its origin can be investigated. That is why I decided to forgo expressing anything that is without significance for the *inferential sequence* ... I called what alone mattered to me the *conceptual content* [*begrifflichen Inhalt*]. Hence this definition must always be kept in mind if one wishes to gain a proper understanding of what my formula language is. That, too, is what led me to the name 'Begriffsschrift'. Since I confined myself for the time being to expressing relations that are independent of the particular characteristics of objects, I was also able to use the expression 'formula language for pure thought' ...

The mere invention of this ideography has, it seems to me, advanced logic. I hope that logicians if they do not allow themselves to be frightened off by an initial impression of strangeness, will not withhold their assent from the innovations that, by a necessity inherent in the subject matter itself, I was driven to make. These deviations from what is traditional find their justification in the fact that logic has hitherto always followed ordinary language and grammar too closely. (*Begriffsschrift, a formula language, modelled upon that of arithmetic, for pure thought*, Preface)

What Frege sought to provide was a language, the grammatical use of which would, of itself, show up logical relationships and certify validity. Using terms derived from Leibniz he emphasized that his language was not simply a *calculus ratiocinator* translating into formulas but requiring to be supplemented by intuitive reasoning; it was a *lingua characterica* directly and immediately appropriate to displaying thought contents in logical relationships:

My intention was not to represent an abstract logic in formulas, but to express a content through written signs in a more precise and clear way than it is possible to do through words. In fact, what I wanted to create was not a mere *calculus ratiocinator* but a *lingua characterica* in Leibniz's sense. (*Ueber den Zweck der Begriffsschrift*, 1882)

In brief, the use of such a language brought thought content into a medium which made it readily subject to logical experience. Speaking picturesquely, it gives thought contents their situations in logical space. It is not likely that Frege would have objected to this metaphor which is a dominating one in Wittgenstein's *Tractatus*. Commenting on the origin of the metaphor, Max Black says:

The basic ideas are suggested by the systems of representation used in 'coordinate geometry'. Any material particle, occupying a point in physical space, can be located, in a way that has become commonplace since Descartes introduced the technique, by means of a set of three numerical co-ordinates (e.g. by the distances of the point from three fixed lines, the 'axes of reference'). Wittgenstein thinks of each point in physical space as a possibility—the possibility of the existence of a material particle at that position. Similarly, he conceives of an elementary proposition as an atomic possibility—a 'point' or 'position' or 'place' (*ein Ort*) in *logical* space: the proposition is the possibility of the corresponding atomic fact. According to this conception, logical space is the ordered system of all atomic situations. The 'logical co-ordinates' of a proposition ought therefore to be a set of specifications sufficient to determine the proposition's sense ... An important implication is the inseparability of a proposition from the 'logical space' in which it is located (3.42). The proposition's logical relations partially determine its sense and are not something superadded when the proposition combines with other propositions in truth-functions. (*A Companion to Wittgenstein's Tractatus*, pp. 154–5)

Just as a solid body denies the use of the space it occupies to any other body, so a proposition may be said to occupy all points of logical space at which it excludes something incompatible with it. Thus if there were only three elementary propositions (*p*, *q*, *r*) in logical space, the proposition *Apq* would occupy the two points *KKNpNqr* and *KKNpNqNr* (there would be a total of eight points, each being a conjunction in which each elementary proposition or its negation occurred). Wittgenstein expresses his point as follows:

4.463 The truth-conditions of a proposition determine the range that it leaves open to the facts.

(A proposition, a picture, or a model is, in the negative sense, like a solid body that restricts the freedom of movement of others, and, in the positive sense, like a space bounded by solid substance in which there is room for a body.)

A tautology leaves open to reality the whole—the infinite whole—of logical space: a contradiction fills the whole of logical space leaving no point of it for reality. Thus neither of them can determine reality in any way.

4.464 A tautolgy's truth is certain; a proposition's possible, a contradiction's impossible.

For Wittgenstein there is one logical space for what can be called 'the world', 'thought' and 'language'. The making-intelligible which our language effects is a verbalization alike of real possibility and of mental conception. The 'logos' of our language is the 'logos' of the world and the 'logos' of thought. One cannot be, and one cannot adopt an intelligible position in thought or language, without being in logical space, subject to its relations. The form of logical space brought into human existence by the design and development of a logical language gives us access also to the structure both of the world and of thought:

5.6 *The limits of my language* mean the limits of my world.
5.61 Logic pervades the world: the limits of the world are also its limits.

Thus just as one could interpret the word, 'physical space', as expressing the set of possible relations generated by quantitative existence, so one could interpret 'logical space' as the set of relations generated in intelligible existence, intelligibility being exemplified in the world, thought and language.

To sum up the comparison between physical space and logical space: It is quantified things that are situated in physical space; the kind of things in logical space are propositions: thus 'proposition' is *the* logical universal, the summum genus, and propositional logic is the basic section of the science.

Wittgenstein writes:

> 5.47 One could say that the sole logical constant was what *all* propositions, by their very nature, had in common with one another.
> But that is the general propositional form.
> 5.471 The general propositional form is the essence of a proposition.
> 5.4711 To give the essence of a proposition means to give the essence of all description, and thus the essence of the world.
> 5.472 The description of the most general propositional form is the description of the one and only general primitive sign in logic.

In physical space a place is the inner surface of surrounding bodies; this surface is made possible and determined by the quantified nature of all the bodies. Correspondingly, the logical place of a proposition is the set of propositions incompatible with it: they are excluded by it, are outside it, diminish its range, box it in. Such a place is *indicated* by the nature of the sign-construct expressing the proposition and, of course, is ultimately *determined* by the sense of the proposition itself. Finally, spatial relationships are intuited in the course of ordinary sense-experience; logical relationships (the relationships of logical space) are experienced best in the course of designing logical language, of forming sign-constructs and of making systematic calculations.

Thus our appreciation and experience of logical space, and of the situations and relationships in it, requires (a) a grasp of the signs and sign-constructs which characterize linguistic competency in logic; and (b) a grasp of the conceptual content which is formalized and processed in logical sentence construction and logical calculation.

Examining modern logical notation we are confronted immediately with the need of a theory of the proposition, explaining what is formalized by the propositional variable, and with the need also of a theory of the operators which are formalized by, e.g. connectives, quantifiers and predicates.

II. The nature of the proposition

Any thought-content which has the form of a potential truth-claim is a proposition. Traditionally, logic has always been concerned with the fact that in our speech and in our thought we can achieve an intelligibility that is appraisable also as a truth-claim. It has not concerned itself with all forms of thought or meaning, e.g. with those that constitute prayers, commands, exclamations. Its notation is such that the grammatical formation of complex meaning is always the processing of a potential truth-claim and the propositional variable is conceived as formalizing the type of entities which are such claims. Thus, technically in calculation, the values which can be substituted for propositional variables are required to possess an invariant aspect of being potential truth-claims.

How is it that a proposition is in principle capable of being asserted, capable of being appraised as true or false? The reason is twofold: firstly, since form (intelligibility) characterizes language and thought as well as reality, a proposition cannot fail to express that which is possible or impossible, actual or non-actual; secondly, since linguistic forms and thought forms are also intentional (i.e. are disclosures), of their nature they can become the content of actual truth-claims. Thought-content is complete and propositional through possessing and disclosing form.

A further characteristic of the proposition is that it can be the object of many attitudes: I can be certain that *p* is the case, doubt it, opine it, assert it, deny it, believe it, be convinced of it, be sceptical of it, assume it, suppose it, surmise it. Indeed propositions exist only in so far as they are brought into existence by psychic and linguistic processes and they are arrived at by analysis of the end-results of these processes. However, a study of, e.g. belief is very different from a study of thought-content. This is evident in the contrast between a grammar of assent such as Newman's classic, and a grammar of rationality, such as a modern standard logic. It is evident also in the impossibility of applying standard logical rules to belief statements: granted that 'John believes that *the Prime Minister of England is going to visit America* it does not follow that John believes that *Mr Heath is going to visit America*'; the familiar rule of substitution cannot be applied to propositions which are linked indissolubly to a belief co-ordinate so that actual equivalence is not sufficient for substitution unless the believer is aware of it. These facts justify the use of a judgment-stroke before theses in logic to signify (a) that one is not dealing with the sign-structure but with its thought-content (we have seen already that the sign-structure of itself does not express anything, it must be *thought*; the symbolism itself is not the proposition); and (b) that one is not subsuming it under any attitude but that of an actual truth-claim. Interpreted in this way the judgment-stroke makes explicit facts that must otherwise be taken for granted. This seems to be essentially the point of Frege's symbol, ⊢. He says, in *Begriffsschrift*:

> If we *omit* the small vertical stroke at the left end of the horizontal one, the judgment will be transformed into a *mere combination of ideas* [*Vorstellungsverbindung*] of which the writer does not state whether he acknowledges it to be true or not ... *The horizontal stroke* that is part of the sign ⊢ *combines the signs that follow it into a totality, and the affirmation*

*expressed by the vertical stroke at the left end of the horizontal one refers to
this totality.* Let us call the horizontal stroke the *content stroke* and the
vertical stroke the *judgment stroke.* The content stroke will in general serve
to relate any sign to the totality of the signs that follow the stroke. *Whatever
follows the content stroke must have a content that can become a judgment.*
(As in *From Frege to Gödel*, pp. 11–12)

It is quite arguable that in setting out logical formulae as theses in a system and
numbering them as such we render a symbol such as Frege's judgment–content
stroke redundant, but Wittgenstein seems to underrate rich facets of its significance when he writes:

> Frege's 'judgment-stroke' ⊢ is logically quite meaningless: in the works
> of Frege (and Russell) it simply indicates that these authors hold the
> propositions marked with this sign to be true. Thus '⊢' is no more a
> component part of a proposition than is, for instance, the proposition's
> number. It is quite impossible for a proposition to state that it itself is true.
> (*Tractatus*, 4.442)

With Frege, proposition is conceived and symbolized as thought-content
that can be appraised as true or false; it may function as content in many
personal attitudes but theses of logic process it in the simple attitude of
assertion or actual truth-claim.

III. The nature of logical operators

Thought-content combines the feature of disclosing intelligibility with that of
being intelligible in itself. From the latter aspect it presents itself as a unity
which is explained in terms of formative processes that have been called,
metaphorically, operations. We have no direct experience of such processes;
indeed conclusions about the existence and nature of the proposition itself are
reached only through reflection on our thought-life and through analysis of it.
We *postulate* logical operations to explain the formation of thought-content
(which it is the business of logical language to process). Accordingly our belief
in them and our theory of them must be mediated by our experience of the
symbols we invent and the sign-constructs which we constitute to express
thought.

Logical language presents propositions in and through its wff's and distinguishes specific wff's as *C*-statements, *K*-statements, predicative statements,
existential statements, modal statements, etc. This suggests that propositions
have specific formations also and the word *operation* is used to connote both
(i) the formative construction of specific wff's; and (ii) the specific formation of
the thought-content signified: 'operation' in this latter sense is a conceptual
construct, a theory grounded in our experience of logical language which is

precisely expressive of propositions. A theory of the general propositional form (i.e. of the generic form of all propositions) focuses, as we have seen, the invariant feature that all propositions have of being intentional and thereby potential truth-claims. The term *operator* connotes any element deemed to be used formatively in making logical sense, general or specific—e.g. (at the level of propositional *signs*) connectives such as *C*, *K*, etc. quantifiers, predicate-letters.

It must always be remembered that a wff has meaning only in use (i.e. only when it is thought by writer, speaker, reader or hearer does it actually signify) and that therefore, of itself, it is not actually expressive of thought. It is interesting to note St Augustine's observation (*De Magistro*) that rational thought cannot be fully exposed in any formal system, that no sign by which a person communicates his thought can make us understand without a personal effort of understanding on our part. In *The Blue Book* Wittgenstein says:

> It seems that there are *certain definite* mental processes bound up with the working of language, processes through which alone language can function. I mean the processes of understanding and meaning. The signs of our language seem dead without these mental processes; and it might seem that the only function of the signs is to induce such processes, and that these are the things we ought really be interested in . . . We are tempted to think that the action of language consists of two parts; an inorganic part, the handling of signs, and an organic part, which we may call understanding these signs, meaning them, interpreting them, thinking. These latter activities seem to take place in a queer kind of mechanism, the mind; and the mechanism of the mind, the nature of which, it seems, we don't quite understand, can bring about effects which no material mechanism could. (p. 3)

Indeed between the *Tractatus* and the *Investigations* Wittgenstein moved, in his understanding of language, from a conception of it as (merely) a system of signs (*Zeichensprache*) to the conception of it as intentional thought, a disclosure of world (*Hermeneutik*) and his objective became one of surmounting the traditional dualism of signs and meaning, language and thought. This objective is widely shared today and makes it entirely natural to construct a theory of logical operations and logical operators *vis-à-vis* thought-content that is grounded in our experience of the linguistic role and behaviour of *C*, *K*, etc. for in thinking and uttering, e.g. *Cpq* the thought-content is formed indissolubly with the sentence.

Certainly as one ranges over the main sections of logic the wff's present meaning in a variety of formations. There is truth-functional meaning, formed by the connectives; predicative meaning, formed simply by the predicator and complexified in generality by the quantifiers; modal meaning, formed by the modal operators; and many-valuate meaning, formed by operators whose force is defined otherwise than by truth-tables. In a wff the function of variables is of course not formal at all; the functor or operator is the formal way by which we both isolate a thought-content and also express it. The more technically precise, in definition, an operator is, the more clearly present is the specific thought-content. An operator need not have a special sign, however; in a predicative sentence logical language symbolizes predicate and argument but not predication (in virtue of which there actually is a predicate and an argument)—it simply juxtaposes predicate-letter and argument conveying in this way that they are now formed into a predicate-argument unity.

One may categorize and analyse the main operators appearing in logical systems as follows:

(a) Truth functional operators. The kind of meaning brought into existence by truth-functional formation is such that its truth-value is always a specific function of the truth-values of the constituent propositions. Of course, strictly speaking the proposition Cpq is a unit and the propositions symbolized p and q do not exist as such. For the purpose of testing and displaying the truth functional relationship one has to analyse it into constituents. 'Logical operation' is a metaphor for formation in the strictest sense of the word; if one likes to use the Aristotelian model of matter/form and echo the medieval tradition one can speak of p and q as potential matter for formations symbolized by Cpq, Apq, Kpq, etc.

(b) The predicator and the quantifiers. Eliminating the verb of existence modern notation has achieved a clear simplicity in the representation of predication, e.g. Fa, and of generality within predication, e.g. (x) Fx, (Ex) Fx. There is a welcome departure also from grammatical symbolism, and generality is displayed as formation, the function Fx being incomplete potential material for generalization. It may be tempting to view atomic thought-content or meaning as being universally predicative. One must remember however that linguistic scholars are not satisfied that all peoples do use their natural language in this topic-comment way. Further, the tradition of logic has always avoided reductionism here. It has been predominantly concerned with that which has 'significance for the inferential sequence' (Frege) and in this context what is basic about every proposition is its character as a potential truth-claim. This basic characteristic does not presuppose a further single basic formation of meaning as is evidenced by the fact that propositional logic functions as the fundamental section of logic.

(c) The negator. Negation is of fundamental importance. It is a remarkable fact that of all the possible statements we can make about the world one half of them is false, for given any meaningful statement we can always form another statement which together with it exhausts logical space. Negation is not (like denial) a psychological event: as Frege pointed out, in criticism of psychologistic interpretations, it is not the opposite of assertion but, rather, is formative of the asserted proposition. Being positive or negative is a feature of meaning and is quite distinct from being true or false which is a feature of *correspondence* between meaning and the facts meant. A positive statement can be denied and can be false; a negative statement can be asserted and can be true. Testing a theory by the method of falsification, by focusing and trying to establish its negation, shows the human importance of negations within logical space.

There is of course no negation in physical space and this gives rise to the need of explaining its significance in logical space. For Plato the force of negating a statement is to both reveal its meaning and to express otherness to it: all forms of meaning refer to facts and opposing forms refer to different facts. He was adhering to Parmenides' principle: 'you will not find thought without being, in whose presence it is uttered'. Technically, for him the 'not' in 'that is not true' is governing the predicate-term rather than forming the proposition as a whole.

The problem of explaining true negative statements is a recurring one in history, discussed in ancient times not only by the Greeks but also by Indian logicians who spoke of 'negative facts', and in modern times by a line of philosophers and logicians before Wittgenstein: Frege, Meinong, Peirce, Russell, Husserl, Moore. Wittgenstein's analysis was very penetrating: of itself negation does not represent anything in reality: 'My fundamental idea is that the "logical constants" are not representatives; that there can be no representatives of the *logic* of facts.' (*Tractatus*, 4.0312) Negation is not something that occurs in the world: it is an operation mapping out the area of logical space. While not providing a new experience of reality it does form and order a content of our thought about reality. Some modern philosophers, such as the phenomenalist Paul Ricoeur, would put it that negation is not part of the given, it is contributed by spirit in the world: 'To know being is not merely to let it appear, it is to shape it intellectually, to order it, to utter it.' Yet negation has a referential force: Wittgenstein speaks of it as casting a shadow on the world:

> That shadow which the picture as it were casts upon the world: How am I to get an exact grasp of it?
> Here is a deep mystery.
> It is the mystery of negation: This is not how things are, and yet we can *say* how things are *not*. (*Note-books*, p. 30)

P and *Np* lead us to the same state of affairs; they have sense through presenting different possibilities, and the state of affairs verifying the asserted proposition falsifies its negation and vice versa. The existence of the state of affairs is a positive fact; its non-existence is a negative fact. Exactly the same investigation tests both propositions:

2.04 The totality of existing states of affairs is the world.

2.05 The totality of existing states of affairs also determines which states of affairs do not exist.

2.06 The existence and non-existence of states of affairs is reality. (We also call the existence of states of affairs a positive fact, and their non-existence a negative fact.) (*Tractatus*)

P and *Np* determine the situation of each other in logical space for they totally exclude each other and thereby surround each other. Thus together they map a state of affairs on to logical space, its logical place being determined according to whether it verifies the positive or the negative proposition:

> 4.064 Every proposition must *already* have a sense: it cannot be given a sense by affirmation. Indeed its sense is just what is affirmed. And the same applies to negation, etc.
>
> 4.0641 One could say that negation must be related to the logical place determined by the negated proposition.
>
> The negating proposition determines a logical place *different* from that of the negated proposition.
>
> The negating proposition determines a logical place with the help of the logical place of the negated proposition. For it describes it as lying outside the latter's logical place.
>
> The negated proposition can be negated again, and this in itself shows that what is negated is already a proposition and not merely something that is preliminary to a proposition.
>
> 4.1 Propositions represent the existence and non-existence of states of affairs. (*Tractatus*)

In summary, negation is a logical operation, a formation of thought-content; it is characterized by revaluing the meaning of the corresponding positive proposition in a formative act which reverses that meaning. It is the resulting proposition as a whole (*Np*) which is negative in form and so performs the function of negating.

(d) Operators in class-calculus and in many-valued logic. Symbols that appear in calculi or logic as functors do not all signify logical operations or logical operators. In e.g. class calculi sign-constructs fall under two main categories: (1) Names of complex classes generated by Boolean operations on simple classes, e.g. '*a* + *b*', '*a* × *b*'. The operation here is not formative of a proposition and so is not a logical one. The unit constructed is, of course, valuable in class calculation. (2) Statements which chart class space by expressing various possible relationships between classes, e.g. '*a* = *b*', '*a* ≠ *o*'. Here the statements are, in their propositional form, predicative, i.e. this is their form as disclosures, the form through which they mean or say something at all and which grounds their appraisability as true or false. The Boolean relationships of class equality or inequality are material or facts expressed through the propositional form of predication: the signs, = and ≠, formalize and represent non-intentional relationships. They are not logical, i.e. processes postulated to explain the formation of a disclosure as such; rather, they construct the stated relationships, i.e. the relationships which we mean, say, intend.

Similarly, in many-valued logic, statements are always subject to bivalent evaluation because the operators which form them as propositions are logical, two-value ones; what many-value operators construct is non-intentional relationships. In two-valued logic a *C*-statement asserts a proposition or thought-content which is formed by the *C*-operator. In many-valued logic the symbol *C* is defined in a framework other than the propositional one of appraisability as true or false; as an operator it is a principle of construction for non-intentional relationships which require to be expressed through logical forms such as predication. A logical operation is one whose whole being consists in forming a disclosure, i.e. an intentional sign which means, discloses, says something. Its origin or ground is in rationality: it is a form of life, specifically of rational competence to think and say something. What is referred to in the disclosure, the *matter* of the disclosure (to use an Aristotelian and medieval image) may be abstract, e.g. mathematical facts. Such facts too have their own construction and symbolic representation; the non-intentional operations which form the sign-constructs may be Boolean, or many-valued, etc.

(e) Modal operators. The operations postulated to explain modal propositions (*Lp*, *Mp*, *Up*, *Zp*) are logical but in a complex sense of the word *logical.* In *Lp* (it is necessary that *p*) the proposition as truth-claim is certified in a special way, i.e. as being necessarily so: *Lp* signifies a proposition under the specific certificate of logical necessitation. Other certifications are of impossibility (*LNp* or *Up*), simple compatibility with necessitation (*NLNp* or *Mp*) and of falling under neither necessitation nor impossibility (*KNLNpNLp*). Clearly, modal operators presuppose formed propositional meaning—they are not postulated as logical operators in the direct, primary sense of the term; what they specify is the *form* of assertion. Since the phenomenon of implication, of necessitation in the context of meaning, is a central concern of logic, modal operators are *material* which it is the direct concern of logic to study. Thus a modal proposition presupposes *formations* of both the proposition and its assertion which, in their different senses, are called logical operations.

Chapter 4

LOGIC AND SUBJECTIVITY

I. Introduction

With Frege modern logic succeeded in moving explicitly and completely away from the influence of a Psychologistic perspective which, for over two hundred years, had stunted its growth and distorted its work. It has not succeeded however in achieving a self-concept which defines the relationship between logic and subjectivity, the link between the science and the life of the human person. Indeed on the whole a fear of being psychologistic seems to have operated against a development of this aspect of the philosophy of logic. For the general philosophies of such logicians as Aristotle and Leibniz might be expected to stimulate interest in this matter, as might also contemporary person-centred philosophies, the movements of Phenomenology and Structuralism, and the development of Wittgenstein's thought between the *Tractatus* and the *Investigations.*

II. Aristotle and Leibniz

For Aristotle, reality is not totally formal. If we use the word, interiority, for that in the individual thing which is furthest away in our knowledge of it, then the most interior aspect of every material thing is its subjectivity. One can 'imitate' the forms of an individual, i.e. reproduce them in the psychic medium of thought through a perfect understanding of them, but one cannot conceive deep subjectivity which is in composition with form but is, in itself, formless— unique, rationally inimitable, incommunicable. This subjectivity is the supposit of predications, designated by the pronoun, *it,* and dignified in the case of human beings with the use of personal pronouns *I, you, he, she.*

Leibniz accepted this pluralistic conception of the world as one of myriads of subjectivities. Predication, the subject-form structure in which we most frequently express our awareness of the world, was important evidence for it. Indeed Leibniz conceived the world to be so truly represented in predication (where the subject *has* all its predicates, comprehending all the predications that can be possibly made of it) that, in his monadology, he endeavours to see the vast changing universe as interiorized in subjectivities—in pre-established generative grammars of activity that were private but harmonious. He used the word, *monad,* to designate subjectivity; everything is condensed and collected in monads: to apply metaphorically the language of his differential calculus, each monad is an integral embracing an unending series of characteristics and events as differentials. Phenomenal development (like predication) is rational through and through, concentrated in antecedently given rules of the monads; nothing happens without a reason and so the science of logic is the analytic mirror of universal rationality.

The general philosophies of Aristotle and Leibniz invite us, then, to consider logic, depth grammar of rationality, as a *form* of life, essentially relativized to a human subject.

III. Wittgenstein

In the *Tractatus* Wittgenstein uses 'world' for reality in so far as we contact it in the medium of language and thought. It is a fact that we can, in the Aristotelian sense of the word, *imitate* it: reproduce it in these media; we can say it, think it, and what we say and think can be evaluated as true or false. Thus reality is amenable to rational imitation: it can be objectified in rational processes and this potentiality to disclose itself in rational media is always there, is pre-linguistic, pre-epistemic. Considered precisely as having this potentiality realities, individually and collectively, are described as *objects*; so considered a reality has not actually any particular character; it cannot be described and is symbolized by a variable:

> 4.1272 Wherever the word 'object' ('thing', etc.) is correctly used, it is expressed in conceptual notation by a variable name.
>
> For example, in the proposition, 'There are 2 objects which . . .', it is expressed by '$(Ex, y) . . .$'.

To know a reality as an object is to conceive it precisely in its potentiality to disclose itself in rational media. In a process of analysis then, actual and possible worlds presuppose objects; or, in other words, actual and possible worlds and everything in them have a radical objectivity—their formal aspects and actual properties as worlds do not exhaust their being: that which through mediation or imitation is this world, is also that which *can* be mediated or imitated and *can* disclose itself in *any* rational medium.

Further it is because actual and possible worlds are objective that they have indispensable characteristics causing irrational propositions about them to be false, and propositions certified by rationality to be true. Thus objectivity, the fact that reality is such that it can disclose itself in any rational medium, guarantees that a grammar of rationality will be an ontology of the possible.

Wittgenstein's theory of objects is difficult, but it is a penetrating grounding of a quality that attaches to logical laws: they express that which *is so*, whether as a possibility, or in all possible worlds, or in any world in which there is at least one individual. The source, guarantee and ground of this quality is that, radically, reality is always and everywhere that which can appear, can be disclosed, in any rational medium: a grammar of rationality can, therefore, speak for it.

It is interesting to note that Aristotle in speaking of reality in its primary state of potentiality to rational form, described it in terms of being subjective. Wittgenstein's context was thought and language where reality is naturally presented at the objective pole of a relationship with a thinker or speaker.

After the *Tractatus* Wittgenstein de-escalated his absorption in the objectivity of reality, in its constitutional amenability to be imitated in any rational medium, its *potential* rationality (not to be identified with *formal* rationality which characterizes reality as mediated, i.e. our *world*). We find instead an escalation of interest in the other pole of life (the subjective one) with language again as the point of departure. Language is not viewed as a medium in which reality is imitated (pictured and thereby said); the emphasis is now on language as a form of personal and social vitality exercised in interaction with reality. Its roots and forms are followed backwards towards the human subject.

This new direction brought balance and completeness into Wittgenstein's philosophy of language. His insight into the objectivity of reality remained as valuable as ever, but the picture theory was abandoned and a much broader conception of language emerged.

We do not use language exclusively to communicate truth, to say what is so and what can be so. Such however was the static *Tractatus* conception of language giving rise to the goal of ideal descriptions by ideal languages, which

> sounds as if these languages were better, more perfect than our everyday language; and as if it took the logician to shew people at last what a proper sentence looked like. All this, however, can only appear in the right light when one has attained greater clarity about the concepts of understanding, meaning and thinking. For it will then also become clear what can lead us (and did lead me) to think that if any one utters a sentence and *means* or *understands* it he is operating a calculus according to definite rules. (*Philosophical Investigations*, 1, § 81)

Further, meaning cannot be explained simply through a correlation of words with things: a word can be used as a name but it can also be used in various other ways:

> ... in fact we do the most various things with our sentences. Think of exclamations alone, with their completely different functions.
> Water!
> Away!
> Ow!
> Help!
> Fine!
> No!
> Are you still inclined to call these words 'names of objects'? (Ibid., § 27)

For Wittgenstein, we have the habit of looking at language without looking at the language-game; we must study language empirically as an ordinary human phenomenon, getting back to 'rough ground', i.e. looking to actual examples and learning from them:

> But how many kinds of sentence are there? Say assertion, question and command? There are countless kinds, countless different kinds of use of what we call 'symbols', 'words', 'sentences'. And this multiplicity is not something fixed, given once for all; but new types of language, new language-games as we may say, come into existence, and others become obsolete and get forgotten.
>
> Here the term 'language-*game*' is meant to bring into prominence the fact that the *speaking* of language is part of an activity, or of a form of life.
>
> Review the multiplicity of language-games in the following examples, and in others:
>
>> Giving orders, and obeying them—
>> Describing the appearance of an object, or giving its measurements—
>> Constructing an object from a description (a drawing)—
>> Reporting an event—
>> Speculating about an event—
>> Forming and testing a hypothesis—
>> Presenting the results of an experiment in tables and diagrams—
>> Making up a story; and reading it—
>> Play-acting—
>> Singing catches—
>> Guessing riddles—
>> Making a joke; telling it—
>> Solving a problem in practical arithmetic—
>> Translating from one language into another—
>> Asking, thanking, cursing, greeting, praying—
>
> It is interesting to compare the multiplicity of the tools in language and of the ways they are used, the multiplicity of kinds of word and sentence, with what logicians have said about the structure of language. (Including the author of the *Tractatus Logico-Philosophicus*.) (Ibid., § 23)

Wittgenstein conceives language as a medium of self-expression in which we live and move and relate to others. There is no such thing as a correct form for language: such an ideal arose from the mistaken conception of language as essentially a depicter of fact:

> . . . it is clear that every sentence in our language is 'in order as it is'. That is to say we are not *striving after* an ideal, as if our ordinary vague sentences had not yet got a quite unexceptional sense, and a perfect language awaited construction by us. (Ibid., § 98)

The form of language derives from the user; as such it is not something private and esoteric, for the user has human life and lives in a social milieu with shared skills and agreements in vocabulary, grammar, tones of expression, gestures, etc. But it is the user who decides how to use words for the purpose of communicating to his hearer and it is this use which is the life, meaning and form of the particular sentence uttered:

> Every sign *by itself* seems dead. *What* gives it life? In use it is *alive.* Is life breathed into it there? Or is the *use* its life? (Ibid., § 432)

It follows that the word, language, refers to an indefinite range of language-games. They have no common defining property but between them is a family resemblance:

> Here we come up against a great question that lies behind all these considerations. For someone might object against me: you take the easy way out. You talk about all sorts of language-games, but have nowhere said what the essence of a language-game, and hence of language, is: what is common to all these activities, and what makes them into language, or parts of language. So you let yourself off the very part of the investigation that once gave you yourself most headache, the part about the *general form of propositions* and of language. (Ibid., § 65)
>
> Don't say: 'There *must* be something common, or they would not be called games'—but *look and see* whether there is anything common to all. For if you look at them you will not see something that is common to *all*, but similarities, relationships, and a whole series of them at that. To repeat: don't think, but look! (Ibid., § 66)
>
> And the result of this examination is: we see a complicated network of similarities overlapping and criss-crossing: sometimes overall similarities, sometimes similarities of detail. (Ibid.)
>
> I can think of no better expression to characterize these similarities than 'family resemblances'; for the various resemblances between members of a family: build, features, colour of eyes, gait, temperament, etc. etc. overlap and criss-cross in the same way. And I shall say: 'games' form a family. (Ibid., § 67)

Speaking a particular language is part of a form of life: it expresses a range of living activities—ordering, questioning, describing, etc. As forms of life, language-activities are logical primitives: they cannot be justified, for they are bedrock:

> It is easy to imagine a language consisting only of orders and reports in battle. Or a language consisting only of questions and expressions for answering yes and no. And innumerable others. To imagine a language means to imagine a form of life. (Ibid., § 19)
>
> If I have exhausted the justifications I have reached bedrock, and my spade is turned. Then I am inclined to say: 'This is simply what I do.' (Ibid., § 217)
>
> What has to be accepted, the given, is—so one could say—forms of life. (Ibid., II, p. 226)

IV. Structuralism

It has been said that everyone is born, intellectually, into the world either a Platonist or an Aristotelian. It could be said with equal justice that anyone who dedicates himself to explanation must identify with either the Wittgenstein of the *Tractatus* or with the Wittgenstein of the *Investigations*, or must become an integral Wittgenstein—the solitary person, perhaps, of real life.

The movement, Structuralism, seems to possess in its own way, at the present day, the main tensions that were felt and pressing in the philosophical development of Wittgenstein. Responsible for *avant garde* movements in the human sciences, with hardly any contemporary scientist or philosopher who does not accept the value of structuralist investigation everywhere, structuralists have been known more for their opposition than for their openness to theories which have recourse to the human subject. The fact is, however, that the question of the origins of structure is a central problem as yet unresolved in the movement.

The concept, *structure*, here is of course a very special one which moves away both from the simple etymology of *structure* (*struere*, to build) and from the static connotation of *form*. Piaget points out:

> ... once we focus on the positive content of the idea of structure, we come upon at least two aspects that are common to all varieties of structuralism: first, an ideal (perhaps a hope) of intrinsic intelligibility supported by the postulate that structures are self-sufficient and that, to grasp them, we do not have to make reference to all sorts of extraneous elements; second, certain insights—to the extent that one has succeeded in actually making out certain structures, their theoretical employment has shown that structures in general have, despite their diversity, certain common and perhaps necessary properties ... In short, the notion of structure is comprised of three key ideas; the idea of wholeness, the idea of transformation, and the idea of self-regulation. (*Structuralism*, pp. 4–5)

Structuralism repudiates the atomistic tendency of many current disciplines to explain structures as 'composites formed of elements that are independent of the complexes into which they enter' (Ibid.) A structure is a whole and it is through the relations among elements that we conceive it properly; the elements of a structure are subordinated to laws which define the whole and explain its overall properties. Through these laws the structure is constituted not only as a whole but also as a whole in process of transformation. Structures are systems of transformation: their laws both structure them and simultaneously govern their transformations:

> ... all known structures—from mathematical groups to kinship systems—are, without exception, systems of transformation. But transformation need not be a temporal process: 1 + 1 'make' 2; 3 'follows hard on' 2; clearly, the

'making' and 'following' here meant are not temporal processes. On the other hand, transformation can be a temporal process: getting married 'takes time'. Were it not for the idea of transformation, structures would lose all explanatory import, since they would collapse into static forms. (Ibid., pp. 11–12)

And transformations of a structure conserve it since the elements to which they give rise always belong to the structure and are always governed by its laws:

These properties of conservation along with stability of boundaries despite the construction of indefinitely many new elements presuppose that structures are self-regulating. (Ibid., p. 14)

In the vision of Structuralism, philosophy, logic, mathematics, the physical sciences, the life sciences, the psychological and social sciences, the humanities (literature, history and linguistics) would form a continuum of knowledge, each discipline employing the structuralist method of investigation and ultimately seeing its sector of reality as a self-regulating transformational system or 'structure'. The successes of the structuralist method (e.g. in anthropology and linguistics), the importance of Structuralists (such as Ferdinand de Saussure, Claude Lévi-Strauss, Roman Jakobson, Jean Piaget, Francois Jacob, Roland Barthes, Edmund Leach, Louis Althusser, Jacques Lacan), the explanatory potency of structure (as a deep rather than a surface reality—that which itself cannot be seen but nevertheless can only be derived from what is seen): these facts compel respect for the Structuralist vision. Indeed standard logic, in the format of a natural deduction system, is a structure in the full Structuralist sense of the word, and in its own domain is already a consistent and complete system of knowledge.

However, at this point, a fundamental problem, on which Structuralist opinion is unclear, unsure and divided, arises. Is structure an ultimate primordial reality? Does it, itself, call for *formation*? What, ultimately, is its genesis or is it an ungenerated whole? It is easy to think of the elements of a structure as changing while the transformation laws applying to them remain immutable. But the very existence of transformation rules poses the same fundamental problem; and the word *innate* poses formidable problems of formation for biology and physiology to answer. Piaget comments:

Now the implicit hope of anti-historical or anti-genetic structuralist theories is that structure in the end be given a non-temporal mathematical or logical foundation (Chomsky has, in fact, reduced his grammars to a formal 'monoid' structure). But if what is wanted is a *general* theory of structure, such as must meet the requirements of an interdisciplinary epistemology, then one can hardly avoid asking, when presented with such non-temporal systems as a mathematical group or a set of subsets, how these systems were *obtained*—unless, of course, one is willing to stay put in the heavens of transcendentalism. One could proceed by postulate, as in axiomatic systems, but from the epistemological point of view this is an elegant way of cheating which takes advantage of the prior labor of those who constructed the intuitive system without which there would be nothing to axiomatize (Ibid., pp. 12–13)

Thus while some contemporary structuralists oppose theories based in any way on the reality of 'subjects' and 'subjectivity', the movement itself, being a method and not a finished doctrine, does not exclude such theories. Piaget, for instance, asserts:

> Structure is simply a system of transformations, but its roots are operational; it depends, therefore, on a prior formation of the instruments of transformation—transformation rules or laws ... The subject exists because, to put it very briefly, the being of structures consists in their coming to be, that is, their being under construction. (Ibid., pp. 140–41)

It is interesting to note two other problems which structuralist investigation cannot fail to encounter. Firstly, since mathematics and logic are used to explain physical laws, what is the relationship between structures in mathematics and logic and structures that are ascribed to the real? Are they the same? Are real structures *there* independently of us? Wittgenstein spoke of the world having logical form but *world* has a specific meaning in his philosophy and *form* is a static concept. The parallel question for the structuralist is whether formal transformations of logic and mathematics account within the observed facts for change and persistence.

The second question concerns the interrelationship between linguistic and logical structures. And here Chomsky's rationalism has replaced the view of logical positivists and of linguistic scholars like Bloomfield who reduced mathematics and logic to linguistics, and mental life to speech. In Chomsky's view since the speaker–hearer's normal use of language is creative he must 'be in control of what is now often called a generative grammar of his language'. The roots of such a grammar are in reason and in an innate reason. Thus rational vitality is the source of language, and logic (the grammar of rationality) is the source of linguistic grammar.

V. Husserl

The broad task which the movement of Phenomenology set before itself was the descriptive investigation of phenomena, both objective and subjective. Those who were phenomenologists in the strictest sense paid particular attention to what it means for objects to appear subjectively in experience, and (on the basis of an operation called phenomenological reduction) studied how the appearances of an object are constituted in and by consciousness. Thus Paul Ricoeur defines the movement as follows:

Fundamentally, phenomenology is born as soon as we treat the manner of appearing of things as a separate problem by 'bracketing' the question of existence, either temporarily or permanently. (*Esprit*, XXI, 821)

It is obviously a movement with a strong belief and interest in subjectivity. With Husserl indeed subjectivity is 'the wonder of wonders', the central mystery:

Whether we like it or not, whether (for whatever prejudices) it may sound monstrous or not, this (the 'I am') is the fundamental fact (*Urtatsache*) to which I have to stand up, which, as a philosopher, I must never blink for a moment. For philosophical children this may be the dark corner haunted by the specters of solipsism or even of psychologism and relativism. The true philosopher instead of running away from them, will prefer to illuminate the dark corner. (*Formale und transcendentale Logik*, p. 209)

Throughout his life (if we disregard his *Philosophie der Arithmetik* of 1891) Husserl was resolutely set against psychologizing, i.e. translating objects into psychological experiences, and as early as 1895, through contact with Frege, abandoning a plan to derive arithmetic from psychology, he had begun his celebrated critique of logical psychologism—the view, as he put it, that 'the theoretical foundation for the construction of logic ... is supplied by psychology, and specifically by the psychology of knowledge.' He was equally opposed to 'objectivism'—failure to take proper account of the subjective aspect of knowledge; and the problem to which he gave his attention, as being the most fundamental one, was reconciling the objectivity of truth with the subjectivity of the act of knowledge. Pivcevic sums up his philosophical development as follows:

If we glance back at Husserl's philosophical development from his *Philosophy of Arithmetic* onward, we shall see that, at root, all his analyses were concerned with one basic problem: the problem of the relation between the objective content of knowledge and the acts of meaning and knowing. Or, to repeat one of his own questions: 'How are we to understand the fact that the "in-itself" of the objectivity can be thought of by us and moreover "apprehended" in cognition, and thus in the end yet become "subjective"?' It was this problem that led the young mathematician Husserl to interest himself in the noetic presuppositions of mathematics and to inquire into the 'origin' of the concept of number. He was made aware by Brentano of the importance of intentional relations, and in exploring these relations he found himself in the domain of that 'object-constituting subjectivity' (*die leistende Subjektivität*, as he came to call it) which was to remain the focal point of his phenomenological analyses. (*Husserl and Phenomenology*, p. 91)

An intentionally active meaning-giving, object-constituting subjectivity—*die leistende Subjectivität*—is central in Husserl. 'Subjectivity' here refers not to particular subjectivities but to subjectivity-as-such (which he finally interprets in the context of a transcendental Ego). He believes it is of fundamental importance to study its constitutive activity, and, for logic, to study in particular the categorial activity which produces logical concepts and logical schemata.

However although Husserl outlined his concept of a Pure Logic (i.e. of a logic that accepted human subjectivity as its source but was free of psychologism) the details of his work were epistemological in character, being concerned with an elucidation of knowledge rather than with a systematic development of logic. Acknowledging that Kant, Herbart, Lotze, Leibniz and Bolzano had also worked on blueprints for a pure logic, Husserl sketched his own two-level structure. Spiegelberg writes:

> The first level is that of the propositions or 'truths' studied by the logic of statements ('*apophantics*') as composed of meanings and their various combinations. The second level consists of the 'things' to which these statements refer, i.e., of the states of affairs (*Sachverhalte*) which they assert, the relations, complexes and other configurations which they can enter and which are to be investigated by what Husserl calls a *formal ontology*.
>
> Actually, this two-level pattern incorporates two one-level conceptions of pure logic, formulated most impressively by Bolzano and by Meinong respectively. Bolzano had organized his pure logic on the propositional level around representational ideas, propositions and truths (*Vorstellung an sich, Satz an sich, Wahrheit an sich*). Meinong knew only of the 'state of affairs,' which he had named '*Objectiv*,' and of other categories of formal ontology. Husserl's conception incorporated both these levels, that of the propositions, which are valid or invalid, and that of the states of affairs, which do or do not 'subsist,' as Bertrand Russell rendered Meinong's term. ('To be the case' might be a less hypostatizing equivalent of the rather harmless German word '*bestehen*'.) (*The Phenomenological Movement: A Historical Introduction*, vol. 1, p. 96)

Later (1929) in his *Formale und Transcendentale Logik* Husserl added a third level: this would be a study of the designata of logical symbols within the context of idealized speech.

Husserl's contribution did not go beyond his argument for the need and possibility of a pure logic. But it is an important point of view. It argues that the science of logic has traditionally been conceived on the basis of a confrontational model of knowledge generally, where science simply faces and observes reality so that its findings are the already-out-there-now-real. Subjectivity is forgotten so that the objectivism is blind.

On final analysis and taking this view in its essentials, there is not in it anything to invalidate modern formal logic and metalogic but its assimilation would force logic to work out a richer philosophical perspective.

VI. Subjectivity in contemporary philosophy

This is a central concept for phenomenologists and existentialists and indeed is frequently burdened with enormous philosophic tasks as when, for instance, Merleau-Ponty speaks of behaviour as 'embodied subjectivity' or speaks of the existence of an 'art hidden in the depths of the human soul and which, like all art, is only known through its results'. In traditional systems which acknowledge their origins in Greek and medieval philosophies, self is also a fundamental concept grounded in conscious activity; for a conscious act presents itself as a subjective act which is object-oriented: concomitant with, e.g. the objective awareness or the objective anger there is a disclosure of self *as subject*. (There never occurs a subjective act which is also subject-oriented; the result is that the concomitant awareness we have of self cannot be elaborated into direct, insightful, thematic knowledge such as we have of objective realities.)

Undoubtedly today's philosophical milieu is suitable and stimulating for exploring the grounding of logic in the human subject.

Of particular interest to logic are some writings of Heidegger (for the parallelism that is evidenced between contemporary philosophy and Wittgenstein) and of Jaspers (for his conception of the highest logic as Reason-becoming-conscious-of-itself).

Heidegger, a student of Husserl and widely regarded as the central figure in contemporary existentialist thought, is representative of the strong movement depicting self not as an isolated (Cartesian) *worldless I* but as inseparable from the world, living authentically only when I make situations vitally *mine* instead of being buried and hidden by surrender to the enslaving tendency of routine life. The programme of Heidegger's *Sein und Zeit* is not unlike that of Wittgenstein's *Investigations*—the bringing back of philosophy to a viewpoint from which one can see the human subject as always participant. For Heidegger himself this means retrieving the Pre-Socratic viewpoint when truth was *alethia*, the unhiddenness of being, before it became with Aristotle a mere property of propositions—correspondence with facts. Language is not simply an instrument for communication: Heidegger rejected such linguistic occasionalism, the conception of language as extraneous to the vitality of thought; for him (*Holzwege*, pp. 60–61) language is our access to being:

> It does not merely present in words and sentences things obvious and things concealed as meant in some particular way; on the contrary, it is language which brings things as such into the open in the first place. Where no language prevails, as in the existence of stones, plants and animals, then there is no access to things either ... Any given language is the occurrence of the word in which its own world dawns historically on a community ... the event in which things as such become intelligible for man in the first place. (F. Kerr's translation, in 'Language as Hermeneutic in the later Wittgenstein', see Bibliography, p. 415 below)

Jaspers writes succinctly of the indissociabillity of subject and object:

> What is then the meaning of this mystery which is implied at each moment by the subject–object–dichotomy? It can only mean that Being as a whole is neither subject nor object but must be the *Enveloping*, which reveals itself in this dichotomy.
>
> Clearly then, Being as such cannot be an object. Everything that becomes an object for me breaks away from the Enveloping in confronting me, while I myself emerge from it as a subject. An object is a definite kind of being for the subject, whereas the Enveloping remains obscure for my consciousness. It is brought to light only through objects, and takes on greater and greater clarity to the extent that the objects become more sharply present to consciousness. The Enveloping itself does not become an object, but it appears in the cleavage of the subject and the object. It is a *background* which is incessantly illuminated through the appearance of objects, while remaining forever the Enveloping. (*Einfuhrung in die Philosophie*, p. 30)

With regard to Jaspers' conception of a higher logic, Sebastian Samay analyses its nature and origin:

> Under the joint impulse of Reason and Existence, thought is able to explore its own transcendental possibilities, possibilities that lie beyond the limits of ordinary logic. Once these limits are transcended, logic is replaced by a-logic.
>
> We must now briefly examine this a-logic, briefly because its principal elements of paradox and contradiction are already known to us from Existence-elucidation. However, we must be prepared to meet some insurmountable difficulties in trying to show the rapport between ordinary logic and rational a-logic. All of these difficulties originate in the fact that the relationship between these two modes of thought is actually transcendental and enveloping. A-logic constantly envelops logic, without really absorbing it, so that their relationship cannot be described logically.
>
> ... it would seem that it is logic itself that demands this final leap of thought into Being where, instead of enveloping its object, itself is enveloped by it. It appears that this last exertion of thinking is made on logical grounds, so that the resulting a-logic is really a rational one. A-logic is not the abdication of Reason, rather the expansion of it. Reason in all its forms is indispensable even for a-logic. This may explain, at least partially, one of Jaspers' often quoted cryptic phrases, 'I have non-knowledge itself only through knowledge, and perfect non-knowledge through a maximum of understanding ...
>
> This process of Reason becoming conscious of itself should not be understood as a simple psychological self-reflection. It requires an act of transcendental reflection. Transcendental reflection forces knowledge to return upon itself, away from its objects. This is not as natural and easy as it may sound, because what Reason finds in returning upon itself is not an

object, but a source (*Ursprung*). Transcendental reflection requires a veritable about-face, inversion (*Umkehrung*), or conversion (*Bekehrung*) of our object-bound natural attitude. This conversion demands a great deal of exertion on the part of Reason. The new logic is a matter of struggle. 'Reason is not easy but difficult to realize,' says Jaspers.

It can be realized only if individuals make it part of their personal formative process. They must become 'wholly involved and interested in it, if this logic is to succeed.' In other words, it cannot be learned or taught from a detached and safe distance. Philosophical logic, as we already know, is an act of Existence. (*Reason Revisited: the Philosophy of Karl Jaspers.* Published by Gill and Macmillan, pp. 210, 214, 220)

VII. Conclusion

Formal logic is a corpus of truths discovered and systematized by methods that are objective in quality. If the objectivism is blind, however, logic as human wisdom will be deficient. It is proper that at the level of philosophical reflection the formal systems be seen not only as an ontology of possibility (grounded in the objective) but as a grammar of rationality (grounded in the subjective). This will not lead, quantitatively, to more theorems within formal logic but it will lead, qualitatively, to a perspective that is integral.

Of course many logicians have difficulties in conceiving logic as having a ground in subjectivity. The fact that this conception does not lead to an enlargement of formal logic is automatically a minus against it. (Since the time of the Greeks it has been explained that subjectivity is not amenable to 'imitation' in rational media so that its functioning as source to logic could not be expressed in a formal system.) Again, conceptions (such as Jaspers) of a logic, higher than traditional and modern logics, in which Reason becomes conscious of itself and which is characterized by paradox and contradiction, may easily appear to lack any real solidity. Further, logicians experience their science as a formal system grounded on itself: to go outside the system and ground it in subjectivity seems to be an exercise in psychologism. Indeed Beth and Cavailles conclude that, for the logician, phenomenology is psychologism developed in a new language.

Notwithstanding the dangers it does not seem impossible to reach a perspective in logic which would do justice to subjectivity. Such a perspective would assimilate, in substance, both the *Tractatus* (which itself summarizes so well the historical tendency of formal logic) and the *Investigations* (which possesses so much of the spirit of contemporary movements to the subjective pole of life).

The *Tractatus* is right in emphasizing that reality is objective in the sense of being amenable to imitation in any rational medium. And logic is the most fundamental science to display this, for it is at the same time both a grammar of rationality and an ontology of the possible. Science supports this view implicitly by its efforts to express the laws of nature in mathematical laws of the greatest rational simplicity and beauty possible; also by its faith that the universe and every event in it is, in principle, patient of rational explanation. This faith is shared broadly, indeed, by ordinary people throughout their daily lives.

When it is the objectivity of reality that is the centre of interest, our concern with language tends to be limited to the descriptive, propositional use of it—to our rational capacity to say what is so or can be so. This is a limited viewpoint from which the clarity and cogency of logic is very impressive. However, just as reality is amenable to rational *description* (description by a human observer) so human life in all its facets is amenable to rational *expression* (i.e. formed communication by the human subject). Looking at language from the direction of the human person, one sees it as a multifaceted expression of life with reality. And from here logic is seen as potentially, for the logician, a glimpse into the art of our own subjectivity.

Chapter 5

LOGIC AND THE IDEAL RATIONAL LIFE

I. Introduction

It is proper that logic should distil from its mass of truth a contribution to perspective in human life. Certainly it is a vantage point from which one can understand the benefits and limitations that occur when life expresses itself in any rational form. For an important part of its work is study of the structure of formal systems; further it formalizes very exactly its own methods and truths; and its role in the creation and operation of our computer world has been very important. For all these reasons it is proper that a contemporary philosophy of logic should have the function of providing perspective on formalism and wisdom in the human disposition to formalize.

This chapter will analyse, firstly, the human value and necessity of formalization and the efficiency of logic as a science here; then it will analyse the limitations of formalization. These analyses will be a basis for presenting a logical ideal for rational living, the ideal being named metaformalism. This ideal has strong affinities to a new contemporary scientific method which will be described.

II. Formalization is inherent to rational living

To be rational is to be operating some formal system; logical procedures in logical language are an extension of natural procedures in natural language. For instance, one aspect of thinking rationally is that we think in accord with what we already know: previous knowledge is a continuous rational constraint—we bring it to bear in a quasi-axiomatic way. We accept systematic consistency as a condition of rationality in daily life, i.e. that principles, explicit or implicit, which are present at the start should be held rigorously throughout the context. The rational expectancies of our daily life have, indeed, the logical character of theorems and instantiations from our *weltanshauung*. Little conscious effort may be involved in the daily exercise of systematic thought, for the knowledge used is habitual and the procedures of judging and testing in the light of that knowledge are habits too.

The very language we use involves a viewpoint, materializes a systematic outlook, is by nature a vehicle of models. Wittgenstein would put it that behind any contemporary language lies the history of a nation's forms of life; in the language of Teilhard de Chardin these constitute a noösphere. It is inherent in human living that we live in particular cultures and that, accordingly, we think systematically. And indeed characteristics of mature, sovereign, thinking are present when we are systematic: commitment to principle and to procedure, generality and tenselessness of statement, precision and consistency in content.

Logic itself bears witness to our strong rational impulse both to elaborate truth, transmitting it to consequences, and to diagnose falsehood, locating its roots in a false principle. If not a definition of the science, it is certainly an important aspect that it is a theory of derivability and that this theory is necessarily operational (to varying degrees) in the other sciences and in daily life.

III. The limitations of formalization

Formalization has, however, important limitations—essentially, historically and psychologically.

A radical incompleteness in human formalizations has been indicated both technically and philosophically. In Aristotle's view material reality is not completely conceptualizable, is not totally formal; this led him to the hylomorphic theory of matter.

For Aquinas, similarly, no reality is known fully in concepts, is completely formalizable; thus our rational point of view shows up the things of our experience as being composite; if one speaks of that in them which is conceptualizable as essence, then one has to say that *to be* is not identical with *being of this essence*—there is a real distinction between the rationality of a thing and its actual be-ing.

An essential point in Frege's theory of predication was the observation that a concept has not the complete reality ('saturation') of the object conceived. Gödel's famous incompleteness theorem established that arithmetic, and any formal system which requires it, is necessarily incomplete. For Wittgenstein an indefinite number of language games is possible, for languages are forms of life and life is too rich for complete formalization. Introducing an abstract computing device, now called a Turing machine, Turing showed that the application of such machines to theories other than arithmetic is effected by an arithmetization process and that there are an uncountable infinitude of non-computable arithmetic functions. These varied and important conclusions point to a common fact, namely that formalization is always an asymptotic movement, if one takes as its goal a complete grasping of reality; they indicate that over-control by any particular formal system or device is not natural to the human mind and underrates the range of its power.

In conceiving the possibility of a science (logic) which would transcend contexts and abstract from the impact of lived experience, Boole implicitly underwrote the importance of not identifying logicality with total rationality. And Leibniz distinguished accurate knowledge and adequate knowledge drawing attention to enormously important elements in our life and in the world which cannot be put in scientific terms. However, the Western world has pursued rationality predominantly in the form of logicality. With its ideal of quantitative exactness and complete objectivity or exteriority in knowledge it has achieved technological control over nature, but its rationality has not been sufficient for understanding the complex unity of human life and the world: it has not integrated into a single culture the clarity and simplicity of exact science with humanistic sensibilities, and it has not retained human properties and values in an era of technology. Rather, mental enquiry and technology has moved forward too much on rigid formal tracks, driven by a logic of intensification and incrementation which prescinded largely from human consequence. According to contemporary thinkers such as Polanyi and Merleau-Ponty we are coming to the end of this epoch of exaggerated objectivism; Marjorie Grene writes:

> We are in the midst of a new philosophical revolution, a revolution in which, indeed, the new physics too has had due influence, but a revolution founded squarely on the disciplines concerned with life: on biology, psychology, sociology, history, even theology and art criticism . . . we have had to free ourselves from the bonds of Newtonian abstraction, to dare, not only to manipulate abstractions, to calculate and predict and falsify, but to *understand.* The revolution before us is a revolution of life against dead nature, and of understanding as against the calculi of logical machines . . . The conceptual reform in which we are now engaged must restore our speech about the world to intelligible discourse and the world it aims at describing to significant and coherent form. Nature must be understood once more as the multifarious scene, not only of an invisible billiards game played by chance against necessity, but of a vast variety of forms, energies and events, living and non-living, sentient and insentient, of processes alive, active and striving, as well as of conditions, dead, passive and inert. (*The Knower and the Known*, pp. 13–14)

The analytic aspect of formalist thinking has been particularly cultivated by the West. This carries with it the habit of dissecting, and of separating everything from everything else, ourselves from the world and from one another. It is natural that this has contributed to the creation of psychic distances, alienating us from the world and from others, and to the felt need for restoring interconnectedness and achieving integrated social living. Certainly, analytic habits can act like an over-efficient grindstone on the cutting surface of the mind. It seems that the great Asiatic cultures have avoided this characteristic of Western thought, have expressed themselves in fluid analogies rather than in well-defined concepts and have sought *union* with nature in an intuitive, subjective, mystical approach.

Psychologically, there is such a thing as mental cramp, the mind being locked in a particular orientation by, e.g. a set of principles that was never fully understood and chosen, by what is implicit in the language system we use, by a less than adequate objective which keeps us moving with considerable intent in one direction (e.g. towards maximum efficiency in locomotion or towards complete computerization). Such 'sets' may be cultural and individuals may be unconscious of the fact that they are not in the nature of things. They may also be generated by personal assumptions or habits never duly examined. Their common result is that under the spell of a deductive compulsion we constantly reapply narrow attitudes of the past, justify repeatedly the characteristic theorems of our lives, relive the same decisions, go through the same behaviour until a good deal of our life is quite spiritless. A most difficult thing for each person is maintaining human proportions, being in all things human—not simply rational and exact on one's own terms, but adequate.

The contrasting logical structures of rationalization and self-deception show, each in its own way, how great an effort is required to confront the fact that we are acting inconsistently with some axiom or rule in our lives. In rationalization, the reasons for an action or decision which we present and acknowledge have the quality of consistency with our principles but they fail to express what really motivates us. Our individual form of life presses us to defend it, in this way, against the inroads of our own freedom. The structure of self-deception displays a different mechanism of defence employed in the same cause. Herbert Fingarette points out that the term, self-deception, invites us to think of the phenomenon as a form of lying to oneself, to conceive it on the model of 'other-deception' and to describe it in terms of belief-and-perception-language:

> For example, it is quite natural to speak of the self-deceiver as one who doesn't *perceive* his own fakery, who can't *see through* the smokescreen he himself puts up. We also say that in a way he sincerely *believes* the story he tells while 'deep inside him' he *knows* it is not true. He makes it *appear* to himself that something is so. We say the self-deceiver is *unaware* of his own deception; and, in straight psychoanalytic language, we speak of his *unconscious* wishes and fantasies. Though in general this is a bag of quite various words, their remarkable interchangeability in the context of self-deception justifies, in this context, our grouping them initially as a single family of terms. (*Self-Deception*, pp. 34–5)

Fingarette takes as a basic fact that to become explicitly conscious of something is to be exercising a certain skill, namely the skill of expressing a particular life situation of ours in language (-like) form.

> We then state that the self-deceiver is one whose life-situation is such that, on the basis of this tacit assessment of his situation, he finds there is an overriding reason for adopting a policy of not spelling-out some engagement of his in the world. As with any reasonably well developed skill, so in this case, too, the action suits the tacit assessment: he does not, therefore, spell-out the matter in question; and, by virtue of this policy, he is further obliged not to spell-out the assessment or the policy. The consequence is that he may be observed as one who is in fact engaged in the world in a certain way such

as carrying out a destructive campaign against some person ... yet he is unable (by virtue of his tacit commitment) to spell this fact out to himself or to anyone else. Thus when the issue is raised, he does not, cannot, express the matter explicitly at all. He is in this respect in no better position than anyone else. He tells us nothing but what he tells himself. (*Self-Deception*, p. 62)

The person has, generally speaking, three options in a situation in which he is strongly inclined to a way of acting which is radically inconsistent with his avowed explicit outlook and aims. One option is to totally forego the way of acting in question; a second is to avow it as *his*. In this second option one becomes a radically divided and vulnerable being; one faces a spiritual crisis in the Kierkegaardian sense of a crisis of the shaping, or the betraying, of the self. The third option is to leave the stalemate between inclination and personality and to move into self-deception—the individual engaging himself in the way to which he is inclined, but the person refusing to acknowledge the engagement as his.

Interpreted in this way as motivated strategy, i.e. as something the ego does rather than as something which happens to the ego, one sees the powerful role of system within human life and the tensions it creates in authentic living. This is especially true if one views the skill (withheld in the situation of self-deception) of spelling-out, of being consciously clear and explicit, as being intimately associated with the highest level of organisation and unification of the individual human life.

Finally, there is such a thing as putting an excessive value on clarity, on the clarity that formalization provides. It is difficult to sustain the excessive clarity of someone else's formalizations: the system (within its own terms of reference) is so wholly present, so cogent that the hearer is robbed of potentiality. No one is clearer in mind than a person with an obsession. And the clarity of our own thinking too may blind us to its narrowness of scope.

IV. Metaformalism as an ideal for rational living

The basic fact is that formalizations neither fully contain the material object's reality nor do they express the human subject's vitality completely. A formalization is incomplete both as description and as expression. This indicates that subjectivity, open to all viewpoints, has a wider receptivity than can be accommodated by a sum total of formal systems, and that the human person is meant to maintain this basic openness and receptivity.

As subject I seem to have an indefinite openness to life. I remain a mystery to myself, in my subjectivity, in that I can never completely formalize myself, to myself. I can objectify and understand the range of capacities I display; with others I can subjugate my environment to myself and constitute social life on our planet as I wish. But while I must live in *some* environment and constitute some particular kind of social life, my subjectivity is not really comprehended in terms of my particular limited circumstances and specific achievements—*I* could be living a very different kind of life and be a very different kind of being, mentally and bodily. There is no bipolar (subject–object) life of which I can say that I could not be subject in it, that it could not be personally my life.

Thus the subjection of life to system is not the rational ideal for life. We demonstrate a greater rationality by looking on form not as fulfilling but as enriching, not as the goal and termination of effort but as a base for further ascent, not as bringing to rest our desire and search for truth but as increasing, endlessly, our potentiality for it. Such a perspective may be called *metaformalism* since it is justified by reflection on the value and limitations of formalization in human life.

It is a striking fact that today studies of diverse sciences are drawing attention to how much of ourselves is in our world: to the process of objectivization and to the fact that the world in which we live and move and have our being is an objective world, encountered by us in a bipolar (subject–object, from–to) experience. The act of being that is formalized in human knowledge is being-revealing-itself-to-human-consciousness; the human view point (sensitive and rational) is an intrinsic part of the formalization. Today interest in the mind's synthetic function in objectivization has displaced and dated the traditional controversy of Idealism and Realism. The complexities of objectivization are conceived to invalidate, as oversimplifications, both poles of this controversy.

The fact is that, as human beings, all we can say is what is or is not objectively so, and to understand the nature and range of objective truth we must understand objectivization. Just as in physical science, relativity theory points out that there is no such thing as a brute fact, the simplest entity in science being an observed fact, so too logical experience at the level of theoretical thought is that an essential relativity or proportion attaches to the world in which we live and move and have our being. Every objective fact is being-revealing-itself-to-consciousness; the simplest fact expresses *a priori* conditions and terms of the rational viewpoint. Experience of formalization has drawn attention, within the science of logic, to rationality as input and, indeed, formal recognition of this input constitutes a radical difference between the axiomatic procedure and that of natural deduction.

Thus logical experience does not support the positivist belief that scientific knowledge possesses a total exteriority, any more than it supports belief in an irrational, arbitrary subjectivity. It suggests to the logician that, as an ideal and master movement in rational living, we should maintain a freedom and mobility of viewpoint (which would be compatible with a further theistic expectancy of, and 'waiting for', a revelation of absolute, unobjectified, unformalized being).

For some philosphers the discovery of so much that is of ourselves in the world, the extended awareness of the raw material from which life is built, has given rise to a sense of emptiness and futility, a pessimism. For Cioran western civilization is in a state of paralysis: every idea and movement works itself out formalistically and then crumbles. Reason is 'the rust of our vitality'—'it is by undermining the idea of reason, of order, of harmony that we gain consciousness of ourselves'. 'An individual, like a people, like a continent, dies out when he shrinks from both rash plans and rash acts, when instead of taking risks and hurling himself towards being, he cowers within it, takes refuge there.'

Logical experience does not support this pessimism. The objective world is our world: it can be as optimal as we make it; always it is *possibly* the best of worlds. Again, the limits of objectivization, sensitive and rational, which are coming more and more into focus, point to ineffable possibilities in unobjectified, undisclosed, being. Further, and very practically, logical experience draws attention to our faculty of transcending the objective, and it suggests that the vitality of transcendence may be of central importance for contemporary well-being. Nowadays the multiplicity of systems (beliefs, values, ways of life) has a pessimising effect—for many people it has become difficult to so believe that it would be logical and a worthy thing to die for their belief. Logical experience, following the natural grain of human life, suggests that the central skill of that life consists in combining a definite choice and dedication in objective living with cultivation of our capacity for transcendence.

Transcendence is threefold. We have the capacity to move out of the gravitational field of our objective circumstances and on to contact, feeling and enjoyment of our own subjectivity. Transcendence of this type may be explicitly practised; it is also implicit in the development of ego strength, the maturation of personality. There is also the transcendence of objectified being that moves towards unobjectified, undisclosed being. It is a function of philosophy to be transcendent in this way. Finally, for the theist, there is the transcendence that moves towards God and divine life, in the hope that our obediential capacity for the ineffable life of God will be actualized.

Thus logical experience is hospitable to the ideal of a life that has bi-polar strength, that integrates dedication and transcendence, temporal achievement and everlasting freedom. Life points to the future. The capacity to assimilate the past as potentiality for the future, to orientate ourselves with great flexibility, with heuristic curiosity about a reality that is only partially disclosed— these are important human qualities at every moment of evolutionary time.

The word, *evolution*, underlines a basic function of any logical system or social structure—to contain an elaborated point of view and to mediate development to a wider point of view with richer content. It is the spirit of a dynamic conservatism to recognize that the past jusifies itself by leading to a better future. Such a spirit needs the service of a section of logic which is pluralistic, i.e. which is a science of integrating different formal orientations, which designs 'system-operators' (analogous to propositional operators) studying the connectivity of systems, and which achieves a technique of systematic and contemporary questioning of structures that mediates genuine development. We tend to use a restricted logic for thinking in closed systems: we prove what we like and we like what we prove, expecting that a principle of logical osmosis will bring others to the same logical consistency. The ground of a pluralistic logic, however, is not the closed system but metaformalism; the space of such a logic is peopled by myriads of (elaborated) viewpoints: it is the grammar of the connectivity and integration of viewpoints, the technical embodiment of magnanimity and love.

V. Metaformalism and the new logic of framework transpositions within science

Current scrutiny of the notion and validity of objectivity has served to present scientific knowledge no longer as a single system expressed in a single language but as a collection of contexts each with its own formal point of departure, conceptual framework, language and elaborated content. The question and need arises: is there a process of integrating whole conceptual frameworks—a formal logical process? Is there a rational grammar for combining context-languages? Important beginnings have been made in working out a new logic of framework transpositions.

With regard to literature on this subject: the writings of Polanyi and Popper are well-known general treatments of the notion of objectivity in science; recent studies by Butterfield, Conant, Kuhn, Agassi, Feyerabend, Hanson, Sellars, Wartofsky and Heelan have criticized relevant assumptions of classical science; the writings of Patrick Heelan are a primary source and the following treatment is based on his extremely lucid presentations.

The situation requiring a new logic arose in the first decades of this century with the replacement of classical physics by quantum physics:

> This involved a conversion from the classical model of a subjectless scientific objectivity to the subject-dependent objectivity of quantum mechanics. Quantum mechanics arose as the outcome of Werner Heisenberg's reflection on the role of observables in science. By an 'observable' he meant a quantity that, though not imaginable in a classical space-time model, was part of the interpretations of a mathematical model and was measurable in principle. His intuition rejected the objectivist presuppositions of classical physics and, in a profoundly significant epistemological shift, he consciously placed the measuring subject or observer at the heart of quantum mechanics. The classical physics of his time presupposed either no observer or one separated from matter and outside of history. The quantum-mechanical observer, on the other hand, is one of human scale who uses instruments of the same scale to observe quantum-mechanical events and processes. Quantum-mechancial observers, then, are as manifold as the kinds of instruments a scientist can use. The most significant discovery of quantum mechanics, however, is the fact that it is not possible to construct an instrument or a panel of instruments that will give simultaneously the values of all the observable properties of a quantum-mechanical system.

Quantum mechanics thus is concerned with contextual observations or descriptions; that is, every observation of a quantum-mechanical system is dependent on the context of the observation, which is, namely, the measuring instrument used to make an observation ... What looks from the classical perspective to be a restrictive principle expressing, namely, our inability to measure simultaneously the precise position and momentum of a system, turns out, with the quantum-mechanical perspective, to be in the first instance a revelation of the context- or observer-dependent character of scientific observations. It also shows that the total scientific horizon is not revealed to any one observer, but that in addition to possible (precise) position states and possible (precise) momentum states there are those imprecise states of position and momentum together revealed in response to mixed contexts of observation. In other words, the synthesis of context results in an enrichment of the horizon vis-à-vis the complementary contexts—taken as thesis and antithesis—in their pure dialectical opposition.

(For example, in a mixed position and momentum context, precise position or precise momentum cannot in principle be observed, but imprecise position (x) and imprecise momentum (p) can be observed and the systematic variabilities (or 'uncertainties') Δx and Δp of x and p respectively will obey Heisenberg's Uncertainty Principle ... which relates the measure of inaccuracy (Δx) of a position measurement (x) with the associated measure of inaccuracy (Δp) of a momentum measurement (p) according to the inequality of $\Delta x \cdot \Delta p \geqslant h/2\pi$—where h is Planck's constant.) (*Nature and its Transformations*, pp. 498–9)

Thus there is no basic set of 'observational facts given immediately and indubitably in experience without the involvement of the subject', and there is no privileged set of basic concepts 'considered as irreformable because received passively from the object':

... the contrast between the observational, on the one hand, as epistemically certain and descriptive of reality, and the theoretical, on the other hand, as tentative, provisional and not descriptive of reality, cannot any longer be sustained. Certainty is found in the use of both types of predicates, and both are used descriptively of the world.... The theoretical explanation of motion becomes an ingredient of our observations of motion. Observational language, in fact, becomes laden with theory. That there is in principle no aspect of observational language that is free from the intrusions of theory is the well known theme of a certain group of authors led by Toulmin, Hanson and Feyerabend. In brief, we might summarize their conclusion and ours, that *observational* and *theoretical* are not characteristics of predicates but of predications or uses of predicates: a *theoretical* use being inferential, mediate and circumspect vis-à-vis realistic intent; an *observational* use being non-inferential, immediate and realistic in intent. (*The Logic of Framework Transpositions*, p. 317)

The progressive theoretical exploration of each domain of fact is stored in a descriptive language which is an historical entity with an historical development. Naturally, over centuries, a vast family of conceptual frameworks and appropriate languages have come into existence. Some deal with the same domain of facts (and historically, perhaps, one replaced another), others do not; some are compatible, some complementary, some incompatible. The question is: what is the logic of relationships between frameworks and the possibility, through logic, of integrating them? This question can be formulated in terms of language, for each framework is a linguistic context, generating necessary and sufficient conditions subjective and objective for the use of a descriptive language. So formulated, the question is: what are logical models for understanding inter-framework relationships and developmental transpositions between frameworks in history? Further, is it possible with the contributing help of a 'context-logic' to integrate all context languages, securing a cumulative field of vision from a single linguistic viewpoint?

One of the examples Heelan gives of the kind of logical understanding a context logic would provide relates to quantum mechanics:

> Quantum mechanics with its complementary languages illustrates a peculiarity of a wide class of context-dependent languages—that they are mutually exclusive yet not absolutely so. They resist combination on the one hand, and on the other, they can be combined within a broader more inclusive language, which, however, is not in a Boolean relation to the original languages, but stands to them in the non-Boolean relation of a non-distributive lattice.
>
> The paradigm case is precise position language L_a and precise momentum language L_b in quantum mechanics. Each corresponds to its own measurement context—precise position language is the linguistic projection of precise position-measurement-contexts, precise momentum language is the linguistic projection of precise momentum-measurement-contexts. Bohr and Heisenberg and most complementarity physicists claim that these languages are subsets of the kinematical language of classical physics. That this is mistaken was pointed out by Feyerabend and the present author ... the position and momentum languages are subsets of a broader quantum mechanical kinematical language L_{ab} in which the space-time description of any quantum system can be formulated, whether or not the system is found in a precise position or precise momentum-measurement-context. The author showed that L_a, L_b, L_{ab} and their complements suitably defined constitute an orthocomplemented non-distributive lattice of languages. L_a and L_b can then be said to be *complementary in L_{ab}*. This is not the same as what Bohr meant, since L_{ab} neither contains nor is contained by the kinematical language of classical physics. It simply replaces it.
>
> The relationships between the three languages L_a, L_b and L_{ab} can be illustrated by means of an analogy taken from biology. Two isolated allopatric stable populations A and B of the same species exist in different

environments, say, on either side of a broad impassable river. Each population has its own set and distribution of genotypes, G_a and G_b respectively. A Boolean union of the two populations would be one where the distribution of the genotypes would be just the set theoretic sum of the genotypes of the two populations. A Boolean union of two such populations if it makes scientific sense at all, makes sense only if the geographical barrier between the two populations remains intact. But if the geographical barrier is removed, say, by building a bridge across the river, each population is able to invade the territory of the other. New selection pressures arise, genes are exchanged, and possibly new hybrids are formed. The exchange of genes, hybridization and natural selection work in the course of time to produce a new steady-state distribution of genotypes G_{ab} in the expanded stabilized population AB, which now occupies the whole territory. G_{ab} will be quite different from a Boolean union of the two original distributions G_a and G_b. The genotypes of populations A and B, even though presumably they all persist among the genotypes of the united stablized population $\bar{A}B$, are in a non-Boolean relation to the latter. The non-Boolean relationships between G_a, G_b and G_{ab} constitute what is called a non-distributive lattice. (*Scientific Objectivity and Framework Transpositions*)

The concluding comment is:

The value of the analysis I have just given over other proposals for the use of a non-classical logic in quantum mechanics and elsewhere is manifold. Firstly, the claim that the context-languages constitute an orthocomplemented non-distributive lattice is a precise, well-defined claim which is subject to falsifying tests. Secondly, it enables classical logic to be retained, if there are good reasons for retaining it, on the level of each of the related object languages, L_a, L_b and the language of the synthetic context L_{ab}. Non-classical logic need enter only when complementary contexts are combined, and in this case, it functions solely on the metalinguistic level of a meta-context-language which is itself a part of the philosophy of the languages concerned and does not affect the use of the languages themselves. Thirdly, the account I have just proposed can be the starting point for many investigations in the philosophy and history of science and in the metascience of science and philosophy. (Ibid.)

VI. General conclusion

Two important insights from the history of logic are that the simplest linguistic act is the sentence (the meaning of words being determined by their roles in sentences) and that the simplest logical act is some exercise of the grammar of propositional logic (formalizing a *whole* proposition, connecting whole propositions monadically, dyadically, etc.). This subordination of parts to a whole may continue to leaven the science of logic. For not only has it seen that propositional, and not terminal, logic is basic within standard logic, it is natural also that it try to situate propositional logic itself within a more general context. Technically, it is quite possible that the basic section of future standard logic will be 'system logic' or 'context logic' (the simplest logical act being regarded as an exercise of its grammar), for it is entirely arguable that a whole framework or system is presupposed and is implicitly present in the formalization and connectivity of propositions. There may then be new Stoic and new Fregean explorers reaching a deeper level in the standard analysis of rationality.

This would bring a qualitative change to modern logic—a science which has been widening itself more than it has been deepening in roots. It would be the kind of technical development which would underwrite the view that logic cannot be fully understood without being seen in its relationship with rational competence and human subjectivity. A 'system logic' would perhaps point to this relationship more strongly than propositional logic.

Section E: Applied Logic

DETAILED CONTENTS OF SECTION E

Chapter 1

THE SCOPE OF APPLIED LOGIC

I. Introduction

While qualities of mind such as clarity, relevance and cogency in reasoning are described as logical, they are also and properly described as qualities of a mind that is judicial, or scientific or mathematical or clinical. They develop quite naturally from any context in which one invests careful thought and therefore do not presuppose a knowledge and application of the science of logic. Logical qualities constitute one aspect of intellectual character and a cursory examination of even ordinary living shows that it challenges us to achieve intellectual asceticism, discernment and decisiveness of a high order. One has to overcome many difficulties, from within and without oneself, in coming to be utterly fair-minded, not least among which is the fact that the average person does not seem to desire a larger measure of good sense than he already possesses. Yet in life the inferential acquisition of knowledge requires the cultivation of both sound intuitive and inferential processes, it being an important insight that we reach truth either by intuition or by inference and predominantly, by a combination of both processes. A valid inferential process does not necessarily bring us to further truth unless the evidence we believe in is true also. Here it requires what Santayana called intellectual chastity to be free of prejudices—convictions which are not based either on consultation with experts or on due examination and yet function as a prior (*prae*) base from which to reach a conclusion (*judicium*). Inherent in life is the challenge, in adulthood, to confront the assumptions that are fundamental in one's outlook and to accept personal responsibility for any attitudes and beliefs one will apply as evidence. Assumptions which have been generated in the course of one's personal history or by the process of cultural osmosis possess great psychic power and thus in becoming reasonably unprejudiced, one inevitably becomes muscular and competent in thought generally.

Competence, of course, includes being properly informed in each and every context in which we presume to reason. To arrive at true conclusions, one must have sound and accurate information to begin with. Further this information cannot be properly subjected to an inferential process, unless it is well formulated. So life challenges us to acquire reasonable linguistic sensitivity and rectitude in our own reasoning, and critical discernment in regard to that of others, particularly where techniques for mass persuasion or mass indoctrination are employed.

There is a further aspect of the human condition which is limiting in itself but demands that we compensate for it by fostering carefulness in processing the thought content of our arguments. It is the fact that reasoning is a human, personal activity in which one may be both feeling deeply and inferring confidently, and everyone is subject daily to propaganda in which agencies emotionalize or de-emotionalize their statements according as they wish to arouse emotion or to mute it. Thus human life challenges us to acquire the habit of disengaging thought content from the context of feelings and to learn to gravitate to conclusions on evidence alone. The detachment achieved is somewhat analogous to that resulting from the design and use of logical language which frees itself from particular contexts to concentrate, as Frege put it, on what has 'significance for the inferential sequence'.

Clearly many forms of life provide the opportunity and the need of developing those qualities of thought that are often called logical. And these qualities need to observe the human proportions of life, for too much clarity may be imported into interpersonal relationships and it is often unrealistic and burdensome to insist on proof—according to a dictum of Aristotle's, indeed, it is a mark of an educated man not to demand in any subject matter more certainty than that subject admits of, humanly. Accordingly, applied logic does not attempt to prescribe formal procedures for living, existential thought: it does not present itself as an art of thinking better and it does not attach special importance to logic for qualities of mind that may be expected to develop through working in this discipline.

The precise content of applied logic follows naturally on the fact that formal logic is a depth grammar of rationality. It consists of (a) a study of the extent to which this grammar can be *identified* in social use (especially in the sciences), and (b) a demonstration of how logical techniques and perhaps logical language too, may be used to clarify and formalize thought content in various contexts of life and science and philosophy.

There is room for the study of existential human thinking and reasoning, sifting its structure and methods for the rules which are present and identifying the rules which translate logical laws and those which do not. It is not controverted that there should be such a formal analysis of basic rationality as it exists. And although, historically, most attention has been given to the empirical sciences and mathematics, the analysis in applied logic touches every area of theoretical thought, i.e. of thought which has as its objective not doing or making things but understanding states of affairs.

History shows that two kinds of people are needed for an analysis to be adequate and concrete: (1) people who are expert and experienced in the particular contexts or subject matters being studied, e.g. empirical scientists when the methods of empirical sciences are being studied, and (2) people who are expert in formal logic. The former are needed to describe the rational structure of their disciplines; the latter contribute by matching these descriptions with forms and structures that formal logic presents in its grammar of rationality. At the points where procedures or structures are not perfectly grammatical, there is, logically speaking, a formal deficiency and therefore what has been traditionally called a 'logical problem'. For many hundreds of years the problem of induction has been, in one form or another, a central problem. Where there is formal deficiency the logician is expected to provide an evaluation both of it and of the steps taken to compensate for it (if it is humanly unavoidable). The essential point, however, is that applied logic represents teamwork, the formal logician being simply the member who provides knowledge of logical forms.

II. Limits in the purpose and functioning of applied logic

Applied logic is concerned with theoretical thought only, i.e. with thought that is intent on understanding reality and on formulating truth-claims rather than with practical thought which is intent on knowing how this or that can be done. Its claim to be concerned here is that theoretical thought is a movement that is (a) inferential, and (b) intent on formulating a coherent system of propositions. Obviously logic has a useful function here, its laws being translatable as directions for the movement of thought, safeguarding truth.

For a conclusion to be true and shown to be true, the evidence must consist of true propositions and the process by which the conclusion is drawn must be logically valid. It is well to bear this double preoccupation in mind as we study existential methods of theoretical thinking; the theoretic process present is not the sole concern in actual life. In empirical science especially the aim is comprehensive—to extend human experience and control of the world as well as to achieve a theoretical mastery of it. Applied logic cannot contribute directly to an experiencing, a technical control or an intellectual mastery of the natural world; it *can* contribute a generalized understanding and evaluation of theoretical processes used.

It is not the function of applied logic to prescribe forms but rather, working within a description given by experts in the discipline whose basic rationality is being examined, to identify those forms which appear in logic as truths or rules or as pertaining to the process of formalization, and to say also what forms do not match with any part of the grammar which logic provides. The main roles of the specialist and the logician are quite distinguishable. It is important above all for the logician not to presume to *describe* the context to which logic is being applied.

For many hundreds of years logicians did presume, with regard to empirical science, both to describe it and to prescribe form and method for it. This was a great weakness in Bacon and Mill who were criticized by scientists for thinking that they could *devise* methods for science and that they could evaluate existing scientific methods without being practising scientists. It would be difficult to surpass Bacon, of course, for a description in broad terms of the empirical and practical nature of science. He understood broadly the direction that science was taking and should take; he divined the technical progress that could come and would come; and he wrote a direct, clear and imaginative analysis of the meaning and utility of science. Also in his works some convictions of contemporary scientists are voiced: science must have the broadest possible basis of fact; the first step in science is to collect facts and to describe them carefully, even with mathematical precision where that is possible. But when he presumed to evaluate actual scientific procedure, in a generalized way, and to advocate a 'new method' (which would be 'such as to leave little to the acuteness and strength of wit, and, indeed, rather to level wit and intellect. For as in the drawing of a straight line or accurate circle by the hand, much depends on its steadiness and practice, but if a ruler or compass be employed there is little occasion for either, so it is with our method.') his writing ceased to be really imaginative and became vague and speculative in quality.

John Stuart Mill was also severely criticized by contemporary scientists for presuming to write a logic of science in complete independence of practising scientists. His methods, particularly, belong to the level of common sense thinking; they are pre-scientific and could not qualify as a description of, or prescription for, scientific methodology.

Of course perspective on logical structure comes most reliably from the formal logician. It is possible for the specialist not to be aware of the full significance of a formal deficiency in his method of investigation or format of explanation. With regard to the empirical sciences, especially, it is possible to put an exaggerated value on their logical unification and to use the method of reduction in a way that does not do justice to their rich conceptual diversity. Indeed nowadays controversies concerning reductionisms and methodological oversimplifications are prominent.

In summary, perhaps the most distinctive feature of contemporary applied logic is that it is interdisciplinary, a new limited role being accepted by the formal logician.

III. The specific contents of applied logic

Since applied logic is concerned solely with theoretical thinking in all its existential forms, its main studies fall naturally into the following categories:
(a) A study of what is positively logical in existential thought. This involves describing the main forms of the latter (especially scientific investigation and explanation, philosophical and mathematical thought) identifying the logical structure that is present and analysing its strength in the light of logical and extralogical experience.
(b) A study of the problems which arise when an evidence-conclusion structure which is in use, existentially, does not correspond to the formal grammar of rationality developed within formal logic. These are called logical problems because they become manifest in the comparison with logical grammar. But of course they are in fact problems for the discipline concerned. Of its nature, contextual reasoning of any variety is not fully logical in its nature. Within empirical science, the processes of verification and induction have been discussed, in one form or another, as logical problems since the time of Plato and Aristotle.

(c) A study of the differences between various existential approaches to reality—the scientific, the philosophic, the aesthetic, the religious, noting the nature of their theoretical concern, their methods, logical strength and logical problems.

(d) A study of logical formalization, i.e. of how techniques and language used within formal logic may be used to clarify and organize extralogical contexts. Thus, for example, the discipline called 'deontic logic' is a logical formalization of theoretical thinking on obligation (*deon* in Greek connoting 'that which is binding'), and the logic of preference is, similarly, an axiomatization of propositions about preference. There are no practical limits to the use that may be made of logical formalization. The study in applied logic is a general one with the presentation of some examples.

(e) A study of formal detachment: whether or not impersonal knowledge is a false ideal and even an impossibility.

Chapter 2

LOGICAL FORMS IN THE EMPIRICAL SCIENCES

I. Introduction

The empirical sciences are sufficiently identified as the present-day range of physical, biological and psychological sciences—they purport to deal directly with ourselves and the world we sense and their conclusions are tested in an appeal made (in experiment or observation) to our world. Extra-experiential or *a priori* sciences, on the other hand, either develop without reference to any particular world (mathematics and logic) or refer to realities that transcend human experience and operate from principles that are acceptable only on the ground of being revealed (supernatural theology).

This chapter will seek to summarize the description which empirical science gives of its own structural growth, and to stress the logical forms which appear in this description and which are the source of the logical strength of the empirical sciences. Problems that arise when the logical formation of scientific argumentation or investigation is not perfect or is not completely explicit will be discussed in the following chapter.

II. An historical survey of the development, structurally, of physical science and of scientific method generally

The Greek contribution to this development. In empirical science today one can distinguish very clearly (1) its field investigations where, by observation and experiment, it tries to reach particular laws; and (2) its theoretical work where it seeks to co-ordinate these laws into a concise explanatory system. A scientist today may be either a field scientist or a theoretical scientist—rarely is the same person both to any really great degree. The Greeks were not empirical scientists in the modern sense of the word. Their interest and insights lay not in methods of investigation but in the theoretical organisation of knowledge— in science as an explanatory system of propositions. Consequently their philosophy and science were not sharply distinguished. It was not that they lacked observation or failed to appreciate its value but simply that the conception of science as an experimental, mathematical enterprise was a later development.

A great achievement of the Greek period was to objectify the human hope of explaining the world, developing a theory of explanation and providing in

Euclid a model of systematic explanation. Primitive types of explanation personified forces in the world and tended to project features of our mental life into things. The Greeks, however, conceived explanation as essentially a logical thing, rooted in evidence and meaning. For them to explain the world would be to reflect it in a system of propositions where less general propositions would be deducible from the more general ones; to explain any particular proposition would be to situate it under the general principle from which it could be deduced.

Thus empirical science is indebted to the Greeks for the development of its deductive and explanatory character; in particular to Socrates for a theory of definitions, to Plato for a general theory of the hypothetical approach—the deducing and verifying of consequences—and to Aristotle for a general theory of induction. Aristotle saw that the world of nature could always be otherwise than it is and, therefore, that a purely deductive science of it is not possible. He emphasized that while scientific *explanation* is deductive (and can always be formulated syllogistically) scientific *investigation* must be an inductive process, a generalization of particular experience. His treatment of the possible types of induction is very important but his description of the rationale of the inductive process indicates how general is the plane of his thought. He does not deal with the process in the concrete modern framework of experiment and mathematical calculation. In his description, the object of the inductive process is to abstract and define forms and a fact (or effect) is explained when it can be shown to be the subject of some defined form, e.g. the phenomenon of falling is explained in terms of it being the nature of a heavy body to fall when unsupported in the atmosphere. Forms vary in degree of abstractness and those displayed in the explanations of Physics, Mathematics and Philosophy represent three different levels of abstractness or generalization.

In his treatment of what modern logicians call intuitive induction (a process in which our sense experience of a particular fact is such as to facilitate direct insight into a general principle), Aristotle points out that science is not self-demonstrating but must originate in intuition. The body of scientific knowledge is generated by two complementary processes—intuition and inference. Intuitions, immediate apprehensions of fact, occur at both the sensory and intellectual levels of knowing. It is the business of sensory intuition to supply science with its data; the role of science is to explain the data by presenting it as deducible from general propositions which, themselves, are ultimately situated under primary principles that do not need to be proved because they are intellectual intuitions. Thus when scientific knowledge is organized into an explanatory system of propositions, sensory intuitions appear as theoretical conclusions, intellectual intuitions as primary explanatory principles; and throughout the system there is a recurring process of demonstration, i.e. explanation through deduction from propositions that are more general and, therefore, intrinsically more intelligible.

In Aristotle's foundational study of physical science, basic commitments are made:

(1) to *a reality principle*: every proposition of science refers to the real world;
(2) to *an evidence principle*: there are indefinable terms (so obvious in meaning as to require no explanation) and indemonstrable truths (so obvious in truth as to require no proof);
(3) to *a truth principle*: to be scientific a proposition must be true;
(4) to *a deductivity principle*: every logical consequence of a scientific proposition is also scientific.

This set of postulates commits science to foundations that coalesce experience and logic, but the coalescence itself is not worked out and clarified—unless one holds that scientific principles are within reach of common intuition and do not require systematic mathematical research. In Aristotle's own day these postulates were attacked by the School of Megara, and paradoxes that have become famous were urged against them (e.g. the Liar paradox against the truth postulate); historians such as Prantl and Zeller have regarded these paradoxes as trivial fallacies but their significance was appreciated in antiquity. In the event Aristotle's theory (presented in his *Prior* and *Posterior Analytics*) was accepted and remained dominant for centuries even while physical science itself changed, becoming experimental and mathematical in character.

Within the Aristotelian framework physical science was not able to come to a clear-cut concept of itself—to see in what precise ways it is an idealizing, logical discipline and an experiencing, discovering one also. The fact is that modern science may be considered from two widely differing aspects: (a) as an enterprise of discovery; and (b) as an explanatory body of propositions, axiomatization being the standard method for consolidating and transmitting knowledge. When modern science is *explaining* (or demonstrating) what it has already discovered, it is an idealizing, logical discipline; for discovering truth, however, it recognizes and practises both an empirical approach, and a purely rational, imaginative one. The former approach examines experiments and expresses the regularity of results in terms of physical laws; it checks new theories at every stage and modifies them when new results demand it—and this is an important way in which physical theories come to be formulated. The latter approach constructs theories, imaginatively; speaking of Einstein's major discovery, Lanczos says:

> He could no longer doubt that nature is much more than a conglomeration of accidental mathematical equations which serve for the description of this or that natural phenomenon. There are great and sweeping principles acting in nature which, when found, show us the unifying links between the confusing variety of single events. Newton's theory of gravitation was age-old, a closed chapter of physics, there was no reason to ponder on it, nothing new came to light in this field for the last hundred years. And yet, purely as the result of a philosophical enquiry, a deep analysis of reference systems, an entirely new light was shed on the old phenomenon, gravitation was something totally different from anything assumed before, a natural and inevitable property of the geometrical structure realized in nature. Would it be imaginable

to make such a discovery by mere observation and trying to fit the observations by a mathematical formula? Not in a million years. Constructive and imaginative mathematical reasoning of greatest profundity was demanded for such a discovery. (*Rationalism and the Physical World*)

Thus, quite understandably, Aristotle's foundational studies did not produce an adequate framework for modern science. In him, the Greeks moved from the foundational research of mathematics (completed by Eudoxus and Theaetetus) to a similar research of physical science. But Greek science was simply observational, neither experimental nor mathematical. And the coalescence of the empirical and the purely rational (so essential and intricate in modern science) was assumed but left uncharted.

The medieval contribution in the development of empirical science. The conception of empirical science as essentially an experimental and mathematical enterprise goes back further than the sixteenth and seventeenth centuries to medieval times. In achieving this conception medieval science advanced beyond the Greek and Arabian stage. The conception itself became more technical and operational in the modern period of science.

In Aristotle, Physics and Mathematics were kept rigidly apart. The concrete world was the province of Physics, and physical questions and answers were non-mathematical in character. From the thirteenth century there was a growing insight into the usefulness of mathematics in explaining the physical world and a gradual penetration of mathematical procedures into physical investigations. By the fourteenth century systematic attempts were being made to express and deal with qualities and motion in quantitative terms. Thus while remaining very limited indeed in mathematical technique, the mathematical physics of the fourteenth and fifteenth centuries developed, conceptually, without a break into that of the sixteenth and seventeenth centuries.

Medieval scientists in Oxford, Paris, Germany and Italy came to understand also that science must become an experimental enterprise, constructing and testing hypotheses. The technical standard of experimentation was not high by modern standards, but Robert Grosseteste, Albert the Great, Roger Bacon, Petrus Peregrinus, Witelo and Themon Judaei were all experimental scientists and introduced the experimental method into European science.

As early as the thirteenth century, in Oxford, Robert Grosseteste (1170–1253) formulated a theory of experimental science: Arriving at scientific knowledge is an inductive process. Induction may be based on a systematic analysis of the phenomena or it may take the form of a sudden leap of intuition or scientific imagination. Both forms of induction lead to a theory, to seeing the data or facts in an intelligible perspective. A further problem arises now: how distinguish between true and false theories? A discrimination can be made only by posing questions to reality itself in the form of special experiments or (where the natural conditions cannot be manipulated as in astronomy) of special observations. By making deductions from various possible theories, it is possible to determine which theories are falsified by experiment or observation but it is not possible to be certain that any particular theory is true. Science must rest content with approaching closer and closer towards certainty. His method of elimination or falsification (and confirmation) was based on two assumptions about the nature of reality: (1) the principle of the uniformity of nature—agents are always uniform in the effects they produce; and (2) the principle of economy: it is an objective characteristic of nature that it operates in the shortest way possible; further, as a pragmatic principle in explanation, one explanation should be preferred to another if it is simpler in content and involves fewer assumptions.

This latter question—what basic assumptions or postulates are made in science?—was also discussed by John Duns Scotus (*c.* 1265–1308) who dealt at length with the principle of the uniformity of nature. He believed that it is implicit in every inductive investigation.

It is interesting to note that the experimental method came to characterize various medieval medical schools where there was a remarkable interest in the logical structure of the procedures used. Galileo derived much of the logic and terminology of his theory of science from Paduan doctors.

The revolutionary development of science in the sixteenth and seventeenth centuries. In weighing up science in any particular period one needs to ask two questions: (1) what principles about the nature of science and of the proper scientific approach to reality, inspired and directed the scientists of that period? (2) what actual scientific work did they accomplish? Galileo Galilei (1564–1642) is often singled out as the father of modern science. The principles that inspire modern science go back further than Galileo, but he used them openly, consistently, successfully and with this general effect that, with him, European science became once and for all highly mathematical, experimental and technological in self-conception and method.

Galileo's conception of scientific method had two main characteristics. Firstly, he eliminated the discussion of essential natures which had characterized Aristotelian Physics and concentrated on describing what he observed. Such words as 'gravity' were for him simply names for certain observed regularities. Secondly, he tried to express the observed regularities in mathematical terms, focusing quantitative relationships in phenomena, studying these, developing mathematical implications and building up a mathematical theory. This abstract mathematical procedure (replacing the effort at immediate and direct generalization about the phenomenon) led to a special kind of experiment—one that would verify or falsify quantitative deductions.

Galileo believed that mathematical theories displayed the enduring substantial reality underlying phenomena. Nature is mathematical; that which is not mathematical is subjective. Indeed the faith that inspired nearly all science until the end of the seventeenth century was that through being mathematical it could discover the basic intelligibility of nature.

With Newton (1642–1727) science was, again, a strictly empirical and mathematical enterprise, characterized by induction and verification. But he did not believe that it could claim to discover the intrinsic structure of the universe or describe natural forces in their concrete reality. Science must concern itself with aspects of reality that can be treated mathematically, with properties of things (at rest or in motion) that vary quantitatively. There may be other methods of approaching reality, with equal logical claims to true knowledge; but this is a successful method, humanly, and there are no others in prospect.

Simplifying phenomena by formulating them under their mathematical aspects, converts complex reality into a machine-like entity—something with definite properties that can be isolated, measured and duplicated, so that in the end the behaviour of the machine can be predicted. This simplification of phenomena gives a wide scope to mathematical reasoning, the objective validity of which is tested, at each stage, by observation or experiment.

Once they are verified the mathematical generalizations become experimental laws. As such they are known to be objective, but they do not reveal to us anything more than mathematical aspects, quantitative relationships. Newton discarded the view, prevalent for two centuries, that the universe is mathematical in its basic structure, and that mathematics is a key opening up the universe in its concrete reality. He felt that there were no grounds to justify this outlook. The mathematical approach to reality was a method, the best one available, with no better one even in prospect. It was saying too much however to describe it as a key. Indeed we do not know that any mathematical deduction gives objective information unless and until we can relate that deduction to the real world by observation or experiment. And the information does not go beyond mathematical aspects, quantitative relationships.

We can speculate of course about the concrete structure of reality, about the real causes or concrete realities behind words like 'gravity'. But speculative hypotheses have no place within science where hypotheses are admissible only in so far as they are amenable to experimental testing.

Newton's conception of scientific method may be summarized as follows: He 'conceived scientific method to be analysable into three essential stages: (1) the determination by experiment of those properties of phenomena that vary quantitatively; (2) mathematical reasoning by means of which these variations may be precisely stated in a form capable of further elaboration; (3) exact experiments by means of which the mathematical reasoning may be verified and extended to further cases in accordance with four rules.' (Susan Stebbing, *A Modern Introduction to Logic*, p. 313) Newton prefixed the four rules to Book III of the *Principia*:

Rule I: 'We are to admit no more causes of natural things than such as are both true and sufficient to explain their appearances.' This rule counsels parsimony or economy in causal explanation.

Rule II: 'Therefore to the same natural effects we must, as far as possible, assign the same causes.' This rests on a belief in the uniformity of nature.

Rule III: 'The qualities of bodies, which admit neither intension nor remission of degrees, and which are found to belong to all bodies within the reach of our experiments, are to be esteemed the universal qualities of all bodies whatsoever.' Newton accepts Galileo's distinction between primary or objective qualities and secondary or subjective qualities. In addition to figure, extension and mobility, he lists as primary qualities, hardness, impenetrability and the inertial powers. Given the simplicity of nature (Rules I and II) and the presence of these properties in all bodies of our acquaintance, we have sufficient theoretical grounds for ascribing them to all bodies in nature.

Rule IV: 'In experimental philosophy we are to look upon propositions collected by general induction from phenomena as accurately or very nearly true, notwithstanding any contrary hypothesis that may be imagined, till such time as other phenomena occur, by which they may either be made more accurate, or liable to exceptions.' In other words, speculative hypotheses, i.e. those for which no experimental evidence is offered, should carry no weight against inductions.

Governing ideas in contemporary physical science. The last 160 years stand out in history as a scientific age, that is to say, as an age in which scientific knowledge is being continually and progressively translated into technology, revolutionizing industrial life and transforming everyday living too. Science never stood in such relationship to life before. Science, of course, includes both technology and pure (theoretical) science. Applied Logic is not concerned with the former. Since 1900, however, the vast development of physical science has produced governing theoretical principles that must be taken into consideration in analysing and evaluating the evidence–conclusion structuring of science. They are:

(1) Modern science is basically mathematical in content and form: its primary idiom is mathematical; so are its most fundamental explanations and concepts; and mathematical formalization is the measure of the full scientific maturity of a discipline (such as biology). Theoretical physics requires the coalescence of the higher systems of mathematics with physical intuition and imagination. The physical scientist himself is guided by an innate conviction of mathematical order in nature.

(2) A radical uncertainty must attach to any mathematical model of nature we may construct at the atomic level. It is impossible to calculate both the position and the velocity of minute particles; thus we cannot assign to them, in our equations, their exact place and velocity, with the result that our model is essentially deficient in basic measurements. This is Heisenberg's principle of uncertainty: the classical picture of a particle moving along a precise trajectory is untenable because it is *in principle* impossible to determine precisely position without generating uncertainty in the value of velocity and vice versa. As a result of this principle 'there is a shift in science from causal to statistical laws. Science is content to predict the future without stipulating any [observable or verifiable causal] mechanism between the present and the future, without claiming that its computation follows the steps of causal law. Its method is

statistical and it recognizes that every prediction carries with it its own uncertainty. But it believes that this uncertainty is measurable and, consequently, that there is room for a scientific prediction which defines its area of uncertainty, as contrasted with unscientific predictions which do not.' (*The Common Sense of Science* by J. Bronowski, Penguin Books)

(3) An unavoidable relativity attaches to the fundamental stage of science, observation. The building bricks of science are observed facts. In Newtonian Physics no distinction was made between the fact itself and the fact as observed. For Einstein the facts that go into the building of science are observed facts and these are relative to the observer—to his position, relative motion etc. As far as any observation is concerned you never have simply a fact or an observer but the joining of the two in an observation. Further, between the event and the observer there must pass a signal—a ray of light, a wave or an impulse—which simply cannot be taken out of the observation. Event, signal, observer: this is the concrete building unit in science. Thus scientific facts—mass, time, space facts—are compound things relative to an observer in a particular system of reference.

The above three principles govern thinking on the degree of certainty and the kind of objectivity attributed by contemporary scientists to their theoretical conclusions.

A summary description of the structure of physical science as it has evolved historically. Scientific investigation has as its end result an explanatory body of propositions which needs to be evaluated in its explanatory force, in the degree of system it introduces into knowledge, and in the evidence-conclusion relationships which structure it. It is a mathematical, experimental enterprise developing itself out of a metrical experience of the world and through the dynamism of rational hypothetical constructions which are verified, falsified and modified through observation and experiment. It does not claim that the metrical approach to reality is the only valid approach, and it does not attach an absolute certainty to its laws but functions as a continuously self-testing, self-correcting enterprise.

III. Structure and method in the biological and human sciences

Scientific concepts of life have changed so much that very little of the nineteenth-century picture remains today. A powerful force in this revolutionary change has been the beginning of an integration of physics, chemistry and biology and the extension to the human sciences of methods of physics and mathematical analysis. The sciences of life have not developed in their revolutionary way by changing scientific method. Just as striking as new discoveries is the continuance of the traditional basic groundwork of mathematical description and analysis, the invention of models and hypothetical mechanisms, logical deduction and testing. Nothing comparable to the methodological changes of the sixteenth and seventeenth centuries has taken place in the twentieth-century development of science.

As in physics and chemistry, conspicuous activities in biology are the making and recording of observations and also experimentation. Observations and experiments are again preceded and followed by the invention of hypotheses which are tested by recourse to further observations.

> At very rare intervals these hypotheses have a tremendous effect: they open up entirely new lines of research—creating new branches of science as well as affecting older existing branches. Familiar examples are the hypotheses introduced into biology by William Harvey, Charles Darwin, Gregor Mendel and Louis Pasteur. The part played by hypotheses in the work of these celebrated men is obscured by the way in which, in histories of science, they are represented not so much as inventors of hypotheses but as discoverers. Thus Harvey is commonly referred to as the discoverer of the circulation of the blood. But what he did was something much more important. He invented a *hypothesis* concerning the action of the heart which had many revolutionary *consequences* for physiology, that there was a circulation of the blood being but *one*. In this way the distinction between the making of observations and the invention of hypotheses tends to be blurred . . . Some new hypotheses also lead to the invention of new apparatus for observation, and the new observations so made possible suggest further hypotheses, and so on. (J. H. Woodger in *Biology and Language: An Introduction to the Methodology of the Biological Sciences including Medicine*: pp. 3–4)

The same basic pattern of operation occurs also in the human sciences, instrumentation being broadened to include statistical techniques, and 'fact' to include that which is reached through the mediation of statistical science (social data being often of this latter nature, and here deduction takes place in a context in which implications are verified or theories falsified against a criterion of 'statistical facts' or probabilities rather than of facts in the classical sense of the word).

As in physics, a higher theoretical development is occasioned in biology by the frequent readjustments between hypothesis and observation and by the need to co-ordinate many hypotheses within a comprehensive theory. At this level the essence of logical process and the objective of logical arrangement is demonstration, explanation and prediction. In physics, which has the most fully developed system of concepts and affords possibilities of axiomatization, rationality is present here to a great extent in the form of logicality. In biology and in the human sciences theoretical rationality is more heavily weighted with the guidance of intuition and its cutting edge has been informal conceptual analysis. Axiomatization has not been applied outside physics. With a growing assimilation of the physicist's experience and exactitude one may expect a greater use of mathematics in the life sciences and the development of an appropriate symbolic language capable of mediating precise analysis and providing scope for calculation. Contemporary biology is not only using some of the branches of mathematics that have been developed to meet the special demands of physics, it is also addressing itself to the task of discovering the special kind of mathematics that is required by itself.

It is also noteworthy that, conceptually, both biology and through it the human sciences are feeling the impact of a reductionist tendency based on the reality of a single scientific method and on the ideal of completely unified knowledge.

IV. The logical forms and logical processes within empirical science

Empirical science combines two distinct objectives and its content is accordingly twofold with a twofold logical formation: (a) Firstly it is, as its name implies, knowledge: an organized and growing body of general laws which provide an ever increasing understanding of nature; (b) secondly, it is an exploratory enterprise, possessing an enormous capacity or methodology for the acquisition of new knowledge, and dedicated to continuous research by methods certified by it as scientific.

(a) As an organized body of knowledge it is explanatory in force, with the logical elements and formation of an axiomatic system. Here is is concerned with consolidating and unifying what has been already discovered: it secures clarity by the primitive quality of its basic technical language, and it demonstrates particular laws by situating them under more general laws or theories. 'Demonstrates' has the force of explaining rather than of proving truth: the process (perfect or imperfect) of proving a particular law is carried out earlier in the work of confirming it and in the effort to falsity it; it is explained now by being subsumed under more general laws from which it can be inferred, i.e. it is absorbed into a vast inferential network through which science both explains and predicts, prediction being understanding and explanation before the event. One must emphasize the meaning-relations that arise (along with truth-relations) when a proposition is subsumed under a more general one; these relations contitute the explanation.

Logical experience of axiomatization underlines the importance, first of all, of having a set of explicit axioms which is a complete and adequate basis for deriving the desired range of theorems. In empirical science a set of theoretical principles or comprehensive theory is sought through which it can describe, explain and predict derivative laws and empirical uniformities (i.e. uniformities that have not been shown to be instances of more general laws). Each empirical science must therefore ask itself whether its theoretical principles are adequate as they stand, whether it needs (and is using) any supplementary principle without formulating and acknowledging it as such. Logicians such as Duns Scotus, in medieval times, and John Stuart Mill, in modern times, have felt that a principle of uniformity in nature must function axiomatically in science. In contemporary times P. A. M. Dirac points out that there is an aesthetic criterion for the selection of possible axiomatic bases in Physics:

It seems to be one of the fundamental features of nature that fundamental physical laws are described in terms of a mathematical theory of great beauty and power, needing quite a high standard of mathematics for one to understand it.

What makes the theory of relativity so acceptable to physicists ... is its great *mathematical beauty*. This is a quality which cannot be defined, any more than beauty in art can be defined, but which people who study mathematics usually have no difficulty in appreciating. The theory of relativity introduced mathematical beauty to an unprecedented extent into the description of nature ... Quantum mechanics [the second revolution in physical thought of the present century] requires the introduction into physical theory of a vast new domain of pure mathematics—the whole domain connected with non-commutative multiplication [where things multiplied in one order do not give the same result as when multiplied in the other order]. This coming on top of the introduction of new geometries by the theory of relativity, indicates a trend which we may expect to continue. We may expect that in the future further big domains of pure mathematics will have to be brought in to deal with the advances in fundamental physics ... The trend of mathematics and physics towards unification provides the physicist with a powerful new method of research into the foundations of his subject ... The method is to begin by choosing that branch of mathematics which one thinks will form the basis of the new theory. One should be influenced very much in this choice by considerations of mathematical beauty. ('The Evolution of the Physicist's Picture of Nature' and 'The Relation between Mathematics and Physics': for full details of these articles see Bibliography p. 417 below.)

Because of their low degree of formalization a principle of uniformity in nature or Dirac's principle may be classified vaguely as perspective and its logical weight pass unnoticed.

Of course in generating a whole network of deductive connections leading to all the particular known laws, not only do the theoretical principles *explain* these laws but they themselves are *confirmed* or re-enforced by them and accordingly are said to *describe* them also. Even as an axiomatic system science regards itself as descriptive of nature.

Logical experience of axiomatization also underlines the importance of scrutinizing the processes of derivation. This is comparatively simple within logic itself where the context is set indefinitely by a language of variables and the processes are purely formal therefore. But in empirical science what one is deriving are descriptions of the world with greater and lesser degrees of generality. Thus what Boole observed in general about contextual reasoning applies here—however logical, it embodies forces that derive from our experience and knowledge of the context: such a reasoning process can never be purely logical, purely theoretic. The rationality of empirical science cannot be completely reduced to the simple logicality of a propositional system; the variables or blanks in a purely formal system are paralleled by populations of concepts in natural science, and the relationships between these concepts are not simply and solely logical ones of implication, conflict etc. Thus an impartial forum of rationality for science must have both formal and informal aspects. Toulmin puts it:

> Any attempt to judge conceptual novelties in science, or to make comparisons across the intellectual boundaries between rival theories, soon drives us beyond the range of a purely formal analysis ... The progressive historical transformation of our ideas—involving the displacement of one proto-arithmetic, physical theory or political doctrine by another—remains to be analysed and judged in other, less formal terms. (*Human Understanding*, vol. 1, pp. 64–5)

A consequence of the strong contextual character in the deductions and reductions within scientific explanation is that reductivism is a genuine hazard and an inevitable topic of controversy: is too much being explained in terms of too little when biology is reduced to physics, personality to behaviour, mind to matter? Scientific controversies of this kind are all the more difficult to resolve because, in general, scientific method has extended to other disciplines from physics, so that method is from one discipline, the problems from another.

(b) As an institution for further discovery, empirical science possesses two methods of making progress: (1) the method of experiment and observation, examining particularly experiments, analysing them through mathematical reasoning and expressing the regularity of results in the form of physical laws; (2) the speculative or dialectical method of creative imagination in which a theory is constructed largely independently of experience. Historically both of these methods have been powerful for the formulation of physical theory, the former (empirical) one being continuously productive in that it modifies theories as new results demand this.

Both methods lead to the formulation of a theory, and at this point, two logical principles become relevant:

(a) the principle that in a valid deduction truth is preserved and transmitted; in virtue of this principle the implications of a true theory must be true also. Granted that q is an implication of p and also that p is true then q is true also; this is an LAF, a natural deduction form or schema referred to traditionally as *modus ponendo ponens*.

(b) the principle that in a valid deduction an implication cannot be false without falsity being present among the premises; in virtue of this principle a theory is falsified when one of its implications is discovered to be false. Granted that q is an implication of p and also that q is false, then p is false: this sequent is proved within propositional logic.

The above are two correct logical principles; the first is invoked in generating the predictions of a theory, the second is used to falsify a theory. The form used in verification is not a logical form; if the theory is true, these consequences of it are realized; but these consequences of it are realized; therefore the theory is true (If *p*, *q*; but *q*; therefore *p*.). The use of this form gives rise to the problem of verification which will be discussed in the next chapter.

Thus the precise logical strength of the hypothetico-deductive method may be defined as follows: when an hypothesis is true the validity of the deductive process constitutes a logical certification that the implications are true, and when an implication is known to be false the validity of the deductive process constitutes a logical certification that the hypothesis is false. These are the only logical principles which are relevant to the method and can constitute it as a formally valid process. Thus logically it is best that the method be conceived and practised primarily in accordance with these principles.

No one has seen this as clearly, perhaps, as Karl Popper. In the eyes of many scientists he is one of the great philosophers of science in history, a philosopher of knowledge whom an experimental scientist can read with complete adherence to his views; his writings are accepted as describing the scientific process with accuracy, veracity and clarity and he presents a very penetrating view of its logic.

In this view it is the task of scientists to produce theories and then to use the two relevant logical principles: (1) by deduction to make the theory yield predictions of what future observations or experiments will show; (2) to make and examine predictions as part of a systematic attempt to falsify the theory. For Popper the essential logic that is available to empirical method is one of disproof rather than of proof: although empirical general statements cannot be proved they are falsifiable; they are essentially a type of proposition that can be tested. Thus Popper would define a scientific proposition through its relationship with the two relevant logical principles: it is the type of proposition which being subject to the deductive process cannot but yield predictions to which also it must transmit its truth, and which is accordingly governed by the second logical principle that a false prediction certifies it also as being false. Thus the primary method of scientific progress is criticism and science is essentially and continuously a self-testing enterprise. Popper sums up his view in *Objective Knowledge: an Evolutionary Approach*:

> As a realist I look upon logic as the *organon of criticism* (rather than of proof) in our search for true and highly informative theories—or at least for new theories that contain more information, and correspond better to the facts, than our older theories. And I look upon criticism, in its turn, as our main instrument in promoting the growth of our knowledge about the world of facts. (p. 318)

He analyses this logic of criticism:

> My theory is briefly this. I look upon logic as the theory of deduction or of derivability, or whatever one chooses to call it. Derivability or deduction

involves, essentially, *the transmission of truth and the retransmission of falsity*: in a valid inference truth is transmitted from the premisses to the conclusion. This can be used especially in so-called 'proofs'. But falsity is also retransmitted from the conclusion to (at least) one of the premisses, and this is used in disproofs or refutations, and especially in *critical discussions* ... Now I should distinguish between two main uses of logic, namely (1) its use in the demonstrative sciences—that is to say, the mathematical sciences—and (2) its use in the empirical sciences. In the demonstrative sciences logic is used in the main for proofs—for the transmission of truth—while in the empirical sciences it is almost exclusively used critically—for the retransmission of falsity ...

Now what I wish to assert is this. If we want to use logic in a critical context, then we should use a very strong logic, the strongest logic, so to speak, which is at our disposal; for we want our criticism to be *severe* ... Thus we should (in the empirical sciences) use the full or classical or two-valued logic. If we do not use it but retreat into the use of some weaker logic—say, the intuitionist logic, or some three-valued logic (as Reichenbach suggested in connection with quantum theory)—then, I assert, we are not critical enough ...

I would assert that not the least important of the achievements of Alfred Tarski is that by introducing two ideas into logic, he has actually made logic very much a realistic affair. The first is Tarski's idea (partly anticipated by Bolzano) that logical consequence is truth transmission. The second, I would say, is the rehabilitation of the correspondence theory of truth, the rehabilitation of the idea that truth is simply correspondence with the facts. (pp. 304–5, 308)

An important source of logical strength to empirical science lies, undoubtedly, in its being a continuously self-testing, disproving enterprise and in the scrupulous and extensive nature of observation and experiment in it. There is a continuous appeal from fact to theory or principle and from theory or principle to fact. In virtue of this continuous give and take everything that is doubtful comes under frequent scrutiny and no hypothesis is regarded as so well supported by evidence that other evidence may not increase or decrease its reliability. The continuous vigilance of an empirical science with regard to fact, and its continuous testing and preparedness to modify theory are important guarantees of its worth. Stebbing comments:

[Pasteur's biographer said] that he had 'a mind, which while pressing forward to establish new facts, was ever seeking arguments against itself, and turned back to strengthen points which seemed yet weak.' It was these self-critical qualities of mind that made Pasteur a great experimental scientist. (*A Modern Introduction to Logic*, p. 326)

Chapter 3

LOGICAL PROBLEMS IN EMPIRICAL SCIENCE

I. Introduction

There are two main kinds of strictly logical problems in empirical science: (1) that which arises when a piece of reasoning is not, and cannot be, *completely* governed by any logical form, i.e. when the reasoning is contextual; (2) that which arises when reasoning is governed by a form which is not perfectly logical, i.e. not of its nature truth-transmitting—this occurs in verification and, more broadly, in the whole inductive development of science. These problems are inescapably part of the human condition: relatively little falls within reach of an absolute human proof. Thus they constitute a challenge to rational skill to compensate, as far as is possible, for the absence of reason's own basic logical forms. And they emphasize that rationality should not be identified with logicality: the ultimate universal challenge and duty with which life confronts us is being rational (which is always possible) rather than being logical (which is often not possible if one defines and relativizes that word to the forms of the existing science).

II. The general problem of contextual reasoning

Contextual reasoning occurs where the reasoning process is not purely logical, i.e. where the power of the evidence (compelling or unconvincing as the case may be) derives indissolubly from both the form of the argument and from experience of the concepts constituting the particular context.

The significant historical facts are: (a) Modern formal logic, being constructive and not abstractive, seeks transcendent, context-free truths or laws and does not concern itself at all with contextual reasoning which is confined to applied logic. Within applied logic itself (which, as we have seen, is teamwork) the main analyses and classifications will be made, naturally, by contextual experts rather than by the formal logician. (b) Traditional logic which was abstractive examined contextual reasoning but produced no really deep systematic study of it; the examination was predominantly concerned with fallacies in reasoning and no general theory was ever achieved. Indeed it was commonly assumed that a complete classification of fallacies would be impossible; the modern logician, Augustus de Morgan, sums up the attitude (in his *Formal Logic*): 'There is no such thing as a classification of the ways in which men may arrive at an error: it is much to be doubted whether there ever can be.' (p. 276)

For over two thousand years fallacies were discussed within the framework presented in Aristotle's *Sophistical Refutations* where he lists thirteen types of fallacies, sophisms or elenchs as they have been variously called. (The framework has been already described in the preparatory section, A, of this textbook.) Aristotle's other accounts, in the *Prior Analytics* and the *Rhetoric*, are briefer; they are concerned, respectively, with breaches of syllogistic law and with observations about arguments that are useful for persuasive speech. The indications from the literature on fallacies (a vast amount of ancient and medieval writings have still to be edited, of course) is that this was a topic of recurrent interest in every century but that discussions were broadly the same and cramped themselves within the Aristotelian framework. Henry Aldrich in his *Artis Logicae Compendium* (1691) ends his conventional treatment as follows:

> These, then, are the thirteen kinds of fallacy familiar to the ancients and normally presented to Logic students as examples. The number could be cut down; for some seem to coincide and, moreover, three of them—Non-Cause, Begging the Question and Many Questions—are not fallacies properly so-called, that is, ill-formed syllogisms, but rather faults of the opponent. The number could also be increased; but since it satisfied Aristotle it has satisfied all later logicians.

There are traditional logicians, like Peter Ramus in the sixteenth century, who anticipated the outlook of modern Mathematical Logic in holding that logic is a science of correct forms and should not concern itself with fallacies. And there were others who altered the framework somewhat. Francis Bacon's list of Idols (of the Tribe, the Den, the Market Place and the Theatre) is particularly psychological. He is interested in the human person reasoning and in the 'false appearances' imposed on him by the general nature of the human mind, by his own individual nature and history, by the very language in which he thinks, and by currently received philosophies and methods of demonstration.

No matter what context a person reasons in he cannot avoid being gravitated towards the invalid and the erroneous, if he lives and thinks under the government of 'false appearances'. The *Port Royal Logic* of 1662 (which was originally entitled *The Art of Thinking* and which was the prototype for textbooks on logic until mathematical logic succeeded in displacing the Rennaissance interpretation of logic) continued Bacon's search for psychological classifications without anything substantial being added. And the efforts of Bentham, Whately and Mill to reclassify fallacies did not produce any substantial alteration either.

Finally, Arabian logic preserved the Aristotelian tradition and otherwise did not concern itself with fallacies. In Indian logic which developed independently of the West, there was a basic interest in inference and in theory of debate. The classical Indian text on logic was the Nyāya sūtra (written during the first three centuries A.D.) and commentaries over more than ten centuries elaborated its classification of fallacies and its subtleties of disputation. With the development, in the fourteenth century, of a new and more formal logic (by the Navya Nyāya, or New Nyāya School) disputation and fallacies were no longer considered within logic.

Thus traditionally, contextual reasoning has been treated in the very limiting area of disputation and, predominantly, within a framework of fallacies. Even within those terms of reference no systematic theory has been achieved. A modern study of contextual reasoning requires the co-operation of the formal logician and experts in the particular contexts. Their basic problem does not consist in discovering the presence or absence of logical form but in describing and assessing the influence of conceptual experience and contextual intuition on the reasoning. Thus the precise problem of contextual reasoning is mainly one for the contextual experts.

III. The problem of verification

When a proposition is true a valid deductive process is, by its very nature, a logical certification that all the implications are true also. The deductive process simply unfolds the meaning of the original proposition and so is truth-preserving, truth-transmitting. But when the original proposition is false a valid deductive process cannot ever constitute a logical certification either of truth or of falsity. As the meaning is deductively unfolded there is no logical basis for saying at any point that there is or is not correspondence with facts; it is thought-content that is implied, not correspondence or lack of correspondence with facts, and many elements implicit in what a false proposition says may happen to be true. Thus when an hypothesis is neither accepted as true nor rejected as false there is no *purely logical basis* for using the results of valid deduction as confirmation of it. In saying that verification is a logical problem, what one means is that the movement from evidence (truth of implications) to conclusion (truth of hypothesis) is not governed by logical form (i.e. the movement is not of its nature truth transmitting) and that this fact—to which logic draws attention—constitutes a problem wherever a verification procedure is used.

Quite clearly the type of rationality present when one accepts an hypothesis as being confirmed cannot be completely identified with logicality. By intuition and experience one may judge it *unlikely* that *this* implication ('X was at the scene of the crime with a gun') would turn out to be true without the hypothesis ('X was the killer') being true. This is an extralogical basis of judgment: the thought content of the conclusion exists not in a framework of *objective logical necessitation* in the light of the evidence but in that of *subjective* rational belief because of the evidence. Judicial enquiries control and define this kind of belief (based on confirmation) when it may be expressed in the form of a court verdict: every effort is required of the defence to *falsify* the affirmations of prosecution or plaintiff (this includes cross-examination of witnesses and questioning their legal weight in the case) and the target of jury deliberations is defined; as defined no more can ever be required than certitude beyond reasonable doubt, and in civil cases judgment on the felt balance of probabilities may suffice. Thus the law admits a systematic procedure of confirmation only in combination with a similar systematic procedure of falsification and it does not identify the outcome of successful confirmation with absolute certitude.

In empirical science the scientist does not wait dependently on experience but confronts the world with conceptions from his own reason. One might say with Popper that science begins effectively with the imaginative proposal of hypotheses. Many logicians believe that in this heuristic movement of reason there is an invisible axiom present, an implicit faith that the world is of such a kind as to correspond with rational expectancies. Historically, this seems to enter into the traditional outlook of western science whether one describes it, logically, as an axiom or, psychologically, as a faith. Science is a search for a plan by a faculty which has, itself, the capacity to conceive plans.

Since the time of the Greeks the term, hypothesis, has come to have four distinct meanings:

(1) *a mere supposition*, a proposition set up to see what its implications are. This movement of reason is behind many contemporary axiomatic systems. Riemann constructed his new geometry on a basis of supposition and at a time when there was no use for it in prospect; it was imensely useful to Einstein later on. Similarly, three-valued logic was worked out and then later used to axiomatize quantum mechanics. Historically, science would have been held back if there were not people prepared to suppose and to work out consistent systems from suppositions, if everyone had as a governing criterion: is this likely to be true?

(2) *a proposition which is being tested* through investigation of its consequences. 'Is virtue knowledge?' asks Socrates of Meno. 'If virtue is knowledge it will be teachable.' But it soon appears that virtue is not teachable at all, at least in the way in which the arts and sciences are teachable. Physicists today use the same procedure in testing mathematical systems for objectivity.

(3) *a fictional entity or proposition* which is not regarded as having objectivity and is never tested against consequences for objectivity but serves simply to unify and systematize a great amount of empirical data. This was a standard device in astronomy from the time of Ptolemy to Galileo. It is used often in the communication of scientific data to the general public—diagrams and mechanical models often function in this way in public relations.

(4) nowadays the word, hypothesis, is being linked up with the study of creative thinking and is *often used with a predominantly psychological meaning* as a bold and penetrating conjecture on the part of some scientist.

Both the use of hypotheses and the method of verifying them vary from science to science, according as the character of the science happens to be purely empirical (e.g. the work of Darwin or Freud), or experimental (e.g. the work of Harvey or Faraday) or a combination of experimentation with mathematical reasoning (e.g. the work of Galileo, Newton, Fourier). Not all scientific work is directed and controlled by hypothesis, but in the absence of well-formulated hypotheses, the research can hardly be better than exploration. In the field of mathematical physics and particularly in astronomy, the meaning of hypothesis is both extended and altered: a whole theory—a complex system of propositions—comes to be regarded as a single hypothesis.

The heuristic approach to the world, the approach by way of hypothesis, is given an empirical value, of course: it is kept under factual control by a process of experimental or observational verification. But quite clearly, in science great confidence is shown in the heuristic function of reason and in the objectivity of what appeals to reason. Where the discrimination cannot be made in experiment or observation, one theory is preferred to its rival if it is superior internally in consistency, mathematical simplicity or explanatory range. Indeed even when an hypothesis is falsified it may still be needed and be retained for rational, explanatory qualities it possesses, and for the way it fits into the existing body of laws.

An hypothesis can be subjected to processes of confirmation and falsification. It is confirmed in the degree to which implications of it are discovered to be true; it is falsified if any implication is discovered to be false. In the latter case we *deduce* its falsity, i.e. the falsity of the implication necessitates, logically, the falsity of the hypothesis and the movement of valid deduction formalizes and expresses this. In the former case no deduction is possible and the language used is that of corroboration. For Popper 'the non-verifiability of hypotheses is methodologically important'. (*The Logic of Scientific Discovery*, p. 253) So important indeed that scientific testing must be structured primarily as a persevering search for negative, falsifying instances. Corroboration must be conceived as the degree to which an hypothesis has stood up to severe testing of this kind and thus proved its mettle:

> It is even quite misleading to regard *every* 'verification' of a prediction as something like a practical *corroboration* of the *explicans*: it would be more correct to say that only such verifications of predictions which are 'unexpected' [without the theory under examination] may be regarded as corroborations of the *explicans*, and so of the theory. This means that a prediction can be used to corroborate a theory only if its comparison with observations might be regarded as a serious attempt at testing the *explicans*—a serious attempt at refuting it. A ['risky'] prediction of this kind may be called 'relevant to a test of the theory'. (*Objective Knowledge: An Evolutionary Approach*, pp. 353–4)

He quotes with approval the remark of Weyl: 'Once and for all I wish to record my unbounded admiration for the work of the experimenter in his struggle to wrest *interpretable facts* [interpretations being equivalent to hypotheses] from an unyielding Nature who knows so well how to meet our theories with a decisive No—or with an inaudible Yes.'

Thus, if in scientific exploration one uses the compass of logic, the fact one must go by is that although hypotheses, being of an unrestrictedly general and empirical content, cannot be proved they can nevertheless be tested. The distinctive character of scientific ideas lies in the boldness of their empirical content, in how disprovable they are, in what tests they attract and what discussions and predictions they stimulate. In guiding us rigorously to disproof (and not supplying us with an instrument of positive proof) logic counsels a human emphasis on learning from mistakes. No one has set out so impressively as Popper the intellectual case for accepting, at the level of methodology, this familiar everyday consequence of the human condition. It is a pathway of disproof that logic lays down for the advance of science:

> The wrong view of science betrays itself in the craving to be right; for it is not his *possession* of knowledge, of irrefutable truth, that makes the man of science, but his persistent and recklessly critical *quest* for truth. (Ibid., p. 281)

Medawar put it:

> The exploratory process is a sort of dialogue between fact and fancy—at least in the sense that it begins with an imaginative conjecture about what the world may be like, and proceeds from that point to, as far as possible, objective observation and criticism. Eventually one builds up a structure of beliefs about the natural world, which is never complete, never beyond the possibility of correction or emendation in some particular. So truth is really a direction in which one is moving: it is not something which one ever finally achieves. One of the greatest strengths of Popper's philosophy is that it gives a plausible and helpful account of what goes on in the head of a scientist when he's actually engaged in the process of exploration ... Popper's methodology has, among other great strengths, the strength of completely abolishing ... cultural distinction ... By 'the tragedy of the two cultures' I mean the entirely erroneous belief that there is an enormous gap between people like artists and poets and writers, who work through the imagination, and scientists, who are, intellectually speaking, rude mechanicals ... Both artists, in the conventional sense, and scientists turn out to rely primarily on the imagination for the generation of their ideas. Both are seekers after truth. (Broadcast on B.B.C., August 1972)

While keeping it responsible to observation and experience, Popper's presentation of scientific method places due emphasis on the understanding provided by hypotheses, on their explanatory power:

> I can therefore gladly admit that falsificationists like myself much prefer an attempt to solve an interesting problem by a bold conjecture, *even (and especially) if it soon turns out to be false*, to any recital of a sequence of irrelevant truisms. We prefer this because we believe that this is the way in

which we can learn from our mistakes; and that in finding that our conjecture was false, we shall have learnt much about the truth, and shall have got nearer to the truth.

I therefore hold that both ideas—the idea of truth, in the sense of correspondence with the facts, and the idea of content (which may be measured by the same measure as testability)—play about equally important roles in our considerations, and that both can shed much light on the idea of progress in science. (*Conjectures and Refutations: The Growth of Scientific Knowledge*, p. 231)

Rationality, when it cannot identify itself with logicality, knows how to define and control its own boldness:

> With the idol of certainty ... there falls one of the defences of obscurantism which bar the way of scientific advance. For the worship of this idol hampers not only the boldness of our questions, but also the rigour and integrity of our tests ... Sciences never pursues the illusory aim of making its answers final, or even probable. Its advance is rather towards an infinite yet attainable aim: that of ever discovering new, deeper and more general problems, and of subjecting our ever tentative answers to ever renewed and ever more rigorous tests. (*The Logic of Scientific Discovery*, pp. 280–81)

IV. Probability values and truth values

Since scientific theories are not logically provable, is it a correct definition of the rationality of science to say that it aims to approximate truth in theories that have high probability value? It is true that as part of the general theory of additive function of sets, pure mathematics provides a calculus (neutral in itself) which can be used and interpreted in any domain or situation that is sufficiently formalized for calculation. Quite clearly science continuously uses probability calculation in its routine work of conjecture, observation and experiment. Also one can take particular scientific hypotheses and, following one's conception of what corroboration is, use the mathematical calculus as a measure of the relative degree of corroboration; the resulting probability evaluation is a function not only, of course, of the abstract mathematical calculus (which is rigorously worked out) but also of the non-mathematical ideas and values which are needed to link the calculus with the particular context (its ideas and values being patient of definition and organization in more ways than one). Thus it is meaningful scientific practice to say both that certain empirical generalizations are very probable and that some hypotheses are more probable than others.

The problem is: how clear are the concepts, *probable* and *probabilistic thinking*, and what part have they in the rationality and aim of science?

On the clarity of the concept of probability, two observations are basic: firstly, there is no accepted theory unifying all nuances of meaning in the common usage of the word, probable; secondly, within science and the philosophy of science, there is no accepted definition of probability: there is no provision of an axiomatic framework for the mathematical calculus, i.e. no agreement and formalization of basic facts within experience to which calculations precisely refer.

In common usage, to express our degree of confidence we use such terms as *probable, likely, plausible, credible, impossible, presumptive, improbable, unlikely*. We also say there is *a good chance*; the *chances* are 1 in 4 (*the odds* there are 1 to 3), there is *a reasonable prospect*, etc., etc.; we say this will *perhaps* happen, or this *usually* happens. Probability statements often refer to 'the long run' purporting to be based on 'a law of large numbers', to give the logic of 'long runs' and 'large numbers'. The ordinary context for a reference to probability is matters of fact, but a probability statement does not refer to any real individual event: it does not *say* that in the next 2 tosses of a penny one will be heads, the other tails. Thus it is neither proved nor disproved by the real outcome here; again it is not affected by past real outcomes: even if I have got 3 consecutive heads, the probability before the next toss is still 1/2. The common sense conception of probability seems, generally, to be a very objective one, reflecting something out there, namely conditions that enable and favour some event, without ensuring its realization; ordinarily one looks to frequency of occurrence as the natural mode of verifying probability statements, but only a rudimentary language of probability values is used.

Theories of probability relativize its meaning, variously, to the mathematical calculus (probability being presented indefinitely as whatever can satisfy the axioms of mathematical theory), to empirical frequency (all agree that knowledge of frequencies can give rise, properly, to probability judgments), to justified degrees of belief, to evidence or warranted assertibility, or to degrees of reasonable confidence (which can vary from person to person without imputation of fault). Each of these theories is regarded as having merits and demerits, no single one being wholly satisfactory. Max Black comments:

> One reason may be that an acceptable philosophy of probability is called upon to perform a number of tasks that are hard to reconcile: to show why some probability judgments are *a priori* whereas others are contingent; to provide a firm basis for a calculus of probability while recognizing probability judgments that are incorrigibly imprecise; to account for and to defend the connection between 'rationality' and specifiable degrees of confidence in conclusions following with probability from given premises; and, above all, to show how and why it is justifiable to act on probabilities. ...
> That all the theories can, with greater or less display of ingenuity, provide a basis for the calculus of chances testifies only to the remarkable economy and simplicity of the needed axioms. (*The Encyclopedia of Philosophy*, vol. 6, pp. 477–8)

Is it substantially accurate and significant to say that the content of science is what is probably so, and the aim of science is to approximate truth through achieving higher degrees of probability in its generalizations and theories?

Popper is emphatic here. When one uses the term, probability, in an absolute sense (as distinct from its relative sense in calculation which of course is a procedure used everywhere in life and science) one cannot relativize either the content or the aim of science to it. Beginning with a minimal description of probability as 'something that satisfies the laws of the calculus of probabilities' it is an elementary consequence of the general multiplication principle for probabilities that the more a statement asserts, the less probable it is:

> This may be expressed by saying that the logical probability of a sentence X on a given evidence Y decreases when the informative content of X increases. (*Conjectures and Refutations: The Growth of Scientific Knowledge*, p. 286)

But scientists do not work by a rule of accepting the most probable hypothesis, the hypothesis which goes as little beyond the evidence as possible. On the contrary they care not for highly probable trivialities but for bold hypotheses with high content that can be more severely and more independently tested:

> This may sound paradoxical to some people. But if high probability were an aim of science, then scientists should say as little as possible, and preferably utter tautologies only. But their aim is to 'advance' science, that is to *add* to its content. Yet this means lowering its probability. And in view of the high content of universal laws, it is neither surprising to find that their probability is zero, nor that those philosophers who believe that science must aim at high probabilities cannot do justice to facts such as these: that the formulation (and testing) of *universal laws* is considered their most important aim by most scientists: or that the intersubjective testability of science depends upon these laws [i.e. the objectivity of scientific statements lies in the fact that having empirical content they can be inter-subjectively tested]. (Ibid., p. 286)

The kind of approach to truth that science makes is that through becoming more comprehensive in its theories, and this means as a rule progress through less familiar and less comfortable or plausible theories. The kind of verisimilitude sought is that based on richness of content, i.e. the similitude sought is to comprehensive truth; it is not a similitude defined by the diminution in it of the risk of being falsified (the limiting case being lack of content), by a high correlation between truth claim and evidence. Popper believes that a clear technical distinction should be drawn between *verisimilitude* (a quality of hypotheses which have proved their mettle in severe testing and which have high empirical content) and *probability* (a term which should be used exclusively in the sense laid down by the calculus of probability). In this language the aim of science would be described, of course, as progress towards truth in verisimilitudes.

Within the framework of this distinction of Popper's, probability language could take on very definite and clear cut meanings in ordinary life and technically. For probabilistic thinking is a clear example of model thinking (handling the complex world from a rational position of less complexity, as when, e.g. one uses a machine model for thinking about living things and living functions or models one's thinking about industrial relations from the conception of factories as small societies of people). The model used here is an abstract mathematical one. Probabilistic thinking consists firstly in working out a mathematical system with elements to which are assigned, *a priori*, probabilities. The only law is that these probabilities sum into unity ($=1$). There may be many systems or models depending on the number of elements and the probabilities assigned to them. Whether any of these systems may or may not relate to the real world is not a mathematical question. How does one choose to operate this or that mathematical model in real life or in science? The system which consists of two elements each with equal probabilities is found to be suitable for predicting the tosses of a coin. It works. In other situations (e.g. the weather over the next four years) one may take a good sample, work out probabilities on the basis of frequency ratios in this sample and use the mathematical model which has the same number of elements and the probabilities that one has worked out.

There may be great difficulty in determining the mathematical model one should use (random sampling is the general technique) but finally in probabilistic thinking there is (1) a model and (2) the real complex world one is investigating. One takes readings of the model which the mathematician provides (he knows the model thoroughly, is *certain* about its features) and one projects these into the real world (predicts they will be true of it, to a useful approximation anyhow). Thus a probability statement purports to be an accurate reading of a chosen mathematical model—in this respect it may be true or false. It is also a projection of this reading into the real world and a heuristic conception of events in terms of it—in this respect it may be successful or unsuccessful. De facto, mathematical calculation underlines the prospect of the reading as being better with things taken in the mass and with long runs.

It is argued that probabilistic thinking makes presuppositions about the world—that the world is intelligible, conforming to human models, that its plan can be represented in samples. In *Probability and Induction*, William Kneale writes:

> The thesis which I wish to dispute [is that] ... probability rules concerning transcendent objects such as electrons are ultimate and presuppose no principles of necessity or impossibility whatsoever. When the notion of probability has become as important as it now is in physical science, the need for a satisfactory definition is urgent ... But what is the definition adopted by those who try to treat probability rules as ultimate? Clearly they

cannot hold any form of the subjectivist theory, and they are debarred from defining probability by reference to ranges or fields of possibility, because they have denied that there can be truths of principle in this domain. They must therefore be committed to the frequency definition, and this by itself is enough to condemn their view. For they are after all assuming laws, but laws of the wildest kind about the convergence of frequency series to limits . . . So long as we believe that there are or may be principles of necessity or impossibility, we have good reason for conjecturing probability rules, whereas without that belief we should have no reason. (pp. 255–6)

V. The problem of induction

The problems of verification and probability evaluation reflect the difficulty of integrating the empirical and the rational in logical evidence-conclusion structures. Such an integration takes place, however imperfectly, every time one subjects an imaginative hypothesis to the control of empirical evidence; also when one reaches a generalization on the basis of limited experience. This latter form of the integration gives rise to the traditional problem of induction. It goes back to the time of Aristotle and has, indeed, been the main logical problem in science for those who have believed that scientific method starts from observation and experiment and proceeds, gradually, to generalizations: there is first, in this narrow Baconian view, the industrious gathering of the 'countless grapes, ripe and in season' from which the wine of science then flows.

Although Aristotle's meaning of the term, *induction*, was more general, it came to mean 'coming to see or believe a general truth through the contemplation of particular instances'. There are three kinds of induction and they are all mentioned by Aristotle:
(1) The process by which we become aware of a particular instance as exemplifying a general truth. For instance in the apprehension of this red patch as being darker than that pink patch we may see that any red patch is darker than any pink patch. Here there is no inference—no relationship of evidence and conclusion; rather the sense experience is such as to facilitate an act of direct insight into a general truth. This kind of induction is called intuitive induction.
(2) The process by which we see the truth of a general proposition by showing that it holds of every instance that is said to fall under it. This process has usually been known as 'induction by complete enumeration', 'perfect induction', 'complete induction'. Another suggested name is 'summary induction' and this brings out the fact that it is not a conclusion from evidence, but rather a shorthand formulation.
(3) A process of reasoning in which we generalize from particular instances. This is called 'induction by incomplete enumeration' or 'induction by simple enumeration'. But it is not to be regarded as a process simply of counting; it is a counting of instances recognized as having certain properties in common:

Everyone makes inferences by simple enumeration. Having met half a dozen Scotsmen all of whom are somewhat lacking in humour, we conclude that no Scotsman can see a joke. This precarious generalization is liable to be upset by the next Scotsman we meet; it could not survive a reading of the works of David Hume. The appearance of a single contradictory instance disproves the conclusion. It is obvious that if the number of observed instances are few in comparison with those that have not been observed, there is considerable likelihood that contradictory instances may be found among the latter. An example of simple enumeration, found in every elementary book of logic, has become famous because contradictory instances were discovered. The conclusion *all swans are white* was derived by many people from their observation of swans in Europe all of which happened to be white. On the discovery of Australia black swans were discovered. (Stebbing, *A Modern Introduction to Logic*, p. 247)

The historical problem of induction arises with the third kind of induction. It arises when we say we can draw general conclusions about the universe, and when we try to justify as strict proof the scientific procedures which end in such conclusions. For it seems, at first sight anyway, that no general conclusion about the universe could be *logically necessitated* by partial experience of it, that evidence covering only some instances could never *implicate* a conclusion about all instances, past, present and future.

Von Wright points out that logically an inductive inference can take place without the conclusion being a generalization:

By an inductive inference we mean roughly this: From the fact that something is true of a certain number of members of a class, we conclude that the same thing will be true of unknown members of that class also. If this conclusion applies to an unlimited number of unexamined members of the class, we say that the induction has led to the establishment of a generalization. As this is the most important type of inductive inference, induction is often defined as the process by which we proceed from particular to general, or from less general to more general propositions.

It is, however, not necessary that an inductive inference should lead to a generalization. We may also extend the conclusion to a limited number of unknown members of the class, e.g. to the next member which turns up, thus proceeding from particulars to a new particular. Both cases of inductive inference, that from particulars to universals and that from particulars to particulars, are covered by the definition of induction as reasoning from the known to the unknown. This definition also includes induction as reasoning from the past to the future. It must be observed that this time-characteristic of inductive inference, which is sometimes mentioned in the definition of it, is of no essential importance, and that induction may also proceed from past cases to other unexamined instances belonging to the past. (*The Logical Problem of Induction*, p. 1)

From the time of Francis Bacon many logicians have tried to validate as proof a process of reasoning from particulars to a universal.

Since medieval times logicians have emphasized that a principle such as the uniformity of nature functions in all inductive reasoning. This strengthens the evidential force of particular instances. For some (e.g. many Scholastics, Newton, Mill and some Neo-Scholastics) it has meant that inductive argumentation is, on ultimate analysis, syllogistic. W. E. Johnson in his *Logic* (Part II, ch. X and XI) maintains that there is a kind of induction that is syllogistic in form and a kind that is not; the former is called formal or demonstrative induction, the latter is called pure or problematic induction. He gives as an example of formal or demonstrative induction: 'Every specimen of argon has the same atomic weight as this specimen of argon; but this specimen has the atomic weight 39.9; therefore every specimen has the atomic weight 39.9.' Here the conclusion follows of necessity from the premises but it is only probably true since the major premiss rests on a problematic induction. 'This species of induction I have called problematic, because in my view, the universal proposition which it establishes must be regarded, not as absolutely certified, but as accepted only with a higher or lower degree of probability depending upon the collective character of the instances enumerated.' (pp. 240, 241)

John Stuart Mill's justification of induction consists essentially in presenting it as a process of analysis. We can never be sure of a generalization for there is always the possibility of an unfavourable instance coming to our knowledge. But the inductive process is not a generalization from particulars, it is a process of analysing particulars. Inconsistently with his extreme Empiricism he assumes that the reality underlying experience is machine-like, and that every phenomenon is the carrying into effect of a set of underlying tendencies. Thus the work of proving a law of nature consists in analysing particulars, identifying tendencies in A and their effects in B.

This work is possible granted two theoretical assumptions and two practical ones. The theoretical assumptions are, firstly 'the whole of the present facts are the infallible result of all the facts which existed at the moment previous', and secondly that each element in the present set of facts is related by causal law to some element in the antecedent set. The two practical assumptions are that we can exhaustively describe the context of a particular phenomenon and that we can decompose this context into its constituent facts. Mill's experimental methods (of Agreement, Difference etc.) are then applied to prove in regard to all but one of these facts that it cannot be the cause of the given effect.

The essential criticism of this theory of induction is its unreality. 'For Mill the universe is already neatly arranged in piles of universals. Consequently the only problem involved in scientific discovery, as he sees it, is the problem of sorting out connections between universals.' (Anschutz, *The Philosophy of J. S. Mill*, p. 110) He held that all inductive investigation is a search for causes— there is 'no other uniformity in the events of nature than that which arises from the law of causation.' (*A System of Logic*, Bk. III, ch. XXI, p. 4, note) But his experimental methods are not really procedures or techniques for determining cause and effect. Rather they formulate separately and conventionally conditions which a cause fulfils: the cause of any effect is so related to it as to occur whenever the effect occurs, and never when it does not, and to vary or be constant as the effect varies or is constant, when susceptible of variations in quantity or degree. Quite clearly if one can reduce a phenomenon to these terms one can identify the members of a causal relationship but Mill's Methods are not procedures helping the scientist to reduce phenomena to these terms. They are pre-scientific, presupposing a situation that can be solved by common sense.

Modern logicians are satisfied that induction cannot be reduced to deduction. It is not governed by implication and theories which aimed at presenting it as a form of strict logical proof have now become pointless. If particular inductive conclusions are to be evaluated it can only be by a use of the calculus of probabilities. However as Von Wright most acutely points out: induction is self-justifying as a 'reasoned policy for purposes of prediction and generalization'; in fact, he points out, there is a tautology here: for the criterion by which we judge a policy of reasoning about the unknown to be a *reasoned* policy can only be that it is grounded in the known, in consummated experience; this is equivalently to *require* that it be an inductive policy. Although Hume was fundamentally right and convincing in all he said about it being impossible to adduce any special fact of nature on which we could ground confidence in inductive inference, he failed to see that the meaning of words 'unknown', 'human faculties', 'reasoned policy', 'inductive policy' make that kind of grounding impossible, irrelevant and unnecessary. The demand for his type of justification of inductive inference, and the problem of a resulting scepticism are solved by an analysis of the contextual language. Von Wright sums up his solution to 'Hume's problem', occasioned by Hume pointing out the impossibility of guaranteeing the truth of any synthetical assertion concerning things outside the domain of our actual or recorded experience:

> Our examination of policies for predicting and generalizing has thus led us to the conclusion that the truth contained in the idea that induction is the best mode of reasoning about the unknown is—a disguised tautology. It is not that the inductive method possesses some features, *besides being inductive*, which give it a superiority over other policies. Its superiority is rooted in the fact that the inductive character of a policy is the very criterion by means of which we judge its goodness. The superiority of induction, in other words, is concealed in the *meaning* of a policy's goodness. (*The Logical Problem of Induction*, p. 175)

The conception of induction as a policy is recent. It appears also in Kneale, Braithwaite, Reichenbach and Wisdom. Von Wright points out that with this conception the problem of the justification of induction may be said to have undergone a transformation. From having been a problem of ascertaining the conditions of truth or of probability in single inductive conclusions, it has become a problem of showing the superiority of the inductive policy, *as such*, over rival policies. (Ibid., p. 224)

A new modern problem of induction has, however, arisen: whether it is possible to assign any probability to the particular inductive conclusions of empirical science without making certain assumptions about the world in which we live. In *Human Knowledge: Its Scope and Limits*, Bertrand Russell says:

From the time of Laplace onwards, various attempts have been made to show that the probable truth of an inductive inference follows from the mathematical theory of probability. It is now generally agreed that these attempts were all unsuccessful, and that, if inductive arguments are to be valid, it must be in virtue of some extra-logical characteristics of the actual world, as opposed to the various logically possible worlds that may be contemplated by the logician. (p. 425)

J. M. Keynes has formulated these extra-logical characteristics which must be assumed, in two principles: a *Principle of Limited Independent Variety* ('the objects in the field, over which our generalizations extend, do not have an infinite number of independent qualities; that, in other words, their characteristics, however numerous, cohere together in groups of invariable connexion, which are finite in number') and a *Principle of Atomic Uniformity* (that natural occurrences can be regarded as compounded of small changes taking place in accordance with enduring mathematical laws). If these principles are false or not justifiable there is no logical ground, it is argued, that any generalization with regard to the existent world is more likely to be true than false. These principles which are not established by science itself, constitute, for the scientist, a faith.

And indeed the scientist is distinguished for his antecedent belief, even passionate belief, in the rationality of what he investigates. Even human pathology is made the subject of science, understanding and therapy. As a lived option 'the real is rational' represents, logically, a strong enduring faith on which the human mind has been growing throughout the history of science. Jacques Monod puts it that

in order to construct knowledge you have got to make a value judgment to begin with ... [And this] is exactly what Popper says in the last chapter of his book *The Open Society* ... Popper doesn't talk about objective versus non-objective knowledge. He talks about the rational versus the irrational attitude. And he admits, as I do, that to choose the rational rather than the irrational attitude is a value judgment—it's not a judgment of knowledge. And therefore it's the basis for an ethic. (B.B.C. Broadcast, July 1972)

Thus the life of science and of scientific education is more than the increase of knowledge: the logical meaning of being a scientist is that one's whole person is involved in a fundamental, magnanimous option.

Nelson Goodman goes so far as to say that, technically speaking, the traditional problem of inductive generalization is a distorted formulation of the really predominant human problem which is one of verification. We should begin with the fact that our mental approach to the world is rational, heuristic and projective; accordingly, our problem should be situated within a theory of projection:

> The reorientation of our problem may be portrayed in ... figurative language. Hume thought of the mind as being set in motion making predictions by, and in accordance with, regularities in what it observed. This left him with the problem of differentiating between the regularities that do and those that do not thus set the mind in motion. We, on the contrary, regard the mind as in motion from the start, striking out with spontaneous predictions in dozens of directions, and gradually rectifying and channelling its predictive processes. We ask not how predictions come to be made, but how ... they come to be sorted out as valid and invalid. Literally, of course, we are not concerned with describing how the mind works but rather with describing or defining the distinction it makes between valid and invalid projections. (*Fact, Fiction and Forecast*, p. 87)

The argument that inductive inference is the best rational approach to the unknown received a substantial corroboration from Peirce. In the *Collected Papers* (vol. II, p. 455 seq.) he speaks of 'the constant tendency of the inductive process to correct itself' as the 'essence' and 'the marvel' of induction. When consistently employed it is, of its nature, self-correcting giving better indications, as it grows, of what a true generalization, a true hypothesis would be. He says (ibid., p. 501):

> the validity of an inductive argument consists, then, in the fact that it pursues a method which if duly persisted in, must, in the very nature of things, lead to a result indefinitely approximating to the truth in the long run.

Reichenbach's Method of Correction reiterates and strengthens Peirce's presentation of induction as an indefinite and self-correcting approximation to the truth.

A minority view held by Donald Williams (*The Ground of Induction*, Harvard University Press, 1947) and Roy Harrod (*Foundations of Inductive Logic*, Macmillan, London, 1956) maintains that the probability of an inductive conclusion is of logical consequence from the inductive procedure itself. Harrod (who wrote his book some years after Williams, saying: 'He alone in the present age believes that the validity of induction can be demonstrated without prior assumptions. I am in complete accord.') points out:

The task before us is simple, but arduous. It is required to show that there can be valid inductions about nature without any prior assumptions about the characteristics of nature whatever. There must be no prior assumption that nature is uniform in whole or in part, or that causes operate. The Principle of Indifference must not be used in any form whatever. No initial prior probabilities must be postulated. We must remain totally open-minded until the accumulation of evidence from experience begins to give guidance. The trouble is that so far logicians have been unable to specify any valid principle or principles justifying argument directly from experience without the aid of some prior assumption. (p. 23)

For Williams there is a principle which justifies, logically and fully, the probability of inductive conclusions about the world. This principle is not a statement about the world. It is a statement about the relationship of any sample to the whole of which it is a sample. What is this statement? 'Given a fair-sized sample, then, from any population, with no further material information, we know logically that it very probably is one of those which match the population, and hence that very probably the population has a composition similar to that which we discern in the sample. This is the logical justification of induction.' (p. 97)

Taking this statement, it may be argued against Williams that the material information from which one proceeds to ascertain the probability of matching—'given' a 'sample', 'fair-sized', from a 'population'—involves some general assumptions about the world, namely that it too is rational, characterized by continuity (so that there is continuity between what is within and what is outside our sense experience), by repetition and by simplicity (it can be represented in human sampling). Harrod indeed seems to make important concessions to this viewpoint on pp. 253 and 261 of his book.

VI. A general conclusion

A twofold concern must characterize the search for true knowledge: a concern to have true propositions as starting points and a concern to have sound theoretic processes for drawing conclusions which must also be true. In purely deductive systems or deductive procedures of science the theoretic processes used translate logical laws, as we have seen; the methodological problem lies in acquiring true or acceptable propositions as starting points.

In empirical science, however, logical problems are created by the theoretic processes used. At first sight the main problem associated with scientific investigation—the problem of verification—may appear different from the main problem associated with science when it is organized into a system of propositions—the problem of inductive generalization. But they are both essentially the problem of integrating the empirical and the rational in a logical evidence-conclusion structure. A scientist in giving some new conclusion to the world may not present it according to his actual method of discovery (e.g. hypothesis, deduction of implications, setting up appropriate experiments to verify these). Rather he often chooses to present his data and experiment first, proceeding then to interpret and generalize them into results. Thus a method that is hypothetico-deductive may be translated as an inductive process where the empirical evidence comes first and the generalization last.

The problems of verification, probability and induction must be examined both as deriving from an absence of logical form and as manifesting the presence of rational skill and of living magnanimous faith in rationality.

Chapter 4

THEORETICAL THOUGHT OUTSIDE THE EMPIRICAL SCIENCES

I. Introduction

The empirical sciences develop a world-picture on the basis of a metrical approach to reality (the term *world-picture* including, as in modern microphysics, a symbolic representation of atomic processes that are in principle inaccessible to sense-perception and imagination). Other approaches to reality also issue in an understanding of it, for instance the philosophic, the aesthetic, the purely mathematical, the religious; and of course every discipline and life itself is an historic process and admits of an enquiry into its history. Each of these approaches has developed its own method and cutting edge; each enriches human experience; each includes the evidence-conclusion structure.

Evidence, inference, conclusion: these terms are used over a vast area of human living; they apply wherever there is a desire for a reasoned approximation to reality. Evidence includes not only the observations and experiments of the physicist, but the documentation of the historian, the statistics of the sociologist, the case histories of the clinical psychiatrist, the testimonies in a court of enquiry, the intuitions of the poet. Similarly, inference can refer to the rigorous deductive processes of a mathematician; to the due process of law (which however can deliberately sacrifice some aids to the reasoning-out of truth in order to serve what are deemed to be more ultimate social values); to clinical reasoning that is based on rapid cross-checking of various models in which different modes of knowledge have found condensation (e.g. models of anatomy, of physiological functioning of body parts, of pathological processes underlying mental neuroses and psychoses); and to the less formal inferences in everyday life. Conclusions, correspondingly, are as diverse in form as the hypotheses of an Einstein, the verdict of a court, the average decisions of life, the diagnosis of a psychiatrist, the poetic vision of a Teilhard de Chardin, the historical explanation of a Toynbee.

One fact that emerges from the whole array of human reasonings is how extremely difficult it is to achieve certitude. Within any given system, on the basis of accepted viewpoints or principles, confidence develops easily as the main issue is the logical soundness of inference. But certitude becomes more difficult according as less can be assumed. Where questions demand the utmost rigour proof may not be feasible; the realistic objective may consist in discerning where the weight of rationality lies. Since the life we are fitted to live is neither more nor less than a rational free life, human life is not attenuated by the absence of full logical proof, provided that among various alternatives rational choices are clearly discernible.

II. Theoretical reasoning that is not subject to control and evaluation by either observation or experiment

The logical structure of mathematics has been made very explicit over the last hundred years. This has been a primary and constant objective in the development of modern mathematical logic which indeed has tended to be content with a language form that could accommodate and formalize mathematical reasoning. Since the time of Boole, the new logicians looked particularly to Mathematics as to the most general and transparent context of human reasoning, developing without reference to our particular world, functioning independently of sense experience and away from any controlling reference to observed facts. This was true whether or not one held the further logistic view that it was a deductive connection with logic itself which guaranteed the rational and objective force of mathematical calculation. Mathematical science was valued for its intrinsic rationality; and, for all who shared the scientists' faith in the rationality of the universe, this grounded a hope in its ultimate utility even though it developed away from the control of observation and experiment.

There have been two different formal ways in which mathematical reasoning and mathematical science (as a body of propositions) have been presented. In the tradition of Frege, Russell and Hilbert the logic implicit in mathematics was displayed best by elaborating mathematics as an axiomatic system. For Gentzen this kind of formalization did not at all express the kind of inferential procedures which mathematicians practise in their proofs, and considerable formal advantages would be obtained if one could do this: 'So I wanted for one thing to establish a formalism which would approximate as far as possible to actual inference. Thus arose a calculus of natural inference.' Thus with Gentzen, one of its two pioneers, the natural deduction approach began as a method of formalizing procedures that are fundamental but informal within mathematics.

With regard to Jaskowski, the other and independent originator, the new approach was a reduction to system of the method of suppositions used in mathematics (and indeed in all reasoning where we prove an implication by making an assumption and obtaining a conclusion). In his paper of 1934, Jaskowski writes:

In 1926 Professor J. Lukasiewicz called attention to the fact that mathematicians in their proofs do not appeal to the theses of the theory of deduction, but make use of other methods of reasoning. The chief means employed in their method is that of an arbitrary supposition. The problem raised by Mr Lukasiewicz was to put those methods under the form of structural rules and to analyse their relation to the theory of deduction. The present paper contains the solution of that problem.

Prescinding from the problem of the precise nature of mathematical science as *knowledge*, and also from all problems raised by the study of the foundations of mathematics, one might summarize the contribution which modern logic makes to the understanding of mathematical reasoning and system as follows: mathematics is the primary existential context in which the grammar of logic is exercised, and there are so many points of similarity between mathematical systems and logical systems that many metalogical insights coincide with metamathematical ones.

With regard to religious doctrines, it is in their nature to be highly axiomatized when they present themselves as based on revealed truths that transcend human experience. Their transcendent character makes it logical that they develop through maintaining continuous deductive contact with their revelation. For a person who transcends the universe in belief or in searching, an inner clarity and consistency is an important logical certification of the worth of religious doctrine. Of course a concrete religious system may also contain an ethics and other theoretical components that are natural and therefore, logically, subject to rational experiential analysis and testing.

Transcending the world in order to explain it is a movement of reason and is not at all discontinuous with the scientific process. The latter proceeds—on the basis that the world is knowable and that there is an explanatory answer for every intelligible question—to frame hypotheses concerning what is unknown about the world. The movement of a natural theology proceeds—on the basis that to exist is to be intelligible, this world being intelligible in virtue simply of being existential—to conclude that the world is not total being (since it does not explain itself completely) and to commit itself to belief in divine creative being. Not to proceed to this commitment is seen, theologically, as an exercise of preference for loss or attenuation of meaning—a type of preference that is not normal in scientific contexts. Thus the movement of transcending is a genuine theoretical effort of understanding with a resultant explanation which science itself is neither called upon to accept nor to oppose. What this movement can mean to the person and what it requires of the person are, of course, questions which concern not the logic of religious faith but the study of its vitality.

III. The logical structure of philosophy and of philosophizing

As one moves from the empirical sciences and mathematics to describe the content and method of philosophy, two basic facts have to be kept in mind:
(1) One of the main tasks of philosophy is to achieve a clear understanding of itself. This requires an appreciation of the difference between it and other disciplines especially the physical sciences and scientific psychology. However,

in the two-thousand-year-old tradition of western philosophy these disciplines were not separate and independent until the last century. A variety of problems and bodies of knowledge were, from time to time, called philosophical that are seen now to be scientific. Further, today there is not consensus on the range of the term 'philosophy' and 'philosophizing' and so even contemporary philosophy may not be totally acceptable as philosophy in the future. The consequence of this lack of precision and self-clarification within the tradition is that the task of describing philosophy must confine itself to the central core. (2) Difficulties arising out of attempts to solve philosophical problems rather than the problems themselves can become central. Thus at any particular time, philosophical method can become a dominant preoccupation and controversy and indeed, in one view, philosophy is conceived best in terms of method or activity rather than of content.

One can discern the general location of philosophic interest and enquiry by considering the logical organization of other disciplines. In each case there is a basis from which one begins, effectively, to demonstrate—there is primitive language and basic truths or axioms. Thus when knowledge is axiomatized—as it is in the empirical sciences, in mathematics, in religious doctrines—one may ask whether (a) primitive language and (b) basic axioms generate a problematique of their own: do they open on to an area of presupposition which, while not exercising any deductive force within axiomatic systems, is logically part of their total meaningfulness and rationality? Is axiomatized knowledge a well constructed raft floating on waters of supposition? Kant developed his philosophy in reaction to the disturbing puzzle of geometry as a body of propositions which, independently of experience, were clear and transparently true and also were confidently and successfully applied to the real world—how was that possible? It is certainly true that the area of human presupposition is also the area of philosophical investigation:

(a) Concepts and terms employed in familiar and scientific explanation—such as 'reality', 'knowledge', 'truth', 'freedom', 'obligation', 'objectivity',—have been subjects for profound wonder and critical enquiry to philosophers. They have been highly controversial too, resistant to any agreed philosophical analysis into unproblematic terms. It was Socrates who first defined and analysed the philosophical function of elucidating concepts. Asked questions about what particular things are right, he moved the enquiry to the more fundamental level it presupposed, asking 'But what is rightness?' This type of fundamental questioning was described by Plato as the mark of the true dialectical philosopher. Aristotle moved the questioning to the most general term of all, asking 'what is it to-be-something?' Since then conceptual questions of this kind have been accepted as central in philosophy. They are second-order questions and their treatment, of its nature, combines conceptual intuition and analysis.

(b) It has always been a function of philosophic enquiry to elucidate ultimate presuppositions in human life, rational investigation and explanatory systems (e.g. what is a *fact*? what can we say about *being real*, as such? what exactly is *knowledge* as a reality in itself? what does it mean to say that human knowledge is *objective*? do our sensations and thoughts disclose a separate external existence of their objects? are there reasons for faith in the human intelligibility of the world?). Traditionally philosophy has also sought to discover what is most basic about the human subject in life (are human beings completely organic or is their vitality spiritual also? what does an analysis of present human life at its highest, i.e. of personal, intelligent, free living, reveal about the possibility that the grave is not the end of a person's life?). And it has enquired into the purpose or lack of it that makes life ultimately meaningful or meaningless, and into the presence of objective values or imperatives in human life (this dimension has given rise to theistic and atheistic doctrine and to varieties of ethical theory).

Of course it must be borne in mind that a good deal of the psychological and ethical content of traditional and contemporary philosophy may, at some future time, be seen as formally belonging to scientific psychology and social science. It has been a recurring feature in the history of philosophy that it recognize sections of its enquiry as belonging to the advancing rationality and axiomatizing range of science. Philosophizing seems to require indeed an attitude of understanding, affirming and valuing the axiomatic power of science while recognizing that it itself works at an underlying level, uncovering and elucidating presuppositions and warrants that, however, do not logically function as axioms for the deduction of theorems. Readjustment of the boundaries of philosophy and science can be, then, a normal continuing feature of the historical development of the two disciplines.

When one looks at the central core of philosophical problems which lie at the roots of objective thought, subjective life and human destiny, and at the variety of philosophical views that have been elaborated in history, it becomes quite clear, firstly, that philosophy is quite different from science in not being a metrical experimental discipline and in not structuring into an axiomatic system. Secondly, while an understanding of how language works is essential, philosophical problems cannot be solved completely and positively by becoming clearer about the way in which an expression is made, by removing ambiguity and unravelling knotted thought. For philosophy is more than problem solving, than the elucidating of presuppositions and basic concepts. The great philosophies have derived from heuristic intuitions of what might be a true perspective on reality and might bring us a deeper understanding of human rationality and human hopes. Philosophizing in its fullest sense seems to consist in asking ultimate questions of life in a profound silence of inner contemplation and in methodically objectifying such personal reflection, bringing it within the reach of critical discussion.

Critical discussion is the aspect of philosophical method that is emphasized today. This is quite understandable. There is no public experiment or objective decision procedure for discriminating between opposing philosophical views. Critical discussion is the medium in which a philosopher experiences the testing of his view and a medium too which stimulates, wakes and energizes others to personal evolution and, possibly, individual appropriation of it. Philosophers in the past have seen philosophical method in aspects that were not overtly socializing: For Plato and Hegel it is dialectical; for Aquinas it consists primarily of conceptual analysis and resolution; for Bergson it is intuitive; for Wittgenstein it is the uncovering of nonsense, for Husserl it is phenomenological description. There are modern thinkers who feel that 'the world' is to be left to the scientist and that philosophical problems must be seen and discussed as problems situated in the language which we use to describe the world; this is somewhat of an extreme from those philosophers, in the past, who believed that philosophy should imitate science—using experimental enquiry (as Hume advocated), axiomatizing like geometry (as Spinoza did) or seeing itself as unified science (as Herbert Spencer felt).

For much of this century, arising from the work of Boole, Frege, Russell and the early Wittgenstein, a consistently held hope and belief was that there is a universal grammar for human thought and communication and that it is possible to master and formalize this grammar and thus bring about a mutation in the quality, clarity and range of philosophical thought. As a case in point, many Polish logicians never lost sight of the fact that their technical work in logic grew out of philosophical concerns and retained their objective of using the new analytic tools to further philosophical enquiry. Indeed Lukasiewicz believed that philosophy must be refashioned and acquire the structure and language that characterize formal logical systems. Since this was generally held, in Poland, to be an impossible development he was called an 'anti-philosopher' there.

Friedrich Waismann indeed argues that the conception of a whole philosophical view is never a matter of logical steps, and being conceived it can neither be proved nor disproved by strictly logical reasoning. What is essential to philosophy is the breaking through to a deeper insight which cannot be lodged in a theorem and cannot therefore be demonstrated:

> Philosophical arguments are none of them logically *compelling* . . . [They] are not deductive; therefore they are not rigorous; and therefore they don't prove anything . . . No philosophical argument ends with a Q.E.D. However forceful it never forces. There is no bullying in philosophy, neither with the stick of logic nor with the stick of language . . . Yet they [philosophic arguments] have force . . . they really screen what actually happens—the quiet and patient undermining of categories over the whole field of thought. Their purpose is to open our eyes, to bring us to see things in a new way— from a wider standpoint unobstructed by misunderstandings . . . Considerations such as these make us see what is already apparent in the use of 'rational', that this term has a wider range of application than what can be established deductively. To say that an argument can be rational and yet not deductive is not a sort of contradiction as it would inevitably be in the opposite case, namely, of saying that a deductive argument need not be rational. (*Contemporary British Philosophy: Personal Statements*, pp. 470, 471, 480)

On the whole it seems clear that in view of the peculiar nature of philoso-phizing, the philosopher must be free of a general dogmatic approach to method, above all from a 'dogmatism of precision'. At the same time one may note various forms of reasoning and refutation which by frequent recurrence demonstrate their distinctive efficiency within philosophy:

The infinite regress argument shows up an unsatisfactory explanation as possessing the crucial obscurity it purports to dissolve. A brief example is an argument of Wittgenstein's in *Philosophical Investigations*:

> How is he to know what colour he is to pick out when he hears 'red'? Quite simple: he is to take the colour whose image occurs to him when he hears the word. But how is he to know which colour it is 'whose image occurs to him'? Is a further criterion needed for that? (§ 239)

An infinite regress in needed criteria means that no criterion is really provided.

Model reasoning is familiar in philosophy. Choosing and working through the details of an analogy is often indispensable for articulating the details of one's view. And rigorously examining analogies is a method of refutation. Berkeley uses it in his *Principles of Human Knowledge*:

> It is said extension is a mode or accident of Matter and that Matter is the *substratum* that supports it. Now I desire that you would explain to me what is meant by Matter's *supporting* extension ... It is evident *support* cannot here be taken in its usual or literal sense, as when we say that pillars support a building. In what sense, therefore, must it be taken? For my part I am not able to discover any sense at all that can be applicable to it. (Part I, par. 16)

Ryle's use of the analogy, 'the ghost in the machine', is a powerful way of focusing the argument against mind–body dualism. In general, analogies play an important part in philosophical reasoning and self-explanation, as the living centre is frequently a broad vision of things.

Criticism that a philosophical view is inconsistent (and therefore false) or self-refuting (and therefore unacceptable) is frequent also; not surprisingly for when one theorizes at the limits of justification one may easily find one's theory subjected to one's own strictures. Thus it was argued that Logical Positivism was self-refuting because its theory of meaning rendered itself meaningless. It is argued similarly that total scepticism is self-refuting.

As a summary one can say that in elucidating concepts and propositions that constitute their concern philosophers describe, divide, define, analyse, make category distinctions and communicate to others by paradigm cases; in reason-ing structures they show, by their example, that their discipline cannot impose a dogmatism of precision and there are philosophic views with a formalistic structure, and others structured quite informally. In its history philosophy has accommodated all forms of argumentation. Popper puts it: 'Philosophers are as free as others to use any method in searching for the truth.'

Philosophy is a limited human enterprise. The fact that it raises ultimate questions does not guarantee it any measure of success in answering them; it is simply its business to formulate such questions and to try to answer them by a purely human investigation. Further the fact that philosophical views are not amenable to experimental confirmation or falsification has, as a practical consequence, that no philosophical view is ever definitely eliminated and a linear development of philosophical insights has proved utopian. Essentially, philosophy takes a more generalized approach to reality than the sciences, and a non-metrical one. Conceptual analysis is the cutting edge in its investigations, and the ability to display a doctrine analytically, as a development out of accepted concepts and intuitions, is the main test of philosophical rectitude.

IV. The use of logical techniques in formal analyses

Organizing knowledge into formal systems is becoming standard procedure in life and in science. Educated people want to see in explicit fashion the primitive terms, postulates and rules of inference in every body of doctrine. They want to force out inconsistencies and vagueness by conceptual improvement and to expose the quality of argument. Further, the widespread use of computers is forcing people to be very analytic and formal as a prerequisite for programming machines. However one may easily fail to distinguish between organizing propositions into a formal system and proving a particular point; as a consequence, one may think one is proving a proposition when all one is doing is situating it in the wider context of one's own formal system. Where the latter is not shared or acceptable, the argument will have little force. Thus while the expert must have a good formal grasp of his subject matter, he needs also the skill of communicating with people to whom his formal system is unfamiliar or even, perhaps, unacceptable. While it relates propositions so that the total intelligibility is organized and transparent, it does not represent the way that individual propositions are actually discovered or the basis on which others will necessarily believe them.

One technique that can be used in formal analysis and exposition is the application of a certain amount of the conceptual apparatus of mathematical logic (e.g. the notation of propositional logic, predicate logic, class logic, modal logic) and of its methods. In 1926, L. Bloomfield, advocating the use of the axiomatic method in linguistics and especially in phonology, wrote:

> The method of postulates (that is, assumptions or axioms) and definitions is fully adequate to mathematics; as for other sciences, the more complex their subject-matter, the less amenable are they to this method, since, under it, every descriptive or historical fact becomes the subject of a new postulate.
>
> Nevertheless, the postulational method can further the study of language, because it forces us to state explicitly whatever we assume, to define our

terms and to decide what things may exist independently and what things are interdependent.

Certain errors can be avoided or corrected by examining and formulating our (at present tacit) assumptions and defining our (often undefined) terms.

Also, the postulational method saves discussion, because it limits our statements to a defined terminology; in particular, it cuts us off from psychological dispute. Discussion of the fundamentals of our science seems to consist one half of obvious truisms, and one half of metaphysics; this is characteristic of matters which form no real part of a subject: they should properly be disposed of by merely naming certain concepts as belonging to the domain of other sciences. ('A Set of Postulates for the Sciences', *Language*, 1926, pp. 153–4)

Since then much work has been done in linguistics on the logical reconstruction of theories. The literature of applied logic also includes the analysis of well-known paradoxes and such famous arguments as St Anselm's Ontological Argument. More importantly, a Temporal Logic (or Logic of Tense) provides the linguistic and inferential apparatus for reasoning that is grounded in change through time; there has been the development of a Deontic Logic—a logic of normative concepts, especially of obligation; and there are logics of preference and of commands, symbolizing conceptual aspects of these entities and formalizing the relationships (especially of implication) which obtain between statements that express them.

Contemporary deontic logic provides a clear and substantial example of the application of logical apparatus and method to theoretical thought. It was initiated by G. H. von Wright whose paper, *Deontic Logic* (1951) and subsequent writings have shaped the contemporary discussions. There were some anticipations of this development: medieval logicians were alive to the possibility of a logic of obligation based on modal logic; in 1926 Ernst Mally, a student of Alexius Meinong, published an axiom system for the notion of *ought*. In *An Essay in Deontic Logic and the General Theory of Action* (1968), von Wright provides perspective on the development over nearly twenty years:

> Deontic Logic, in its modern form, was born as an off-shoot of modal logic. Its point of departure was the observation of a formal analogy between the concepts of possibility, impossibility and necessity on the one hand and the notions of permission, prohibition and obligation on the other hand.
>
> I soon realized that a deontic logic analogous to a propositional modal logic is inadequate as a proposed formalization of norms (rules) of action. It does not permit expression of the distinction, for example, between an obligation to destroy a certain state of affairs and a prohibition against producing this same state. In order to express this distinction, symbolic means for differentiating between the 'active' and the 'passive' mood of behaviour have to be created. This, in turn, requires means of expressing that

a state of affairs comes into being, continues or passes away. What is required is thus a Logic of Action founded upon a Logic of Change.

In *Norm and Action* (1963) I tried to meet these requirements. The rudiments of a formal theory of change and of action were developed and used as a basis for deontic logic. The new fabric presented a rather different look from the original one. In particular, the close analogy with modal logic threatened to break down. As a consequence, the building of a deontic logic came to appear to me as 'a much more radical departure from existing logical theory than I at first realized . . .'

It was not without surprise that I found that the analogy between deontic and modal logic which in *Norm and Action* had seemed to me to break down, was restored when the formal theory of action was given a more accomplished shape. Deontic logic, as I see the subject now, is essentially a branch or facet of modal logic. *Permissibility* as deontic possibility of acting closely parallels *ability* as human (and naturalistic) possibility of doing things. The various conditional permission concepts, moreover, suggest as their analogues a variety of relative modalities. If these suggestions turned out to be fruitful for the study of modal concepts, one could perhaps say that deontic logic had paid off the debt it owes to modal logic for its birth.

The applications of deontic logic are in ethics and the philosophy of law. It would seem that applications to ethics require, in order to be fruitful, a complement in the form of a logic of value concepts. The applications to legal theory are, I believe, of a more direct nature. Two problems for the treatment of which deontic logic seems to provide a useful basis, are those of *completeness* of normative (legal) systems and of the *hierarchy* of norms of a legal order. (pp. 3–5)

Much work has been done in devising an appropriate semantical basis. At first von Wright applied deontic operators (the Greek *deon* means that which is binding) to action-describing sentences only. In *Norm and Action* he constructs such sentences in this way: pTq expresses the transformation of a state of affairs p into a state of affairs q; $d(pTq)$ expresses the bringing about of this transformation, and $f(pTq)$ expresses the forbearing from bringing it about. Deontic operators such as O (obligation) and P (permissibility) are attached to such *df*-sentences. His system was strictly speaking a logic of act-names rather than of propositions, the notion of truth-value being replaced by that of *performance-value*. Since then he has accepted a wider application of deontic operators, namely to closed and open sentences which can be descriptions of states of affairs or statements about act-individuals.

The notion of permission is the primitive deontic operator, obligation being defined by it:

$$Op \equiv \sim P \sim p.$$

There are three principles or axioms: a principle of permission, that for any act p, either p or $\sim p$ is permitted:

$$Pp \vee P \sim p.$$

The second principle is one of deontic distribution:

$$P(p \vee q) \equiv Pp \vee Pq.$$

There is a principle of deontic contingency, stating that

$$O(p \vee \sim p) \text{ and } \sim P(p \& \sim p) \text{ are not valid.}$$

The rules of inference of propositional logic are used along with a *rule of extensionality*:

If p and q are logically equivalent, Pp and Pq are logically equivalent. The validity of deontic formulae can be determined by a truth-table method; thus the system is a decidable one.

A. R. Anderson sought to simplify and reduce deontic logic by translating 'It is obligatory that p' into 'If p is not done then—necessarily some sanction or penalty will be applied.' Sören Hallden has developed a deontic system in which the basic type of sentence is 'it is better if p than if q'; he defines 'it ought to be the case that p' as 'it is better if p than if not-p'. These approaches fail to include and formalize the notion of moral commitment which von Wright, Nicholas Rescher and other logicians regard as essential for a deontic system. The difference in approach underlines the fact that a formal system, achieving an intelligibility that is intrinsic in basis, cannot determine its own applicability.

Concerning the axiomatic work that was done, R. Hilpinen observes:

> In this approach, plausible-looking candidates for logical truth are selected as axioms for the notions studied, a sample of consequences (or theorems) is derived from these axioms, and the adequacy of the axiom system is decided by considering these consequences. Deontic formulae are normally interpreted simply by translating them to sentences of ordinary language. The plausibility of putative theorems is judged on the basis of the intuitive plausibility of their ordinary-language counterparts ... The formulation of our intuitions concerning deontic notions in ordinary language often involves ambiguous expressions such as 'implies', 'requires', etc. ... Recent studies by Stig Kanger, Saul A. Kripke, Jaakko Hintikka, Richard Montague, W. H. Hanson and others indicate that the application of modern semantical methods (model theory) to deontic logic gives a more fruitful basis for understanding deontic formulae and judging their acceptability. (*Deontic Logic: Introductory and Systematic Readings*, pp. 15–16)

Jaakko Hintikka points out the basic formal importance of distinguishing deontic consequence and logical consequence:

> What does the validity of a statement of the form $(p \supset q)$ mean? According to our definitions above it means that the statement $(p \& \sim q)$ is

not satisfiable. The intuitive meaning of this fact can be expressed by saying that p cannot be realized without *ipso facto* realizing q, too. When we are thinking of or discussing normative matters, we often—unwittingly—slip into discussing something else. Without noticing it, we concentrate our attention, not on what can or cannot be realized, but rather on what can or cannot be realized *without violating any obligations*. In the case at hand, we are tacitly considering whether p can be realized without realizing q *while all norms are satisfied*. In other words, we are interested in whether $(p \& \sim q)$ can be true, not in any old possible world, but in a *deontically perfect* world. This means that we are considering, not the satisfiability of $(p \& \sim q)$, but the satisfiability of $P(p \& \sim q)$, in other words, not the validity of $(p \supset q)$, but the validity of $O(p \supset q)$. (*Deontic Logic: Introductory and Systematic Readings*, p. 78)

In $p \supset q$ we state that the realization of p involves q as a logical consequence and therefore in any arbitrary world; in $O(p \supset q)$ we state that as the force of a norm (in a world where all norms are fulfilled) the realization of p involves q. In the latter case q is a deontic consequence rather than a logical consequence of p. A system of purely deontic consequences does not provide an adequate basis for solving the ethical problems of actual human living, many of which arise because previous obligations have been neglected. Further fallacies arise when the distinction between logical consequence and deontic consequence is not observed. In the first edition of his *Formal Logic*, Prior put forward as an evident truth of logic: 'If we are obliged to do A, then if our doing A implies that we ought to do B, we are obliged to do B.' However the obligation of doing B arises *as a consequence* because not only are we obliged to do A but also we are in a world where, all norms being satisfied, we actually do A. If we did not do A the basis for concluding that we are obliged to do B would be gone.

It seems that the formal problems encountered by deontic logic clarify the nature and difficulties of ethical thought itself. In summary one may say that in constructing a deontic logic one encounters difficulty in devising satisfactory linguistic forms for deontic content; in reaching a set of axioms whose derivatives are at no point in conflict with moral intuition, or, alternatively, in establishing an independent decision procedure for deontic statements which claim to be formally true but are not simply instances or applications of truths in formal logic.

This section on the application of logical techniques must, finally, give due prominence to the fact that at the present time formal analyses and expositions of all kinds make as much use as possible, in inference, of the *formalistic method* which is based on the fact that one may deal with words in two entirely different ways: one may be concerned with them materially (as a set of waves in the air, or as a series of ink marks, governed by *syntactical* rules which refer exclusively to their material form and never to their meaning) or one may be concerned with them as having meaning (and as coming therefore under the rules of semantics). One of the most important achievements of modern methodology is the realization that operating with language on the syntactic level can make the work of thought considerably easier. Such a method is called *formalism*. It consists in ignoring every meaning of the signs employed and considering the signs exclusively according to their written form. The method is based on the clear distinction between a language in itself with its purely syntactic rules and the giving of meaning to this language. It would be easy to construct a language without attaching any meaning to it and different interpretations could be assigned to the same formalized language. Indeed formalism consists essentially in the extension of a method known for centuries, namely that of calculation which occurs in the language of numbers.

Thus a sign may be said to have a twofold meaning:

(1) it has *an operational meaning* for us if we know how to use it, know the syntactical rules which are applicable to it;

(2) it has an *eidetic meaning* for us if we know what it refers to and connotes. When an eidetic meaning is given, an operational meaning is always given along with it but not vice versa. Bochenski notes: 'There are two extreme positions in philosophy today: on the one hand it is held that human knowledge is limited to eidetic meanings, and on the other that it is limited to the purely operational. In the first case all formalism is excluded, or at any rate systems which cannot be fully interpreted are rejected. On the other side, it is maintained that there is no such thing as eidetic meaning, and that only operational meaning is at our disposal. Both views are erroneous. It is perfectly clear that in certain cases there is an eidetic meaning. On the other hand, however, there seems to be parts of mathematics, physics, astronomy, etc. which cannot be given any eidetic meaning, although on the whole they lead to consequences which it is possible to interpret eidetically.' (*The Methods of Contemporary Thought*, p. 39)

Formalism is used in many spheres of modern research, including Logic. It has been humorously put that in formalism one does not know what one is saying, nor whether what one is saying is true. But Bochenski notes:

(1) The goal of formalism is always knowledge. A formalistic system only fulfils its task, therefore, if it is ultimately possible to interpret its results eidetically.

(2) The rules governing formalistic operations must make sense eidetically. They prescribe what we are to do and it must be possible to understand them, ultimately.

(3) In practice, formalized systems are nearly always developed by first establishing meaningful signs, then abstracting from their meaning and building up the system formalistically and finally giving a full interpretation to the finished system. (This holds in particular for logic.)

(4) Although it would not be impossible to have a science whose system had no meaning except a syntactic one, this cannot be the case with logic. For logic has to provide rules of deduction for all indirect thinking and if its rules were not eidetically meaningful no deduction could be carried out.

Accordingly most contemporary logicians hold that systems which do not permit any known eidetic interpretation are not really logic.

Formalism is a very useful method to use in conjunction with other methods, for the following reasons:
(a) in very complicated matters our eidetic understanding may break down and be helped on by formalistic processes;
(b) the use of formalism (which handles signs according to their written shape) helps to exclude tacit presuppositions about objects;
(c) the process of formalistic deduction is suitable for delimiting and clarifying primitive concept or terms;
(d) a system that is developed purely formalistically may permit of many interpretations and therefore of many uses.

It is important to note that while the extensive use of artificial symbols has occurred at the same time as the development of formalism, artificial symbols need not be regarded formalistically. For example, the primitive parts of the language of mathematical logic are usually not regarded formalistically.

Chapter 5

FORMAL DETACHMENT: IDEAL OR MYTH?

I. Introduction

The sense in which our knowledge may be said to be objective is a matter of great contemporary discussion in both science and philosophy. Added to this interest is an unprecedented grasp and power of formalization which has created a technology of computerization. Against this background the contemporary writings of Michael Polanyi and (from the last century) the *Grammar of Assent* of John Henry Newman are particularly important for their argument that human knowing is *basically* informal, that it is not true to say either that, ideally, human knowledge should be purely formal or that, factually, one could know in a completely formal way. In contrast, objectivist writings are concerned with scientific knowledge as something which, being stated and formalized in human language, is no longer part of ourselves, and grows through being subject to universal criticism. All these writings are valuable for developing an overall perspective. They are not in direct conflict and indeed it may emerge that they combine in any full account of knowledge, both formal and informal.

II. Michael Polanyi

In 1958 Michael Polanyi, a distinguished physical chemist, published his Gifford lectures (1951–2) as *Personal Knowledge: Towards a Post-Critical Philosophy*. He wrote:

> I start by rejecting the ideal of scientific detachment. In the exact sciences, this false ideal is perhaps harmless, for it is in fact disregarded there by scientists. But we shall see that it exercises a destructive influence in biology, psychology and sociology, and falsifies our whole outlook far beyond the domain of science. I want to establish an alternative ideal of knowledge, quite generally.
>
> Hence the wide scope of this book and hence also the coining of the new term I have used for my title: Personal Knowledge. The two words may seem to contradict each other: for true knowledge is deemed impersonal, universally established, objective. But the seeming contradiction is resolved by modifying the conception of knowing.
>
> [Personal participation of the knower in all acts of understanding] does not make our understanding subjective. Comprehension is neither an arbitrary act nor a passive experience, but a responsible act claiming universal

validity. Such knowing is indeed objective in the sense of establishing contact with a hidden reality; a contact that is defined as the condition for anticipating an indeterminate range of yet unknown (and perhaps yet inconceivable) true implications. It seems reasonable to describe this fusion of the personal and the objective as Personal Knowledge. (Preface)

In this and subsequent writings Polanyi argues that the urge to have an impersonal knowledge has made science disjoin subjectivity and objectivity, has made it seek a quality of total exteriority which is impossible for human understanding and has made prediction rather than understanding its central criterion.

In his view, with regard to all explicit formalized knowledge there is always a tacit dimension—unformalized knowing. Tacit thought is an indispensable part of all knowledge, and the ideal of eliminating all unformalized elements from scientific knowing and establishing a strictly detached, objective knowledge never was realized and could not be:

> I think I can show that the process of formalizing all knowledge to the exclusion of any tacit knowing is self-defeating. For, in order that we may formalize the relations that constitute a comprehensive entity, for example, the relations that constitute a frog, this entity, i.e. the frog, must be first identified informally by tacit knowing; and, indeed, the meaning of a mathematical theory of the frog lies in its continued bearing on this still tacitly known frog. Moreover, the act of bringing a mathematical theory to bear on its subject is itself a tacit integration of the kind we have recognized in the use of a denotative word for designating its object. And we have seen also that a true knowledge of a theory can be established only after it has been interiorized and extensively used to interpret experience. Therefore: a mathematical theory can be constructed only by relying on *prior* tacit knowing and can function as a theory only *within* an act of tacit knowing, which consists in our attending *from* it to the previously established experience on which it bears. Thus the ideal of a comprehensive mathematical theory of experience which would eliminate all tacit knowing is proved to be self-contradictory and logically unsound. (*The Tacit Dimension*, pp. 20–21)

Formalized knowledge has the great value of being patient of critical reflection; it is an external, explicit, articulate system and we can examine its derivation from specifiable premises according to clear rules of inference. This is its logical difference from knowledge which, being acquired and held tacitly, is *a-critical*. It does not follow, however, that the ideal is a completely precise and strictly logical representation of knowledge and that the presence of tacit thought is a flaw to be eliminated. For tacit operations are of their nature necessary for the production and the renewal of articulate frameworks. Further, formulating our knowledge not only makes us better informed, it also increases our mental power to re-organize, tacitly, our knowledge from ever new points of view; thus it maintains the supremacy of our tacit powers:

> In the last few thousand years human beings have enormously increased the range of comprehension by equipping our tacit powers with a cultural machinery of language and writing. Immersed in this cultural milieu, we now respond to a much increased range of potential thought. (*The Tacit Dimension*, p. 91)

Humanly we can only see the universe from a centre within ourselves and we must give existence to our vision in the imitation, the medium, of human language. Human perspective cannot be eliminated from human knowledge or human expression:

> In the Ptolemaic system, as in the cosmogony of the Bible, man was assigned a central position in the universe, from which position he was ousted by Copernicus. Ever since, writers eager to drive the lesson home have urged us, resolutely and repeatedly, to abandon all sentimental egoism, and to see ourselves objectively in the true perspective of time and space.
>
> What is the true lesson of the Copernican revolution? Why did Copernicus exchange his actual terrestrial station for an imaginary solar stand-point? The only justification for this lay in the greater intellectual satisfaction he derived from the celestial panorama as seen from the sun instead of the earth. Copernicus gave preference to man's delight in abstract theory, at the price of rejecting the evidence of our senses, which present us with the irresistible fact of the sun, the moon and the stars rising daily in the east to travel across the sky towards their setting in the west. In a literal sense, therefore, the new Copernican system was as anthropocentric as the Ptolemaic view, the difference being merely that it preferred to satisfy a different human affection. (*Personal Knowledge: Towards a Post-Critical Philosophy*, pp. 3–4)

Thus in considering theoretical knowledge to be superior to immediate experience we are not ceasing to be anthropocentric; what we are doing is favouring an anthropocentrism of our reason, believing that rationality commands universal acceptance by rational creatures everywhere, and enables us to make even prophetic contact with reality: 'In this whole indeterminate scope of its true implications lies the deepest sense in which objectivity is attributed to scientific theory.' (Ibid., p. 5) The prophetic power inherent in abstract theory has been shrunk and distorted into the concept of scientific theory as 'a convenient contrivance, a device for recording events and computing their future course' whereas the true nature and core of theory is the *understanding* that it gives:

> To say that the discovery of objective truth in science consists in the apprehension of a rationality which commands our respect and arouses our

contemplative admiration; that such discovery, while using the experience of our senses as clues, transcends this experience by embracing the vision of a reality beyond the impressions of our senses, a vision which speaks for itself in guiding us to an ever deeper understanding of reality—such an account of scientific procedure would be generally shrugged aside as out-dated Platonism: a piece of mystery-mongering unworthy of an enlightened age. Yet it is precisely on this conception of objectivity that I wish to insist. (Ibid., pp. 5–6)

Further, intellectual passion is a reality *in* science: it has a logical function within scientific understanding, serving as a guide to what is precious to science, to what is of higher and what of lesser interest:

Scientific discovery reveals new knowledge, but the new vision which accompanies it is not knowledge. It is less than knowledge, for it is a guess; but it is more than knowledge, for it is a foreknowledge of things yet unknown and at present perhaps inconceivable. Our vision of the general nature of things is our guide for the interpretation of all future experience. Such guidance is indispensable. Theories of the scientific method which try to explain the establishment of scientific truth by any purely objective formal procedure are doomed to failure. Any process of enquiry unguided by intellectual passions would inevitably spread out into a desert of trivialities. Our vision of reality, to which our sense of scientific beauty responds, must suggest to us the kind of questions that it should be reasonable and interesting to explore. It should recommend the kind of conceptions and empirical relations that are intrinsically plausible and which should therefore be upheld, even when some evidence seems to contradict them, and tell us also, on the other hand, what empirical connections to reject as specious, even though there is evidence for them—evidence that we may as yet be unable to account for on any other assumptions. In fact, without a scale of interest and plausibility based on a vision of reality, nothing can be discovered that is of value to science; and only our grasp of scientific beauty, responding to the evidence of our senses, can evoke this vision. (Ibid., p. 135)

A problem arises when we acknowledge the participation of the knower in shaping his knowledge and accept personal rather than impersonal knowledge as the ideal: is knowledge then 'something that we could determine at will, as we think fit?':

I have argued that personal knowledge is fully determined, provided that it is pursued with unwavering universal intent. I have expounded the belief that the capacity of our minds to make contact with reality and the intellectual passion which impels us towards this contact will always suffice so to guide our personal judgment that it will achieve the full measure of truth that lies within the scope of our particular calling. (*The Study of Man*, p. 27)

The existence, in every act of knowing, of a tacit and passionate contribution of the person, means that in knowing we exercise commitment and responsibility:

> Within its commitments the mind is warranted to exercise much ampler powers than those by which it is supposed to operate under objectivism; but by the very fact of assuming this new freedom it submits to a higher power to which it had hitherto refused recognition. Objectivism seeks to relieve us from all responsibility for the holding of our beliefs. That is why it can be logically expanded to systems of thought in which the responsibility of the human person is eliminated from the life and society of man. In recoiling from objectivism, we would acquire a nihilistic freedom of action but for the fact that our protest is made in the name of higher allegiances. We cast off the limitations of objectivism in order to fulfil our calling, which bids us to make up our minds about the whole range of matters with which man is properly concerned. (*Personal Knowledge: Towards a Post-Critical Philosophy*, pp. 323–4)

Once one acknowledges understanding rather than prediction as the core of knowledge the whole range of disciplines from physics to the fine arts are seen to arise from the same tacit powers. Rationality in science is akin to rationality in ethics, in politics, in jurisprudence and law. Creative thinking in science is akin to intuition in art and literature. As formal intellectual beauty is a criterion of truth in science, so is it a criterion of excellence in aesthetics. And science resembles religion, too, in resting on belief that leads to understanding:

> We must now recognize belief once more as the source of all knowledge. Tacit assent and intellectual passions, the sharing of an idiom and of a cultural heritage, affiliation to a like-minded community: such are the impulses which shape our vision of the nature of things on which we rely for our mastery of things. No intelligence, however critical or original, can operate outside such a fiduciary framework. (*Personal Knowledge: Towards a Post-Critical Philosophy*, p. 266)

So closely linked is the formal explicit rationality of science with its sources that Polanyi speaks of it as 'dwelling in' them as we are said to dwell in our own bodies:

> I suggest now that the supposed pre-suppositions of science are so futile because the actual foundations of our scientific beliefs cannot be asserted at all. When we accept a certain set of pre-suppositions and use them as our interpretative framework, we may be said to dwell in them as we do in our own body. Their uncritical acceptance for the time being consists in a process of assimilation by which we identify ourselves with them. They are not asserted and cannot be asserted, for assertion can be made only within a

framework with which we have identified ourselves for the time being; as they are themselves our ultimate framework, they are essentially inarticulable.

It is by his assimilation of the framework of science that the scientist makes sense of experience. This making sense of experience is a skilful act which impresses the personal participation of the scientist on the resultant knowledge. (Ibid., p. 60)

Through their common personal involvement there is an inescapable solidarity of science with all other cultural provinces.

At this point one may cite as support another contemporary scientist, C. H. Waddington, who argues that art absorbs central insights and concerns of science not through formal learning but by a kind of empathy which has important effects on the ways in which painters have worked. In his book, *Behind Appearance: A study of the relations between painting and the natural sciences in this century*, he points out that both art and science have, at times, dealt with tangible objects and familiar experiences; together they have also engaged in dissolving familiar reality, in fusing space and time into a single continuum; they have responded to the impossibility of a single unified description of nature by complementary approaches at various levels; and now artists like scientists are becoming preoccupied with the nature of their own activities and materials. Art and science now consciously share the same epistemological foundation: 'The observer does not wholly make what he observes, but his intrinsic character colours it. There is no strict objective-subjective dichotomy. The painter is *in* his painting, the scientist is *in* his science.' (p. 240) Examining the common tendency of twentieth-century painting and science towards probing behind appearances and their relationships at levels of conscious connections and unconscious reflections, Waddington concludes:

> The scientist does not go to the painter for a representation of scientific objects, but for the enrichment and deepening of his consciousness, which comes when he finds a painter in whom the climate of scientific thought has penetrated into the spirit, leading to the production of works in which some of the deeper, less easily expressible features of the scientific outlook are 'shown forth'. (p. 155)

It may well be that one of the greatest recurring mistakes in history has been to take philosophic systems and scientific systems as the paradigm case of knowledge, assuming a simple identity between perfect knowledge and wholly explicit truth. Polanyi insists that it is in the very nature of human knowing to be a kind of groping that combines both *focal* and *subsidiary* awareness, that knows, in a specifiable way, that which we attend to and, in an unformalized way, that which we are relying upon: no knowledge is, or can be, wholly focal. Essentially this means that knowledge is studied best within a theory of life (indeed of evolving life) rather than within a theory of form or system.

Impersonalized knowledge exists only in the neutral process of transference; in the sender it arises out of a living process, in the receiver it returns to a living process—that of another centre, another subjectivity. Marjorie Grene puts it as follows:

> ... only the explicit, formulable core of knowledge can be transferred, neutrally, from person to person. Its implicit base (since it is not verbalized and cannot be formulated and so impersonalized) must be the groping *of someone*.

> But while personal, the subsidiary, or tacit, root of knowing is primarily directed away *from* the inner core of my being *to* the focal centre of my attention. All knowledge consists in a *from-to* relation. Of course, subsidiary knowledge is mine: indeed, it is what, relevantly to the present focal point of my attention, I have assimilated to my very self: it is what, out of my being-in-the-world, I have interiorized to the point where I can rely on it to guide me towards a distally located goal. All knowing—whether tacit, as in perception or in skills, or explicit (though never totally so), as in the mastery of an intellectual discipline—displays this dual structure. I attend from a proximal pole, which is an aspect of my being, to a distal pole, which, by attending to it, I place at a distance from myself. All knowing, we could say, in other words, is orientation. The organism's placing of itself in its environment, the dinoflagellate in the plankton, the salmon in its stream or the fox in its lair, prefigures the process by which we both shape and are shaped by our world, reaching out from what we have assimilated to what we seek.

> Unlike the traditional ideal of a wholly explicit, self-guaranteeing truth, from-to knowledge cannot be instantaneous; it is a stretch, not only of attention, but of effort, effort must be lived, and living takes time. Knowledge, therefore, is imbedded both in living process (as Piaget, too, has argued in *Biologie et Connaissance*, and as Suzanne Langer is arguing in her study of *Mind*) and in the uniquely human form of living process: in history. (*Knowing and Being*, Introduction, pp. x–xi)

The human living process must be seen not as automatic, not as arbitrary but as responsible. Responsibility is part of the human hope of achievement: the human way of being an active centre is characterized by a sense of calling and by a responsibility.

Situating his view within contemporary thinking, Polanyi concludes that while it diverges from the common analyses of science, it does respond to many facets of general scientific thought and to what Merleau-Ponty has called 'the philosophical mission of the twentieth century'—'to explore the irrational and to integrate it into an enlarged reason'.

> [The common analysis of science] assumes that the logical foundation of empirical knowledge must be capable of definition by explicit rules. While the difficulties of this enterprise have not gone unnoticed, the reluctance to

abandon it in principle still seems universal. My own attempts to acknowledge tacit powers of personal judgment as the decisive organon of discovery and the ultimate criterion of scientific truth, have been opposed by describing these agencies as psychological, not logical, in character. But this distinction is not explained by my critics. Is an act of perception which sees an object in a way that assimilates it to past instances of the same kind, a psychological process or a logical inference? We have seen that it can be mistaken and its results be false; and it certainly has a considerable likelihood of being true. To me this suggests that it is a logical process of inference even though it is not explicit. In any case, to perceive things rightly is certainly part of the process of scientific inquiry and to hold perceptions to be right underlies the holding of scientific propositions to be true. And, if, in consequence, we must accept the veridical powers of perception as the roots of empirical science, we cannot reasonably refuse to accept other tacit veridical processes having a similar structure. This is what I have been urging all along since I first wrote '. . . that the capacity of scientists to guess the presence of shapes as tokens of reality, differs from the capacity of our ordinary perception only by the fact that it can integrate shapes presented to it in terms which the perception of ordinary people cannot readily handle'. ('Tacit Knowing: Its Bearing on Some Problems of Philosophy', in *Knowing and Being*, pp. 172–3)

Current writings on the history of science have confirmed the view I put forward years ago that the pursuit of science is determined at every stage by unspecifiable powers of thought, and I have shown here how this fact forms my starting point for developing a theory of non-explicit thought. You may call such a theory—using a term coined by Gilbert Ryle—an informal logic of science and of knowledge in general. Alternatively, you may call it a phenomenology of science and knowledge, by reference to Husserl and Merleau-Ponty. This would correctly relate my enterprise both to analytic philosophy and to phenomenology and existentialism. ('The Logic of Tacit Inference', in *Knowing and Being*, p. 155)

III. John Henry Newman (1801–90)

Reading Newman's classic *Essay in Aid of a Grammar of Assent*, one cannot fail to be struck by the fact that in its treatment of inference, it is in complete accord with Polanyi's *Personal Knowledge*. Although the language is that of an Illative Sense rather than of tacit and focal awareness the perspective, substance and emphases are the same.

For Newman it is fundamental that everyone who reasons is his own centre and that no development of logic can reverse this truth:

The authoritative oracle, which is to decide our path, is something more searching and manifold than such jejune generalizations as treatises can give, which are most distinct and clear when we least need them. It is seated in the mind of the individual, who is thus his own law, his own teacher, and his own judge in those special cases of duty which are personal to him. It comes of an acquired habit, though it has its first origin in nature itself, and it is formed and matured by practice and experience; and it manifests itself, not in any breadth of view, any philosophical comprehension of the mutual relations of duty towards duty, or any consistency in its teachings, but it is a capacity sufficient for the occasion, deciding what ought to be done here and now, by this given person, under these given circumstances. It decides nothing hypothetical, it does not determine what a man should do ten years hence, or what another should do at this time. It may indeed happen to decide ten years hence as it does now, and to decide a second case now as it now decides a first; still its present act is for the present, not for the distant or the future. (pp. 354–5)

Newman is concerned here with reasoning in concrete life. Reasoning may also be brought to bear on notions. In one important aspect, the nature of reasoning is determined by its constituent propositions. A proposition may be expressive of things, our apprehension of such a proposition being called *real* and our assent and belief real also; or it may be expressive to us of notions, our assent and belief being described as notional also. It is a paradox that while assent is most perfect when it is a *real* one, inference is *clearest* when it is exercised on notions—and ends, therefore, in a conclusion to which we give notional assent. One can see therefore an inescapable limitation in the method of logical inference which pursues the objective of public clarity as a common measure between mind and mind, as a means of joint investigation and as a recognized intellectual standard:

> What we desiderate [in the method of logical inference] is something which may supersede the need of personal gifts by a far-reaching and infallible rule. Now, without external symbols to mark out and to steady its course, the intellect runs wild; but with the aid of symbols, as in algebra, it advances with precision and effect. Let then our symbols be words: let all thought be arrested and embodied in words. Let language have a monopoly of thought; and thought go for only so much as it can show itself to be worth in language. Let every prompting of the intellect be ignored, every momentum of argument be disowned, which is unprovided with an equivalent wording, as its ticket for sharing in the common search after truth. Let the authority of nature, commonsense, experience, genius, go for nothing. Ratiocination, thus restricted and put into grooves, is what I have called Inference, and the science, which is its regulating principle, is Logic. (p. 263)

In practice, logic can succeed only insofar as words can in fact be found for representing 'the countless varieties and subtleties of human thought'; this means that it must fail, for it is not true that whatever can be thought can be adequately expressed in words:

> Even when argument is the most direct and severe of its kind, there must be those assumptions in the process which resolve themselves into the conditions of human nature; but how many more assumptions does that process in ordinary concrete matters involve, subtle assumptions not directly arising out of these primary conditions, but accompanying the course of reasoning, step by step, and traceable to the sentiments of the age, country, religion, social habits and ideas, of the particular inquirers or disputants, and passing current without detection, because admitted equally on all hands! And to these must be added the assumptions which are made from the necessity of the case, in consequence of the prolixity and elaborateness of any argument which should faithfully note down all the propositions which go to make it up. We recognize this tediousness even in the case of the theorems of Euclid, though mathematical proof is comparatively simple.
>
> Logic then does not really prove; it enables us to join issue with others; it suggests ideas; it opens views; it maps out for us the lines of thought; it verifies negatively; it determines when differences of opinion are hopeless; and when and how far conclusions are probable; but for genuine proof in concrete matter we require an *organon* more delicate, versatile and elastic than verbal argumentation. (pp. 270–71)

The simplicity and exactness of science, generally, makes it impossible for it to be ever a measure of fact, and so it is in the nature of things that the particular science of logic can never contain or properly represent real inference in its formulas:

> As to Logic, its chain of conclusions hangs loose at both ends; both the point from which the proof should start, and the points at which it should arrive, are beyond its reach; it comes short both of first principles and of concrete issues. Even its most elaborate exhibitions fail to represent adequately the sum-total of considerations by which an individual mind is determined in its judgment of things; even its most careful combinations made to bear on a conclusion want that steadiness of aim which is necessary for hitting it. As I said when I began, thought is too keen and manifold, its sources are too remote and hidden, its path too personal, delicate and circuitous, its subject-matter too various and intricate, to admit of the trammels of any language, of whatever subtlety and of whatever compass. (p. 284)

The method by which we become certain of what is concrete is a multiform and intricate process of ratiocination:

> First, it does not supersede the logical form of inference, but is one and the same with it; only it is no longer an abstraction, but carried out into the

realities of life, its premisses being instinct with the substance and the momentum of that mass of probabilities, which, acting upon each other in correction and confirmation, carry it home definitely to the individual case, which is its original scope.

Next, from what has been said it is plain, that such a process of reasoning is more or less implicit, and without the direct and full advertence of the mind exercising it ... [The mind is] unequal to a complete analysis of the motives which carry it on to a particular conclusion, and is swayed and determined by a body of proof, which it recognizes only as a body, and not in its constituent parts. (p. 292)

It seems to be a law of our minds that we recognize that certitude can correlate with an argument that is implicit, tacit, baffling our powers of analysis and incapable of being brought under logical rule:

... the processes of reasoning which legitimately lead to assent, to action, to certitude, are in fact too multiform, subtle, omnigenous, too implicit, to allow of being measured by rule, that they are after all personal—verbal argumentation being useful only in subordination to a higher logic. (p. 303)

Methodical processes of inference are only instruments of the mind; the complete, living *organon* of reasoning must be a person and not a mere method or calculus. Further the personal dimension includes such elements as a sober purpose of discovering truth, a moral earnestness and patience, with freedom from attachment to system:

Thus a proof, except in abstract demonstration, has always in it, more or less, an element of the personal, because 'prudence' is not a constituent part of our nature, but a personal endowment ... [Our language frequently signifies] that we have arrived at these conclusions—not *ex opere operato*, by a scientific necessity independent of ourselves—but by the action of our own minds, by our own individual perception of the truth in question, under a sense of duty to those conclusions and with an intellectual conscientiousness. (pp. 317–18)

Thus it is the mind that reasons and controls its own reasonings responsibly, the ultimate test of truth being the testimony borne to truth by the mind itself. Newman gives the name, Illative Sense, to our living, spontaneous energy of judging and concluding, when it develops fully into an intellectual mastery of some particular field of enquiry:

It is the mind that reasons, and that controls its own reasonings, not any technical apparatus of words and propositions. This power of judging and concluding, when in its perfection, I call the Illative Sense ... In no class of concrete reasonings, whether in experimental science, historical research, or theology, is there any ultimate test of truth and error in our inferences besides the trustworthiness of the Illative Sense that gives them its sanction; just as there is no sufficient test of poetical excellence, heroic action, or gentleman-like conduct, other than the particular mental sense, be it genius, taste, sense of propriety, or the moral sense, to which those subject-matters are severally committed. Our duty in each of these is to strengthen and perfect the special faculty which is its living rule, and in every case as it comes to do our best. And such also is our duty and our necessity, as regards the Illative Sense. (pp. 353, 359)

IV. Conclusion

In *The Physicist's Conception of Nature* Werner Heisenberg writes:

> When we speak of the picture of nature in the exact science of our age, we do not mean a picture of nature so much as a *picture of our relationship with nature*. The old division of the world into objective processes in space and time and the mind in which these processes are mirrored—in other words, the Cartesian difference between *res cogitans* and *res extensa*—is no longer a suitable starting point for our understanding of modern science. Science, we find, is now focused on the network of relationships between man and nature, on the framework which makes us as living beings dependent parts of nature, and which we as human beings have simultaneously made the object of our thoughts and actions. Science no longer confronts nature as an objective observer, but sees itself as an actor in this interplay between man and nature.

It seems clear that in this interplay an understanding is humanly developed which is in part a tacit mental vitality, in part an explicit objective account. Until now applied logic has been objectivist in confining itself to determining the logical status of explicit accounts. This is an inevitable result of an historical development which assigns to a logic of statements the basic position in the science, and which, indeed, technically and fully justifies that assignation in respect of the other sections of existing logic. But a question arises now: what is the logical status of scientific understanding viewed, totally, in both tacit and explicit dimensions? what are the limits of logical clarification and explication here? And a further question develops: is there a section of logic more basic than the logic of propositions—a 'system logic' in which statements are no longer disjoined (simply something else in the world) but are symbolized as the world interiorized within a unique personal *weltanshauung*? Against the background of scientific relativity and of social personalism, must a grammar of rationality not acknowledge and—to the extent possible—formalize as rules the exercise of rational vitality at its personal depth? The interest in theory comparison within science, the contemporary development (for scientific purposes) of a new logic of framework transpositions, the conception (presented in the philosophy of logic section of this book) of metaformalism rather than formalism as the logical ideal for human living—there are positive indications of the value of considering the technical possibility of such a development within formal logic.

Section F: A Bibliography of Logic

(Note: the three sections of this bibliography overlap somewhat.)

Introductory Note

At times it is not easy to decide whether a book or paper should be classified as a contribution to logic rather than to mathematics, or philosophy or linguistics. In his bibliography of symbolic logic Alonzo Church notes the particular difficulty of drawing the line between modern logic and mathematics; he defines symbolic logic as 'the formal structure of propositions and of deductive reasoning investigated by the symbolic method' and uses as a criterion of symbolic method 'substantial use, explicit or implicit, of formal criteria of inference, so that the symbolism becomes a calculus rather than a mere shorthand'. Accordingly he includes treatises on foundational questions connected with the axiom of choice, foundational investigations of proof by recursion and of definition by recursion, the Zermelo axiomatic set theory and topics closely related to Boolean algebra. In the present bibliography, the objective is to display as forcibly as possible the specific nature of logic (even as it develops over the various periods of its history and gives rise to various sections of the contemporary science) and to underline the logical perspective as such. Thus a division is made between logic and mathematics which is sharper than that of Church.

Again, it is often not easy to decide whether a work should be included in the bibliographical section on the history of logic or in the section on the science of logic. Books are in the former section because they elucidate the historical development of logic; books in the latter section are valued for their exposition of some section of the science of logic.

1. TREATISES AND PAPERS OF FOUNDATIONAL IMPORTANCE IN THE HISTORY OF LOGIC
(in chronological order)

Aristotle, *Aristotle's Categories and De Interpretatione*, translated by J. L. Ackrill, Oxford, 1963.

Aristotle, *Prior and Posterior Analytics*: A revised text with Introduction and Commentary by W. D. Ross, Oxford, 1949.

Aristotle, *Topica et Sophistici Elenchi*, W. D. Ross, ed., Oxford, 1958.

Abelard, Peter, *Dialectica*, L. M. de Rijd, ed., Assen, Netherlands, 1956.

William of Sherwood, Introductiones in Logicam—Treatise 6: 'On the Properties of Terms' (edited by Martin Grabmann in *Die Introductiones in Logicam des Wilhelm von Shyreswood*, Munich, 1937).

William of Sherwood, *Syncategoremata*, J. R. O'Donnel, ed., Medieval Studies, Notre Dame, Indiana, 1941.

William of Ockham, *Summa Logicae*, Philotheus Boehner, ed., New York, 1951–4.

Burleigh, Walter, *De Puritate Artis Logicae Tractatus Longior, with a Revised Edition of the Tractatus Brevior*, P. Boehner, ed., Franciscan Institute Publications, Text Series, No. 9, St Bonaventure, N.Y., 1955.

Leibniz, Gottfried Wilhelm, *Philosophical Papers and Letters*, Leroy Loemker, ed.,
Paper 24: On the General Characteristic (*c.* 1679),
Paper 26: Two Studies in the Logical Calculus (1679)
        1. Elements of Calculus
        2. Specimen of Universal Calculus
Paper 41: A Study in the Logical Calculus (*c.* 1690),
Dordrecht-Holland, 1969.

Boole, G., *The Mathematical Analysis of Logic*, Cambridge, 1847; reprinted, Oxford, 1948.

De Morgan, Augustus, 'On the Syllogism, No. IV, and on the Logic of Relations', *Transactions of the Cambridge Philosophical Society*, vol. 10 (1864).

Frege, Gottlob, *Begriffsschrift, eine der arithmetischen nachgebildete Formelsprache des reinen Denkens*, Halle, 1879.

Frege, Gottlob, *Die Grundlagen der Arithmetik, eine logisch-mathematische Untersuchung über den Begriff der Zahl*, Breslau, 1884.

Peirce, C. S., 'On the Algebra of Logic: Contribution to the Philosophy of Notation', *American Journal of Mathematics*, vol. 7 (1885).

Frege, Gottlob, *Grundgesetze der Arithmetik, begriffsschriftlich abgeleitet*, vol. 1, Jena, 1893.

Zermelo, Ernst, 'Beweis, dass jede Menge wohlgeordnet werden kann', *Mathematische Annalen*, vol. 59 (1904).

Hilbert, David, *Über die Grundlagen der Logik und der Arithmetik. Verhand-lungen des Dritten Internationalen Mathematiker-Kongresses in Heidelberg vom 8. bis 13. August 1904*, Leipzig, 1905.

Brouwer, L. E. J., 'De onbetrouwbaarheid der logische principes' (The untrust-worthiness of the principles of logic), *Tijdschrift voor wijsbegeerte*, vol. 2 (1908).

Russell, Bertrand, 'Mathematical Logic as based on the Theory of Types', *American Journal of Mathematics*, vol. 30 (1908).

Zermelo, Ernst, 'Untersuchungen über die Grundlagen der Mengenlehre I', *Mathematische Annalen*, vol. 65 (1908).

Russell, Bertrand, and Whitehead, A. N., *Principia Mathematica*, 3 vols., Cambridge, 1910–13; 2nd edition 1927.

Lesniewski, S., *Logical Studies* (in Russian), St Petersburg, 1913.

Sheffer, H. M., 'A Set of Five Independent Postulates for Boolean Algebras', *Transactions of the American Mathematical Society*, vol. 14 (1913).

Löwenheim, Leopold, 'Über Möglichkeiten im Relativkalkül', *Mathematische Annalen*, vol. 76 (1915).

Lesniewski, S., *Zasady ogólnej teorii mnogości*, 1 (Foundations of the General Theory of Sets), Moscow, 1916.

Post, E. L., 'Introduction to a General Theory of Elementary Propositions', *American Journal of Mathematics*, vol. 43 (1921).

Wittgenstein, Ludwig, 'Logisch-philosophische Abhandlung', *Annalen der Naturphilosophie* (1921). This was translated into English by C. K. Ogden in 1922 under the title *Tractatus Logico-philosophicus*. A new translation by D. F. Pears and B. F. McGuinness appeared in 1961, London and New York.

Schönfinkel, Moses, 'Über die Bausteine der mathematischen Logik', *Mathematische Annalen*, vol. 92 (1924). (This paper was the origin of Combinatory Logic. Schönfinkel became ill shortly after writing this paper and never developed a deductive theory. H. B. Curry was the first to do so.)

Bernays, Paul, and Schönfinkel, Moses, 'Zum Entscheidungsproblem der mathe-matischen Logik', *Mathematische Annalen*, vol. 99 (1928).

Gödel, Kurt, 'Die Vollständigkeit der Axiome des logischen Funktionen-kalküls', *Monatshefte für Mathematik und Physik*, vol. 37 (1930).

Herbrand, Jacques, 'Recherches sur la théorie de la démonstration', *Travaux de la Société des Sciences et des Lettres de Varsovie*, Classe III, No. 33 (1930).

Gödel, Kurt, 'Über formal unentscheidbare Sätze der Principia Mathematica und verwandter Systeme 1', *Monatshefte für Mathematik und Physik*, vol. 38 (1931). Translations in *The Undecidable*, Martin Davis, ed., New York, 1965, and in *From Frege to Gödel*, van Heijenoort, ed., Cambridge, Mass., 1967.

Tarski, Alfred, 'Pojecie Prawdy w Jezykach Dedukcyjnyck' (The Concept of

Truth in the Languages of the Deductive Sciences), *Travaux de la Société des Sciences et des Lettres de Varsovie*, Classe III (Sciences mathematiques et physiques), No. 34, Warsaw, 1933. This was translated into German in *Studia Philosophica*, vol. 1, 1936. An English translation by J. H. Woodger appears in *Alfred Tarski: Logic, Semantics and Metamathematics*, Oxford, 1956.

Carnap, Rudolf, *Logische Syntax der Sprache*, Vienna, 1934. Translated by Amethe Smeaton, with revisions, as *The Logical Syntax of Language*, New York and London, 1937.

Gentzen, Gerhard, 'Untersuchungen über das logische Schliessen', *Mathematische Zeitschrift*, vol. 39 (1934–5).

Heyting, Arend, *Mathematische Grundlagenforschung, Intuitionismus, Beweistheorie*, Berlin, 1934.

Jaskowski, Stanislaw, 'On the Rules of Suppositions in Formal Logic', *Studia Logica*, No. 1 (Warsaw, 1934).

Church, Alonzo, 'A Note on the Entscheidungsproblem', *Journal of Symbolic Logic*, vol. 1 (1936).

Henkin, Leon, 'Completeness in the Theory of Types', *Journal of Symbolic Logic*, vol. 15 (1950).

Ackermann, Wilhelm, *Solvable Cases of the Decision Problem*, Amsterdam, 1954.

2. BIBLIOGRAPHY OF THE HISTORY OF LOGIC

(a) General Treatises

Beth, E. W., 'Hundred Years of Symbolic Logic', *Dialectica*, 1 (1947).

Beth, E. W., 'The Origin and Growth of Symbolic Logic', *Synthese*, 6 (1947–8).

Bochenski, J. M., O.P., 'L'état et les besoins de l'histoire de la logique formelle', *Proceedings of the Tenth International Congress of Philosophy*, vol. 1, part 2, Amsterdam, 1949.

Bochenski, J. M., O.P., *A History of Formal Logic*, translated and edited by Ivo Thomas, Notre Dame, Indiana, 1961.

Bochenski, J. M., O.P., 'Notes historiques sur les propositions modales', *Revue des sciences philosophiques et théologiques*, 26 (1937).

Bochenski, J. M., O.P., 'Notiones historiae logicae formalis', *Angelicum*, 13 (1936).

Church, Alonzo, Brief bibliography of formal logic, in *Proceedings of the American Academy of Arts and Sciences*, 80 (1952).

Kneale, William, and Kneale, Martha, *The Development of Logic*, Oxford, 1962.

Kotarbinski, Tadeusz, *Wyklady z Dziejón Logiki* (Lessons in the History of Logic), Warsaw, 1957, translated into French as *Leçons sur l'histoire de la logique*, Warsaw and Paris, 1964.

Lewis, C. I., *A Survey of Symbolic Logic*, Berkeley, 1918.

Lukasiewicz, Jan, 'Zur Geschichte der Aussagenlogik', *Erkenntnis*, 5 (1935).

Nidditch, P. H., *The Development of Mathematical Logic*, London, 1962.

Scholz, Heinrich, *Geschichte der Logik*, Berlin, 1931.

Scholz, Heinrich, *Geschichte der Logik: Geschichte der Philosophie in Längsschnitten*, Heft 4, Berlin, 1931.

Wang, H., *A Survey of Mathematical Logic*, Pekin, 1962, and Amsterdam, 1963.

(b) Ancient Logic

Texts (in chronological order)

Aristotle, *Categoriae et Liber de Interpretatione*, L. Minio-Paluello, ed., Oxford, 1949.

Aristotle, *Aristotle's Categories and De Interpretatione*, translated by J. L. Ackrill, Oxford, 1963.

Aristotle, *Aristotle's Metaphysics*: A revised text with Introduction and Commentary by W. D. Ross, Oxford, 1924.

Aristotle, *Aristotle's Prior and Posterior Analytics*: A revised text with Introduction and Commentary by W. D. Ross, Oxford, 1949.

Aristotle, *Topica et Sophistici Elenchi*, W. D. Ross, ed., Oxford, 1958.

Stoicorum Veterum Fragmenta, H. von Arnim, ed., 4 vols., Leipzig, 1903–24.

Galen's Institutio Logica, English translation, Introduction and Commentary by John S. Kieffer, Baltimore, 1964.

Boethius, *Opera Omnia*, ii, J. P. Migne, ed., Patrologia Latina, lxiv, Paris, 1860.

Minio-Paluello, L., *The genuine text of Boethius' translation of Aristotle's Categories*, Medieval and Renaissance Studies, 1, 1943.

Philodemus, *On Methods of Inference*, P. and E. A. De Lacy, eds., Lancaster, Pa., 1941.

Minio-Paluello, L., 'Gli Elenchi Sofistici: redazioni contaminate . . ., frammenti dell'ignoto commento d'Alessandro d'Afrodisia tradotti in latino', *Rivista di Filosofia Neosc.*, 46, 1954.

Secondary Sources

Bochenski, J. M., o.p., *Ancient Formal Logic*, Amsterdam, 1951.

Bochenski, J. M., o.p., *Elementa Logicae Graecae*, Rome: Anonima Libraria Cattolica Italiana, 1937.

Bochenski, J. M., o.p., *La Logique de Théophraste*, Collectanea Friburgensia, n.s. fasc. xxxvii, Fribourg, 1947.

Bochenski, J. M., o.p., 'Non-Analytical Laws and Rules in Aristotle', *Methodos*, 3 (1951).

Dürr, K., *The Propositional logic of Boethius*, Amsterdam, 1951.

Kapp, E., *Greek Foundations of Traditional Logic*, New York, 1942.

Mates, Benson, *Stoic Logic*, Berkeley and Los Angeles, 1961.

Miller, J. W., *The Structure of Aristotle's logic*, London, 1938.

Patzig, G., 'Die Aristotelische Syllogistik', *Abhandlungen der Akademie der Wissenschaften in Göttingen*, Phil. Hist. Klasse III, No. 42, Göttingen (1959).

Porphyry, *Isagoge et in Aristotelis Categorias Commentarium*, A. Busse, ed., Commentaria in Aristotelem Graeca, iv (i), Berlin, 1887.

Ross, W. D., *Aristotle*, 5th ed., London, 1968.

Ross, W. D., 'The Discovery of the Syllogism', *Philosophical Review*, 48 (1939).

Solmsen, Fr., 'The Discovery of the Syllogism', *Philosophical Review*, 50 (1941).

Stocks, J. L., 'The Composition of Aristotle's Logical Works', *Classical Quarterly* (1933).

Thomas de Vio Caietanus, *Commentaria in Porphyrii Isagogen ad Praedicamenta Aristotelis*, I. M. Marega, ed., Rome, 1934.

Thomas de Vio Caietanus, *Commentaria in Praedicamenta Aristotelis*, M. H. Laurent, ed., Rome, 1939.

(c) Medieval Logic

Texts (in chronological order)

Avicenna, *La logique du fils de Sina, communement appelé Avicenne*, translated by Vattier, Paris, 1658.

Anselm of Canterbury, *Monologion, Proslogion* and *De Veritate, Opera Omnia*, i, F. S. Schmitt, ed., Edinburgh, 1946.

Abelard, Peter, *Abaelardiana Inedita*, L. Minio-Paluello, ed., Twelfth Century Logic: Texts and Studies, ii, Rome, 1958.

Abelard, Peter, *Dialectica*, L. M. de Rijk, ed., Assen, 1956.

Adam of Balsham, *Adam Balsamiensis Parvipontani Ars Disserendi (Dialectica Alexandri)*, L. Minio-Paluello, ed., Twelfth Century Logic: Texts and Studies, i, Rome, 1956.

John of Salisbury, *Metalogicon*, C. C. J. Webb, ed., Oxford, 1929.

John of Salisbury (Saresberiensis), *The Metalogicon of John of Salisbury*, translated with an Introduction by D. D. McGarry, Berkeley, 1955.

William of Sherwood, *Die Introductiones in Logicam des Wilhelm von Shyreswood*, M. Grabmann, ed.; *Sitzungsberichte der Bayerischen Akademie der Wissenschaften, Phil.Hist.Abteilung*, Jahrgang 1937, Heft 10, Munich, 1937.

William of Sherwood, Introductiones in Logicam—Treatise 6: 'On the Properties of Terms' (edited by Martin Grabmann in *Die Introductiones in Logicam des Wilhelm von Shyreswood*; Munich, 1937).

William of Sherwood, *Syncategoremata*, J. R. O'Donnell, ed., Medieval Studies, Notre Dame, Indiana, 1941.

Peter of Spain, *Petri Hispani Summulae Logicales*, J. M. Bochenski, ed., Rome: Domus Editorialis Marietti, 1947.

Mullalley, Joseph P., *The Summulae Logicales of Peter of Spain*, Medieval Studies 8, Notre Dame, Indiana, 1945.

William of Ockham, *Summa Logicae*, Philotheus Boehner, ed., New York, 1951–4.

Boehner, P., ed., *The Tractatus de praedestinatione et de praescientia dei et de futuris contingentibus of William Ockham*, with a study by the editor on the medieval problem of three-valued logic, Louvain, 1945. English translation by Adams and Kretzmann, New York, 1969.

Burleigh, Walter, *De Puritate Artis Logicae Tractatus Longior, with a Revised Edition of the Tractatus Brevior*, P. Boehner, ed., Franciscan Institute Publications, Text Series, No. 9, St Bonaventure, N.Y., 1955.

Buridan, Jean, *Sophismata*, Paris, undated, per Johannem Lambert impressa.

Buridan, John, *Sophisms on Meaning and Truth*, New York, 1966.

Paul of Venice, *Logica Magna*, Venice, 1499.

Ralph Strode, Richard Ferabrich and William Heytesbury, *Consequentiae Strodi cum Commento Alexandri Sermonetae*, Venice, 1517.

Nelson, N., *Peter Ramus and the Confusion of Logic, Rhetoric and Poetic*, Michigan, 1947.

Johannes a Sancto Thoma, *Ars Logica*, B. Reiser, ed., Turin, 1930.

Secondary Sources

Bochenski, J. M., o.p., 'De consequentiis Scholasticorum earumque origine', *Angelicum*, 15 (1938)

Bochenski, J. M., o.p., 'Duae consequentiae Stephani de Monte', *Angelicum*, 12 (1935).

Bochenski, J. M., o.p., 'Sancti Thomae Aquinatis de Modalibus opusculum et doctrina', *Angelicum*, 17 (1940).

Boehner, P., *Medieval Logic, An Outline of its Development from 1250– c. 1400*, Manchester, 1952.

De Rijk, L. M., *Logica Modernorum, a Contribution to the History of Early Terminist Logic*, i, Assen, 1962.

Doyle, J., 'John of St. Thomas and Mathematical Logic', *The New Scholasticism*, 27 (1953).

Grabmann, Martin, 'Bearbeitungen und Auslegungen der aristotelischen Logik aus der Zeit von Peter Abaelard bis Petrus Hispanus', *Abhandlungen der Preussischen Akademie der Wissenschaften*, Phil-hist.Klasse Nr. 5 (1937).

Kristeller, P. O., *Latin Manuscript Books before 1600*, New York, 1948.

Lachance, J., 'Saint Thomas dans l'histoire de la logique', *Et. d'hist. littér. et doctr. du XIIIe siècle*, 1, 1932.

Moody, E. A., *The Logic of William of Ockham*, New York and London, 1935.

Moody, E. A., *Truth and Consequence in Mediaeval Logic*, Amsterdam, 1953.

Ong, W. J., *Ramus, Method and the Decay of Dialogue*, Cambridge, Mass., 1958.

Salamucha, Joseph, 'Die Aussagenlogik bei Wilhelm Ockham', *Franzis- kanische Studien*, 32 (1950).

Styazhkin, N. I., *Elements of the algebra of logic and the theory of semantic antinomies in later medieval logic*, Logicheskie issledovaniya (Studies in logic), Moscow, 1959.

Wilson, C., *Medieval Logic and the Rise of Mathematical Physics*, Madison, Wisconsin, 1956.

(d) Period between Medieval and Modern Logic

Texts (in chronological order)

John of St. Thomas, *The Material Logic of John of St. Thomas: Basic Treatises*, translated by Simon, Glanville and Hollenhorst, Chicago, 1955.

Leibniz, Gottfried Wilhelm, *Logical Papers*, translated by G. H. R. Parkinson, Oxford, 1966.

Junge, J., *Logica Hamburgensis*, Hamburg, 1638; reprinted 1957.

Arnauld, A., and Nicole, P., *La logique ou l'art de penser*, Paris, 1662, Amsterdam 1675, Paris, 1752.

Leibniz, Gottfried Wilhelm, *Philosophical Papers and Letters*, L. E. Loemker, ed.,
Paper 24: On the General Characteristic (*c.* 1679)

Paper 26: Two Studies in the Logical Calculus (1679)
        1. Elements of Calculus
        2. Specimen of Universal Calculus
Paper 41: A Study in the Logical Calculus (*c.* 1690),
Dordrecht-Holland, 1969.

Aldrich, H., *Artis Logicae Compendium*, Oxford, 1691.

Leibniz, Gottfried Wilhelm, *Opera Omnia*, 6 vols., L. Dutens, ed., Geneva, 1768.

Bolzano, Bernard, *Theory of Science*, translated by Rolf George, Oxford, 1972.

Mill, J. S., *A System of Logic, Ratiocinative and Inductive, being a Connected View of the Principles of Evidence and the Methods of Scientific Investigation*, London, 1843.

Hamilton, Sir William, *Lectures on Logic*, 2 vols., H. L. Mansel and J. Veitch, eds., Edinburgh, 1860.

Jevons, W. S., *Pure logic, or the logic of quality apart from quantity: with remarks on Boole's system and on the relation of logic and mathematics*, London, 1864.

Keynes, J. N., *Studies and Exercises in Formal Logic*, London and New York, 1884; last ed., 1906.

Secondary Sources

Bar-Hillel, Yehoshua, 'Bolzano's Propositional Logic', *Archiv für mathematische Logik und Grundlagenforschung*, vol. 1 (1952).

Berg, J., *Bolzano's Logic*, Stockholm Studies in Philosophy, 2, Stockholm, 1962.

Couturat, L., *La Logique de Leibniz d'après des documents inédits*, Paris, 1901.

Jourdain, P. E. B., 'The logical work of Leibniz', *The Monist*, 26 (1916).

(e) Modern Logic

Texts (in chronological order)

Boole, G., *The Mathematical Analysis of Logic*, Cambridge, 1847. Reprinted, Oxford, 1948.

De Morgan, Augustus, *Formal logic or the calculus of inference, necessary and probable*, London, 1847; new edition (by A. E. Taylor), Chicago and London, 1926.

Boole, G., *An Investigation of the Laws of Thought, on which are founded the Mathematical Theory of Logic and Probabilities*, London, 1854.

Boole, G., *Studies in Logic and Probability*, R. Rhees, ed., London, 1952.

De Morgan, Augustus, *On the Syllogism and Other Logical Writings*, Péter Heath, ed., London, 1965.

De Morgan, Augustus, 'On the Symbols of Logic, the Theory of Syllogism, and in particular of the Copula, and the Application of the Theory of Probabilities to some Questions of Evidence', *Transactions of the Cambridge Philosophical Society*, vol. 9 (1856).

De Morgan, Augustus, 'On the Syllogism, No. iii, and on Logic in General', *Transactions of the Cambridge Philosophical Society*, vol. 10 (1864).

De Morgan, Augustus, 'On the syllogism, No. iv, and on the logic of relations', *Transactions of the Cambridge Philosophical Society*, vol. 10 (1864).

De Morgan, Augustus, *Syllabus of a Proposed System of Logic*, 1860.

De Morgan, Augustus, *Formal Logic*, London, 1926.

Schröder, Ernst, *Der Operationskreis des Logikkalküls*, Leipzig, 1877.

Van Heijenoort, Jean, ed., *From Frege to Gödel, A Source Book of Mathematical Logic 1879–1931*, Cambridge, Mass., 1967.

Frege, Gottlob, *Begriffsschrift, eine der arithmetischen nachgebildete Formelsprache des reinen Denkens*, Halle, 1879.

Frege, Gottlob, *Conceptual Notation and Related Articles*, translated and edited with a biography and introduction by Terrell Ward Bynum, Oxford, 1972.

Peirce, C. S., 'On the Algebra of Logic: Contribution to the philosophy of Notation', *American Journal of Mathematics*, vol. 7 (1885).

Peirce, C. S., 'On the Algebra of Logic: A Contribution to the Philosophy of Notation', Paper 13 of *Collected Papers*, vol. III, Cambridge, Mass., 1931–58.

Geach, Peter and Black, Max, *Translations from the Philosophical Writings of Gottlob Frege*, Oxford, 1960.

Frege, Gottlob, *Die Grundlagen der Arithmetik, eine logisch-mathematische Untersuchung über den Begriff der Zahl*, Breslau, 1884.

Frege, Gottlob, *The Foundations of Arithmetic*, translated by Austin, J. L., Oxford, 1959.

Peano, Giuseppe, *Arithmetices principia, nova methodo exposita*, Turin, 1889.

Schröder, Ernst, *Vorlesungen über die Algebra der Logik* (*exakte Logik*), vol. 1, Leipzig, 1890.

Schröder, Ernst, *Vorlesungen über die Algebra der Logik*, Leipzig, 1890–95.

Schröder, Ernst, *Vorlesungen über die Algebra der Logik* (*exakte Logik*), vol. 2, part 1, Leipzig, 1891.

Peano, Guisseppe, 'Sul Concetto di Numero', *Rivista di Matematica* (Turin), vol. 1 (1891).

Frege, Gottlob, *Grundgesetze der Arithmetik, begriffsschriftlich abgeleitet*, vol. I, Jena, 1893, vol. II, 1903.

Peano, Giuseppe, *Notations de logique mathématique. Introduction au Formulaire de Mathématique*, Turin, 1894.

Schröder, Ernst, *Vorlesungen über die Algebra der Logik* (*exakte Logik*), vol. 3: *Algebra und Logik der Relative*, part 1, Leipzig, 1895.

Peano, Giusseppe, *Formulaire de Mathématique*, 5 vols., Turin, 1895–1905.

Burali-Forti, Cesare, 'Una questione sui numeri transfiniti', *Rend. di Palermo*, vol. 11 (1897).

Peano, Giusseppe, *Opere Scelte*, ii, U. Cassina, ed., Rome, 1958.

Peano, Giusseppe, *Studii di logica matematica*, Atti Acad., Torin, vol. 32 (1897).

Whitehead, A. N., *The Algebra of Symbolic Logic: A Treatise of Universal Algebra with Applications*, Cambridge, 1898.

Husserl, Edmund, *Logical Investigations* (2 vols.), London, 1970.

Russell, Bertrand, *Logic and Knowledge, Essays 1901–1950*, R. C. Marsh, ed., London, 1956.

Frege, Gottlob, *Grundgesetze der Arithmetik, begriffsschriftlich abgeleitet*, vol. 2, Jena, 1903.

Russell, Bertrand, *The Principles of Mathematics*, vol. 1, Cambridge, 1903.

Huntington, E. V., 'Sets of independent postulates for the algebra of logic', *Transactions of the American Mathematical Society*, vol. 5 (1904).

Zermelo, Ernst, 'Beweis, dass jede Menge wohlgeordnet werden kann', *Mathematische Annalen*, vol. 59 (1904).

Hilbert, David, *Über die Grundlagen der Logik und der Arithmetik. Verhandlungen des Dritten Internationalen Mathematiker-Kongresses in Heidelberg vom 8. bis 13. August 1904*, Leipzig, 1905.

Hadamard, Jacques, 'Cinq lettres sur la theorie des ensembles', *Bulletin de la Société Mathématique de France*, vol. 33 (1905).

Richard, Jules, 'Les principes des mathématiques et le problème des ensembles', *Revue générale des sciences pures et appliquées*, vol. 16 (1905).

Russell, Bertrand, *Logic and Knowledge*, R. C. Marsh, ed., London, 1956. Contains his papers 'On Denoting' (1905), 'Mathematical Knowledge as based on the Theory of Types' (1908), 'The Philosophy of Logical Atomism' (1918) and 'Logical Atomism' (1924).

McColl, H., *Symbolic Logic and its Applications*, London, 1906.

Brouwer, L. E. J., *Over de grondslagen der wiskunde* (On the foundations of mathematics), Dissertation, Amsterdam and Leipzig, 1907.

Richard, Jules, 'Sur la logique et la notion de nombre entier', *L'Ens. math.*, vol. 9 (1907).

Brouwer, L. E. J., 'De onbetrouwbaarheid der logische principes' (The untrustworthiness of the principles of logic), *Tijdschrift voor wijsbegeerte*, vol. 2 (1908).

Russell, Bertrand, 'Mathematical Logic as Based on the Theory of Types', *American Journal of Mathematics*, vol. 30 (1908).

Zermelo, Ernst, 'Untersuchungen über die Grundlagen der Mengenlehre 1', *Mathematische Annalen*, vol. 65 (1908).

Russell, Bertrand, and Whitehead, A. N., *Principia Mathematica*, 3 vols., Cambridge, 1910–13; 2nd edition, 1927.

Brouwer, L. E. J., *Intuitionisme en formalisme*, Groningen, 1912.

Chwistek, Leon, *Zasada sprzeczności w świetle nowszych badań Bertranda Russella* (The Principle of contradiction in the light of recent investigations of Bertrand Russell), Kraków, 1912.

Lewis, C. I., 'Implication and the Algebra of Logic', *Mind*, vol. 21 (1912).

Lewis, C. I., 'Interesting Theorems in Symbolic Logic', *Journal of Philosophy*, vol. 10 (1913).

Lesniewski, S., *Logical Studies* (in Russian), St Petersburg, 1913.

Sheffer, H. M., 'A Set of Five Independent Postulates for Boolean Algebras, with Application to Logical Constants', *Transactions of the American Mathematical Society*, vol. 14 (1913).

Wittgenstein, Ludwig, *Notebooks 1914–1916*, translated by G. E. M. Anscombe, Oxford, 1969.

Löwenheim, Leopold, 'Über Möglichkeiten im Relativkalkül', *Mathematische Annalen*, vol. 76 (1915).

Lesniewski, S., *Zasady ogolnej teorii mnogosci.* 1 (Foundations of the General Theory of Sets), Moscow, 1916.

Nicod, J. G. P., 'A Reduction in the Number of the Primitive Propositions of Logic', *Proceedings of the Cambridge Philosophical Society*, 19 (1917–20).

Brouwer, L. E. J., *Begründung der Mengenlehre unabhängig vom logischen Satz vom ausgeschlossenen Dritten. Erster Teil: Allgemeine Mengenlehre*, Amsterdam, 1918.

Hilbert, David, 'Axiomatisches Denken', *Mathematische Annalen*, vol. 78 (1918).

Lewis, C. I., *A Survey of Symbolic Logic*, Berkeley, Cal., 1918.

Lukasiewicz, Jan, 'O logice trojwartosciowej' (On the Three-Valued Logic), *Ruch Filozoficzny*, V, 1919, 1920.

Russell, Bertrand, *Introduction to Mathematical Philosophy*, London, 1919.

Lewis, C. I., 'Strict Implication—an Emendation', *Journal of Philosophy*, vol. 17 (1920).

Chwistek, Leon, 'Antynomje Logiki Formalmej' (Antinomies of Formal Logic), *Przeglad Filozoficzny*, vol. 24 (1921).

Post, E. L., 'Introduction to a General Theory of Elementary Propositions', *American Journal of Mathematics*, 43 (1921).

Sheffer, H. M., 'The General Theory of Notational Relativity', 1921 (unpublished).

Wittgenstein, Ludwig, *Tractatus Logico-Philosophicus*, London, 1922.

Wittgenstein, Ludwig, *Prototractatus: An Early Version of Tractatus Logico-Philosophicus by Ludwig Wittgenstein*, edited and translated by McGuinness, Nyberg, von Wright, Pears, London, 1971.

Hilbert, David, 'Neubegründung der Mathematik', *Abhandlungen aus dem Mathematischen Seminar der Hamburgischen Universität*, vol. 1 (1922).

Lukasiewicz, Jan, 'Interpretacja liczbowa teorii Zdan' (Numerical Interpretation of the Theory of Propositions), *Ruch Filozoficzny*, VII, 1922/23.

Chwistek, Leon, 'The theory of constructive types (Principles of logic and mathematics)', *Annales de la Société Polonaise de Mathématique*, vol. 2 (1924).

Schönfinkel, Moses, 'Über die Bausteine der mathematischen Logik', *Mathematische Annalen*, vol. 92 (1924).

Fraenkel, Adolf, 'Untersuchungen über die Grundlagen der Mengenlehre', *Mathematische Zeitschrift*, vol. 22 (1925).

Ramsey, F. P., Review of Whitehead and Russell's *Principia Mathematica*, 2nd edn., vol. 1, *Nature*, vol. 116 (1925).

Chwistek, Leon, 'Über die Hypothesen der Mengenlehre', *Mathematische Zeitschrift*, vol. 25 (1926).

Hilbert, David, 'Über das Unendliche', *Mathematische Annalen*, vol. 95 (1926).

Sheffer, H. M., 'Notational Relativity', *Proceedings of the Sixth International Congress of Philosophy*, New York, 1927.

Bernays, Paul, and Schönfinkel, Moses, 'Zum Entscheidungsproblem der mathematischen Logik', *Mathematische Annalen*, vol. 99 (1928).

Brouwer, L. E. J., *Intuitionistische Betrachtungen über den Formalismus*, Sitzungsberichte der Preussischen Akademie der Wissenschaften, 1928.

Husserl, Edmund, *The Paris Lectures*, translated with Introductory essay by Peter Koestenbaum, The Hague, 1970.

Lesniewski, S., 'Grundzüge eines neuen Systems der Grundlagen der Mathematik', *Fund. math.*, 14, 1929.

Curry, H. B., 'Grundlagen der kombinatorischen Logik', *American Journal of Mathematics*, vol. 52 (1930).

Gödel, Kurt, 'Die Vollständigkeit der Axiome des logischen Funktionenkalküls', *Monatshefte für Mathematik und Physik*, vol. 37 (1930).

Herbrand, Jacques, 'Recherches sur la théorie de la démonstration', *Travaux de la Société des Sciences et des Lettres de Varsovie*, Classe III (Sciences Mathématiques et Physiques), No. 33, 1930.

Heyting, Arend, 'Die formalen Regeln der intuitionistischen Mathematik', *Sitzungsberichte der Preussischen Akademie der Wissenschaften*, Physikalisch-mathematische Klasse, 1930.

Lesniewski, S., 'Über die Grundlagen der Ontologie', *Comptes rendus des séances de la Société des Sciences et des Lettres de Varsovie*, Classe III, Vol. 23 (1930).

Tarski, Alfred, 'Fundamentale Begriffe der Methodologie der deductiven Wissenschaften', I, *Monatshefte für Mathematik und Physik*, vol. 37 (1930). English translation in *Logic, Semantics and Metamathematics*, Oxford, 1956.

Gödel, Kurt, *On Formally Undecidable Propositions of Principia Mathematica and Related Systems*, translated by B. Melzer, with an Introduction by R. B. Braithwaite, Edinburgh, 1962.

Peirce, C. S., *Collected Papers*, 8 vols., C. Hartshorne, P. Weiss and A. W. Burks, eds., Cambridge, Mass., 1931–58.

Ramsey, F. P., *The Foundations of Mathematics and Other Logical Essays*, R. B. Braithwaite, ed., New York and London, 1931.

Church, Alonzo, 'A Set of Postulates for the Foundation of Logic', *Annals of Mathematics*, vol. 33 (1932).

Gentzen, Gerhard, 'Über die Existenz unabhängiger Axiomensysteme zu unendlichen Satzsystemen', *Mathematische Annalen*, vol. 107 (1932).

Church, Alonzo, 'A Set of Postulates for the Foundation of Logic' (Second paper), *Annals of Mathematics*, vol. 34 (1933).

Curry, H. B., 'Apparent Variables from the Standpoint of Combinatory Logic', *Annals of Mathematics*, vol. 34 (1933).

Gödel, Kurt, 'Zur intuitionistischen Arithmetik und Zahlentheorie', *Ergebnisse eines mathematischen Kolloquiums*, Heft 4 (1933).

Tarski, Alfred, 'Pojecie Prawdy w Jezykach Dedukcyjnyck' (The Concept of Truth in the Languages of the Deductive Sciences), *Travaux de la Société des Sciences et des Lettres de Varsovie*, Classe III (Sciences mathematiques et physiques), No. 34, Warsaw, 1933. This was translated into German in *Studia Philosophica*, Vol. 1, 1936. An English translation by J. H. Woodger appears in *Alfred Tarski: Logic, Semantics and Metamathematics*, Oxford, 1956.

Wittgenstein, Ludwig, *The Blue and Brown Books*, Oxford, 1969.

Carnap, Rudolf, *Logische Syntax der Sprache*, Vienna, 1934. Translated by Amethe Smeaton, with revisions, as *The Logical Syntax of Language*, New York and London, 1937.

Gentzen, Gerhard, 'Untersuchungen über das logische Schliessen', *Mathematische Zeitschrift*, 39 (1934).

Heyting, Arend, *Mathematische Grundlagenforschung. Intuitionismus. Beweistheorie*, Berlin, 1934.

Hilbert, D., and Bernays, P., *Grundlagen der Mathematik*, Berlin, vol. 1: 1934, vol. 2: 1939 (both vols. reprinted: Ann Arbor, Michigan, 1944).

Jaśkowski, Stanislaw, 'On the Rules of Suppositions in Formal Logic', *Studia logica*, No. 1 (Warsaw 1934).

Lukasiewicz, Jan, 'Z historii logiki Zdan' (On the History of the Logic of Propositions), *Przeglad Filozoficzny* (Philosophical Review), 1934.

Church, Alonzo, 'A Note on the Entscheidungsproblem', *Journal of Symbolic Logic*, vol. 1 (1936).

Wittgenstein, Ludwig, *Remarks on the Foundations of Mathematics*, translated by G. E. M. Anscombe, Oxford, 1967.

Tarski, Alfred, 'The Semantic Conception of Truth', *Philosophy and Phenomenological Research*, 4 (1944).

Tarski, Alfred, 'The Semantic Conception of Truth', *Readings in Philosophical Analysis*, New York, 1949.

Hilbert, D., and Ackermann, W., *Grundzüge der theoretischen Logik*, New York, 1949.

Austin, J. L., *Philosophical Papers*, Urmson and Warnock, eds., Oxford, 1970.

Henkin, Leon, 'Completeness in the Theory of Types', *Journal of Symbolic Logic*, vol. 15 (1950).

Wittgenstein, Ludwig, *Philosophical Investigations*, translated by G. E. M. Anscombe, Oxford, 1953.

Ackermann, Wilhelm, *Solvable Cases of the Decision Problem*, Amsterdam, 1954.

Austin, J. L., *How to do things with Words* (The William James Lectures delivered in Harvard University in 1955), Oxford, 1962.

Russell, Bertrand, *An Inquiry into Meaning and Truth*, London, 1963.

Russell, Bertrand, *My Philosophical Development*, London, 1969.

Secondary Sources

Ambrose, Alice and Lazerowitz, Morris, *Ludwig Wittgenstein: Philosophy and Language*, London, 1972.

Anschutz, R. P., *The Philosophy of J. S. Mill*, Oxford, 1953.

Anscombe, G. E. M., *An Introduction to Wittgenstein's Tractatus*, London, 1959.

Anscombe, G. E. M. and Geach, P. T., *Three Philosophers*, Oxford, 1961.

Bernstein, Richard, ed., *Perspectives on Peirce*, Yale University Press, New Haven, Conn., 1965.

Beth, E. W., 'Hundred Years of Symbolic Logic', *Dialectia*, 1 (1947).

Beth, E. W., 'The Origin and Growth of Symbolic Logic', *Journal of Symbolic Logic*, 13 (1848).

Black, Max, *A Companion to Wittgenstein's Tractatus*, Cambridge, 1964.

Boehner, Philotheus, *Medieval Logic*, Manchester University Press, 1952.

Bogan, James, *Wittgenstein's Philosophy of Language*, London, 1972.

Boll, M., and Reinhart, J., 'Logic in France in the Twentieth century', *Philosophic thought in France and the United States*, M. Farber, ed., Buffalo, 1950.

Briere, O., s.j., *Fifty years of Chinese Philosophy 1898–1950*, London, 1956.

Copi, Irving, and Beard, Robert, eds., *Essays on Wittgenstein's Tractatus*, London, 1966.

De Mauro, Tullio, *Ludwig Wittgenstein: His Place in the Development of Semantics*, Dordrecht-Holland, 1967.

Fann, K. T., *Wittgenstein's Conception of Philosophy*, Oxford, 1969.

Furbery, Mats, *Saying and Meaning: A Main Theme in J. L. Austin's Philosophy*, Oxford, 1971.

Fumagalli, Maria Teresa Bronio-Brocchieri, *The Logic of Abelard*, Dordrecht-Holland, 1969.

Goodstein, R. L., *Development of Mathematical Logic*, London, 1971.

Griffin, James, *Wittgenstein's Logical Atomism*, Oxford, 1964.

Hallett, Garth, *Wittgenstein's Definition of Meaning as Use*, New York, 1967.

Hartnack, Justus, *Wittgenstein and Modern Philosophy*, London, 1962.

Henry, Desmond Paul, *The Logic of Saint Anselm*, Oxford, 1967.

Hesse, M. B., 'Boole's Philosophy of Logic', *Annals of Science* (London), 8, 1952.

Howell, Wilbur Samuel, *Eighteenth-Century British Logic and Rhetoric*, Princeton, New Jersey, 1971.

Howell, Wilbur Samuel, *Logic and Rhetoric in England, 1500–1700*, New York, 1961.

Hu Shih, *The Development of the Logical Method in Ancient China*, New York, 1968.

Jackson, Reginald, *An Examination of the Deductive Logic of John Stuart Mill*, London, 1941.

Jordan, Z., *The Development of Mathematical Logic and of Logical Positivism in Poland between Two Wars* (Polish Science and Learning, 1945, Number 6), New York, Oxford University Press.

Kneale, William, 'Boole and the Revival of Logic', *Mind* 57 (1948)

Lejewski, Czeslaw, 'On Lesniewski's Ontology', *Ratio*, vol. 1 (1958).

Luschei, E. C., *The Logical Systems of Lesniewski*, Amsterdam, 1962.

McGuinness, B. F., 'The Mysticism of the Tractatus', *The Philosophical Review*, 75 (1966).

Malcolm, Norman, *Ludwig Wittgenstein, a Memoir*, London, 1966.

Metz, R., 'Mathematical Logic', *A Hundred Years of British Philosophy*, New York and London, 1938.

Muirhead, J. M., ed., *Contemporary British Philosophy*, 1st and 2nd series, London, 1965.

Nidditch, P. H., *The Development of Mathematical Logic*, London, 1962.

Pitcher, George, *The Philosophy of Wittgenstein*, New Jersey, 1964.

Pitcher, George, ed., *Wittgenstein: the Philosophical Investigations*, London, 1968.

Pole, David, *The Later Philosophy of Wittgenstein*, London, 1958.

Potter, Vincent, *Charles S. Peirce on Norms and Ideals*, Amherst, Mass., 1967.

Raju, P. T., *The Philosophical Traditions of India*, London, 1971.

Ramsey, F. P., Critical notice of Ludwig Wittgenstein's *Tractatus Logico-Philosophicus*, *Mind*, 32 (1923).

Rhees, R., *Discussions of Wittgenstein*, London, 1970.

Royal Irish Academy, 'Celebration of the Century of *The Laws of Thought* by George Boole', *Proceedings of the Royal Irish Academy*, 57, A, 6, 1955.

Russell, Bertrand, *A Critical Exposition of the Philosophy of Leibniz*, London, 1967.

Shwayder, D. S., *Wittgenstein's Tractatus: a Historical and Critical Commentary*, unpublished D.Phil. dissertation, Oxford, 1954.

Skolimowski, Henryk, *Polish Analytical Philosophy*, A Survey and a Comparison with British Analytical Philosophy, London, 1967.

Sobocinski, B., 'In Memoriam Jan Lukaziewicz', *Philosophical Studies* (National University of Ireland), vol. 6 (1956).

Specht, Ernst Konrad, *The Foundations of Wittgenstein's Late Philosophy*, Manchester, 1969.

Stenius, E., and Stegmüller, W., *Wittgenstein's Tractatus: a Critical Exposition of its Main Lines of Thought*, Oxford, 1960.

Sternfeld, Robert, *Frege's Logical Theory*, Illinois, 1966.

Styazhkin, J. I., *History of Mathematical Logic from Leibniz to Peano* (translated from the Russian), Cambridge, Mass., 1969.

Thiel, Christian, *Sense and Reference in Frege's Logic*, Dordrecht-Holland, 1965.

Thomas, I., 'Introductory Notes to Modern Logic', *Blackfriars*, 33 (1952).

Thomas, I., 'Logica moderna y logica clasica', *Estudios filos.*, 3 (1953).

Urmson, J. O., *Philosophical Analysis, Its Development between the two World Wars*, London, 1969.

Van Peursen, C. A., *Leibniz*, London, 1969.

Van Peursen, C. A., *Ludwig Wittgenstein: an Introduction to his Philosophy*, London, 1969.

Von Wright, Georg H., 'Special Supplement: the Wittgenstein Papers', *Philosophical Review*, 78 (1969).

Walker, Jeremy D. B., *A Study of Frege*, Oxford, 1965.

Watling, John, *Bertrand Russell*, Edinburgh, 1970.

Winch, Peter, ed., *Studies in the Philosophy of Wittgenstein*, London, 1969.

Wittgenstein, Ludwig, *Ausgewählte Konkordanz zu Wittgensteins Philosophischen Untersuchungen* (Zusammengestellt von Alastair McKinner), Oxford, 1972.

Wrenpohl, Paul, 'Wittgenstein and the Naming Relation', reprint from *Inquiry*, No. 4 (Winter, 1964).

(f) Non-Western Logic

Fung, Yu-lan, *A History of Chinese Philosophy*, translated by Derk Bodde, vol. 1, Princeton, 1952.

Ingalls, D. H. H., *Materials for the Study of Navya-Nyāya Logic*, Cambridge, Mass., and London, 1951.

Ingalls, D. H. H., 'The Comparison of Indian and Western Philosophy', *The Journal of Oriental Research* (Madras), 22 (Sept. 1952–June 1953), Parts I–IV, Madras, 1954.

Randle, H. N., *Indian Logic in the Early Schools*, Oxford, 1930.

Rescher, Nicholas, *The Development of Arabic Logic*, Pittsburgh, 1964.

Sugiura, S., *Hindu Logic as Preserved in China and Japan*, Philadelphia, 1900.

Vidyābhūsana, S. C., *Indian Logic. Mediaeval School*, Calcutta, 1909.

Vidyābhūsana, S. C., *A History of Indian Logic, Ancient, Mediaeval and Modern Schools*, Calcutta, 1921.

3. BIBLIOGRAPHY OF THE SCIENCE OF LOGIC

(a) Formal Logic

Ackermann, Robert, *Introduction to Many-Valued Logics*, London, 1967.

Ackermann, Robert John, *Modern Deductive Logic: An Introduction to its Techniques and to its Significance*, London, 1970.

Ackermann, Robert, *Nondeductive Inference*, London, 1966.

Acta Philosophica Fennica, Fascicule 16 (1963) (Proceedings of a colloquium on modal and many-valued logics held at Helsinki, 1962).

Alexander, Peter, *An Introduction to Logic: The Criticism of Arguments*, London, 1969.

Ambrose and Lazerowitz, *Fundamentals of Symbolic Logic*, New York, 1959.

Angell, Richard B., *Reasoning and Logic*, New York, 1964.

Basson, A. H., and O'Connor, D. J., *Introduction to Symbolic Logic*, London, 1959.

Bird, Otto, *Syllogistic and Its Extensions*, New Jersey, 1964.

Black, Max, *Critical Thinking*, New Jersey, 1952.

Blyth and Jacobson, *Class Logic: A Programmed Text*, New York, 1961.

Bochenski, J. M., O.P., *A Precis of Mathematical Logic*, translated from the French and German editions by Otto Bird, Dordrecht-Holland, 1959.

Carnap, Rudolf, *Introduction to Symbolic Logic and its Applications*, New York, 1958.

Carney, J. D. and Sheer, R. K., *Fundamentals of Logic*, London, 1964.

Carroll, L. (Dodgson, C. L.), *Symbolic Logic, a Fascinating Mental Recreation for the Young*, Oxford, 1896.

Church, Alonzo, *Introduction to Mathematical Logic*, i, Princeton, 1956.

Copi, Irving M., *Introduction to Logic* (with self-instructional supplement), New York, 1961.

De Bono, Edward, *Practical Thinking*, London, 1971.

Dickoff and James, *Symbolic Logic and Language, A Programmed Text*, New York, 1965.

Dopp, M. Joseph, *Formal Logic*, New York, 1960.

Dopp, M. Joseph, *Notions De Logique Formelle*, Louvain, 1967.

Éditions de L'Académie de la République Socialiste de Roumanie, *Logique Automatique Informatique*, Bucharest, Roumania, 1971.

Faris, J. A., *Quantification Theory*, London, 1964.

Feys and Fitch, *Dictionary of Symbols of Mathematical Logic*, Amsterdam, 1969.

Fisk, Milton, *A Modern Formal Logic*, New Jersey, 1964.

Fuchs, Walter R., *Eltern entdecken die neue Logik*, Munich and Zürich, 1971.

Gardner, Martin, *Logic Machines and Diagrams*, New York, 1958.

Gilby, Thomas, *Barbara Celarent: A Description of Scholastic Dialectic*, London, 1949.

Hamblin, C. L., *Fallacies*, London, 1970.

Hilbert, D., and Ackermann, W., *Principles of Mathematical Logic*, London, 1950.

Hughes, G. E., and Cresswell, M. J., *An Introduction to Modal Logic*, London, 1968.

Hughes, G. E., and Londey, D. G., *The Elements of Formal Logic*, London, 1965.

Iseminger, Gary, *An Introduction to Deductive Logic*, New York, 1968.

Jeffrey, Richard C., *Formal Logic: Its Scope and Limits*, New York, 1967.

Kalish, Donald and Montague, Richard, *Logic: Techniques of Formal Reasoning*, New York, 1964.

Kearns, John T., *Deductive Logic: a Programmed Introduction*, New York, 1969.

Keene, Geoffrey B., *First-Order Functional Calculus*, London, 1964.

Keene, Geoffrey, B., *The Relational Syllogism: A Systematic Approach to Relational Logic*, Exeter, 1969.

Kneebone, G. T., *Mathematical Logic and the Foundations of Mathematics*, London, 1963.

Langer, Susanne K., *An Introduction to Symbolic Logic*, New York, 1953.

Leblanc, Hugues and Wisdom, William A., *Deductive Logic*, Boston, 1972.

Lee, Harold Newton, *Symbolic Logic: an Introductory Textbook for Non-Mathematicians*, New York, 1961.

Lemmon, E. J., *Beginning Logic*, London, 1965.

Lewis, C. I., *A Survey of Symbolic Logic: the Classic Algebra of Logic*, New York, 1960.

Lewis, C. I., and Langford, C. H., *Symbolic Logic*, New York, 1959.

Lorenzen, Paul, *Formal Logic*, Dordrecht-Holland, 1965.

Lukasiewicz, Jan, *Aristotle's Syllogistic: From the Standpoint of Modern Formal Logic*, Oxford, 1957.

Lukasiewicz, Jan, *Elements of Mathematical Logic*, translated by Wojtasiewicz from Polish, Oxford, 1963.

Lukasiewicz, Jan, 'On Variable Functors of Propositional Arguments', *Proceedings of Royal Irish Academy*, Dublin, 1951.

Massey, Gerald J., *Understanding Symbolic Logic*, New York, 1970.

Mates, Benson, *Elementary Logic*, New York, 1965.

Mendelson, E., *Introduction to Mathematical Logic*, London and New York, 1964.

Meredith, C. A., 'On an Extended System of the Propositional Calculus', *Proceedings of the Royal Irish Academy*, Dublin, 1951.

Mitchell, David, *An Introduction to Logic*, London, 1962.

Moody, Ernest A., *Truth and Consequence in Mediaeval Logic*, Amsterdam, 1953.

Neidorf, Robert, *Deductive Forms: An Elementary Logic*, New York, 1967.

Nidditch, P. H., *Introductory Formal Logic of Mathematics*, London, 1957.

Olson, Robert G., *Meaning and Argument*, New York, 1969.

The Open University, *Introduction to Logic*, 2 vols. (Parts 1–9 and 10–18), Bletchley, Bucks, 1971.

The Open University, *Logic (1) Boolean Algebra*, Bletchley, Bucks., 1971.

The Open University, *Logic (II) Proof*, Bletchley, Bucks., 1971.

Polya, G., *How to Solve It*, New York, 1957.

Prior, A. N., *Formal Logic*, 2nd edition, Oxford, 1961.

Quine, W. V., *Elementary Logic*, New York, 1941.

Quine, W. V., *Mathematical Logic*, 1st edition, New York, 1940; revised edition, Cambridge, Mass., 1951.

Rescher, Nicholas, *Many-Valued Logic*, London, 1969.

Reichenbach, H., *Elements of Symbolic Logic*, New York, 1948.

Rosser, J. B., and Turquette, A. R., *Many-valued Logics*, Amsterdam, 1952.

Ruby, Lionel, *The Art of Making Sense: A Guide to Logical Thinking*, Philadelphia, 1954.

Russell, Bertrand, and Whitehead, A. N., *Principia Mathematica* (3 vols.), London, 1968.

Salmon, Wesley C., *Logic*, New Jersey, 1965.

Schragrin, Morton L., *The Language of Logic: A Programed Text*, New York, 1968.

Smullyan, R. M., *First-Order Logic*, Berlin: Heidelberg: New York, 1968.

Stebbing, L. Susan, *A Modern Elementary Logic*, London, 1960.

Stebbing, L. Susan, *A Modern Introduction to Logic*, London, 1958.

Stoll, Robert R., *Sets, Logic and Axiomatic Theories*, London, 1961.

Strawson, P. F., *Introduction to Logical Theory*, London, 1952.

Suppes, Patrick, *Introduction to Logic*, London, 1964.

Tarski, Alfred, *Introduction to Logic and the Methodology of the Deductive Sciences*, New York, 1946.

Thomason, Richmond H., *Symbolic Logic: An Introduction*, London, 1970.

Von Wright, G. H., *An Essay in Modal Logic*, Amsterdam, 1951.

Zeman, J. Jay, *Modal Logic: The Lewis-Modal Systems*, Oxford, 1973.

(b) Metalogic

Ackermann, W., *Solvable Cases of the Decision Problem*, Amsterdam, 1954.

Alston, William P., *Philosophy of Language*, New Jersey, 1965.

Barker, Stephen F., *Philosophy of Mathematics*, New Jersey, 1964.

Black, Max, *The Labyrinth of Language*, London, 1968.

Black, Max, *Margins of Precision*, New York, 1970.

Black, Max, *The Nature of Mathematics: A Critical Survey*, London, 1933, New York, 1934.

Black, Max, 'The Semantic Definition of Truth', *Language and Philosophy*, Ithaca, 1949.

Blumenthal, Arthur L., *Language and Psychology: Historical Aspects of Psycholinguistics*, New York, 1970.

Bochenski, J. M., O.P., 'Logistique et logique classique', *Bulletin Thomiste*, 10 (1934).

Breal, Michel, *Semantics: Studies in the Science of Meaning*, New York, 1964.

Brouwer, L. E. J., 'Historical Background, Principles and Methods of Intuitionism', *South African Journal of Science*, 49 (1952/3).

Carnap, Rudolf, *The Formalization of Logic*, Cambridge, Mass., 1943.

Carnap, Rudolf, 'Foundations of Logic and Mathematics', *International Encyclopedia of Unified Science*, vol. 1, no. 3, Chicago, 1939.

Carnap, Rudolf, *The Logical Syntax of Language* (translation from the German with additions), London, 1937.

Carnap, Rudolf, *Meaning and Necessity, a Study in Semantics and Moda Logic*, Chicago, 1947.

Carroll, John B., *Language and Thought*, New Jersey, 1964.

Chao, Yuen Ren, *Language and Symbolic Systems*, London, 1968.

Chappell, V. C., *Ordinary Language*, New Jersey, 1964.

Chomsky, Noam, *Cartesian Linguistics: A Chapter in the History of Rationalist Thought*, New York and London, 1966.

Chomsky, Noam, *Current Issues in Linguistic Theory*, The Hague, 1969.

Chomsky, Noam, *Language and Mind*, New York, 1968.

Allen, J. P. B. and Van Buren, Paul, *Chomsky: Selected Readings*, London, 1971.

Chomsky, Noam, *Syntactic Structures*, The Hague, 1969.

Church, Richard, *The Wonder of Words*, London, 1970.

Cohen, L. Jonathan, *The Diversity of Meaning*, London, 1966.

Cohen, Morris R., *A Preface to Logic*, London, 1946.

Copi, Irving M., *The Theory of Logical Types*, London, 1971.

Crawshay-Williams, Rupert, *The Comforts of Unreason*, London, 1947.

Crawshay-Williams, Rupert, *Methods and Criteria of Reasoning: An Inquiry into the Structure of Controversy*, London, 1957.

Crystal, David, *Linguistics*, Harmondsworth, Middlesex, 1971.

Crystal, David, *Linguistics, Language and Religion*, London, 1965.

Crystal, David, *What is Linguistics?*, London, 1971.

Curry, H. B., and Feys, R., *Combinatory Logic*, i, Amsterdam, 1958.

Curry, H. B., *Foundations of Mathematical Logic*, New York, 1963.

Curry, H. B., *Theory of Formal Deductibility*, Notre Dame, Indiana, 1957.

Dixon, Robert, *What is Language? A New Approach to Linguistic Description*, London, 1965.

Doughty, Pearce and Thornton, *Language in Use*, London, 1971.

Douglas, Mary, *Natural Symbols: Explorations in Cosmology*, London, 1970.

Geach, Peter, *Mental Acts*, London, 1957.

Geach, Peter, *Reference and Generality*, New York, 1962.

Gödel, Kurt, *On Formally Undecidable Propositions of Principia Mathematica and Related Systems*, translated by B. Meltzer, Edinburgh and London, 1962.

Greenberg, Joseph H., ed., *Universals of Language*, Cambridge, Mass., 1968.

Gross, M., and Lentin, A., *Introduction to Formal Grammars*, London, 1970.

Hayukawa, S. I., *Language in Action*, New York, 1946.

Heyting, Arend, 'Formal Logic and Mathematics', *Synthese* (Amsterdam), 6 (1947/8).

Heyting, Arend, *Intuitionism, an Introduction*, Amsterdam, 1956.

Hilbert, D., and Ackermann, W., *Grundzüge der theoretischen Logik*, 3rd edition, Berlin, 1949.

Hildum, Donald C., ed., *Language and Thought*, London, 1967.

Hintikka, Jaakko, *The Philosophy of Mathematics*, Oxford, 1969.

Holloway, John, *Language and Intelligence*, London, 1955.

Holt and McIntosh, *The Scope of Mathematics*, Oxford, 1966.

Hunter, Geoffrey, *Metalogic: An Introduction to the Metatheory of Standard First Order Logic*, London, 1971.

Jourdain, P. E. B., 'The Function of Symbolism in Mathematical Logic', *Scientia* 21 (1917).

Kac, Mark and Ulam, Stanislaw, *Mathematics and Logic*, London, 1968.

Kilmister, C. W., *Language, Logic and Mathematics*, London, 1967.

Kleene, S. C., *Introduction to Metamathematics*, Amsterdam, 1952.

Körner, Stephan, *The Philosophy of Mathematics*, London, 1960.

Lambert, Karel, ed., *The Logical Way of Doing Things*, New Haven and London, 1969.

Lehrer, Adrienne and Keith, eds., *Theory of Meaning*, New Jersey, 1970.

Lemmon, E. J., *Introduction to Axiomatic Set Theory*, London, 1968.

Lewis, Clarence I., 'Notes on the Logic of Intension', *Structure, Method and Meaning: Essays in Honor of Henry M. Sheffer*, New York, 1951.

Linsky, Leonard, ed., *Reference and Modality*, Oxford, 1971.

Lukasiewicz, Jan, *Aristotle's Syllogistic from the Standpoint of Modern Formal Logic*, 2nd edition, enlarged, Oxford, 1957.

McLuhan, Marshall, *The Gutenberg Galaxy*, London, 1967.

McLuhan, Marshall, *Understanding Media: The Extensions of Man*, London, 1967.

Malmberg, Bertil, *New Trends in Linguistics*, Stockholm, 1964.

Martin, Robert L., ed., *The Paradox of the Liar*, New Haven, 1970.

Mascall, E. L., *Words and Images: A Study in Theological Discourse*, London, 1957.

Miller, Robert L., *The Linguistic Relativity Principle and Humboldtian Ethnolinguistics*, The Hague, 1968.

Minnis, Noel, ed., *Linguistics at Large: The fourteen Linguistic Lectures presented by the Institute of Contemporary Arts, London 1969–1970*, London, 1971.

Mostowski, Andrzej, *Thirty Years of Foundational Studies* (Lectures on the

Development of Mathematical Logic and the Study of the Foundations of Mathematics, 1930–64), Oxford, 1966.

Nagel, Ernest and Newman, James, *Gödel's Proof*, London, 1971.

Nicod, Jean, *Geometry and Induction* (with prefaces by Roy Harrod, Bertrand Russell and André Lalande), London, 1969.

Ogden, C. K., and Richards, I. A., *The Meaning of Meaning*, London, 1966.

Palmer, Frank, *Grammar*, Harmondsworth, Middlesex, 1971.

Pap, Arthur, *Semantics and Necessary Truth*, New Haven, 1966.

Pitcher, George, ed., *Truth*, New Jersey, 1946.

Quine, W. V., *From a Logical Point of View*, Cambridge, Mass., 1953.

Quine, W. V., *Methods of Logic*, 1st edition New York, 1950; revised edition, London, 1958.

Quine, W. V., *Set Theory and Its Logic*, Harvard, 1969.

Quine, W. V., *A System of Logistic*, Cambridge, Mass., 1934.

Quine, W. V., *The Ways of Paradox*, New York, 1966.

Quine, W. V., *Word and Object*, Cambridge, Mass., 1960.

Ramsey, F. P., *The Foundations of Mathematics and Other Logical Essays*, R. B. Braithwaite, ed., London, 1931.

Reeves, Joan Wynn, *Thinking about Thinking*, London, 1965.

Reid, Louis Arnaud, *Meaning in the Arts*, London, 1969.

Rogers, Robert, *Mathematical Logic and Formalized Theories*, Amsterdam, 1971.

Rosser, J. B., 'A Mathematical Logic without Variables', *Annals of mathematics*, vol. 36 (1935).

Russell, Bertrand, *Introduction to Mathematical Philosophy*, London, 1919.

Russell, Bertrand, *The Principles of Mathematics*, i, Cambridge, 1900.

Ryle, Gilbert, 'A Puzzling Element in the Notion of Thinking', *Proceedings of British Academy*, vol. XLIV, Oxford.

Salmon, C., ed., *Zeno's Paradoxes*, Indiana and New York, 1970.

Scholz, Heinrich, 'Die Klassische und die moderne Logik', *Blätter für deutsche Philosophie*, 10 (1937).

Searle, J. R., *Speech Acts: an Essay in the Philosophy of Language*, Cambridge, 1969.

Sigel, Irving, and Hooper, Frank, eds., *Logical Thinking in Children*, New York, 1968.

Stoll, Robert R., *Set Theory and Logic*, San Francisco and London, 1963.

Strawson, P. F., *Meaning and Truth*, Oxford, 1970.

Sturtevant, E. H., *An Introduction to Linguistic Science*, New Haven and London, 1967.

Suppes, Patrick, *Axiomatic Set Theory*, New York and London 1960.

Tarski, Alfred, *Logic, Semantics, Metamathematics: Papers from 1923 to 1938*, translated by J. H. Woodger, Oxford, 1956.

Ullmann, Stephen, *Semantics: An Introduction to the Science of Meaning*, Oxford, 1970.

Viand, Gaston, *Intelligence: Its Evolution and Forms*, London, 1960.

Vygotsky, Lev Semenovich, *Thought and Language*, Cambridge, Mass., 1962.
Von Wright, Georg H., *Logical Studies*, London, 1967.
Waismann, F., *The Principles of Linguistic Philosophy*, London, 1968.
Weiss, Paul, 'The Nature of Systems', *The Monist*, vol. 39 (1929).
White, Alan R., *Truth*, London, 1970.
Whitehead, A. N., *An Introduction to Mathematics*, Oxford, 1958.
Wilson, John, *Language and the Pursuit of Truth*, London, 1967.
Wisdom, John, *Logical Constructions*, New York, 1969.

(c) Philosophy of Logic

Aaron, Richard I., *Knowing and the Function of Reason*, Oxford, 1971.
Bennett, Jonathan, *Rationality: an Essay towards an Analysis*, London, 1964.
Boon, James A., *From Symbolism to Structuralism: Lévi-Strauss in a Literary Tradition*, Oxford, 1972.
Brown, G. Spencer, *Laws of Form*, London, 1969.
Browne, G. D., *Philosophy of Logic*, New York, 1966.
Charbonnier, G., *Conversations with Claude Lévi-Strauss*, London, 1969.
Clack, Robert J., *Bertrand Russell's Philosophy of Language*, The Hague, 1969.
Crowe, F. E., ed., *Collection: Papers by Bernard Lonergan*, London, 1967.
Dickinson, D. R., *Operators: An Algebraic Synthesis*, London, 1967.
Edgley, Roy, *Reason in Theory and Practice*, London, 1969.
Erickson, Stephen A., *Language and Being: An Analytic Phenomenology*, New Haven and London, 1970.
Foucault, Michel, *The Order of Things: An Archaeology of the Human Sciences*, translated from the French, London, 1970.
Hintikka, Jaakko, *Logic Language Games and Information: Kantian Themes in the Philosophy of Logic*, Oxford, 1973.
Husenjaeger, G., *Introduction to the Basic Concepts and Problems of Modern Logic*, Dordrecht-Holland, 1972.
Hörmann, Hans, *Psycholinguistics: An Introduction to Research and Theory*, Berlin, Heidelberg, New York, 1971.
Husserl, Edmund, *Formal and Transcendental Logic*, translated by Dorion Cairns, The Hague, 1969.
Jaffé, Aniela, *The Myth of Meaning in the work of C. G. Jung*, translated by R. F. C. Hull, London, 1970.
Jaspers, Karl, *Way to Wisdom: an Introduction to Philosophy*, New Haven and London, 1954.
Kerr, F., 'Language as Hermeneutic in the later Wittgenstein', *Tijdschrift voor Filosofie*, Belgium, September 1965.
Kiefer and Munitz, eds., *Language, Belief and Metaphysics*, New York, 1970.
Körner, Stephen, *Categorial Frameworks*, Oxford, 1970.
Küng, Guido, *Ontology and the Logistic Analysis of Language*, Amsterdam, 1967.

Landesman, Charles, ed., *The Foundations of Knowledge*, New Jersey, 1970.
Langer, Susanne K., *Philosophical Sketches: A Study of the Human Mind in Relation to Feeling, Explored through Art, Language and Symbol*, New York, 1964.
Leach, Edmund, *Lévi-Strauss*, London, 1970.
Lewis, H. D., *Clarity is not Enough*, London, 1969.
Lonergan, Bernard, *Metaphysics as Horizon*, reprint from *Gregorianum*, vol. XLIV, 1963, Fasc. 2.
Lonergan, Bernard, *Method in Theology*, London, 1972.
Luchins, Abraham and Edith, *Logical Foundations of Mathematics for Behavioural Scientists*, New York, 1965.
Lyas, Colin, ed., *Philosophy and Linguistics*, London, 1971.
Macksey, Richard, and Donato, Eugenio, eds., *The Languages of Criticism and the Sciences of Man: The Structuralist Controversy*, Baltimore, 1970.
Malet, Andre, *The Thought of Rudolf Bultmann*, Shannon, Ireland, 1969.
Martin, Wm. Oliver, *The Order and Integration of Knowledge*, Michigan, 1957.
Mascall, E. L., *The Openness of Being: Natural Theology Today*, London, 1971.
Moravcsik, J. M. E., ed., *Aristotle: a Collection of Critical Essays*, London, 1968.
Mundle, C. W. K., *A Critique of Linguistic Philosophy*, Oxford, 1970.
Piaget, Jean, *The Principles of Genetic Epistemology*, translated by Wolfe Mays, London, 1972.
Poole, Roger, *Towards Deep Subjectivity*, London, 1972.
Prior, A. N., *Objects of Thought*, Oxford, 1971.
Quine, W. V., 'Designation and Existence', *Readings in Philosophical Analysis*, New York, 1949.
Quine, W. V., 'Ontological Remarks on the Propositional Calculus', *Mind*, 43 (1934).
Quine, W. V., 'On What There is', *The Review of Metaphysics*, 1 (1948).
Quine, W. V., *Philosophy of Logic*, New Jersey, 1970.
Rescher, Nicholas, *Topics in Philosophical Logic*, Dordrecht-Holland, 1968.
Royal Institute of Philosophy Lectures, vol. 3 (1968–9): *Knowledge and Necessity*, London, 1970.
Searle, J. R., ed., *The Philosophy of Language*, Oxford, 1971.
Sprigge, Timothy L. S., *Facts, Words and Beliefs*, London, 1970.
Strawson, P. F., *Logico-Linguistic Papers*, London, 1971.
Strawson, P. F., *The Bounds of Sense: An Essay on Kant's Critique of Pure Reason*, London, 1966.
Strawson, P. F., *Philosophical Logic*, Oxford, 1967.
Toms, Eric, *Being, Negation and Logic*, Oxford, 1962.
Tracy, David, *The Achievement of Bernard Lonergan*, New York, 1970.
Veatch, Henry, 'Aristotelian and Mathematical Logic', *The Thomist*, 13 (1950).

Veatch, Henry, 'Basic Confusions in Current Notions of Propositional Calculi', *The Thomist*, 14 (1951).

Veatch, Henry, 'Concerning the Ontological Status of Logical Forms', *The Review of Metaphysics*, 2 (1948).

Veatch, Henry, 'Formalism and/or Intentionality in Logic', *Philosophy and Phenomenological Research*, 11 (1951).

Veatch, Henry, *Intentional Logic*, New Haven and London, 1952.

Parker, Francis H., and Veatch, Henry, *Logic as a Human Instrument*, New York, 1959.

The Verb 'Be' and its Synonyms: Philosophical and Grammatical Studies (4 parts), Dordrecht-Holland, 1967–9.

Waddington, C. H., *Behind Appearance: a Study of the Relations between Painting and the Natural Sciences in this Century*, Edinburgh, 1969.

Zinov'iev, A. A., *Philosophical Problems of Many-valued Logic*, New York, 1963.

(d) Applied Logic

Achinstein, Peter, *Law and Explanation: an Essay in the Philosophy of Science*, Oxford, 1971.

Arthurs, A. M., *Probability Theory*, London, 1965.

Batog, Todeusz, *The Axiomatic Method in Phonology*, London, 1967.

Beveridge, W. I. B., *The Art of Scientific Investigation*, London, 1961.

Bochner, Salomon, *The Role of Mathematics in the Rise of Science*, Princeton, N.J., 1966.

Borger, Robert and Cioffi, Frank, eds., *Explanation in the Behavioural Sciences: Confrontations*, Cambridge, 1970.

Brody, Baruch A., *Readings in the Philosophy of Science*, New Jersey, 1970.

Carnap, Rudolf, *Logical Foundations of Probability*, London, 1950.

Christian, William, *Meaning and Truth in Religion*, Princeton, New Jersey, 1964.

Chwistek, Leon, *The Limits of Science: Outline of Logic and the Methodology of the Exact Sciences*, New York, 1949.

Cohen, L. Jonathan, *The Implications of Induction*, London, 1970.

Craik, K. J. W., *The Nature of Explanation*, Cambridge, 1967.

Davies, J. T., *The Scientific Approach*, Academic Press, 1965.

De Jouvenal, Bertrand, *The Art of Conjecture*, translated from the French by Nikita Lary, London, 1967.

Dirac, P. A. M., *The Development of Quantum Theory*, London, 1971.

Dirac, P. A. M., 'The Evolution of the Physicist's Picture of Nature', *Scientific American*, 208/5 (May 1963).

Dirac, P. A. M., 'The Relation between Mathematics and Physics', *Proceedings of the Royal Society of Edinburgh, Session 1938–39*, LIX/II (1939).

Feigl, Herbert, and Brodbeck, Mary, eds., *Readings in the Philosophy of Science*, New York, 1953.

Ferré, Frederick, *Language, Logic and God,* London, 1970.

Fisher, Alden and Murray, George, *Philosophy and Science as Modes of Knowing,* New York, 1969.

Fodor, Jerry A., *Psychological Explanation: An Introduction to the Philosophy of Psychology,* New York, 1968.

Gardiner, Patrick, *The Nature of Historical Explanation,* Oxford, 1952.

Gartmann, Heinz, *Science as History,* translated from the German by Alan G. Readett, London, 1960.

George, Frank, *Models of Thinking,* London, 1970.

Good, John Irving, *The Estimation of Probabilities, An Essay on Modern Bayesian Method,* Massachusetts, 1965.

Goodman, Nelson, *Fact, Fiction and Forecast,* New York, 1965.

Goodman, Nelson, *Language of Art: An Approach to a Theory of Symbols,* Oxford, 1969.

Gottlieb, Gidon, *The Logic of Choice, An Investigation of the Concepts of Rule and Rationality,* London, 1968.

Grene, Marjorie, ed., *Interpretations of Life and Mind: Essays around the Problem of Reduction,* London, 1971.

Griffiths, A. Phillips, ed., *Knowledge and Belief,* Oxford, 1967.

Hanson, Norwood Russell, *Patterns of Discovery,* Cambridge, 1965.

Hare, R. M., *Essays in Philosophical Method,* London, 1971.

Hare, R. M., *Practical Inferences,* London, 1971.

Harré, R., ed., *Scientific Thought: 1900–1960,* Oxford, 1969.

Harris, Errol, *Hypothesis and Perception,* London, 1970.

Heelan, Patrick A., 'Complementarity Context—Dependence and Quantum Logic', *Foundations of Physics,* 1 (1970).

Heelan, Patrick A., 'Horizon, Objectivity and Reality in the Physical Sciences', *International Philosophical Quarterly,* 7 (1967).

Heelan, Patrick A., 'The Logic of Framework Transpositions', *International Philosophical Quarterly* (1971).

Heelan, Patrick A., 'Towards a Hermeneutic of Natural Science', *British Journal for Phenomenology* (1972).

Heimbeck, Raeburne Seeley, *Theology and Meaning: A Critique of Metatheological Scepticism,* London, 1969.

Hemple, Carl C., 'Fundamentals of Concept Formation in Empirical Science', *International Encyclopedia of Unified Science,* vol. 2, no. 7, Chicago, 1952.

Hick, John, and McGill, Arthur, *The Mny-faced Argument: Recent Studies on the Ontological Argument for the Existence of God,* London, 1968.

Hilpinen Risto, ed., *Deontic Logic: Introductory and Systematic Readings,* Dordrecht-Holland, 1971.

Hintikka, Jaakko, *Models for Modalities: Selected Essays,* Dordrecht-Holland, 1969.

Katz, Jerrold J., *The Problem of Induction and its Solution,* Chicago, 1962.

Kneale, William, *Probability and Induction,* Oxford, 1949.

Körner, Stephan, *Abstraction in Science and Morals,* Cambridge, 1971.

Körner, Stephan, *Experience and Theory: An Essay in the Philosophy of Science*, London, 1966.

Kyburg, Henry E., *Probability and Inductive Logic*, London, 1970.

Lakatos, Imre, and Musgrave, Alan, eds., *Criticism and the Growth of Knowledge*, Cambridge, 1970.

Larrabee, Harold A., *Reliable Knowledge: Scientific Methods in the Social Studies* (revised edition), Boston, 1964.

Lerner, Daniel, ed., *Evidence and Inference: The Hayden Colloquium on Scientific Concept and Method*, New York, 1959.

Levi, Isaac, *Gambling with Truth; An Essay on Induction and the Aims of Science*, London, 1967.

Lucas, J. R., *The Concept of Probability*, Oxford, 1970.

Lukasiewicz, Jan, *Die logischen Grundlagen der Wahrscheinlichkeitsrechnung*, Crackow, 1913.

Madden, Edward H., *The Structure of Scientific Thought*, Boston, 1960.

Medawar, P. B., *The Art of the Soluble: Creativity and Originality in Science*, London, 1969.

Medawar, P. B., *Induction and Intuition in Scientific Thought*, London, 1969.

Mitchell, Basil, ed., *Faith and Logic: Oxford Essays in Philosophical Theology*, London, 1957.

Mosteller–Rourke–Thomas, *Probability and Statistics*, Reading, Mass., 1961.

Nagel, Ernest, *The Structure of Science: Problems in the Logic of Scientific Explanation*, London, 1961.

Nidditch, P. H., ed., *The Philosophy of Science*, Oxford, 1968.

O'Neil, W. M., *An Introduction to Method in Psychology*, Melbourne, 1962.

Passmore, John, *Philosophical Reasoning*, London, 1961.

Piaget, Jean, *Insights and Illusions of Philosophy* (translation from the French), London, 1971.

Polanyi, Michael, *Intellect and Hope: Essays in the Thought of Michael Polanyi*, Durham, N.C., 1968.

Polanyi, Michael, *Knowing and Being: Essays by Michael Polanyi*, London, 1969.

Polanyi, Michael, *The Logic of Liberty: Reflections and Rejoinders*, London, 1951.

Polanyi, Michael, *Personal Knowledge: Towards a Post-critical Philosophy*, London, 1962.

Polanyi, Michael, *The Study of Man*, London, 1959.

Polanyi, Michael, *The Tacit Dimension*, London, 1967.

Popper, Karl R., *Conjectures and Refutations: The Growth of Scientific Knowledge*, London, 1963.

Popper, Karl R., *The Logic of Scientific Discovery*, London, 1959.

Popper, Karl R., *Objective Knowledge; An Evolutionary Approach*, Oxford, 1972.

Pörn, Ingmar, *The Logic of Power*, Oxford, 1970.

Prezelecki, Marian, *The Logic of Empirical Theories*, London, 1969.

Prior, A. N., *Logic and the Basis of Ethics*, Oxford, 1949.

Prior, A. N., *Papers on Time and Tense*, Oxford, 1968.

Prior, A. N., *Past, Present and Future*, Oxford, 1967.

Prior, A. N., *Time and Modality, The John Locke Lectures*, 1955–56, Oxford, 1957.

Reichenbach, Hans, *Experience and Prediction, An Analysis of the Foundations and Structure of Knowledge*, Chicago, 1938.

Rescher and Urquhart, *Temporal Logic*, Vienna and New York, 1971.

Rescher, Nicholas, *The Logic of Commands*, London, 1966.

Schlegel, Richard, *Completeness in Science*, New York, 1967.

Schlesinger, G., *Method in the Physical Sciences*, London, 1963.

Schon, Donald A., *Invention and the Evolution of Ideas*, London, 1967.

Sikora, Joseph J., s.j., *The Scientific Knowledge of Physical Nature*, Paris, 1966.

Stone, Kenneth, *Evidence in Science*, Bristol, 1966.

Stover, Robert, *The Nature of Historical Thinking*, North Carolina, 1967.

Swain, Marshall, ed., *Induction, Acceptance and Rational Belief*, Dordrecht-Holland, 1970.

Theobald, D. W., *An Introduction to the Philosophy of Science*, London, 1968.

Toulmin, Stephen, *Foresight and Understanding: An Enquiry into the Aims of Science*, London, 1961.

Toulmin, Stephen, *The Uses of Argument*, Cambridge, 1964.

Toulmin, Hepburn and MacIntyre, *Metaphysical Beliefs*, London, 1970.

Von Wright, Georg Henrik, *An Essay in Deontic Logic and the General Theory of Action*, Amsterdam, 1968.

Von Wright, Georg Henrik, *Explanation and Understanding*, London, 1971.

Von Wright, Georg Henrik, *The Logical Problem of Induction*, Oxford, 1965.

Von Wright, George Henrik, *The Logic of Preference*, Edinburgh, 1963.

Von Wright, George Henrik, *Time, Change and Contradiction*, Cambridge, 1969.

Winch, Peter, *The Idea of a Social Science: and its Relation to Philosophy*, London, 1958.

INDEX OF PROPER NAMES

References are to the body of the text; none are given for Section F, the special bibliography of logic.

INDEX OF SUBJECTS

This index is designed as a supplement to the tables of contents.